IN TIME OF WAR

IN TIME OF WAR

HITLER'S TERRORIST ATTACK
ON AMERICA

PIERCE O'DONNELL

Introduction by Anthony Lewis

THE NEW PRESS

NEW YORK
LONDON

Requests for permission to reproduce selections from this book should be mailed to:
Permissions Department, The New Press, 38 Greene Street, New York, NY 10013

Published in the United States by The New Press, New York, 2005
Distributed by W. W. Norton & Company, Inc., New York

LIBRARY OF CONGRESS CATALOGING-IN-PUBLICATION DATA

O'Donnell, Pierce.
    In time of war : Hitler's terrorist attack on America / Pierce O'Donnell ; introduction by
Anthony Lewis.
        p. cm.
    Includes bibliographical references and index.
    ISBN 1-56584-958-2
    1. World War, 1939–1945—United States. 2. Sabotage—United States—History—
20th century. 3. World War, 1939–1945—Secret service—Germany. 4. Nazi Saboteurs Trial,
Washington, D.C., 1942. I. Title.

D769.1.O46 2005
940.53'73—dc22   2004060958

The New Press was established in 1990 as a not-for-profit alternative to the large, commercial
publishing houses currently dominating the book publishing industry. The New Press operates
in the public interest rather than for private gain, and is committed to publishing, in innovative
ways, works of educational, cultural, and community value that are often deemed insufficiently
profitable.

www.thenewpress.com

Composition by Westchester Book Composition

Printed in the United States of America

2 4 6 8 10 9 7 5 3 1

To Harry O'Donnell,
my best pal, who helped liberate
Nazi-occupied Europe—
may you rest in peace

Inter arma silent leges (In time of war the laws are silent).

—LATIN MAXIM

They that can give up essential liberty to obtain a little temporary safety deserve neither liberty nor safety.

—BENJAMIN FRANKLIN

MORE: And go he should, if he was the Devil himself, until he broke the law!

ROPER: So now you'd give the Devil the benefit of the law!

MORE: Yes. What would you do? Cut a great road through the law to get after the Devil?

ROPER: I'd cut down every law in England to do that!

MORE: (*Roused and excited*) Oh? (*Advances on Roper*) And when the last law was down, and the Devil turned round on you—where would you hide, Roper, the laws all being flat? (*He leaves him*) This country's planted thick with laws from coast to coast—man's laws, not God's—and if you cut them down—and you're just the man to do it—d'you really think you could stand upright in the winds that would blow then? (*Quietly*) Yes, I'd give the Devil benefit of law, for my own safety's sake.

ROBERT BOLT, *A MAN FOR ALL SEASONS:*
A PLAY IN TWO ACTS (1960)

Contents

Acknowledgments

This book would not have been possible without the terrific support of literally dozens of people. I am deeply grateful to everyone who helped me in so many ways. Naturally, I take full responsibility for the contents of the book.

I am most grateful to Anthony Lewis not only for his introduction but also for his lifelong commitment to civil liberties.

My dear friend and former law partner Michael Flaherty, along with Eveline Ruehlin, introduced me to the then obscure German saboteurs' case in late 1999 by way of an informative article in the *Washington Legal Times*, "Death Sentence Behind Closed Doors," by Sam Skolnik.

Patrick Girardi (Columbia, 2003), Danny Walsh (Loyola Marymount, 2005), and Thomas Weigandt (Yale, 2007) were resourceful, enthusiastic researchers. Harry Silberman, one of my ace paralegals, was masterly in finding literally thousands of documents, articles, and artwork in government archives, Internet databases, and library collections. Crystal Joseph did helpful research on civil liberties and treatment of prisoners of war. Danielle DeRosa, Jessica Wahl, and Kelly Baccaro skillfully verified the source citations.

My assistant, Dolores Valdez, deserves special recognition. She patiently typed and helped edit seemingly endless revisions of the manuscript without losing a sentence or her infectious enthusiasm.

Dolores's unflagging encouragement helped me get through some rough times.

My colleagues at O'Donnell & Shaeffer LLP were patient listeners even when they were a captive audience.

The book was materially benefited by the comments of numerous friends and colleagues. I am deeply grateful to Stuart Benjamin, David Burcham, Ken Carano, Erwin Chemerinsky, David Cole, the Rev. Robert F. Drinan, S.J., the Rev. Michael Engh, S.J., Bert Fields, Nikki Finke, Michael Flaherty, Tom Girardi, Susan Grode, Carole Handler, Clyde Hettrick, Brian McMahon, H.R. McMasters, Howard Miller, Kendra Morries, Ann Marie Mortimer, Tom Mortimer, Dawn O'Donnell, Mary Eileen O'Donnell, Dennis Perluss, Jefferson Rees, Barry Richard, Mark Robinson, Walt Rose, Lynn Roth, Liz Shannon, Harry Silberman, Robert Silverman, Tim Toohey, Dolores Valdez, Jonathan Varat, Nick Winslow, and Jerry Zeitman.

Many libraries and repositories were most helpful. I owe a debt of gratitude to the dedicated staffs of the Library of Congress, National Archives, Los Angeles Public Library, United States Supreme Court Library, University of North Carolina at Chapel Hill Wilson Library, Georgetown University Library, University of California at Los Angeles Library, University of Southern California Library, and Franklin D. Roosevelt Library at Hyde Park.

My unsinkable agent, Alice Martell, has been a wise counselor and enthusiastic advocate for this book. Thanks to Alice, I found James O'Shea Wade, who brilliantly edited the manuscript. Alice's and Jim's passion for the subject sustained me as we raced together to the finish line.

The staff at The New Press—executive director Diane Wachtell and editorial assistant Joel Ariaratnam—unstintingly supported this project. I also appreciate the excellent assistance of associate editor Sarah Fan and copy editor Sue Warga.

Finally, my beloved wife, Dawn, has been a beacon of encouragement throughout this project. I stole too many hours from her and our five children, but Dawn constantly saw value in the undertaking. Over the four years of researching and writing this book, I lost my father and then my mother. Without Dawn's loving, tender support as well as not-so-gentle prodding, I would not have been able to persevere.

Montecito, California
December 2004

Introduction

Anthony Lewis

In 1942, at a dangerous time in World War II, German submarines landed eight Nazi saboteurs on the beaches of Long Island and Florida. One quickly decided to inform the FBI. The other seven were rounded up and, on President Roosevelt's orders, tried by a specially appointed military commission. Six were executed, and the other two were sent to prison. In a case called *Ex parte Quirin*, the United States Supreme Court upheld the president's power to order a military trial.

The case of the Nazi saboteurs is not just a curious piece of history—not anymore. President George W. Bush's lawyers have used the decision in *Ex parte Quirin* to justify his extraordinary claims of power to override long-established civil liberties because of the threat of terrorism.

In Time of War is a thrilling account of the saboteurs' story, from their training on a farm in Prussia to their end. But it is much more than that, and much more important. Pierce O'Donnell has uncovered the secrets of the legal process used against the Nazis: the lies of J. Edgar Hoover, the determination of President Roosevelt to execute the saboteurs whatever the law, the unethical behavior of Supreme Court justices.

Hoover held a press conference to announce the capture of the eight saboteurs. He said nothing about the real reason for the capture: the decision of one of the eight to turn himself in. Instead he left it to the press to think—and write—that masterly FBI sleuthing had done the trick. At Congress's urging, President Roosevelt gave Hoover a medal. His false bravado went uncorrected for years.

Three days after the Nazis were all in custody, President Roosevelt sent a memo to his attorney general, Francis Biddle, saying that all eight should be given the death penalty. Biddle, and probably other administration figures, conveyed Roosevelt's views to the members of the Supreme Court. Justice Owen Roberts told his colleagues that Biddle had suggested to him "that Roosevelt would execute the Germans no matter what the Court did." Roberts added: "I believe FDR intends to have all eight men shot if we do not acknowledge his authority."

Two of the justices had close relationships with the Roosevelt administration that raised questions about their sitting in the *Quirin* case. James F. Byrnes had been working as a virtual member of the government for months, and before long he left the Court to be the president's top war administrator. Felix Frankfurter's ethical position was far more shocking. In a conversation with the secretary of war, Henry L. Stimson, he had actually recommended the use of a military commission to try the Nazis.

The Supreme Court's handling of the case was a blot on the Court's history apart from what went on behind the scenes. The Court heard argument on the issue of presidential power to have the Germans tried by military commission without knowing how the commission had actually performed, and before its verdict. The Court decided the case in a day. It upheld the president's power in a unanimous order, without an opinion explaining its reasoning. The opinion, by Chief Justice Harlan F. Stone, was issued months later. Justice Hugo Black's law clerk at the time, John P. Frank, said later: "If the judges are to run a court of law and not a butcher shop, the reasons for killing a man should be expressed before he is dead."

"The process by which the Supreme Court reached judgment in *Ex parte Quirin* was illegitimate," Pierce O'Donnell concludes. It was "tainted," he writes, "by the justices' conflicts of interest, bias, and President Roosevelt's ex parte threats to execute the German saboteurs if the Supreme Court did not uphold his actions." For those reasons, O'Donnell urges, the *Quirin* decision should not be treated as a valid precedent in today's tests of presidential power.

But even if one accepts the *Quirin* decision on its face, it is unconvincing for the Bush administration to rely on it in support of repressive tactics now. The Bush lawyers note that two of the *Quirin* defendants were American citizens but were held subject to trial by military commission. That, they say, justifies Bush's detention of Americans without trial or counsel.

But the situations are entirely different. There was no doubt about the facts in 1942—that the eight were sent by Hitler to sabotage American installations, that they shed their military uniforms and wore civilian clothes, and so on. But in the case of Americans detained by President Bush as "enemy combatants"—terrorists—Bush claimed the power to determine the facts himself. His lawyers said the courts should have virtually no power to examine his determinations.

Moreover, the Bush administration claimed the power to hold its prisoners in total isolation, forbidding them in particular to speak with a lawyer and violating the Geneva Convention on prisoners of war (POWs). The German saboteurs were given a prompt trial and afforded lawyers for their defense, and superb lawyers they were— military officers who saw it as their duty to represent their clients zealously even if that meant challenging the orders of their commander in chief.

The story of the principal defense lawyer in the case, Colonel Kenneth C. Royall, is a main subject of this book, and a remarkable tale. In practical terms, Royall had an unwinnable case. But he persevered, to his honor and that of American law. Later he became secretary of the army. As a result of this book, he will be remembered for performing a lawyer's duty under overwhelmingly adverse circumstances. It is an uplifting theme—and a fitting reminder of how much the safety of our country depends on the morality, commitment to the rule of law, and good faith of lawyers.

Tragically, President Bush has not had the wise counsel of a Kenneth C. Royall in the wake of the 9/11 terrorist attacks. In a series of extraordinary legal analyses by Bush administration lawyers between late 2001 and 2003, the president was advised that he had the constitutional authority to override international treaties and congressional laws prohibiting torture of enemy soldiers and requiring hearings to determine if they are entitled to POW status. These conclusions are startling—and wrong.

Federal law and the international Convention against Torture and Other Cruel, Inhuman, Degrading Treatment or Punishment clearly prohibited the degrading treatment of al-Qaeda and Iraqi prisoners at the U.S. prison in Guantánamo Bay, Cuba, and the Abu Ghraib prison in Baghdad. Article 5 of the Third Geneva Convention of 1949 requires a prompt hearing before a competent tribunal for captured enemy forces to determine if they are innocent civilians who must be released, lawful combatants who must be held as prisoners of war until the end of hostilities, or persons (such as saboteurs or terrorists) who are subject to war crimes prosecutions. These basic requirements of international humanitarian law—officially adopted by the United States—are intended to set a minimal code of conduct for treating captives in time of war.

Article 5 status hearings have proven to be highly effective in sorting out how captives should be classified. In the 1991 Gulf War, the United States held 1,196 such hearings before military tribunals, and almost 75 percent of these prisoners were freed after being found to be innocent civilians. Contrary to Pentagon claims, not all of the Guantánamo Bay detainees were picked up on the Afghan battlefield—some were arrested in countries as far away as Zambia and shipped to Guantánamo Bay by American authorities, while others were handed over to U.S. forces for the bounty. Informed intelligence officers admit that many of those held in Cuba were civilian Afghans rounded up by mistake during the war. Similarly, the International Committee of the Red Cross estimates that between 75 and 90 percent of Iraqi civilians apprehended by coalition forces were "arrested by mistake," often with the use of brutal tactics.

On the advice of his lawyers, President Bush determined that the Geneva Conventions did not cover prisoners held at Guantánamo Bay because they were "unlawful combatants"—a term not found in the Geneva Conventions. This decision was strongly opposed by Secretary of State Colin Powell, who correctly argued that the Third Geneva Convention should cover the Afghan conflict. The prisoners could still be found to be "unlawful combatants," Powell noted, but only after individual hearings for those requesting them. The secretary of state—a former top military officer himself—was profoundly alarmed at the administration's radical reversal of "over a century of US policy and practice [that would] undermine the protections of the law for our troops." The widespread condemnation of the United States by the world legal community in the wake of our repudiation of international humanitarian law—predicted by Powell—was dismissed by Secretary of Defense Donald Rumsfeld in 2002 as "isolated pockets of international hyperventilation."

Similarly, Bush administration lawyers, invoking a sweeping notion of impervious presidential power, counseled the president that extremely harsh interrogations of suspected terrorists were justified because they might elicit information that could prevent future attacks by foreign enemies. One Justice Department memorandum in August 2002 declared: "Any effort to apply [the criminal law against torture] in a manner that interferes with the President's direction of such core matters as the detention and interrogation of enemy combatants thus would be unconstitutional."

The president's lawyers paved the way for the shocking abuses that have occurred in the military's treatment of prisoners in the war on terror. International and U.S. legal obligations and the rule of law were put aside. Like it or not, the Taliban, certainly a cruel and violent movement, controlled virtually all of Afghanistan, thereby entitling its captured soldiers to POW status—or, at a minimum, to status hearings under the Third Geneva Convention. Cruel and humiliating interrogation techniques have heightened resentment of America in the Arab world and mocked our commitment to democratic values.

Official U.S. government reports—as well as investigations by the International Committee of the Red Cross, Human Rights Watch, and others—have found that people in American military custody have been murdered, tortured, and subjected to inhuman and degrading treatment while being interrogated. The army has admitted that at least thirty-nine prisoners in Iraq and Afghanistan died, some while being interrogated. Among other things, male detainees at Abu Ghraib were paraded naked, ordered to do jumping exercises and sing "The Star-Spangled Banner" in the nude, made to stand on boxes with their arms outstretched, forced to maintain physically painful positions for hours, compelled to masturbate in front of women, and subjected to unmuzzled military dogs to make them involuntarily urinate out of fear of the menacing dogs. Prisoners released from Guantánamo Bay have alleged that they were systematically abused by American military personnel in similar ways, including being beaten, deprived of sleep, shackled in painful positions, threatened with death to coerce confessions, and continually subjected to humiliation—all violations of the Geneva Conventions if true.

The issues raised by the Bush administration's unprecedented legal assertions in its war on terror are numerous and troubling. They reduce to one fundamental proposition: presidential power is unconstrained by law. Using the 9/11 attacks as the excuse for breathtakingly expanded and unreviewable executive authority, President Bush has broken with the American principle, first expressed by John Adams, that ours is meant to be a government of laws, not men.

The need to return to the Constitution is emphasized in O'Donnell's book. It shows President Bush's misguided reliance on the German saboteurs' case, the government's massive violations of international law, federal statutes, and military regulations, and the fallacy of the administration's constitutional argument that presidential power is unconstrained by law in wartime. The Supreme Court's three detainee cases in June 2004—rejecting President Bush's most extreme position of unreviewable powers—are analyzed with an eye toward future court battles over how much due process will be afforded citizen and noncitizen terrorist suspects. *In Time of War* is required reading for everyone who cherishes the American dream of a nation that lives up to the promises of freedom—that all men and women are in fact created equal in the eyes of the law and that the purpose of government is to preserve and protect their inalienable rights of life, liberty, and pursuit of happiness—in times of peace and war.

IN TIME OF WAR

Part I

MILITARY NECESSITY

In war countries act out of self-interest.

—HERMANN GOERING

Are all the laws, but one, to go unexecuted, and the government itself to go to pieces, lest that one be violated?

—ABRAHAM LINCOLN

Experience should teach us to be most on our guard to protect liberty when Government's purposes are beneficent. Men born to freedom are naturally alert to repel invasion of their liberty by evil-minded rulers. The greatest dangers to liberty lurk in insidious encroachment by men of zeal, well-meaning but without understanding.

—JUSTICE LOUIS D. BRANDEIS, DISSENTING IN

OLMSTEAD V. UNITED STATES, 277 U.S. 438, 479 (1928)

Chapter 1

A World at War

The grunts and groans could be heard hundreds of yards away. In the chilly April morning, a dozen men, wearing several layers of sweaters and speaking in English, were training hard in hand-to-hand combat.

The sun had not been in the sky long enough to make its warming presence felt. But the aches and pains, bruises and sprains were felt by the commandos in training. As they struggled to get through the grueling training program, they voiced the complaints of all young men whose freedom had been involuntarily exchanged for sixteen hours a day of running, climbing, and calisthenics. Theirs was the universal brotherhood of sweating, swearing raw recruits crawling in mud.

The incongruity of the setting was not lost on the men in the unit. In those rare moments when they could pause and enjoy a brief respite, they marveled at their idyllic surroundings among the green fields and stately pine forests of what had formerly been a private estate and now served as a training facility.

Young men like them on five continents were undergoing a similar ordeal. From Japan to Germany, America to Russia, the scene was the same: conscripts and volunteers being indoctrinated in the lethal art of war, preparing to kill—or be killed. It was April 1942, and the world was at war.

* * *

The men training that day were being taught techniques of sabotage. For a month, the recruits received intensive theoretical and practical instruction in the manufacture and use of explosives, incendiary material, and various types of chemical, mechanical, and electrical delayed-timing devices. They were being prepared to inflict damage on the enemy's infrastructure and spread terror throughout the general population. To make the exercises realistic, the school provided railroad tracks and bridges of differing construction and materials to blow up. The training facility was also equipped with rifle and pistol shooting ranges, a gymnasium for boxing, judo, and wrestling, and fields for group calisthenics, soccer, and hand-grenade tossing. A nearby airfield was available for practicing parachute jumps.

The second floor above the gymnasium had been converted into a lecture room and laboratory large enough to accommodate twenty students and an instructor. Here the recruits learned about explosives as well as the techniques of invisible writing, creating and operating under false identities, and the use of secret codes. They carefully studied maps of vital canals, waterways, and railroad lines used for transporting the enemy's raw materials; they familiarized themselves with the locations and layouts of principal aluminum and magnesium plants as well as other strategic war industries. No note taking was allowed at this school for sabotage—everything had to be memorized.

All of this could have been taking place in the south of England, and the dirty-faced trainees could well have been elite British and/or American soldiers. Winston Churchill had created the Special Operations Executive (SOE) and ordered its personnel to "set Europe ablaze." SOE agents—British and foreign nationals committed to the Allied cause—would be trained at facilities like this one and infiltrated into occupied Europe.

But this training was being conducted in Nazi Germany—the ruler of most of Europe and currently engaged in the Russian campaign. These were German soldiers, all of whom spoke English and had lived in the United States—indeed, two had become American citizens. And this was a remote, secret saboteur school at Quenz Lake, Brandenburg, the capital of the state of Prussia, located some thirty miles from Berlin.

Once a luxurious working farm owned by a wealthy Jewish shoe manufacturer, Quenz Lake had been transformed into a secluded military campus for specialized sabotage training. For the past several years, its alumni had undertaken many successful military and industrial sabotage missions in Europe, weakening the resistance of Hitler's eventual targets and escalating sabotage to a formidable military tool. Among its most effective graduates were pro-Nazi civilians—so-called fifth columnists—from many nations.

These days, cows, chickens, pigs, and ducks, along with the caretaker's children, roamed free on the tranquil property dotted with a main farmhouse, barn, two smaller houses, a greenhouse, and assorted sheds. They kept well away from the current twelve trainees, several guards behind the stone wall around the central part of the facility, and an ill-tempered sergeant with a sawed-off shotgun and three German shepherd guard dogs.

The main farmhouse—a solid two-story, twelve-room stone building resembling a country club—stood more than a hundred feet from the main gate and high stone wall facing a narrow dirt road. A fifteen-minute walk from the last bus stop in Brandenburg, the farm was ideally isolated from prying eyes and inquisitive neighbors. It was a perfect place to boldly plot the destruction of critical American industrial facilities and transportation systems.

Lieutenant Walter Kappe presided over the school with an iron hand. A fanatical Nazi in charge of American sabotage, Kappe was attached to the Abwehr II, a part of Germany's military intelligence service (Amt Auslands Abwehr) of the German Armed Forces High Command (Oberkommando der Wehrmacht or OKW).[1] Before the war, he had been an official of the Ausland Institute at Stuttgart—an organization charged with recruiting Germans abroad for the Nazi Party and exploiting them as sources of military, economic, and political intelligence.

Kappe was fluent in English and highly knowledgeable about the United States, having lived there from 1925 to 1937. He had first worked at a farm implement factory in Kankakee, Illinois. In Chicago, he organized Teutonia, the first Nazi organization on American soil. Kappe then graduated to forming Friends of the New Germany, the precursor of the German-American Bund. Editing the Bund's newspaper in the United States, he distinguished himself as an effective press agent and propagandist. In 1933 Kappe moved to New York, where he became a leader in the Friends of Hitler movement.[2]

Internal Bund politics forced Kappe's return to Germany in 1937, just as Hitler's war preparations were intensifying. Joining the Ausland

Institute, the stocky thirty-two-year-old was assigned to head the American section. For the next four years, Kappe indoctrinated repatriated Germans who were heeding the Führer's summons to return to the glorious fatherland. When the Japanese attacked Pearl Harbor and the United States entered the war, he was transferred to the Abwehr and put in charge of recruiting and training English-speaking Germans to wage a sophisticated terrorist campaign inside the United States.

A university dropout, Kappe was a smooth talker and self-promoter. He was hardly the most qualified man for the job of devising and implementing an elaborate sabotage operation. Nevertheless, "Kappe had always fancied himself as having more talent and ability than he actually possessed, and he had a knack of convincing others of the same thing."[3]

By the time the United States and Germany had declared war on each other, the German High Command had developed detailed plans for sabotaging some of the critical components in America's industrial war capacity. Years of information gathering had yielded detailed transportation maps and plant designs. The primary target was the light metals industry, the backbone of airplane manufacturing.[4] So the planners targeted plants operated by the Aluminum Company of America in East St. Louis, Illinois, Alcoa, Tennessee, and Massena, New York. The Germans also wanted to destroy a cryolite plant in Philadelphia in order to cripple the supply of an essential raw material for aluminum production. They believed that if aluminum and magnesium production could be disrupted, America would produce fewer aircraft and eventually lose the war to superior German airpower.

Disruption of vital transportation corridors was also a high priority. The Germans devised detailed plans to disable several waterways and blow up hydroelectric plants at Niagara Falls and in the Tennessee Valley. Significant stretches of railroad track—such as the Horseshoe Curve in Altoona, Pennsylvania, the Hell Gate Bridge linking New York City and New England, and the Chesapeake and Ohio Railway's coal-carrying lines—were also targeted for destruction. The saboteurs could select other targets so long as they severely retarded the production or transportation of war materials.

The plan also had propaganda and psychological warfare objectives. The saboteurs were instructed to set explosive devices in railroad stations and department stores to incite public panic. And for good measure, Jewish-owned businesses such as Macy's department store were fair game.[5]

By late 1941, German intelligence knew considerably more about America's Achilles' heels than the United States knew about Germany's industrial vulnerabilities. As Germany under Hitler moved inexorably toward war, the High Command had mastered the bitter lessons of World War I. The activation of a special section of military intelligence—focused on sabotage and the encouragement of minority uprisings in enemy countries rather than espionage—was a logical step for the German army.

The Abwehr spared no effort in training an elite corps of saboteurs. In the Berlin suburb of Tegel, a laboratory for experimenting with new and improved explosives and other techniques for sabotage was established. Two especially useful inventions developed there were innovative detonators—one that blew planes out of the sky at preselected altitudes based on changes in air pressure and another resembling a cigarette lighter that had a time delay of up to forty days.

The officer placed in charge of Abwehr II was Colonel (later General) Erwin von Lahousen. A professional soldier since 1916, his strengths were organization and intrigue—two essential talents for a man in his position. Yet the Austrian native was also a realist. "[T]he perpetration of any considerable act of sabotage on the enemy country is among the most difficult tasks of a secret service," he constantly reminded his colleagues.[6]

Lahousen had proven to be an ace saboteur. In addition to sabotage operations, the Abwehr had masterminded a string of successes against the Allies. One of their most notorious coups was Operation North Pole. Starting with the arrest of two Dutch underground agents infiltrated from England, the operation eventually blossomed into a grand deception (*Funkspiele*, or "radio game") using captured Allied radio operators under Nazi control, in which falsified messages were used to lure additional Allied agents into entrapment as soon as they landed on the Continent.

A meticulous planner and stickler for detail, Lahousen selected his targets with great care. Given the inherent difficulties of sabotage, he wanted to maximize his efforts. It was critical to inflict extensive damage on strategic targets that would be time-consuming to repair.

"Only . . . [then] can it be said that an act of sabotage has had any operational value in the military sense or has been really effective from the industrial point of view," he insisted.[7]

The American sabotage campaign had special urgency. Hitler himself was demanding action. Not only had America been militarily weakened by the surprise Japanese attack on Hawaii and the Philippines, Hitler reasoned, but its people were fearful of further Japanese and German attacks. Hitler and his planners envisioned a steady, unrelenting wave of terrorist attacks. These surprise explosions, train wrecks, and electrical and communications disruptions would serve as continuing, demoralizing reminders of American vulnerability to a superior German power that, despite being a vast ocean away, could nevertheless attack with impunity and without warning at any time and any place. This random terrorism would strike fear in the hearts of the enemy.

While senior military leaders privately entertained serious reservations about the feasibility of the plan, Hitler's reasoning was not totally absurd by any means. Demolished factories in the heart of a city—blown up by enemy secret agents striking seemingly at will—would be a military and propaganda victory at the same time. If a sufficient number of these operations were successful, many in the panic-stricken civilian population would begin to lose confidence in their leaders and, as Hitler had demonstrated in Europe, begin to accept the inevitability of defeat. With their morale at ebb tide, the American people might well pressure Roosevelt and Congress to make "an honorable peace" with Germany.

But when Germany declared war on the United States, Hitler faced one major obstacle in realizing his dream. Remarkably, Germany lacked a single reliable agent in the United States. Trying to keep America out of the war and not gratuitously arouse anti-German sentiment, the German Foreign Office had given strict orders to Abwehr II to stay out of the United States during the uneasy years of "peace." The discovery of German espionage would be regarded as a hostile act—a prelude to sabotage—and only strengthen the hand of FDR and his "Jew advisors" who wanted America to enter the war.[8]

Germany also lacked reliable agents for another reason. In early 1941, the Federal Bureau of Investigation (FBI), led by J. Edgar Hoover, had arrested the most important German spies in the United States. Assisted by William Sebold, a naturalized American of German descent who had been recruited as a German spy and trained by the Gestapo, federal agents pulled off a well-planned sting at the old Knickerbocker Hotel off Times Square in New York. This loss of thirty-three intelligence assets escalated the pressure on Abwehr II to mount an externally generated sabotage mission against the United States.

Lahousen personally selected Lieutenant Kappe to recruit the men for the American sabotage mission. Using a cover operation of a Berlin publication named *Der Kaukasus* ("The Caucasus") notable for publishing nothing, Kappe had file drawers full of interviews with Germans repatriated from the United States. The Third Reich was able to maintain such detailed dossiers because all returning Germans had to fill out forms that eventually reached Kappe at the Ausland Institute. These files had been fertile sources for recruits for Abwehr assignments.

From thousands of candidates who could speak English and were familiar with America, Kappe winnowed the list down to twelve recruits, nine of whom would eventually be selected at the conclusion of training. They were Hitler's terrorists. Their mission to cripple American airplane production and create panic among the people was admittedly audacious. But so, too, was the notion that Germany could rule most of Europe. In the spring of 1942, Hitler's Third Reich was off to an impressive start. In some eyes, Germany appeared invincible.

Chapter 2

Fear Itself

Some five thousand miles from Quenz Lake—across the U-boat-infested North Atlantic—Franklin Delano Roosevelt sat in the War Room in the southwest corner of the White House main floor studying maps of various theaters of operations. He had spent many anxious hours in that room over the past six months. No American president since Lincoln had faced such a desperate wartime situation. Not only was most of Europe occupied by Nazi forces (with only a handful of exceptions, including Spain, Portugal, Switzerland, and Sweden), Russia was reeling under a savage German assault, and Great Britain stood alone, its lifeline to the United States under constant threat of being severed by German U-boats.[1] The relatively small number of submarines deployed not only were sinking thousands of tons of shipping in the transatlantic convoys keeping Britain alive and able to fight, but also were sinking U.S. and Allied ships within sight of observers on the shores of the Atlantic Coast and in the Caribbean. By the end of April 1942, not only had Britain lost an appalling number of merchant ships, but the Royal Navy "had lost five capital ships, equal to a third of its original strength," four fleet aircraft carriers, sixteen cruisers, and seventy-eight destroyers.[2]

Everywhere he looked, the beleaguered thirty-second president of the United States saw not only the Third Reich's menacing swastikas covering one country after another but also Japanese forces extending a vast perimeter of conquest over the Pacific and threatening Australia. FDR was hardly in a position to offer much immediate aid to the Royal Navy. He had made a deal in 1940 for the transfer of fifty American World War I–vintage destroyers, in exchange for which the British granted "the United States 99-year leases of land on eight British possessions in the Caribbean and western Atlantic on which to establish naval and air bases"—an arrangement that left many of the warships still being refitted.[3]

The U.S. Navy was stretched to the limit in the Pacific. As one naval historian noted bluntly: "After Pearl Harbor the serviceable strength of the United States Navy in battleships amounted to only three, all hitherto with the Atlantic Fleet but now transferred to the Pacific Fleet. With these ships and four fleet carriers . . . the Americans had to confront Japan's eleven battleships and six fleet carriers; gruesome odds."[4]

Both Allied navies were desperately short of the escort ships needed in the Atlantic to fend off the U-boat offensive. Churchill and Roosevelt knew that if the Battle of the Atlantic was lost, Britain simply could not survive.[5] April 1942 indeed seemed to be the cruelest month for the Allies.

With setbacks and defeats coming one after the other, the news had been unrelentingly dismal. The American people were genuinely fearful that the Japanese would bomb and quite possibly invade the West Coast. And with enemy submarines sinking ships with impunity in American waters, it seemed equally possible that the United States would face any number of threats from Germany, ranging from infiltration of saboteurs to an invasion on the East Coast.[6]

The first months of 1942 had been a nightmarish winter of despair for Americans. "Even Roosevelt was not always as buoyant and self-confident as he tried to appear . . . he was testy, suffering from war nerves."[7] FDR's legendary calmness under crisis was being sorely tested, and his "fear-soaked anxieties had had to be sternly repressed."[8] The president had to appear calm and confident to the nation and even among his closest advisors. Roosevelt knew the truth of what Thomas Jefferson had written in 1810: "In time of peace the people look most to their representatives; but in war, to the executive solely."[9]

Whatever demons of despair haunted him, Roosevelt had to be the people's pillar of strength. They had trusted him for nine years to lead them out of the nation's worst depression. Now he had to command the armed forces and convert the peacetime economy to wartime production at a speed unprecedented in history. FDR had the vision to see that America, given time, would truly become the "arsenal of democracy," its shipyards and factories churning out staggering quantities of ships, aircraft, tanks, and all the other armaments required for victory. But even as he looked to the future, his thoughts must have occasionally turned to another difficult period four years earlier, when he first had begun to prepare for the day that America would have to go to war—a time when he had faced another sort of enemy: the enemy within.

Germany's rearmament under Hitler and Japan's rising imperialism after the 1932 elections alarmed the new president of the United States, who had been elected to lift his countrymen out of the Great Depression with his New Deal. As he enacted his bold domestic program of social and financial legislation, Roosevelt kept a watchful eye on developments in Germany and Japan. As time passed, he realized that America would have to boost defense spending dramatically and convert more of its civilian production capacity to manufacturing tanks, planes, guns, and ammunition. But he would have to proceed cautiously.

Even with war clouds gathering in the late 1930s, American participation in any "foreign wars" had powerful enemies. Isolationist sentiment had spread like a prairie fire in Congress and among the American people. Before Pearl Harbor, the American public was totally against entering into "Europe's war." The isolationist movement in America—spearheaded by American aviation hero Charles A. Lindbergh and the America First Committee—was at an all-time high, with 80 percent of the public favoring nonintervention.[10] A 1939 poll showed only 2 percent supporting declaring war and fighting the Nazis.[11]

Roosevelt also had to contend with the limitations imposed on him by the Neutrality Act. The gradual steps he took to come to the aid of Great Britain reflected both a necessary caution and a firm conviction that it was in the interest of the national security of the United States to help Britain survive. But he also knew that the only way the country could become effectively involved in the conflict was if it was directly attacked.[12]

Roosevelt's realization of the inevitability of American involvement in the spreading global conflagration was a decisive factor in his decision to run for an unprecedented third term. Despite his weariness from eight grueling years trying to put America back to work and a tradition of serving for only two presidential terms, FDR chose to run for a historic third term in 1940. He feared the self-destructive potential of continued isolationism and the fact that none of the other likely candidates in either party "could be counted on to stand up to Hitler and the Japanese while carrying on what was left of the New Deal."[13]

But until America was actually attacked, Roosevelt had to deal with America's reluctance to be involved. His 1940 campaign platform highlighted his public commitment to keep the country out of the war. "Your boys are not going to be sent into any foreign wars," the president solemnly assured the electorate in a stump speech.[14] And he meant it—it was his intention to help Britain as much as possible while avoiding direct American involvement in the war, at least until the country's military preparedness was far more advanced.

In September 1939 Roosevelt had written to Winston Churchill, welcoming him back to his old post as first lord of the Admiralty and asking Churchill to keep in touch. Thus began a remarkable relationship, in part a genuine and growing friendship, in part complex negotiations between two pragmatic and wily political leaders, each bent on protecting his country's interests.[15] From the very first day of becoming prime minister in May 1940, Churchill schemed in every way imaginable to get the United States to enter the war and, until that inevitable day, to supply Britain with vital armaments essential to resist the German onslaught. In his famous February 9, 1941, broadcast, Churchill made a fervent plea for American military aid: "[G]ive us the tools and we will finish the job."[16]

Roosevelt had no intention of allowing Hitler to take over the world. Yet FDR also mistrusted British imperial motives and wanted to limit costs to the United States. He hoped almost until Pearl Harbor that "aid short of war, or war short of ground forces, would do the job."[17] As time passed, however, Roosevelt had no delusions that the United States could (or should) remain neutral.

In the summer of 1940, when Britain stood alone after the fall of France and the earlier debacle in Norway, the new British prime minister despaired of victory for his island nation. Britain faced the threat of an imminent cross-Channel invasion and was under daily attack by the Luftwaffe. Even more perilous were the immense losses of shipping to German submarines. If unchecked, the loss rate, Churchill wrote to FDR on December 8, 1940, would be "fatal."[18]

By the time of Pearl Harbor, Germany and Italy ruled Europe.[19]

British defeats and retreats in North Africa and the Middle East had further expanded German-Italian domination over critical areas. Following the surprise attack on Soviet Russia on June 22, 1941—"by far the most gigantic collision of military forces in all of world history"[20]—Hitler was so confident of victory by early autumn, he confided to close associates, that all he needed to do was "kick in the door" to topple the rotten Jewish-Bolshevist state.[21] Churchill feared that Russia could not repel the Nazi invaders and that Germany, with its eastern front secure, would turn its military might to finishing off Great Britain.[22] In Churchill's words, his nation's very "life and survival hung in the balance."[23]

Americans could hardly believe the unrelenting stream of "terrifying news of the apparently unstoppable sweep of German armor across the face of Europe." Fear and anxiety took hold of the popular consciousness. Concern about a Nazi occupation of Britain and annexation of the Western Hemisphere was mounting in the general American population.[24]

In this darkest hour for Britain and the Soviet Union, Roosevelt confided to Churchill his resolve to "look for an incident" that would justify America joining these embattled nations in the hostilities.[25] In 1941, therefore, FDR authorized U.S. Navy escorts of ships bound for Britain as far as Iceland to protect against deadly German U-boats. In September an American ship, the *Greer*, sustained a Nazi torpedo attack, the latest in a series of provocations in the North Atlantic. Seizing on the opportunity, Roosevelt addressed the American people on radio:

> [T]hese acts of international lawlessness [revealed] . . . the Nazi design to abolish the freedom of the seas and to acquire absolute control and domination of these seas for themselves. . . . The American people can have no further illusions about it. No tender whisperings of appeasers that Hitler is not interested in the Western Hemisphere, no soporific lullabies that a wide ocean separates us from him, can long . . . have any effect on the hard-headed, far-sighted, and realistic American people. . . . We have sought no shooting war with Hitler. We do not seek it now. . . . But when you see a rattlesnake poised to strike, you do not wait until he has struck before you crush him. These Nazi submarines and raiders are the rattlesnakes of the Atlantic.[26]

But the isolationist opposition to Roosevelt's policies, principally represented by America First, remained formidable. In response to Roosevelt's fireside chat about the *Greer* attack, Charles A. Lindbergh told a national audience that the three most prominent groups of war agitators—a very small minority of people—"are the British, the Jewish, and the Roosevelt Administration." While lamenting the persecution of Jews in Nazi Germany, Lindbergh nevertheless chastised American Jews for supporting U.S. intervention in Europe, suggesting that "they will be among the first to feel" the consequences of bigotry at home. After all, he added, the Jews' "greatest danger to this country lies in their large ownership and influence in our motion pictures, our press, our radio, and our government."[27]

Lindbergh's blunder was vigorously exploited by FDR and his interventionist allies. America First and its spokesman—roundly condemned for their anti-Semitism and un-Americanism—lost significant credibility as 1941 drew to a close. In a stunning reversal of public opinion, by October 1941, 70 percent of those responding to a Gallup poll thought defeating Hitler was more important than staying out of the war.[28]

Despite cabinet members such as Secretary of War Henry L. Stimson and other top advisors urging a more aggressive stance, Roosevelt stayed the course of gradualism. By 1941, his top priority was "to hold the Atlantic as a shield protecting the Western Hemisphere."[29] The president's instincts and intelligence reports suggested that a Japanese attack—likely on a British territory in the Pacific, an onslaught that Germany was urging Japan to undertake—would be the precipitating crisis dragging the United States into war.

Meanwhile, FDR wanted to mobilize to the maximum the nation's resources for defense "while also preserving and even extending the social gains that the New Deal had made."[30] War production meant rapid conversion and expansion of manufacturing plants. The president had been moving as quickly as he could in light of the staunch resistance from Congress and the isolationist forces.

In what may have been his most conspicuous triumph in moving America closer to war, Roosevelt had secured the passage of the Lend-Lease Act in March 1941. With this stark departure from all pretense of neutrality to open support of Britain, FDR was following through on his mid-1940 promise that the United States would "extend to the opponents of force the material resources of the nation." American military aid to Britain—at a cost far greater than could ever be repaid—had furnished the materials that allowed the brave defenders of freedom to hold on until the United States entered the war. But in the last months of 1941, the United States—whose war production was not yet at full capacity—lagged "far behind what was absolutely necessary for the preservation of the British and American democracies."[31]

Gradualism and isolationism came to an abrupt end on December 7, 1941.

The devastation at Pearl Harbor was horrific. Two waves of Japanese aircraft—launched one hour apart from carriers two hundred miles north of Hawaii—hit the naval base at Pearl Harbor. The Japanese severely damaged or destroyed 8 battleships, 3 light cruisers, 4 other vessels, 188 airplanes, and shore installations. They inflicted 3,435 casualties (including 2,395 deaths) while suffering the loss of fewer than 100 people, 28 of the 343 aircraft launched, and 5 midget submarines. For all intents and purposes, the Pacific Fleet had almost been obliterated.[32] (By great good fortune, the fleet's aircraft carriers were at sea and unharmed.) Simultaneously, the Japanese also attacked Hong Kong, Wake Island, and Midway Island.

Roosevelt and Churchill—while heartsick over the loss of life at Pearl Harbor—were nonetheless visibly relieved after the helpless uncertainty and indecision of the prior two years.[33] The leaders of the two great democracies were committed to waging war to a final total victory. Despite inevitable tensions between Roosevelt and Churchill over military strategy and the complexion of the postwar world, their admiration and genuine affection for each other grew deeper.[34] Regular debate and compromise—facilitated by nine face-to-face meetings and summits lasting 120 days and almost two thousand wartime messages between them—was the hallmark of their collegial decision making.[35]

Through the darkest days as well as the dawn of better times, Roosevelt and Churchill "marvelously kept their heads and their tempers, cheered each other up, differed with candor and grace, and handled a bewildering variety of strategic and diplomatic questions with impressive virtuosity."[36] "It is fun to be in the same decade with you," Churchill once wrote to FDR.[37] These extraordinary men—"indissolubly joined by the sense of sharing a historic stage during a mortal crisis"—would be called upon to furnish extraordinary leadership in desperate times.[38]

* * *

On December 8, 1941, a resolute FDR spoke to a joint session of Congress and the nation via radio. It was a concise, memorable address of less than five hundred simple words that he had dictated himself, with Harry Hopkins, one of FDR's most trusted advisors and the U.S. administrator for lend-lease, adding a sentence to the peroration.[39]

"Yesterday, December 7, 1941—a date which will live in infamy—the United States of America was suddenly and deliberately attacked by the naval and air forces of Japan. . . . No matter how long it may take us to overcome this premeditated invasion, the American people in their righteous might will win through to absolute victory."

The president then asked Congress to declare that this "unprovoked and dastardly attack" had created a state of war between the United States and Japan. The resounding cheers in Congress echoed the collective outrage and surge of patriotism that swept the nation with the incredible news of Pearl Harbor. Men—young and older—flocked to recruiting stations, each expressing in one fashion or another a steely resolve "to beat them Japs with my own bare hands."[40] By the Monday evening after Pearl Harbor, three times as many men had enlisted at the New York City army recruiting center than on April 6, 1917, the day the nation entered World War I.[41]

One of those who volunteered was Kenneth Claiborne Royall, a forty-seven-year-old North Carolina lawyer and former state senator who had fought in World War I. The lanky Harvard Law School graduate was commissioned a colonel and placed in charge of breaking the army's contract logjam. Giving up a successful private law practice, Royall went to Washington, D.C., to help his country defeat Nazi Germany, Italy, and imperial Japan. He could never have imagined what history had in store for him in the spring of 1942.

The tidal wave of patriotic sentiments notwithstanding, a mood of uncertainty gripped anxiety-ridden America. Countless rumors of invasion, spies, and intrigues spread like wildfire. Sensational news reporting prompted FDR to chide newspapers and radio stations not "to deal out unconfirmed reports in such a way as to make people believe they are gospel truth."[42]

On the Pacific coast, Americans feared that the Japanese at any moment might attack them next. The near hysteria was fueled by unfamiliar blackouts and sandbags piled around critical facilities such as telephone exchanges. Japanese neighbors—both citizens and aliens—became the convenient targets of hatred, suspicion, and even destruction of their property. In the Los Angeles area alone, a hundred Japanese-owned businesses were sold or shuttered within the first few days after Pearl Harbor.[43]

In the immediate wake of Pearl Harbor, the territorial governor of Hawaii issued a proclamation turning over all governmental functions to the military. The military governor, Lieutenant General Walter C. Short, closed the civilian courts and replaced them with two forms of military tribunal: lower provost courts for crimes punishable up to five years and a military commission for more serious offenses, including those carrying the death penalty.[44] The territorial governor of Hawaii also suspended the writ of habeas corpus—a wartime expediency upheld by the federal courts.[45]

Now America was at war with Japan, but what about Germany?[46] FDR feared that he could not get a war declaration out of Congress, the isolationists arguing that Japan, not Germany, was the enemy that had attacked America. Yet he knew that Nazi Germany was the most dreaded adversary "because of its armed might, industrial production, and technological innovations."[47] Hitler came to the rescue, however, when he had Germany and Italy declare war on the United States on December 11, 1941.

In his speech to the Reichstag, Hitler betrayed his deep hatred of Roosevelt, contending he was "the main culprit" urged on by diabolical American Jews and resorting to war to camouflage the New Deal's failures at home. "I cannot be insulted by Roosevelt, for I consider him mad, just as Wilson was," Hitler proclaimed.

It would prove to be Hitler's fatal miscalculation: the American people were now united against Germany as well as Japan.

As he reacted to the dreadful news on December 7, 1941, the president knew that the road ahead would be rocky, demanding of the American people "hard work—grueling work—day and night, every hour and every minute."[48] He had tried to avoid a two-front war, he told his wife, Eleanor, because "we haven't got the navy to fight in both the Atlantic and the Pacific . . . [and thus we would now have] to take a good many defeats" while the nation's naval, air, and ground forces were greatly strengthened.[49]

With the Allied war effort careening from one calamity to another, Americans were understandably nervous. The last foreign invasion of

U.S. soil had occurred during the War of 1812—ironically by the British. Now the nation that had never lost a war was looking alarmingly vulnerable.

Nazi submarines were particularly dangerous and demoralizing. Unprotected oil tankers and cargo ships were easy prey along the Atlantic coast. In March 1942 alone, U-boats sank twenty-eight vessels; in November 1942, total Allied losses reached a staggering record of 600,000 tons of shipping. In May 1941, Churchill had anxiously told Roosevelt that British shipping losses could rise to 4.5 million tons over the next year, with sinkings outpacing new construction.[50] From Maine to Miami, oil spills, lost cargo, and corpses washed onto the beaches. Shortages of oil, coffee, sugar, and other goods were being felt every day.[51] "My Navy has been definitely slack in preparing for this submarine war off our coast," Roosevelt wrote to Churchill on March 18, 1942. America was essentially defenseless at sea.

By late spring 1942, the news was no better. Russia teetered on the brink of seemingly inevitable collapse, and German field marshal Erwin ("the Desert Fox") Rommel and his Afrika Korps tanks were ravaging North Africa. The military picture on all fronts was bleak. With Hitler's armed forces demonstrating "apparent invincibility time and again," Roosevelt and Churchill agreed to meet in Hyde Park in June 1942.[52]

As he left the Oval Office at the end of that dreary day in late spring 1942, Roosevelt knew that there would be even rougher times ahead. In the weeks after Pearl Harbor, FDR took decisive steps to unleash "a production and mobilization machine with a potential beyond any the world had seen."[53] As much as anything, the president realized that a geometric increase in airplane production was essential to winning a two-front war. The trick was to hold off the Axis onslaught for the couple of years required to mount a winning counteroffensive.

Lifting the sagging American spirit was an equally monumental task for FDR. The deep-seated trauma over Pearl Harbor—sending convulsive shock waves through the national psyche—was in part the result of "an enormous failure of the imagination. Americans could not believe that a country overseas ever would attack American territory."[54] Reeling from this unthinkable, devastating blow, the public suddenly began to realize that the continental United States was no longer immune to attack by a foreign power.[55]

The morale of the American people and fighting forces was critical to the nation's survival. Even for the Great Communicator, it was a daunting challenge. Through his regular fireside chats and public appearances, FDR had lifted his fellow Americans out of their worst economic emergency, employing his considerable powers of persuasion and empathy. All they had to fear was fear itself, he told them. But now there was a new enemy and a new fear. And one of the greatest fears of the president and his advisors was enemy sabotage.

In a May 6, 1941, radio address, Secretary of War Stimson warned Americans about the grave risks posed by Nazi Germany's utter lack of respect for human life. "Today a small group of evil leaders have taught the young men of Germany that the freedom of other men and nations must be destroyed. Today those young men are ready to die for that perverted conviction."[56]

FDR needed a win—something to lift the sagging American spirit—to demonstrate that the nation's borders and manufacturing facilities would be defended at all costs.

Chapter 3

Hitler's Terrorists

While Roosevelt brooded over America's vulnerability, Hitler and his senior advisors were putting the finishing touches on Operation Pastorius. The Nazis had a fondness for invoking history in their cause. So the inaugural sabotage operation would be named after Franz Pastorius, leader of the first German immigrant community in America in 1683.

Hitler's personal involvement in the mission's planning was hardly unusual. A student of war, he reveled in tactical details, often to his generals' consternation. More than anything, Hitler relished the audacity of his plan.

The commandos would leave occupied France on two U-boats, land units on Long Island and the Florida coast, and then proceed by different routes to rendezvous in New York City. Equipped with explosives, detailed maps and plans of critical defense plants, and plenty of American money, they would destroy their strategic transportation, manufacturing, and hydroelectric plant targets in a rapid series of morale-sapping attacks that would provoke a general panic. In their spare time, they would blow up several railroad stations and businesses such as department stores and other places where large numbers of civilians were present.

Operation Pastorius was by no means a quixotic venture. The German High Command justifiably feared that America's industrial might and its awesome capacity, once in high gear, would produce large numbers of high-quality warplanes, ships, and munitions for the Allies. The Nazis knew firsthand that America's steady influx of weapons and supplies to England during the nominal neutrality period had kept hope alive that Germany would not overrun England. The war would be won as much in the air as on the ground. America's warplane manufacturing had to be interrupted.

Hitler wanted to strike a devastating blow at the heart of his enemy's industrial capacity. Indeed, he envisioned launching sabotage missions every four to six weeks until the United States had been widely penetrated and the American public demoralized by the war being brought to the home front. So this first operation was a trial run—a precursor of devastation and mayhem to follow.

Germany had already endured three years of war, and, objectively viewed, its hope for ultimate victory seemed to be waning by the day. The *Sicherheitsdienst*, the intelligence division of the SS and commonly referred to as the SD, frequently gathered German morale or "mood" reports, documenting everything from rumors currently circulating to criticism of the Nazi government or the war effort. The SD reported a significant decline in popular optimism after news of the hardships on the Russian front coupled with the massive air raids on German cities.[1] It would be a real morale booster if German saboteurs were able to strike back and carry the battle to the American heartland.

Those selected to undertake these high-risk operations really had no choice:[2] accept the assignment or face swift and implacable Nazi retribution, possibly through the machinery of one of Hitler's "special courts," or tribunals, established to preside over matters in which he wanted a specific outcome.[3] In 1942, less then 8 percent of the accused before the tribunals received verdicts of not guilty. Hitler validated these courts and their seemingly predetermined outcomes with his characteristic twisted logic: "[I]t is necessary that justice not conserve the negative elements but rather eradicate the rotten elements."[4]

Germany would not be the only country in 1942 to bypass the constitutionally ordained judicial system to achieve a political objective.

By late May, the men in the two saboteur teams had been trained. The nine volunteers—one named Schmidt later dropped out while en route to the French coast because of venereal disease—then went on a three-day tour around Germany during which they surveyed aluminum and magnesium plants, railroad shops, canals and river locks, and other facilities similar to those they would be destroying in the United States. They were instructed in the most vulnerable points to be sabotaged. It was now only a matter of time before they would embark on their historic mission.

The saboteurs were a motley crew recruited by Kappe from various elements of German society. They all had one thing in common—long-term residency in the United States between the wars. They also shared an aversion to being sent to the Eastern Front, where German forces were already suffering ferocious casualties. Hitler had indeed "kicked in the door," and a massive German army was streaming through it. The Wehrmacht reached the outskirts of Moscow—but got no further. Hitler's soldiers, 250,000 of them, took Stalingrad, but three months after Russia counterattacked in November 1942, only 90,000 had survived. Few of them would manage to return to Germany.

Did these eight "volunteers" have more promising prospects?

George John Dasch

George John Dasch was born in 1903 in Speyer am Rhein, Germany—a city near Frankfurt.[5] One of twelve children, Dasch was educated in a Catholic seminary in Düsseldorf and soon fell in love with America as a young boy. In 1922, the desperate nineteen-year-old stowed away on the SS *Scholarie* of the Kerr Line bound for Philadelphia, hiding for sixteen days in the galley coal bin.

Once in Philadelphia, Dasch worked for a German baker for only a week before hitchhiking to New York City. There he worked as a waiter, took night classes with other immigrants, and lived with an Irish family named Callahan on 145th Street near Amsterdam Avenue.

In 1925 Dasch and some buddies drove across the United States and worked as waiters in California. Two years later, he joined the U.S. Army Air Corps while attempting to become a U.S. citizen. He shipped out to Honolulu. A year later, he got out of the army, receiving an "excellent" character rating.

For a few years, Dasch moved around the country, stopping in St. Louis, St. Peters, Missouri, and Chicago. By 1930, back in New York City, he became a waiter at the New Yorker Hotel. That spring, he met his future wife, Snooks—a beautician from Philadelphia whose real name was Rose Marie Guillie. They were married in September 1930.

After experiencing the pervasive misery and poverty of the early Depression years, the newlyweds made a brief trip to Europe to meet Dasch's mother. He had lost his waiter job, and Snooks had suffered a miscarriage. On their return to New York City, they worked in hotels and restaurants. By September 1939, Dasch had qualified for U.S. citizenship and was supposed to go to court for the final swearing in, but he never showed up.

In August 1939, while his mother was visiting, Dasch's family heard over the radio the news about Hitler's nonaggression pact with the Soviet Union. His worried mother rushed back to Germany in time for the start of the war on September 1, 1939. She urged her son to return home to get a better, steadier job than being a waiter.

On Christmas Eve, in 1940, Dasch informed his incredulous wife that he wanted to return to more prosperous Germany and start a new life. "To find the dignity and pride in work that has eluded me in the United States," he insisted.

In order to repatriate to Germany, however, he was forced to register as an alien in America—something that hurt his feelings. The Daschs received their passports in January 1941, but because Snooks was a U.S. citizen, the Neutrality Act barred her from traveling into a war zone. Soon thereafter, she became very ill and had to have a hysterectomy. Bound for Germany in late March 1941, Dasch left his wife behind in the United States and arrived in Berlin on May 13, 1941.

Berliners were celebrating the incredible string of German victories, but Dasch was not caught up in the general enthusiasm. While he was a socialist and fond of reading Norman Thomas, he had never belonged to a political party or joined the Bund. In fact, he later claimed that he hated Hitler and the Nazis and that he was a member of groups that broke up Bund and Nazi meetings. The ubiquitous Nazi flags and constant refrain of "Heil Hitler" supposedly made him uncomfortable, yet Dasch had to pretend to be a loyal Nazi in order to make a decent living and not attract the sinister interest of the Gestapo.

Upon his return in 1941, Dasch was told to see Walter Kappe, who helped Dasch land a job at a radio station where he became responsible for monitoring American broadcasts. Whether out of a wry sense of humor or a morbid death wish, Dasch—at nights when radio reception was poor—would denounce Hitler on the air, using an American name. When he heard about the Japanese attack on Pearl Harbor, Dasch became depressed because he had been stationed in Honolulu and could imagine what it must have been like when war came to the beautiful island. Now enraged by Hitler and Nazi Germany, he decided that he would fight against them in his own little way.

When Kappe first attempted to recruit him for the sabotage operation, Dasch was less than enthusiastic. "I just arrived from that terrible country," he reminded Kappe. "Why would I want to go back? I came here to fight."

Apparently he was all too successful at playing the part of the loyal Nazi to avoid suspicion. Indeed, Kappe—impressed by the volatile and eccentric Dasch's facile intelligence and his American manners and speech—became convinced that he was just the man to lead the mission against America.[6]

Dasch would later claim that he always intended to sabotage the sabotage mission as his way of striking back at Hitler. Once safely in America, he planned to fight for the United States and even serve as the leader on a mission to sabotage Germany. From the very first day he heard about it, Dasch would later insist, he was determined to make sure that the German mission failed. He had visions of becoming an American hero. Grandparents would tell their grandchildren about his brave deeds. He would have a place in history.

Edward John Kerling

Born on June 12, 1909, in the Rhineland, Edward John Kerling was a disaffected youth who was attracted, like so many others, to Hitler's National Socialism. By June 1928 he was a proud member of the Nazi Party. Indeed, he was one of the first seventy thousand supporters of Hitler.

When he was twenty, Kerling came to the United States, but he remained an active Nazi. Friends back home continued to pay his Nazi Party dues while he established residency and joined the German-American Bund. Kerling never even thought of becoming a U.S. citizen—he was a German and a Nazi first, last, and foremost.

While he lived in America, Kerling's jobs were menial—smoking hams in Brooklyn and working as a shipping clerk for a Jewish-owned packing company in Manhattan. He married Marie Sichart, who had emigrated to the United States from Munich and then joined the Bund. As a team of cook and butler-chauffeur, they worked for affluent families in the suburbs of New York—Greenwich, Connecticut, and Short Hills, New Jersey. But after a few years their marriage fell apart and they separated. Contrary to Kerling's wishes, they were never divorced.

After seven years in America, Kerling returned to Germany in 1936 for a vacation to watch the Olympic games. He joined many fellow Bund members who saw the spectacle as a glorious triumph for Hitler. After returning to the United States, he had relationships with several women. The most significant was with Hedwig "Hedy" Engemann, a German who worked as a waitress in Miami in the early 1940s. With her, Kerling would share his hopes and his bed. The occasional appearance of his wife, Marie, did not disrupt their relationship.

With Germany at war, Kerling and some friends decided to return to Germany to defend the fatherland. They bought a yawl named *Lekala* for under $2,000. While they were sailing from New York to Miami, the U.S. Coast Guard intercepted the boat off Atlantic City and, under the provisions of the Neutrality Act, stopped them from going on to Europe. One of Kerling's crewmen on the aborted cruise to Deutschland would also end up as one of the eight saboteurs.

After wavering about returning to Germany, largely because of his romance with Hedy in Miami and New York, Kerling sailed home on the SS *Exchordia* in late July 1940. Since he had been one of Hitler's earliest supporters, Kerling immediately got a job at an army listening post in Deauville, France, where he translated English-language broadcasts into German.

Three months later, Kerling became the stage manager for the theaters in Berlin controlled by Joseph Goebbels's Ministry of Propaganda. He was instrumental in the production of shows promoting Nazi ideology in the sort of entertainment that Goebbels considered suitable for German audiences. His stint lasted for eighteen months; it was a comfortable sinecure, but Kerling wanted to see action in the army. In his spare time, he wrote many letters to Hedy, telling her that he was happy to be back home but was desperately lonely without her.

Kerling got his wish, after a fashion, in March 1942, when Walter Kappe interviewed Kerling at the Ministry of Propaganda. Taking an instant liking to Kerling, Kappe was impressed by this committed Nazi's "intelligence, strength of character, and loyalty to the Nazi cause."[7] At five feet nine inches and 170 pounds, Kerling made a favorable impression, with wavy brown hair parted in the middle, heavy brows over calm gray eyes, and an ingratiating smile. With his perfect Aryan good looks, he was the very image of a soldier of the Third Reich.

Kerling immediately accepted Kappe's invitation to join the team. Finally, he had found the ideal way to serve—and, if necessary, to die for—his country.

Ernest Peter Burger

Born in 1906, Ernest Peter Burger had an unremarkable childhood in Essex, Germany. His Nazi Party credentials were impeccable. Present at the creation, he participated actively in Hitler's first attempt to seize power at the Munich beer hall putsch.

In the 1920s, Burger proved to be a better street fighter than a student in a technical school. One particularly violent brawl led to his leaving Germany rather than face the Bavarian courts. He arrived in the United States in February 1927.

Burger held many jobs during his six years in America. While he studied English and went to night school, he was a machinist for several companies in the Midwest. Burger joined the Michigan and Wisconsin National Guards. Eventually, he became an American citizen.

When the Depression hit, Burger joined the growing ranks of millions of other unemployed Americans. By late 1933, Hitler was in power.[8] Burger's parents wrote to him about the new prosperity in Germany under Hitler and urged him to return home. His parents paid for his passage back to Germany in 1933, and Burger resumed his former role as an active Nazi Party member. He was appointed aide-de-camp to Ernest Roehm, a homosexual who happened to be one of Hitler's closest associates and leader of the Nazi Sturmabteilung—or SA, the Storm Troopers, who were ultimately supplanted by the SS. By sheer luck, Burger escaped the Night of the Long Knives, when Roehm and hundreds of Storm Troopers were brutally executed by the SS in a bloody purge on June 30, 1934, largely because of pressure by the German army. Burger had left two days before the start of the decimation of the SA on an assignment to assist the chief of the Medical Division of the Storm Troopers.

After the purge, Burger bounced around, taking a minor post in the party's domestic propaganda division in Berlin, attending classes and graduating from the University of Berlin, and marrying his secretary. At the university, Burger met Professor Karl Haushofer, a prominent exponent of geopolitics and a favorite of Hitler. The professor took a liking to Burger and gave him a somewhat ticklish assignment. Burger undertook an analysis of material on the German dismantling of Czechoslovakia. His report contained some derogatory comments about the Gestapo.

Haushofer also assigned Burger to do a similar study of German rule in Poland. The Poland report got into the hands of the Gestapo, and Burger was arrested on March 4, 1940. Burger was accused of falsifying government documents, but none of Burger's friends in power could acknowledge their association with him. Burger was put in a concentration camp for nearly seventeen months. Eventually, the charges against him were dropped.

In July 1941, Burger returned to the army as an infantry private in a unit assigned to guard Yugoslavian and British soldiers in POW camps outside Berlin. In February 1942, Kappe interviewed Burger, and early in April of that same year, Burger was released from guard duty and sent to the sabotage school at Quenz Lake.

Kappe felt as though he was giving Burger a chance for redemption, rescuing him from the tender mercies of the Gestapo and the revenge of those he accused of betraying the National Socialist revolution. When Burger and Dasch first met, Dasch readily accepted Burger as a loyal and disciplined Nazi, although he was not sure why he had agreed to work for Germany after what the Gestapo had done to him. For his part, Burger did not think that Dasch would make a good leader—he was too talkative, inattentive, and undisciplined.

The two men worked closely together but, not surprisingly, no real trust or friendship developed. They were an odd couple. Burger's job in the sabotage mission was to establish a front in Chicago, either as a violin instructor or as a commercial artist. Using one of these jobs as a cover, he would put classified ads in the *Chicago Tribune* on the first and fifteenth of each month. The assumption was that the Abwehr would obtain copies of the *Tribune* and, seeing the advertisements, conclude that conditions were favorable for Kappe to leave for America to oversee the sabotage operation.

This clandestine method of communication was never employed because at the last minute, one of the men in Dasch's group, the hapless Schmidt, dropped out, having allegedly caught a dose of gonorrhea. Burger was forced to take over his assignment and sacrifice his central communications point. Instead, the saboteurs would use the addresses of loyal Bundists and active Nazi members in the United States for secret communications.

Herbert Hans Haupt

Herbert Hans Haupt was twenty-two years old at the time of the sabotage mission. Kappe thought that Haupt—a tall, broad-shouldered young man with extraordinary good looks who had taken boxing lessons—would be invaluable to the mission because of his six-foot, 190-pound frame. Haupt would be a great asset for another reason: he acted like an American. He wore flashy jewelry and used a lot of American slang.

Haupt was born in Stettin, Germany, on December 21, 1919. When he was only five years old, he was brought to Chicago, remaining there for nearly the rest of his life. At age ten, he became an American citizen as a part of his father's naturalization. Herbert went to a public school and found his niche as a scrawny kid who loved to work out on playground gymnastic equipment, "trying to build up his biceps as if he had visions of making himself into a superman."[9]

During his sophomore year, he decided to become an optician's apprentice at the Simpson Optical Manufacturing Company rather than continue to attend school. Like other impressionable youth, Haupt "took to strutting around the neighborhood in the brown-shirt uniform that the German-American Bund adopted from the Nazis."[10]

Later, his girlfriend, Gerda Stuckmann Melind, became pregnant, and Haupt was under pressure to comply with the requirement that he register for the American draft. Haupt was only twenty-one years old, and Gerda had been a widow for four years. Haupt told his mother that he was going on a vacation, while he told Gerda that he was taking a short trip to California.

Instead, he panicked and split for Mexico. In June 1941, with about

$160 between them, Haupt and two friends drove down to Mexico City in a 1933 Chevy. During their stay in Mexico, they found that they could not get jobs without work permits since they were foreigners. After about three weeks, they met a man named Hans Sass, who took them to the German consulate. The German officials suggested that they could find work in a Japanese monastery, of all places, and that the consulate would pay for their fare.

So in late July 1941, Haupt, a friend, and several other Germans from Central American countries departed for Yokohama. The "monastery" turned out to be a labor camp. Haupt and his buddy tried to rebel at first, but it was useless. The German officials told them that they would have to earn their living—if not in the labor camp, then somewhere else where they could contribute to Germany's war effort.

Rising to the challenge, they qualified as seamen, taking a three-week course on a German liner. Soon afterward, they were put aboard a German freighter headed for Germany. They were expected to continue working their way while on the passage to Germany. Haupt performed duties as an oiler and a lookout. Once they reached Germany and got to Saarbrucken, they were given some freedom. In March 1942, Haupt received a medal and commendation for successful blockade running. Acting as a German freighter's lookout, he had spotted a British warship, enabling his ship to evade the British blockade.

Haupt was pleased that he had returned to Germany; he even considered becoming a pilot in the Luftwaffe. This was easier said than done. The Gestapo was not convinced about his explanation for his return to Germany, which sounded too naive to be true.

Claiming to be a magazine editor, Walter Kappe wrote Haupt a letter telling him to come to Berlin to discuss an article about his trip to Germany. Haupt went to Berlin and told Kappe his story. Two weeks later, Haupt was again asked to come to Berlin, and this time Kappe turned the conversation to Haupt's problems in Germany, including the continued questioning by the Gestapo and his difficulty finding any quality work. Kappe remarked that the only thing left for Haupt to do was to return to the United States. Haupt readily agreed, although Kappe mentioned that "certain unspecified duties for Germany might be expected of him in the United States."[11]

Haupt was soon off to the school for saboteurs at Quenz Lake. His problems of the draft and his pregnant girlfriend seemed far behind him. In fact, they would prove to be the least of his worries.

Richard Quirin

Richard Quirin was born in 1908 in Berlin. After attending trade schools, he became a machinist's apprentice. In 1927, with jobs scarce in the Berlin area, he borrowed some money from his uncle for passage to the United States. While residing in the United States, Quirin lived with another uncle in Schenectady, New York, working as a tinsmith, studying English at night school, and landing a job with the maintenance department of General Electric. He later applied for American citizenship.

During the Depression, Quirin was laid off from his job at General Electric and settled in New York City, working as a house painter. He joined the German-American Bund and its version of the Storm Troopers. In the process, he dropped the idea of becoming an American citizen.

In 1939, when Quirin heard that Germany was paying the way for those who wanted to return to the fatherland, he repatriated for several reasons. His German-born wife was homesick and desperately wanted to return, Hitler had gained power in Germany, and the promise of the Third Reich was high. Once he returned, he got work as a Volkswagen machinist.

Kappe was impressed with Quirin because of his "knowledgeable, uncomplicated approach to . . . [his] work and . . . [his] stubborn devotion to duty."[12] Kappe also liked the fact that Quirin was a dyed-in-the-wool Nazi who would not let his imagination carry him beyond the job at hand. Two months after Kappe spoke with Quirin, his papers were processed for his transfer to Quenz Lake.

Heinrich Heinck

Heinrich Heinck was born in 1907 in Hamburg. Like Quirin, Heinck also attended trade schools and became a machinist's apprentice, and he left Germany in 1927, when jobs were extremely hard to find. While

Heinck was working as an oiler and machinist's helper on the Hamburg-American Line's SS *Westphalia*, he jumped ship in New York.

Just like Quirin, he stayed in America for twelve years. Heinck's stay in the United States, however, was illegal. During his dozen years there, Heinck remained in New York, associating almost exclusively with other German nationals. Heinck refused to leave his safety net, even at work, where he progressed from a busboy to a handyman and then to an elevator operator, and finally to his own trade as a machinist.

Like his counterpart, Heinck also joined the German-American Bund and became a Storm Trooper. Not long after he joined, non–U.S. citizens were ordered to leave the Bund. Nevertheless, Heinck continued to attend its social functions and applied for membership in the Nazi Party in Germany.

Along with thousands of others, Heinck also allowed Germany to pay his way back to his homeland in 1939. Coincidentally, when he began work that year in Germany, he found himself at a workbench next to Quirin. Kappe liked Heinck for the same reasons that he recruited Quirin—he displayed stubborn devotion to his duty, and he was knowledgeable but not imaginative. Heinck and Quirin made the trip together to the school at Quenz Lake.

Hermann Otto Neubauer

Neubauer was born in 1910 in Hamburg, emigrating to the United States in 1931, when he was twenty-one. With some training as a cook, he found employment in restaurants and on ships. In 1934, Neubauer worked in a concession at the Chicago World's Fair and in several hotels.

The same year, he joined the Nazi Party and became a member of the Bund in the United States. In 1939, Neubauer joined Kerling in his efforts to sail the *Lekala* to Germany. After his brief stay in Miami, Neubauer married a German American girl, Alma Wolf, whom he had known from Chicago, and they returned to Germany in 1940.

Almost immediately upon his arrival in Germany, Neubauer was drafted into the German army. Three days after Hitler's invasion of Russia, an artillery shell exploded near his billet, embedding shrapnel in his face and leg. The doctors removed as much of it as possible, but the piece over his right eye was too close to his brain for the doctors to risk an operation. For the rest of his life, Neubauer had a metal fragment resembling the shape of a lima bean in his cheek and smaller pieces of metal in his forehead and leg.

In March 1942, Neubauer received a cryptic note from Kappe saying that he would like Neubauer to go on a special assignment to a country where he had been before. Fearing he would soon be sent off to the Russian front once more, he replied immediately. Three weeks later, his company commander gave him the money to go to his home in Hamburg and then to Berlin, where he was to report to Kappe at the editorial offices of *Der Kaukasus*. Kappe liked Neubauer for the same reason that he recruited Quirin and Heinck: Neubauer was eager to obey his orders and to please his superiors.

Werner Thiel

The eighth and final recruit was Werner Thiel. Born in 1907 in Augsburg, Germany, he first went to the United States when he was twenty years old. He traveled to Detroit, where he found work as a machinist at the Ford plant and then at General Motors. By 1930, however, he worked only intermittently and was unable to find a permanent job anywhere.

In New York, where machinists were in even less demand than in Detroit, Thiel found a job as a handyman and then spent three years as a porter at the Home for the Aged and Infirm on Central Park West. Just across Central Park was Yorkville, the Friends of the New Germany, and its successor, the Bund. Thiel later moved to Hammond, Indiana, for a better job and helped establish a new Bund chapter there.

After losing his job in Hammond, Thiel traveled all over the country looking for jobs and found work for short periods in cities such as East Chicago, Los Angeles, San Diego, San Francisco, Hammond again, and Fort Myers. By now, he had heard of the beginning of Hitler's promised thousand-year reign in Germany, and he applied for passage to Germany at the German consulate. He met Dasch on his return trip to Germany.

Once in Germany, Thiel found steady work in a Berlin war plant for nearly eight months, until Kappe interviewed him. At a second meeting, one week after his first interview in March 1942, Kappe said that it would be nice "for some of us fellows who knew the United States to go back and do something." On April 1, 1942, Thiel left his job at the war plant to go home for a few days during Easter before reporting for duty at Quenz Lake two days later.[13] Like the rest, he completed his abbreviated saboteur training and went on the postgraduate tour of German industrial plants and critical transportation facilities similar to those they would be attacking in the United States.

The saboteurs' spirits were high as they embarked for France with their fake names and backgrounds. The Führer had entrusted them with this historic responsibility for Deutschland. America was weak, demoralized; Germany's world domination was inevitable. These eight English-speaking Germans—two of them U.S. citizens—would be responsible for the first successful wave of Hitler's terrorist attacks on America.

Chapter 4

"Just a Scrap of Paper"

"Good morning, Mr. Commander in Chief," Henry L. Stimson greeted his boss.

The secretary of war knew that FDR preferred his military title to "Mr. President." In fact, Roosevelt "relished the role, which he wore with the same ease as he did the naval cape in which he was so memorably photographed, the wind in his hair, on the deck of the cruiser *Houston* in San Francisco Bay, reviewing the fleet."[1]

A man who "took his position as head of the armed services more seriously than did any other President but Lincoln"[2] was now responsible for the security of his 135 million fellow Americans—and the fate of the free world. Roosevelt, in Winston Churchill's exaggerated assessment, was "that great man whom destiny has marked for the climax of human fortune."

Roosevelt was sound on grand military strategy—indeed, Churchill considered him America's "most skilful strategist."[3] Stimson was "wholly certain that the Army had never had a finer Commander in Chief" than Roosevelt—"the best war President the United States has ever had."[4] Stimson and FDR disagreed on many issues, but over time "Stimson never wavered in his admiration for Mr. Roosevelt's great qualities," and he had increasing "affection for the man who carried his burdens with such buoyant courage" and "determination . . . in time of threatened disaster."[5]

On this day in early June, the sixty-year-old president was huddling with three of his principal homeland security advisors: Stimson, Attorney General Francis B. Biddle, and Federal Bureau of Investigation director J. Edgar Hoover. The commander in chief continued to be worried about domestic sabotage by German and Japanese combatants and American sympathizers. His fears were anything but irrational.

Each of the men at the meeting remembered incidents before and during World War I of suspected German sabotage within the United States.[6] For example, on July 30, 1916, more than two million pounds of munitions stored on Black Tom Island in New York Harbor had exploded, causing some $14 million in damage and killing three men and a child. The munitions were bound for Russia to be used against Germany. German agents were believed to be responsible.

Roosevelt had also been warned by Churchill to beware of fifth columnists in his midst. Churchill had firsthand experience to share with his friend. Immediately after Churchill became prime minister in May 1940, he took decisive action to counteract fifth columnists in Great Britain at the considerable expense of civil liberties. Holland had just fallen to the Nazis, France would soon follow, and German troops were gathering across the English Channel. Churchill feared a Nazi invasion assisted by enemy agents within Britain. He had heard "rampant rumours of European 'Fifth Columnists' who had opened doors for the Nazis."[7]

Fantasy reports about Nazi spies and sympathizers within Great Britain fueled near-hysterical concern about internal security. While Churchill would later admit that no serious fifth column was at work in Britain during the war, he acted otherwise when his nation trembled under the darkening shadow of German occupation. "Very considerable numbers" of British fascists, communists, and other suspicious persons should be detained, Churchill urged.

Using broad powers granted by Parliament, Churchill—invoking national security to extirpate "the malignancy in our midst"—eventually arrested and interned thousands of German and Italian aliens and British subjects. By late July 1940, some twenty-seven thousand—most of them innocent of any wrongdoing or pro-Axis sympathies—had been rounded up and imprisoned in makeshift camps scattered around the country.[8] With Britain in mortal peril, Churchill did not fret much about the suspension of habeas corpus or massive civil liberties violations.

In his very first message to Roosevelt as prime minister, Churchill reported that he expected attacks by parachutes and airborne troops in Britain and Ireland similar to those launched against Belgian and Dutch targets in 1940 and the British in Crete in 1941. FDR in turn warned Congress of a fifth column threat. In a fireside chat with the American people, as France was falling to the Nazis, he "spoke darkly of the new methods of war involving spies, saboteurs and traitors."[9] The American people, he warned, must be on guard for "[t]he Trojan Horse. The Fifth Column that betrays a nation unprepared for treachery."[10]

Both Roosevelt and Churchill faced "enemies within" before and after war broke out. Churchill had to contend with the British fascists, led by Sir Oswald Mosley. (Mosley and his fellow admirers of Hitler would have made up the core of Britain's puppet government in event of German occupation.) The prime minister also had to contend with those who wanted to appease Germany, sympathizers such as the duke of Windsor (the former King Edward VIII) and others highly placed in the British establishment—not a few of whom wanted to come to terms with Germany even well after war was declared.[11] Britain's foreign secretary, Lord Halifax—whom Chamberlain had wanted instead of Churchill to be his replacement as prime minister—was initially more often than not of little help to Churchill in the war cabinet during Churchill's tenure as first lord and then as prime minister. Lord Halifax was emblematic of far too many in the British aristocracy, the Conservative Party, and the other components of the ruling class in Britain—proponents of appeasement before the war and defeatist (or inclined to be conciliatory and make some sort of deal with Hitler) after the war broke out.[12]

Roosevelt was fully aware of what his friend Churchill had endured at the hands of enemies "both foreign and domestic." Roosevelt had been forced to contend with one of his own diplomatic appointees—Joseph P. Kennedy, ambassador to the Court of St. James—who believed that Germany would overwhelm Britain and that America should stay out of the war. FDR eventually but firmly neutralized Kennedy, but he was somewhat less successful with his bitter enemy, the staunchly isolationist and anti-British Colonel Robert McCormick. His *Chicago Tribune* would later print information revealing the greatest secret of the war, the successful breaking of the enemy's codes—a revelation fortunately ignored by the Japanese and the Germans.

The Bundists in America and Oswald Mosley's fascists in Britain had their parallels in Europe—the Rexists in Belgium, Quisling and his followers in Norway, the Vichy collaborators in France, and other pro-Nazi groups as well as Communists (before Hitler's invasion of the Soviet Union)—all of whom provided more than sufficient grounds for Churchill's and Roosevelt's apprehension about the possibilities of internal subversion. Such gloomy realities intensified the atmosphere of fear of fifth column betrayals. The British government dealt firmly with potential "enemies within." Mosley and his wife and associates were imprisoned or interned along with Germans and Italians as well as other British subjects.

When America entered World War II, Roosevelt did not hesitate to implement sweeping homeland security measures. Shortly after Pearl Harbor, the president issued a series of orders making the eastern seaboard a military zone. Warning signs were conspicuously posted along the beaches.

National security entailed more than defending against external military threats. One critical area was ensuring labor-management peace during the war to avert crippling interruptions of vital military equipment production. A summit of labor and industry leaders before Christmas 1941 led to a pledge of no strikes and no lockouts for the duration of the emergency. All labor-management disputes would be settled by peaceful means. Soon thereafter, FDR appointed a War Labor Board to make certain that production was not paralyzed by debilitating work stoppages.[13]

With Britain's example no doubt in mind, Roosevelt was terribly concerned about internal threats to the nation's security. Thus on the afternoon after the Japanese attack, Attorney General Biddle brought to the White House presidential proclamations authorizing the arrest of German and Italian aliens in the country. It was classic FDR, thought Biddle at the time. As he sat in his office, taking another Camel from a tarnished, dented silver cigarette case, Roosevelt leaned back, blowing a cumulus of smoke across the desk toward his visitor. Roosevelt wanted to know how many Germans were in the country and whether his attorney general planned to intern all of them. Biddle balked at the idea of mass internment of Germans, but Roosevelt was less hesitant.

"I don't care so much about the Italians," he explained. "They are a lot of opera singers, but the Germans are different; they may be dangerous."[14]

It was one thing to incarcerate enemy aliens who enjoyed little or no constitutional protection. But the president was being pressured by the military, California governor Culbert Olson, California attorney general Earl Warren, West Coast business leaders and politicians, editorial writers, and many others to remove all Japanese Americans in the western United States and relocate them to interior detention centers.

Earl Warren's attitude epitomized the public clamor for removal of Japanese Americans from the West Coast. He was convinced that the military had wartime authority "to tell me to get back 200 miles if it wants to do it, and as a good American citizen I have no right to complain. . . . Now," Warren concluded, "if a good American citizen cannot complain, I don't see why the Japanese should complain."[15]

This unprecedented proposal posed a serious question of presidential authority. The United States Constitution offered little guidance about the full extent of the president's powers in such exigent circumstances. As commander in chief, he was the warlord with supreme powers over the military. As president, he ran the executive department of the three coequal branches of government, and he took an oath of office to faithfully "preserve, protect, and defend the Constitution of the United States." From the dawn of the Republic, scholars had debated the chief executive's inherent powers to suspend civil liberties during wartime, especially without congressional authorization and in the face of such constitutional guarantees as the writ of habeas corpus, due process of law, and trial by jury.

While he generally respected constitutional tradition,[16] Roosevelt was first and foremost a man of action, not an ideologue but an inveterate pragmatist with an awesome job to do.[17] He would let nothing—including the Bill of Rights—stand in the way of achieving success. And when it came to protecting national security, he would countenance no temporizing. After all, had he not been elected three times by the American people to protect the nation from all enemies, foreign and domestic?

America was at war, in a desperate fight for her life. For the first time in any living American's lifetime, foreign aggressors threatened the physical safety of the nation. Certain security measures, however expedient or harsh, had to be taken in the national interest.[18]

Roosevelt also felt that the First Amendment's guarantee of freedom of the press had to be balanced against the needs of national security. In his fireside chat two nights after Pearl Harbor, he warned against hysterical rumor mongering by the media:

> To all newspapers and radio stations . . . I say this:
> You have . . . no right in the ethics of patriotism to deal out
> unconfirmed reports in such a way as to make people believe
> they are gospel truth.[19]

As the war progressed, Roosevelt grew increasingly hostile toward what he perceived as seditious criticism in the press.[20] FDR pressed Biddle for court action against the most vocal critics of his war policies. His antipathy to newspaper attacks put him in such illustrious company as George Washington, Thomas Jefferson, and Abraham Lincoln. When his attorney general insisted on clear evidence of sedition, Roosevelt intensified his pressure to take criminal action against his detractors.

Roosevelt had little tolerance for "the theory of sedition, or in the constitutional right to criticize government in wartime," Biddle found. "He wanted this antiwar talk stopped."[21] FDR was, after all, a man who did not allow abstract principles to stand in the way of his goals.

Biddle was enough a student of American history to know that a nation at war made compromises in respecting the rights of its own citizens.

During the American Revolution, loyalists were treated harshly. Branded traitors, some were stripped naked, tarred and feathered, and then dragged around town to the local patriots' mocking taunts. In patriot-controlled colonies, British supporters could not vote, sell land, sue debtors, or work as lawyers, doctors, or schoolteachers. Vocal critics of the insurrection were also stripped of their property and goods, and some were banished upon pain of death if they returned. This intolerance of sharp political dissent spilled over into the new federal government's enactment of the notorious Sedition Act of 1798, which made it a crime to speak or write anything "false, scandalous and malicious" about the government, Congress, or the president. Numerous individuals were sent to prison.[22] The Alien Act of the same year gave the government sweeping powers to deport any alien deemed dangerous to the nation's welfare.

The status quo for a large segment of the population did not change during or after the Revolutionary War. African Americans constituted almost 20 percent of the colonists, and 95 percent of them were slaves for whom the inalienable rights of life, liberty, and the pursuit of happiness were merely words on parchment. The few free slaves (like women) had no right to vote, and they were restricted by curfews and other discriminatory measures. Near the end of hostilities, racism temporarily yielded to expediency—the ban on African Americans enlisting as soldiers had been lifted in all states except Georgia and South Carolina. The new Constitution, however, perpetuated slavery, and each African American counted as only three-fifths of a person for purposes of allocating seats in the House of Representatives among the states.[23]

The War of 1812—sometimes called the Second Revolutionary War—arose from British maritime practices during the Napoleonic Wars blocking American cargo headed for France and impressing some six thousand American seamen alleged to be British navy deserters. In the lead-up to war, President Thomas Jefferson halted trade with European countries in 1807, enraging New Englanders whose businesses were bankrupted by the trade embargo. With New England talking secession from the Union, the author of the Declaration of Independence ruthlessly enforced the Embargo Act, arresting Americans for opposition to the law and employing treason trials in the Lake Champlain area to quell an insurrection.

When James Madison became president in 1809, he tried to persuade the British to cease interfering with American shipping. When they persistently refused, America declared war and suffered heavy casualties and property damage in the first part of hostilities. The British invaded America and burned the White House.

The state and federal courts decided several cases involving citizens' rights in wartime. Samuel Stacy Jr. was arrested for treason in Watertown, New York, and held by the military without trial. A lower state court issued a writ of habeas corpus, but the military defied the order by pretending that each officer to whom the writ was presented did not have physical custody of the prisoner. In 1813, the New York Supreme Court of Judicature issued an order freeing Stacy. In the face of the pretextual charge of treason without any proof and the military's usurpation of civil authority to try a citizen for treason, the court proclaimed its "indispensable duty . . . to act as a faithful guardian of the personal liberty of the citizen, and to give ready and effectual aid to the means provided by law for its security."[24]

Before the decisive Battle of New Orleans in 1815, General Andrew Jackson imposed martial law on the city. Not only did Jackson ignore a writ of habeas corpus issued on behalf of a local newspaper editor arrested for fiercely criticizing the general, he arrested the judge who issued the order. Following the Treaty of Ghent ending the war, Jackson restored civil authority and paid a $1,000 fine issued by one angry judge who had not appreciated the defiance of his authority and arrest.

The United States Supreme Court decided a significant case involving property rights in time of war. In *Brown v. United States*, the fledgling high court held that the military cannot condemn property as belonging to the enemy merely on the order of the executive without an act of Congress. A declaration of war by Congress was not sufficient to authorize the confiscation of timber bought by U.S. citizens before the war.[25]

The Mexican-American War (1846–48) marked the first time that the United States was the invader. Following the annexation of the Republic of Texas by what resentful Mexicans called "land-hungry" America, soldiers clashed at the Rio Grande. President James Polk told Congress that Mexicans had "shed American blood on American soil"—an incitement to war for a war-happy Congress. One dubious congressman, Abraham Lincoln, challenged Polk to show him the spot where blood had been shed.

The Mexican-American War polarized the nation, providing the genesis for American traditions of conscientious objection and civil disobedience. This war of aggression was unnecessary and degrading for a democratic country, its opponents claimed. The abolitionists increasingly demanded that the newly acquired territories—all of Mexico's vast land north of the Rio Grande and Baja California—be declared slavery-free states. The war and slavery prompted Henry David Thoreau in 1849 to write his classic "On the Duty of Civil Disobedience," in which he protested the corruption of American democracy:

[W]hen a sixth of the population of a nation which has undertaken to be the refuge of liberty are slaves, and a whole country is unjustly overrun and conquered by a foreign army, and subjected to military law, I think that it is not too soon for honest men to rebel and revolutionize. What makes this duty more urgent is the fact that the country overrun is not our own, but ours is the invading army.[26]

The Civil War marked a low tide for civil liberites in wartime. President Abraham Lincoln suspended the writ of habeas corpus, arresting anyone who expressed sympathy for the rebellious South and detaining them without charges or a trial. Draft resisters by the hundreds—along with more than thirteen thousand newspaper editors, judges, lawyers, legislators, and others—were imprisoned. Newspapers voicing pro-South views were shut down.[27] In 1861, Lincoln even ignored Chief Justice Roger Taney's ruling in *Ex parte Merryman* that Lincoln's suspending habeas corpus without congressional authorization was unconstitutional.[28] In fact, the president was so upset with Taney that he reportedly issued a presidential warrant for his arrest.[29]

The Spanish-American War in 1898 was a boon to freedom of the press. Sometimes dubbed "the Correspondents' War," so-called yellow journalists from Joseph Pulitzer's *New York World* and William Randolph Hearst's *New York Journal*—aided by advances in long-distance communications—fomented as much as reported the short-lived hostilities against Spain in Cuba and the Philippines. One by-product of the war—opposed by Mark Twain and others as imperialistic—was American occupation of Cuba and the 1903 Platt Amendment to the Cuban constitution demanded by the United States as a condition of granting independence. That is how the United States obtained its perpetual lease to the naval base at Guantánamo Bay.[30]

In resisting FDR's impulse to imprison his most virulent critics, Biddle was determined not to repeat the abuses perpetrated during and immediately after World War I—another dark hour in the protection of civil rights in times of turmoil. Nervous about German spies, Congress had enacted legislation—the Espionage Act (1917) and Sedition Act (1918)—making it a crime to circulate false statements intended to interfere with military success or to utter or publish words intended to bring into contempt the government, Constitution, or flag of the United States. In other words, it was a crime to express disloyal or antiwar sentiments.

Nearly a thousand persons were convicted under these laws, reminiscent of the infamous Sedition Act of 1798.[31] Socialist presidential candidate Eugene V. Debs was imprisoned for a decade. In *Schenck v. United States*, the Supreme Court in 1919—with Justice Oliver Wendell Holmes applying for the first time his "clear and present danger" test for protecting free speech under the First Amendment—unanimously upheld the convictions of socialists who had violated the Espionage Act by distributing antiwar circulars to men accepted for military service in World War I.[32]

Toward the end of the war, President Woodrow Wilson appointed A. Mitchell Palmer to be his attorney general. Once associated with the Democratic Party's progressive wing for his support of trade union rights and women's suffrage, Palmer became the scourge of civil liberties advocates. With ambitious J. Edgar Hoover as his special assistant and alarmed by the Russian Revolution, he launched a fierce crusade to rid the country of anarchists, socialists, and communists. The attorney general's fears of communist agents plotting the overthrow of the U.S. government were fueled by the discovery of thirty-eight bombs sent to leading politicians and by the Italian anarchist who blew himself up outside Palmer's home.

Employing the Espionage and Sedition Acts, Palmer and Hoover declared war on "alien radicals" and left-wing groups.[33] On November 7, 1919, the second anniversary of the Russian Revolution, more than ten thousand suspected communists and anarchists were arrested. While the government found no evidence of a conspiracy, a large number of innocent people were imprisoned without trial for long periods, while others were deported to Russia. In January 1920, the infamous "Palmer Raids" in thirty-three cities led to the arrest and detention without trial of another six thousand people—many of whom were members of the Industrial Workers of the World (IWW). Palmer's Red scare was ultimately exposed as a fraud,[34] but the damage to the civil liberties of thousands of law-abiding citizens and noncitizens—including the executions of Sacco and Vanzetti, whose innocence was protested by Felix Frankfurter[35]—was a terrible reality.[36] Radicalized by these flagrant violations of the Bill of Rights, Roger Baldwin and other East Coast liberals founded the American Civil Liberties Union in 1920.

President Roosevelt was supremely confident that he knew what he was doing in the conduct of the war. Indeed, he was more certain than he had been during his famed Hundred Days, when he launched the New Deal after his election in 1932.

The war, the overriding necessity to win it, simplified everything conceptually. It provided him with clearly perceived goals, a sharply defined set of priorities, and a pattern of action. It reduced the number and restricted the range of choices open to him, thereby lessening the pangs of indecision and lightening the burden of decision.[37]

If nothing else, Roosevelt was the consummate politician of his age. A great listener, he had an uncanny knack for synthesizing public opinion into a popular plan of action. His "dominant instinct was to unify the nation."[38] On the issue of internal security, FDR—haunted by Churchill's chilling warning about the danger of a fifth column—listened attentively to the massive outpouring of concern about rampant disloyalty among Japanese Americans.

In the hours, days, and weeks after Pearl Harbor, Americans, particularly on the West Coast, were gripped by an explosive mix of fury and fear. The wave of U.S. defeats in the wake of Pearl Harbor left the American people demoralized and feeling vulnerable.[39] Panic over an imminent invasion was widespread as soldiers occupied aircraft plants and the Coast Artillery units steeled themselves for air attacks. "Enemy Planes Sighted over California Coast," the *Los Angeles Times* warned in a banner headline on December 9, 1941. All military leaves were canceled as soldiers, sailors, and marines rushed back to their posts.

On the night of the Pearl Harbor attack, Los Angeles was blacked out, and the next day, San Francisco followed with a partial blackout that went total within a few days. The next day, a rumor spread that Japanese aircraft had buzzed the Golden Gate Bridge but had been turned back by floodlights from the Presidio. (After a report of Japanese aircraft over the coast near San Jose, later shown to be false, Western Defense Command's head, General William Ord Ryan, claimed that they were from a carrier and that his fighter planes had driven them off.) On December 20, the tanker *Emido* was the first merchant shipping victim in the Pacific when she was sunk off Crescent City, California, by a Japanese submarine, the I-58.[40] By December 22, 1941, nine Japanese submarines reigned supreme from Washington to California, harassing American shipping along the Pacific coast. And on February 23, 1942, while President Roosevelt was addressing the nation by radio, a Japanese submarine—unnoticed eight miles offshore—shelled oil fields north of Santa Barbara.[41]

Eleanor Roosevelt, joined by her civil defense protégé, New York City mayor Fiorello La Guardia, flew to the West Coast immediately after Pearl Harbor. In addition to finding little or no civilian defense preparations except in San Diego, she also witnessed firsthand the widespread public feeling of insecurity. "[C]oastal Californians were in a state of extreme jitters over the possibility of Japanese air attacks, even of landings by Japanese troops."[42]

The passage of time only heightened the collective sense of dread and vulnerability. The horror of the Japanese attack on Pearl Harbor was burned into the collective American consciousness, a national trauma with long-lasting effects. Six months later, Congress still debated how the epicenter of U.S. naval operations for the Pacific Fleet—with its ships sitting like ducks on a pond and its air force lined up on the ground for target practice—could have been so utterly caught off guard.[43] Americans genuinely feared a Japanese invasion on the West Coast.

Nowhere was the feeling of insecurity more acute than in California. There a prevalent "mood of willfully oblivious, even defiant, well-being" and aloofness from the wars in the Pacific and Europe "ended abruptly on the morning of 7 December 1941."[44] With Congress' declaration of war the next day, and Germany declaring war on the United States a few days later, the cries for isolationism and neutrality were drowned out by the chorus of Californians fully supporting the war effort.

Widespread anti-Japanese sentiment was fueled by another, less lofty consideration: "the deep and fearsome antipathy between the peoples of Japan and the United States" for four decades in the nation and particularly in California, where a xenophobic campaign had primarily been waged.[45] Exclusionary laws and restrictions on alien citizenship reflected the strong community prejudice against Japanese.[46] Thus, the attack on Hawaii "had struck the deepest possible chord in the collective psyche of California."[47] Reprisals against the Japanese— vilified in the press as "mad dogs, yellow vermin and nips"[48]—were politically popular.[49]

The antipathy against the Japanese in California dated back to the early years of the century. In 1906, the San Francisco City Council had "called for a halt to [Japanese] immigration and for segregation between Oriental and white children." And when Theodore Roosevelt sent the U.S. "Great White Fleet" around the world, German agents tried to stir up trouble by spreading rumors that Japan was about to send troops "disguised as Mexican peons into Arizona." Kaiser Wilhelm also generously offered to send Germany's High Seas Fleet "to protect the East Coast in the event that Britain was dragged into a war by some incident between the Americans and the Japanese."[50]

FDR's decision to take extraordinary, and arguably unconstitutional, measures to deal with the perceived threat of the Japanese "enemy within" was made easier by the high-level government report on Pearl Harbor,[51] citing accounts (mostly fake) of "widespread espionage by resident Japanese before the attack."[52] Fuel was added to the bonfire of anti-Japanese feelings by recurring false rumors of treachery and bogus reports about strange-looking men with maps or shore-to-ship signaling.[53] Some claims were sheer lunacy on their face: "hordes of Japanese soldiers in disguise were about to pounce on San Diego from across the Mexican border . . . and . . . hundreds of Japanese spies were hiding out on Oahu."[54]

The coup de grâce came from the military. In early 1942, Lieutenant General John L. de Witt, the officer in charge of the Western Defense Command, recommended the evacuation of all Japanese from the coastal areas of California, Oregon, and Washington because they posed a substantial threat to national security. General de Witt characterized all persons of Japanese descent as "subversives," belonging to "an enemy race," and "potential enemies." The military's exclusion recommendation was all the more remarkable since no hard evidence of sabotage or treachery supported this conclusion, General de Witt admitting that "nothing had been proved against Japanese-Americans." But in a mad twist of logic, and operating on the principle that "a Jap is a Jap," he argued that this only provided "a disturbing and confirming indication that such action *will* be taken."[55]

This was the same General de Witt whose army intelligence branch at the Presidio in San Francisco had falsely reported thirty Japanese planes over the city the night after Pearl Harbor. This fabrication led to a blackout and a false nationwide news alert that the city was being bombed.[56] The same unit falsely claimed the next day that thirty-four Japanese ships were menacing the California coast between San Francisco and Los Angeles. These and other bogus reports fanned the flames of popular unrest over a Japanese fifth column.

The widespread public apprehension about a Japanese invasion—coupled with the strong military recommendation—led to the president's Executive Order 9066 of February 19, 1942, directing the army to remove all persons of Japanese ancestry from the Pacific coastal area.[57] The decree claimed that "the successful prosecution of the war requires every possible protection against espionage and against espionage to national-defense material, national-defense premises, and national-defense utilities." Several weeks later, Congress enacted a statute imposing criminal penalties for violations of the order, including a curfew imposed on Japanese Americans.

In all, 117,000 Japanese American men, women, and children—none of whom had been shown to be disloyal, two-thirds of whom were United States citizens by birth on American soil, and many of whom were elderly[58]—were forcibly removed to ten relocation centers in the remote interior, "where they lived uncomfortably behind barbed wire."[59] Like the Jews of Europe, they were hurriedly herded onto trains with only the belongings they could carry, and they lost their homes, farms, and livelihoods. Like prisoners of war, they were prohibited from leaving these camps for more than three years.[60] None was accused of any crime.

Roosevelt had no illusions about the legality of his draconian measure.[61] "The President caved in to the panic."[62] He knew that many of the internees were U.S. citizens. Thus, "any action against aliens and citizens alike would stand on shaky constitutional ground and . . . a failure to take similar action against all Germans and Italians would encourage charges of racial discrimination."[63] But this was, Roosevelt insisted, a "military necessity," and he vigorously supported the plan, giving Stimson and the War Department carte blanche to do whatever was necessary.[64]

Even though the country was at war with Germany and Italy, Roosevelt did not intern all Americans of German and Italian descent. Indeed, FDR did not even incarcerate all German or Italian enemy aliens—who had the benefit of "investigations and hearings to separate the loyal from the disloyal."[65] Yet, without even a modicum of due process, American citizens of Japanese extraction were effectively stripped of their citizenship and interned.

Notwithstanding his liberal credentials, Roosevelt had a war to win. Civil liberties had to take a backseat to national security. FDR was not "much concerned with the gravity or implications of this step," Biddle observed. "He was never theoretical about things. What must be done to defend the country must be done. . . . The military might be wrong. But they were fighting the war. Public opinion was on their side."[66]

In any event, this was a question of law for the Supreme Court to decide sometime in the future. "And meanwhile—probably a long meanwhile—we must get on with the war."[67]

Remarkably, this radical measure did not generate any significant congressional or cabinet debate.[68] Biddle was the sole cabinet officer who opposed the evacuation. As the secretary of the interior, Harold Ickes, recalled: "There was practically no discussion of the plan and I interjected nothing."[69] No court declared the program unconstitutional.[70] The War Department's invocation of "military necessity" all but silenced any government critics of the plan. Apparently, no one pointed out the hypocrisy of the United States fighting Nazi "barbarism" with, as FDR was fond of claiming, "the great upsurge of human liberty" and individual freedom embodied in the Bill of Rights while blatantly violating numerous constitutional guarantees of tens of thousands of American citizens.[71]

FDR's request that the military's measures also be "as reasonable and as humane as possible"[72] did little to mitigate the harshness of the wholesale physical relocation of so many loyal citizens of Japanese descent to what the president himself admitted were "concentration camps."[73] While their sons and brothers were fighting (and dying) for America,[74] the internees—some of whom barely knew a word of Japanese—were forced to live in tar-papered, military-style barracks encircled by barbed wire and sentry guards with machine guns.

For example, at the Manzanar War Relocation Center between Lone Pine and Independence, California, ten thousand detainees lived in eight hundred buildings with little privacy and "only sheets hanging, separating each family . . . [and] common latrines with no partitions and showers with no stalls."[75] While the residents tried to fashion normal lives amid the harsh winter cold and searing summer heat of this desolate area of the Owens Valley, internment at Manzanar (and the nine other camps) was for most "a place of woe"—"a dreadful, humiliating experience, a brutal reminder of America's racism and its historic demonization of Asian immigrants."[76]

The internees—while certainly treated better than the Jews under Hitler and not physically brutalized or murdered—were nonetheless deprived of all freedom and much human dignity. Families were given tags with identifying numbers that had to be worn on coat lapels and affixed to suitcases. They could not travel or leave the camps, and they were forced to sell their homes and businesses.

At the time, few Americans spoke out against what the American Civil Liberties Union later condemned as "the worst single wholesale violation of civil rights of American citizens in our history."[77] Eleanor Roosevelt, a renowned, tireless civil rights advocate, "made but a single feeble protest to her husband."[78] FDR was unapproachable on the subject, his traditional liberalism yielding to a fierce pragmatism. Internment was popular and seemed to be an effective way "to relieve feelings of powerlessness toward Japan and quiet a potentially divisive issue."[79] This drastic measure went largely unchallenged.[80]

In the end, Roosevelt lost little sleep over curtailing civil liberties in World War II.[81] As Biddle perceptively observed: "[T]he Constitution has never greatly bothered any wartime President."[82] Arbitrariness in wartime was a distasteful but necessary evil for the attainment of the greater good—preservation of the nation. FDR felt he was on solid ground. After all, eighty-one years earlier, another wartime president had taken drastic actions—including suspending the writ of habeas corpus—to save the Union.

"Was it possible," Abraham Lincoln asked, "to lose the nation and yet preserve the Constitution? A limb may be amputated to save a life, but a life is never wisely given to save a limb."[83]

Unconcerned about the judgment of history, Roosevelt opted for expediency over morality. When it came to the nation's very survival, the end always justified the means. "I am perfectly willing to mislead and tell untruths," he told the secretary of the Treasury, Henry Morgenthau Jr., in May 1942, "if it will help win the war."[84]

Ironically, while liberal Attorney General Biddle could be expected to oppose internment,[85] the staunchest opponent of this unprecedented dislocation of American citizens—without even a hearing or evidence of disloyalty—was none other than FBI director J. Edgar Hoover. Reporting nominally to Biddle, Hoover was already a legendary law enforcement official and the federal civilian official most responsible for hunting down enemy spies and saboteurs. His most conspicuous fault, his critics claimed, was a penchant for publicity that often influenced—and sometimes compromised—the performance of his duties.

The tough-talking Hoover—hardly considered a card-carrying civil libertarian—told FDR that his agents had no evidence that the Japanese American community was disloyal or giving aid and comfort to Japan. Hoover's opposition may have been less motivated by sensitivity to civil liberties than his feeling that the mass arrests were an affront to the FBI. After all, Hoover "felt the bureau had already arrested any likely spies in the first seventy-two hours after the [Pearl Harbor] attack."[86]

In the bureaucratic infighting over evacuation, Secretary of War Henry L. Stimson sided with his generals and Assistant Secretary John J. McCloy. Internment of Japanese Americans was a nonissue for this distinguished Republican member of Roosevelt's cabinet. America was at war. The entire state of California, the western halves of Washington and Oregon, and the southern part of Arizona had all been designated as military zones. The military claimed evidence of disloyalty among this class of residents in the coastal area, and invasion of the West Coast seemed "probable in the first months of the war."[87] Thus, Stimson and McCloy drafted a blanket presidential order that required the forced evacuation of all people of Japanese descent from any military zone.[88]

A brilliant administrator, McCloy's support for internment was a major influence not only on Stimson but also on President Roosevelt. Once he was convinced by U.S. military leaders that the evacuation was necessary for national security, McCloy had no serious qualms about the legality of arresting 117,000 people without any judicial process. As he bluntly told Attorney General Biddle during a heated meeting between high-level Justice and War Department officials on February 1, 1942: "You are putting a Wall Street lawyer in a helluva box, but if it is a question of safety of the country, [or] the Constitution of the United States, why the Constitution is just a scrap of paper to me."[89]

McCloy's boss, Henry L. Stimson, was born in New York City on September 21, 1867. Graduating from Yale and then Harvard Law School, he became a member of the bar in New York in 1891. Stimson was a devoted and extremely active Republican in New York City, organizing voters to turn out to vote for Republican candidates whom he thought best represented Republican ideals without sacrificing too much ground to appease the city's overwhelmingly Democratic populace.[90]

A prominent attorney and public citizen, Stimson became highly involved in the Association of the Bar of the City of New York as well as local politics. Calling legal practice the "noble . . . profession of the law," he felt that "the American lawyer should regard himself as a potential officer of his government and a defender of its laws and constitution." Stimson also believed that "the practice of the law is conducive to good citizenship and the lawyer is a stabilizing force in the body politic."[91]

Republican president Theodore Roosevelt, FDR's cousin, appointed Stimson to the prestigious post of United States attorney for the Southern District of New York in 1906. Stimson served in the National Guard. President William Howard Taft, another Republican, appointed him secretary of war in 1911, the first of several prominent government positions to which he would be assigned: governor of the Philippines in 1927, secretary of state under President Herbert Hoover in 1929, and secretary of war under President Roosevelt in 1940. FDR appointed Stimson—by then a prominent member of the Republican Party—in order to gain bipartisan political support for his policies on preparing for possible war. By mid-1942, Stimson had already been highly successful in rallying the American public to support the war effort and organizing the nation's industrial sector and economic resources in the fight against Japan and Germany.[92]

With the war news still relentlessly dreadful in the late spring of 1942, Roosevelt, while remaining confident of ultimate victory and the end of "this dark season of defeat" in a few months, nevertheless felt besieged.[93] The wolf packs of lethal German U-boats controlled the North Atlantic and terrorized the eastern seaboard. The greater part of the Pacific was under Japan's control, and the threat of invasion was real and demoralizing. While the Doolittle bombing raid on Tokyo on April 18 had been successful in bringing the war to the Japanese people, it was more of a symbolic victory than a strategic military one.[94]

Internal security was also problematic. While the West Coast had been cleansed of all Japanese, FDR knew that Germany would try to recruit spies and fifth columnists among German-American Bund loyalists. And while his FBI director had confidently boasted in early January that "spy and sabotage activity against the United States has been virtually halted so far in this war," the risk of terrorism was omnipresent.[95]

But where would they strike? How would the terrorists enter the country? How much more horrible news and reminders of their vulnerability at home would Americans tolerate?

The president of the United States would not have to wait long for an answer.

Chapter 5

The Landing

On their very last night in Germany, the graduates of Quenz Lake enjoyed an elaborate celebratory dinner at a popular restaurant in the Tiergarten, Berlin's famous park. Officers from the High Command gave speeches emphasizing the importance of the mission and wishing them success. The head of the Abwehr, Admiral Wilhelm Franz Canaris, was not present. After signing their orders, he had remarked: "This will cost these poor men their lives."[1]

On May 22, the men traveled to Paris via an express train en route to the departure site—Lorient on the Atlantic coast near Brest. The former French naval base had become one of the main operating ports for U-boats. Before reaching Lorient, however, the team spent a weekend in Paris. They stored their luggage—filled with explosives and fuses, fatigues, shovels, and American currency—under guard at the Hôtel des Deux Mondes on the Rue de l'Opera and went off to enjoy the threadbare amenities of the occupied city. Some were content to spend Kappe's money on a good meal and take in the usual tourist sights, visiting the Eiffel Tower, the Tuileries, and the Louvre and strolling along the Seine.

But Heinrich Heinck, the former machinist, got drunk in a bar and started blurting out "I am a secret agent" to everyone around him. The sheer absurdity of his remark spared Heinck. No one actually believed him. When Ernest Burger and Richard Quirin, who had accompanied

Heinck, realized that their compatriot was considered a buffoon, they remained calm, blending in with the crowd and laughing at him like everyone else.

Herbert Haupt, the handsome boxer, either thought that he was exempt from the "fee for service" of a prostitute because of his new position with the German High Command or simply ran out of money. Whatever the reason, screams in French came pouring out of his hotel room, and soon all the men rushed into Haupt's room. They gathered enough money to pay her, and she eventually quieted down and left the premises.

After their adventures in Paris, Kappe and his men took their places in two adjacent first-class compartments on an overnight train to Lorient. Their mood was somber. As their departure drew closer and the danger of their mission was fully appreciated, a brooding feeling of anxiety overtook the men. They had passed the point of no return.

Upon arrival at Lorient, Dasch was so eager to leave the train that he forgot his pipe, tobacco pouch, and wallet containing his false draft and social security cards bearing the name George John Davis. Realizing his blunder, Dasch raced from their hotel, Jour de Rêve, to the railroad station in the hope that he could retrieve his lost goods without any confrontation. In his frenzied attempt to reclaim his items, Dasch caught the suspicious eye of the soldier in charge. Understandably, Dasch the secret agent did not have proper German identification papers, and the soldier summoned his captain.

Dasch was not supposed to have German identity documents because Kappe did not want them carrying anything that would identify them as Germans. This departure from normal procedure, Kappe felt, would not become an issue so long as they all traveled together under his supervision. But Kappe was not there at the station to explain matters. In fact, Kappe had given new false identities to all the men except Haupt and Burger, who were naturalized U.S. citizens and had their own legitimate papers.

Dasch pleaded with the captain to no avail. Since he did not have the requisite identity papers, he would have to be taken into custody. Dasch told the captain to call Lieutenant Kappe at the hotel, which he did, but he also called the Gestapo just to be sure.

A little while later, Kappe, accompanied by a Gestapo agent, arrived at the railroad station. "Gentlemen, let this man go, he is under my control," Kappe stated in his most assertive voice as he displayed his authority from the High Command. "He is involved in a very secret and volatile mission. I apologize for the inconvenience." Dasch was released in Kappe's custody, and the Gestapo agent, who had wasted his time, reprimanded the hapless Dasch "on [his] negligence, especially in time of war."

This "negligence" was trivial compared to what happened the very next day. Each team—one headed by Dasch and the other by Edward John Kerling—had been given $80,000 in American currency. In the course of giving Kerling's group advice about the money, Kappe told them not to open any bank accounts, change their money at a bank, or spend more than one $50 bill at a time. "The bills are numbered sequentially, and were part of a series that Germany obtained from the United States years earlier," Kappe explained. Kappe was afraid that the numbers on the bills would be known in the United States.

While Kappe was doling out this advice, Herbert Haupt was looking through his money bag. Suddenly, he noticed a gold certificate, a worthless and incriminating piece of paper because the United States had taken them out of circulation nine years earlier, in 1933. The gold certificate would have certainly aroused suspicion in the United States. An embarrassed Kappe blamed it on an intelligence officer from whom he had accepted the money. He dismissed his error, telling his shaken men "not to worry about little things like that."

Despite their qualms about Kappe's leadership, Kerling's group—Haupt, Hermamn Neubauer, and Werner Thiel—changed into their uniforms and gathered their belongings: civilian clothes, sea bags, shovels, four crates of explosives and fuses, and their money belts. It was now May 27. Kerling's group was to leave first, since their trip to Florida would take longer than Dasch's group's voyage to New York.

Before they embarked on their mission, all eight men were required to sign contracts furnished by Kappe. These specified how much they would be paid for undertaking the operation. In turn, each man agreed, upon penalty of death, not to tell anyone about their mission.[2]

Hurrying all the way, Kappe drove the four men to the dock from the hotel. They did not get a chance to say good-bye to the other four or to wish each other good luck. The four saboteurs, apprehensive and tired, boarded the U-584, a type VIIC submarine, met Lieutenant Commander Joachim Deecke, who would be in command of the submarine, and were on their way.

When Kappe returned to the hotel from dropping off Kerling's group, he had a minor quarrel with Dasch. Both men were frustrated with the occurrences of the last couple of days and took it out on each other. Later on, Dasch retreated to his room, and with nothing else to do, he examined the money that Kappe had given to him. A large number of bills had oriental block symbols stamped on the backs. This currency had been circulated in Japan before it got to Germany and thus was of no use. Dasch confronted Kappe, yelling at him: "This money I don't want. You should be ashamed of having supplied us with money like that."

His nerves were frazzled and he was too tired to argue at this point, so Kappe simply took the marked money back from Dasch. Figuring that he had hammered Kappe enough on the subject of outdated and marked bills, Dasch decided to confirm their instructions that once in the United States, they would not actually commit any forms of sabotage for several months.

"That was originally my plan," Kappe conceded. "However, I now want at least some minor diversionary sabotage efforts—like maybe blowing up Macy's." He also suggested planting bombs in railroad and bus station lockers.

While Dasch could conceive of no reason for these mindless acts of violence, he grudgingly agreed to follow his revised orders.

Dasch's team should have departed the next day for New York, but Kappe received a call notifying him that submarine U-202 was still in dry dock. They would have to wait for at least twenty-four hours. So, with nothing else to do in Lorient, the remaining four men—tempers frayed—fell to arguing with each other.

Heinck accused Dasch of being a disloyal German because Dasch did not have a certified prewar record of loyalty to the Bund or Nazi Party. Then they argued over whether it would be a good idea to contact a friend of Heinck's who resided on Long Island. After much wrangling, Dasch reluctantly accepted the address of Heinck's friend, promising to use it if necessary.

The submarine was finally ready to get under way late on the evening of May 28. Kappe drove them to the dock. The sub was docked behind a freighter in order to prevent anyone on shore from seeing it. The Germans were extremely cautious whenever they were about to send out a U-boat or embark on a sabotage mission. After all, there were spies everywhere.

The crew on U-202, also a type VIIC submarine, was under the command of Lieutenant Commander Hans-Heinz Lindner. An older veteran at age thirty-eight, the six-foot Lindner had blond hair, blue eyes, a mustache, and beard. Clad in the sort of outfit typically worn by U-boat officers on patrol—a cap, khaki pants, suspenders, and a gray sweater—and with an Iron Cross on a chain hanging from his neck, this highly experienced submarine captain exuded the confidence, if not arrogance, characteristic of Admiral Karl Dönitz's elite. He was also ruthless. Lindner participated in the U-boat massacre of Allied vessels in the vital eastern seaboard shipping lanes that would result in the sinking of 259 ships in 1942 alone.[3]

With the war going so well for Germany, Lindner was hardly surprised when he was ordered to transport the four new men to the United States on a secret mission and to make sure they were not bothered or asked questions while on board. On the way back from the United States, Lindner warned his crew that any reference to their trip or talk of the passengers on the submarine would subject the offender to punishment—a death sentence.

For the most part, the fifteen-day trip across the Atlantic was uneventful, if not downright boring. The sub was submerged during the day and glided on the surface at night. The highlight of every day seemed to be alarm drills: the U-boat quickly submerged as each man rushed to his station. At this stage of the war, however, Lindner took no special precautions during most of the Atlantic crossing. Britain's Coastal Command and American forces could not yet provide the long-range aircraft coverage of the Atlantic that would make life utter hell for U-boats later in the war. Apart from drills, Lindner allowed the crew to remain on a low state of alert. This would change when the submarine could be spotted from the North American coast.

Dasch and his compatriots had a difficult time adjusting to a sailor's life. The quarters were tight and overly crowded, making it impossible for the men to talk among themselves about their assignment. Several also became seasick. Dasch and his team were free to roam through the various compartments of the U-boat, except for the communications and torpedo rooms. Pulling rank, Dasch was allowed in the communications room after convincing the captain that he should be aware of any breaking news in the United States and radio warnings to residents near the shore about any submarines at sea.

A dense fog provided cover for the submarine until it reached the banks off Newfoundland. At about the same time, the submarine crew started to become anxious. As relaxed as the submariners had originally been, they now proceeded with utmost caution since none of them had ever been this close to the coast of the United States before.

It was thirty minutes past midnight, early on the morning of Saturday, June 13. Luckily, the fog rolled in again, obscuring their landing on Amagansett Beach near the tip of Long Island and 105 miles east of New York City.[4] Dasch handed out the money belts and distributed $1,000 in smaller bills among his men. It was now time to get the contingent of saboteurs ashore.

"Okay, boys, follow my lead, and we'll be fine," Dasch assured them.

These had to be some of the most famous last words ever uttered by a commando leader in World War II.

Dressed in German marine infantry uniforms, the four men scrambled out of the conning tower and into a heavy rubber boat, lowering themselves along with their sabotage gear, shovels, explosives, detonators, fuses, a duffel bag containing civilian clothes, and Dasch's sea bag with all their money. Two sailors from the crew paddled the four men and four crates to the beach in the inflatable. While they were almost certain that no one would be near this remote area, they remained on the lookout for any midnight bathers, vagrant fishermen, or a romantic couple on the lonely, fog-ridden beach. If they actually encountered anyone, whether civilian or military, the sailors' orders were to detain them and forcibly put them on the rubber boat going back to the submarine—where they would be fed to the fish.

The fog was so thick that almost as soon as they paddled away from the sub it was no longer visible. The anxious crewmen in the boat were not even sure they were headed in the right direction. Then, through a momentary rift in the fog, Dasch spotted a vast expanse of white sand.

"We made it, boys," Dasch announced, a tad prematurely.

A little too eager to get to shore, their leader jumped out of the boat, thinking he could wade up to the beach. But he underestimated the depth, and he sank below the water. He had to be dragged back into the boat—an auspicious start for the mission.

A few moments later, the bottom of the boat grazed sand. Dasch ran up onto the beach, looking around for anyone or anything. The night was quiet, except for the waves crashing behind them.

"Come, let's go," he urged the other three.

The men started carrying the containers of explosives and equipment from the boat to the beach, and Burger retrieved the money belt. Dasch was helping the sailors from the submarine empty out some water that had splashed in as they came to shore. All of a sudden, he glanced behind him. A light was moving slowly down the beach.

Dasch froze in terror. Taking a deep breath, he calmed himself and hastily devised a plan. Dasch made out the figure of a man and hoped to avoid detection. That would save him from forcing whoever was coming along to get in the boat. Neither Burger nor the other two men could see this innocent-looking young man, dressed in some kind of sailor uniform, on the beach. They had gone in the opposite direction to reach higher ground, and in any event, the fog was too thick to see anything without a flashlight.

Dasch desperately wanted to prevent the intruder from seeing the others carrying explosives and wearing German uniforms. So he took the initiative and approached the interloper. Dasch was unarmed, and so was the other man, John C. Cullen, a twenty-one-year-old seaman second class in the United States Coast Guard.[5]

"Who are you?" Cullen asked.

"Coast Guard?" Dasch responded sheepishly, hoping that he was not.

"Yes, sir. Who are you?" Cullen now demanded.

Dasch collected his thoughts and said: "We're fishermen from Southampton and ran ashore here."

Believing Dasch, but still curious, Cullen queried, "What do you intend to do about it?"

Dasch was too far into his lie now to stop.

"Stay here until sunrise and then we'll be all right."

In theory, Dasch had given a plausible response, but there remained at least four more hours of darkness. So Cullen, who readily accepted Dasch's story, graciously offered the Coast Guard station, about a third of a mile away, as refuge for these stranded fishermen until sunup. Dasch agreed to go, then realized this was the last thing he wanted, and declined. It was one thing for him to appear as a fisherman in the dense fog, quite another for him to pass as one inside the Coast Guard station.

Cullen was perplexed by this curious response. Dasch then declared that he had no fishing permit or form of identification, for that matter. Then Cullen, growing suspicious, told Dasch that he would have to accompany him—he had no choice in the matter. Dasch brushed Cullen's arm aside and stopped him.

"Now, wait a minute," Dasch asserted. "You don't know what this is all about."

Just then, Burger, who was clad in swimming trunks that he had worn under his German navy uniform and was dragging the duffel bag, looked up and saw Dasch with another man. Without thinking, Burger called to him in German. Stunned, Dasch turned around and rebuked him for his carelessness.

"Shut up, you damn fool," Dasch barked in English to Burger. Composing himself, Dasch quickly added, "Everything is all right. Go back to the boys and stay with them."

This was exactly the sort of situation in which Dasch was supposed to kill anyone who discovered his landing party (particularly someone from the U.S. military) and bury the body. "Instead, Dasch, a garrulous loudmouth, but no tough guy," tried to bluff his way out of this jam.[6] That turned out to be a great mistake.

Meanwhile, Quirin and Heinck had been sipping from a bottle of German brandy that Heinck had smuggled onto the submarine. Burger came back to them and told them to lie low, informing them that Dasch had been confronted by an American sailor. Upon hearing this news, Quirin nearly bolted for Dasch with the intent of knocking Cullen unconscious and sending him out to the U-boat. Burger restrained him, however.

After Burger and Dasch's strange exchange, Cullen grew nervous. He was not sure what foreign language Burger had spoken (though he had his suspicions) or how many men were actually there. Cullen was all by himself and without any sort of weapon or communications device. Sensing Cullen's fear, Dasch took control.

"How old are you?"

"Twenty-one," replied Cullen.

"Do you have a father?"

"Yes."

"Do you have a mother?"

"Yes."

"Well, I wouldn't want to have to kill you."

There was a long, tense pause. *Who is this guy?* Cullen kept asking himself. *Why is he threatening to kill me?*

Dasch cut the tension. "Forget about this, and I'll give you some money and you can have a good time," he said, as he held out two $50 bills.

Cullen did not accept the bribe.

"Here's three hundred dollars. Take this."

Cullen now accepted the money, counted only a few bills, and then stuffed the currency in his pocket.

"No, it's all right," Cullen replied as he started to walk away, pretending that the bribe had worked.

Dasch believed that the money would buy Cullen off, but then he realized he should make one thing clear.

"Wait a minute," he yelled as he grabbed Cullen. "Take a good look at me."

Cullen shone the flashlight in Dasch's face.

"Look in my eyes," Dasch commanded. "Look in my eyes."

After a long, hard stare, Dasch exclaimed, "You'll be meeting me in East Hampton sometime. Do you know me?"

"No, sir, I never saw you before in my life."

Seemingly content with Cullen's answer, Dasch wanted to drive his point home.

"My name is George John Davis. What's yours?"

"Frank Collins," murmured Cullen as he slowly backed away. And then he abruptly pivoted and began running down the beach toward the Coast Guard station.

Relieved that the confrontation was over, Dasch nonetheless wanted to leave the beach in a hurry. He suspected that "Frank Collins," or whoever he was, would be coming back shortly—and this time he would not be alone or unarmed.

Dasch ran back to his men, who were all eager to hear what happened.

"Everything is fine for now, but we have no time to waste."

He ordered them to dig a trench and bury the explosives, the shovels, and their clothes. They had all already changed into civilian clothes except for Dasch, who was still wearing the trousers of his uniform.

The Germans were wearing their uniforms while landing because, they believed, they would be treated as prisoners of war, according to the Espionage Act of 1917, if they were captured while dressed as enemy combatants. And as prisoners of war they would be treated humanely and imprisoned for the remainder of the war or until exchanged for American prisoners of war. At least that was what they had been told back in Germany. That the treatment they would receive would be less cordial if they were apprehended later, while disguised as civilians with explosives and spy paraphernalia on their persons, apparently never crossed their minds.

Dasch hastily changed into his civilian clothes, complete with nonmatching socks and wet trunks underneath his pants. After they finished burying their sabotage materials, Dasch led his men further inland. It was still dark and foggy, but they made it up to the road, where they rested for a while. After about an hour, the sun began to rise, and the headlights of oncoming cars startled the men, especially when a military truck drove by carrying several men in uniform.

Each man was extremely worried. They were on American soil and thousands of miles from home, they had already been discovered by the Coast Guard, and enemy soldiers were nearby. A series of subsequent incidents did nothing to allay their fears.

First, they heard their submarine, U-202, switch its motors from electric to diesel shortly after four o'clock in the morning. Lindner had already sent a signal to Admiral Dönitz that his four passengers had safely landed.[7] Now the saboteurs' only ready means of escape was gone, and they fully realized that they were on their own. At any moment, as the Cullen encounter had shown, they could be apprehended or killed. Somehow, this sabotage business did not seem as exciting as it had at Quenz Lake or the farewell dinner.

Then they heard a telephone ringing from a house roughly fifty yards down the road. Their hearts stopped dead as they saw a light go on and then heard a man talking. They could not make out what the man was saying, but Dasch feared it was the Coast Guard calling. The man stopped talking after about a minute or so and then walked to his door. Glancing outside, he then returned to the telephone and continued speaking. Soon thereafter, the lights in the man's house went out, and the four men breathed sighs of relief.

Pulling themselves together, they followed Dasch down a dirt road in search of a major highway. Dasch wanted to get to Amagansett since he knew that trains ran from there to New York City. They found the main highway, but Dasch was not sure in which direction they should proceed. He did not want the others to know this, however.

As it turned out, Dasch went in the wrong direction, and the men were forced to sneak by a trailer camp. Outside the camp were railroad tracks; when he stumbled upon them, he finally figured out where he was in relation to the Long Island Rail Road. They headed west down the tracks toward the small station at Amagansett.

By this time, it was past five o'clock in the morning, and the men were completely worn out, sodden, and grimy. The railroad station was deserted, and no timetable was posted. New York City was a long three hours away.

When dawn came, there was nowhere for them to hide. It was an uncomfortable feeling. An hour later, after the men had changed out of some of their damp clothes, and after listening to Dasch speculate that there might be no train service on Saturday morning, they saw smoke billowing from the station house chimney.

The ticket agent, Ira Baker, had the early Saturday morning shift, and he was getting ready to start his day. At half past six, he opened the front door to the station and raised the shutter over the ticket window. When the four disheveled men came up to the window, Baker was not too surprised, since he was accustomed to seeing unkempt fishermen taking the early morning trains.

Dasch walked up to the ticket window. "Four one-way tickets to Jamaica, please," he requested in his best English. Just to make sure that there was no suspicion, Dasch quickly volunteered, "The fishing's been pretty lousy lately."

Baker did not say anything, merely nodded and pushed the tickets over the counter. Their train was scheduled to depart for New York in twenty-five minutes. Dasch paid $20 and took the tickets, congratulating himself on passing as a fisherman and not arousing any suspicion.

Dasch bought newspapers for each of his men as they boarded the train. The headlines announced an important victory by the Americans over fifteen Japanese warships in the Coral Sea, at the cost of only one aircraft carrier, the USS *Lexington*. The paper also carried an ad in which President Roosevelt asked the American people to contribute to the war effort and donate old tires since rubber was now a scarce commodity.

In an ironic twist, the newspaper also ran a review for a motion picture debuting that day. Entitled *Nazi Agent*, the movie had just opened at the Rialto Theater in New York City, and it starred Conrad Veidt playing German twins: one a naturalized and loyal American, the other a German consul. Much to the chagrin of any loyal German-American Bund member and Hitler himself (the Führer was very fond of the American films procured for him by Goebbels), the American murders his German twin at the end.

Their German-American drama would have a happier ending, the saboteurs thought. Germany's finest—Dasch, Burger, Quirin, and Haupt—were on their way to New York City to wreak havoc on the American wartime economy. And while they were at it, they would blow up Jewish-owned Macy's for good measure.

Chapter 6

"The Real McCoy"

Fearful that he might be shot in the back, John Cullen ran as fast as he could back to the Coast Guard station. A flare gun and a flashlight offered no defense against men he assumed to be armed and dangerous. Pretty certain that he had heard one man speak in German, he quickly made the connection with the U-boats prowling off the coast. Like thousands of Coast Guardsmen forming the first line of coast defense against invasion, Cullen shared the apprehensions of most Americans. He had joined the Coast Guard (formed in 1790 and now under the command of the U.S. Navy for the duration of the war) to play his part in the service's dual mission—to protect shipping off the East Coast and to prevent enemy infiltration from the sea.[1]

It was impossible, of course, to secure the country's twelve thousand miles of coastline and the seventy-five hundred miles of porous Canadian and Mexican borders against enemy spies and saboteurs. The Atlantic seaboard alone—from Eastport, Maine, to Key West, Florida—zigzagged in and out of hidden harbors, isolated inlets, and backwater beaches where no one lived or worked. The presence of Coast Guard shore patrolmen such as Cullen, walking his assigned six miles of coastline, was essentially a public relations campaign to calm the public. But Cullen, by sheer chance, had been in the right place at the right time.

Breathing hard, he arrived at the station and reported his encounter to his incredulous superior, Boatswain's Mate Carl R. Jennett.

"Boat," he yelled, bursting into the sleeping Jennett's room at the Amagansett Coast Guard station. "Get up, people landed on the beach! Two Germans held me up on the beach. . . . They gave me this."

Cullen handed Jennett the wad of money from the man who'd called himself Davis.

"Oh, my God, we've got the real McCoy here," Jennett exclaimed.[2]

Fumbling to get on his clothes as he awoke the rest of his men, Jennett sprang into action. He armed his four young recruits, none of whom had ever before fired a gun. After sending a dispatch to the Coast Guard's district headquarters, Jennett headed for the beach with his men. Cullen led the way, trying to find the area where he had discovered the landing party.

"Be careful not to shoot each other," Jennett warned them. All he needed was for his guys to start firing away when it was so foggy you could hardly see your hand in front of your face.[3]

While searching the area, they suddenly heard the unmistakable sound of powerful diesels and got a whiff of the familiar smell of diesel fuel as the submarine started up its engines. The engines revved as the captain tried to release his grounded submarine from a sandy shoal.

"Look, over there!" one of the rookie Coast Guardsmen shouted.

Through the dense fog, Jennett could dimly discern the superstructure of a submarine with a blinker light, run aground and trying to free itself. Not wanting to be shelled, he ordered his men to duck behind a sand dune until the U-boat made its escape with the help of the rising tide.[4]

As the light from sunrise began to burn through the fog, the Coast Guardsmen searched the beach area. Eventually, they recovered a treasure trove—a buried canvas bag of Nazi uniforms, a pack of German cigarettes, and four tin-covered crates containing what appeared to be explosives and incendiary devices. This would be critical evidence in the event of the German saboteurs' capture.

The Coast Guard notified the navy, army, and FBI. By noon, the news had spread to the FBI's large New York City office and the headquarters in Washington, D.C. Bureau director J. Edgar Hoover was promptly notified and personally organized the largest manhunt in FBI history.

* * *

Hoover's agency traced its origins to the appointment of thirty-four special agents within the Justice Department in 1908—the year the Boy Scouts had been founded and Henry Ford introduced the Model T. Historically, law enforcement was a local matter, but Congress began to federalize more crimes—such as prohibiting the interstate transport of women for prostitution in 1910. With the enactment of the Espionage Act in 1917, the Bureau of Investigation was tasked with arresting spies and protecting the nation's internal security—a responsibility that Hoover regarded as the exclusive province of his agency. He neither asked for nor wanted help from the military or any other agency of the government.[5]

John Edgar Hoover was born in Washington, D.C., on New Year's Day in 1895. Of German and English extraction, he was the youngest of three children of Dickerson Naylor Hoover, the chief of the printing division of the U.S. Coast and Geodetic Survey, and Annie Marie Scheitlin, the granddaughter of the first Swiss consul general in America. As a young boy, J. Edgar was known as "Speed," but not because of any athletic attribute—the nickname referred to his quick wit and sharp mind.[6]

At five feet ten inches, Hoover's physical appearance resembled something of an inverted triangle—a heavy torso held up by spindly legs. His nose had been flattened in childhood when a baseball smashed into it. Though he may have resembled Babe Ruth physically, that was the extent of the comparison.

During high school, Hoover never had a regular girlfriend or dated. Instead, he devoted himself entirely to his work, foreshadowing his fifty-five years with the Department of Justice. J. Edgar became the captain of the school's military drill team—his devotion was so total that friends joked he was "in love with Company A." He lived with his mother—who called him Edgar—until she died in 1938.

While he graduated as his high school's valedictorian, he turned down a scholarship to the University of Virginia. Instead, Hoover took a job as a clerk at the Library of Congress, enrolled at George Washington University in night school, and eventually earned his bachelor's and master of laws degrees there in four years. Hoover passed the bar and took a clerk's job for $990 per year at the Department of Justice. It would be his one and only employer until he died.

Jack Alexander, Hoover's profiler at the *New Yorker* in 1937, wrote that Hoover, who enjoyed betting on horses, "dressed better than most and a bit on the dandyish side." A perfectionist, Hoover also "had an exceptional capacity for detail work, and he handled small chores with enthusiasm and thoroughness. He constantly sought new responsibilities to shoulder, and welcomed chances to work overtime." Later, his sheer will and dogged determination would inspire his agents to get their man.

A soprano in the church choir before his voice changed, Hoover taught Sunday school and attended church regularly. "He believed deeply in God, in his country, and in the value of integrity, and he made sure everyone around him knew it."[7] And despite being afflicted with a stutter, the strong-willed Hoover dominated conversations and was used to getting his way.

Harlan Fiske Stone—a former Columbia Law School dean who would later serve as the chief justice of the United States—became the attorney general in 1924 under President Calvin Coolidge. One of his top priorities was to rebuild the image of the Bureau, which he discovered was "filled with men with bad records . . . many convicted of crimes. . . . [The] organization [is] lawless . . . [undertaking] many activities without any authority in federal statutes. . . . [Its] agents engaged in many practices which are brutal and tyrannical in the extreme."[8] Stone offered the top job to the twenty-nine-year-old Hoover.

Quickly demonstrating his legendary political shrewdness, J. Edgar, instead of leaping at the opportunity, said he would accept only if he had sole control over merit promotions and the department was totally divorced from outside politics. Stone agreed, and Hoover took the job. Stone quickly concluded that Hoover was a wise choice—a man of "exceptional intelligence, alertness, and executive ability."[9]

Hoover totally transformed the agency. When he took charge, the bureau had merely 441 agents, 216 support employees, and an annual budget of only $2.3 million. The new director insisted that most new recruits have legal or accounting backgrounds. Hoover made assignments based on merit—but he was particularly susceptible to flattery. Agents knew that fulsomely complimenting the director went a long way, but at the same time they "quaked at the thought of the director's disapproval." According to one agent, "the first rule" was "do not em-

barrass the director," which in turn became the unwritten command-
ment "never embarrass the Bureau." Hoover instilled a pervasive fear of
failure in his agents. When a mistake was made, heads rolled.

With no civil service or union to protect them, Hoover's employees
were totally subject to his whims. Agents were transferred for being fat
and chastised for reading pinup magazines; one was even fired for
playing with a yo-yo in the hallway. A twenty-six-year-old clerk was
fired for letting his girlfriend sleep over at his apartment. There were
no coffee breaks, and FBI personnel affairs were not to be discussed
outside the office. Men were allowed to smoke, but not women, who
were confined to internal and clerical jobs. (Only in the later years of
his tenure were women allowed to become special agents.)

Hoover was an absolute monarch in his kingdom, actually referring
to FBI headquarters as "the seat of government." Anyone who wanted
to speak to the director had to visit him—Hoover rarely ventured
outside his office. He sat behind a raised desk, polished and always
sparkling, at the end of a thirty-five-foot office. Huge flags flanked his
sides. All who were granted an audience with him sank deep into leather
chairs, peering up at the throne before them, as Hoover sat majesti-
cally above his subjects. He hated sweaty palms, so agents always pat-
ted their hands on their pants legs before entering his office and
shaking hands with him.[10]

Hoover ran the Bureau without much publicity until June 17, 1933,
when Charles "Pretty Boy" Floyd and his gang killed five men, including an FBI agent. After observing the press and radio coverage accorded
to the colorful gangster, Hoover was quoted as saying: "If there is going
to be publicity, let it be on the side of law and order."[11] From then on,
Hoover's FBI was frequently in the papers, garnering fame for none
other than J. Edgar himself. His PR operation was matched by no other
federal agency—there were even radio (and later television) programs
devoted to glorifying "G-men," as FBI agents came to be known.

Starting with the capture of Bruno Hauptmann, the infamous
Lindbergh baby kidnapper, Hoover publicized the role of the agency
in the case, fighting off several other agencies to secure public credit
for his men in Hauptmann's capture. Walter Winchell, a widely read
Broadway gossip columnist and radio broadcaster, was the mouth-
piece for the Bureau and Hoover, who rarely held a press conference.
Frequently traveling with an FBI escort, Winchell wrote something
flattering about "G-man Hoover" nearly every day.[12]

Hoover managed to turn himself into a folk hero. By the time Roosevelt took office in 1933, *Collier's* magazine noted that Hoover's "appetite for publicity is the talk of the capital."[13] Senator George Norris once called Hoover the "greatest hound for publicity on the American continent." Chief Justice Stone echoed the criticism of the Bureau and the director he had appointed, making the acid comment that "one of the great secrets of Scotland Yard has been that its movements are never advertised."[14]

Soon other criticisms of the FBI surfaced, aimed specifically at the director. In the spring of 1936, Senator Kenneth D. McKellar spoke before Congress, rebuking the director for never actually making an arrest himself. Hoover never directly responded to the statement—he took action. Less than a month later, Hoover personally led a raid in New Orleans that captured the most prominent figure in the Ma Barker mob, Alvin "Kreepy" Karpis. The press spin was that J. Edgar was on the scene organizing the arrest all by himself. Thirty-five years later, however, Karpis wrote in his book that Hoover hid until Karpis was safely covered by many guns. Waiting until he was told the coast was clear, Hoover came out to reap the glory.[15]

Soon after he took control, Hoover started amassing secret files. These included tidbits of information about the politics and personal and sex lives of public officials and prominent citizens, from Charles Lindbergh to Supreme Court justices to celebrities.[16] Hoover even maintained dossiers on FDR and Churchill.[17] This compromising information—much of it "raw" or completely unverified—"would guarantee that Hoover would remain director as long as he wished."[18]

Hoover was well known to maintain files particularly on anyone who criticized his directorship. Unflattering portions of these ten million secret dossiers were leaked to the public if any attacks became overly critical.[19] FBI agents were so afraid of the director's notorious vindictiveness that they never voiced any public criticisms of the agency or Hoover.

Attorney General Francis B. Biddle insightfully noted that behind Hoover's "absolute self control" was a "temper that might show great violence if he did not hold it on leash, subject to the domination of a will that is the master of his temperament."[20] Hoover seemed to strike only after being struck first.

Roosevelt kept Hoover in office throughout his four presidential terms. Roosevelt saw him as a fellow pragmatist who was more intent on getting a job done than worrying about legal niceties or moral ambiguities. Thus, in April 1942, the president wanted to know if Hoover had succeeded in cleaning out "the alien waiters in the principal Washington hotels." The president was concerned about eavesdropping spies: "Altogether too much conversation in the dining rooms!" he complained to Hoover, who was more than happy to oblige.[21]

Shortly after he got the report of German saboteurs landing on Long Island, Hoover informed his nominal boss, Biddle. The attorney general then notified President Roosevelt: "[A]t 1:30 A.M. an unarmed Coast Guard patrolman near Amagansett, Montauk Point, Long Island, discovered two men placing material in a hole they had dug; one of them covered the patrolman with a gun, gave him $260 and told him to keep his mouth shut. I shall, of course, keep you informed."[22] Somehow Dasch had acquired a gun when in fact he was unarmed.

Hoover met with Biddle to lay out his plan to track down the German saboteurs.[23] Despite his penchant for publicity, Hoover recommended a total news blackout to Biddle and FDR. An announcement might alert the saboteurs, Hoover argued. The president agreed, and for the next two weeks, the press and American people had no inkling of terrorists in their midst.[24]

Biddle had earlier wondered about Roosevelt's "long-standing preoccupation with sabotage [which] now seemed validated."[25] Showing his concern over German spies loose in America, Biddle "had a bad week trying to sleep as . . . [he] thought of the possibilities. The saboteurs might have other caches hidden, and at any moment an explosion was possible."[26]

Biddle was an outstanding attorney general with impeccable credentials. He was a descendant of Colonel William Randolph, who had come to Virginia in 1673 and whose son married a granddaughter of Pocahontas. A former federal appellate judge and solicitor general, Biddle had a brilliant legal mind and was widely regarded as a political liberal in his day. A short, dapper man sporting a thin, neatly trimmed mustache, he was, like his subordinate Hoover, a natty dresser. After graduating from Harvard College and Harvard Law School, he served as private secretary (law clerk) to legendary Supreme Court justice Oliver Wendell Holmes Jr. in 1911–12.

Following military service in World War I, he had a successful law practice in Philadelphia for twenty years. In the early 1920s, he served in the United States attorney's office, sharpening his formidable skills as a trial lawyer while prosecuting Prohibition and other federal law violations. Unlike far too many federal officials in those days, he was incorruptible, refusing bribes from opposing counsel representing the breweries.

An avid reader, he was an accomplished writer, devoting his spare time to writing eight books, including a well-received biography of his mentor, Holmes, and a novel set in Philadelphia. Biddle had a keen analytical bent. Contemporaries marveled at how quickly he was able to grasp the essence of complex legal issues.

Biddle caught the eye of a president who needed a great deal of high-powered legal talent to defend and implement his New Deal policies. Following a brief tour as chairman of the National Labor Relations Board in 1934–35 and membership on the Philadelphia Board of Public Education for three years, Biddle was appointed to the United States Court of Appeals for the Third Circuit in 1939. A year later, President Roosevelt named him solicitor general, the government's chief advocate in the Supreme Court. As he had done his entire career, he distinguished himself in that coveted post. When FDR needed his fourth attorney general in 1941 to replace Robert Jackson (whom he had appointed to the Supreme Court), he turned to Biddle. As the nation's fifty-eighth attorney general, Biddle became the president's chief legal counsel and served his client and the nation with great distinction.

Roosevelt was fond of Biddle. Shortly after Pearl Harbor, he played a joke on his attorney general that spoke volumes about the president's attitude toward civil liberties in wartime. In the presence of several aides, he told Biddle that he wanted to issue a proclamation "abrogating as far as possible all freedom of discussion and information during the war. It's a tough thing to do, but I am convinced that it is necessary." (Like many jokes, it may well have concealed an unconscious expression of anger—in this instance FDR's resentment of the ferocious criticism he had endured as the architect of the New Deal.)

When the thunderstruck Biddle saw that the others were keeping a straight face, and mindful of some of the vicious false attacks on the president in the press over FDR's three terms, Biddle made an impassioned speech defending civil liberties. Finally, when everyone broke out laughing, Biddle realized Roosevelt was teasing him and took it in good humor. That Biddle initially believed his president was serious "suggest[ed] a disturbingly casual attitude" toward civil liberties and foreshadowed FDR's support for rounding up all Japanese Americans on the West Coast.[27]

Biddle's strong opposition to internment was not surprising in light of his progressive political philosophy and distinguished legal background.[28] Throughout the war, Biddle's Justice Department waged a determined but doomed campaign against the War Department on various civil liberties issues, including Japanese internment. Supported by such capable aides as James H. Rowe Jr. and Edward J. Ennis, Biddle forcefully opposed the suspension of the writ of habeas corpus and the systematic deprivation of constitutional rights of loyal Japanese American citizens, including the violation of restrictions against warrantless searches and seizures, the deprivation of liberty after only indictment, suspension of the right to trial by jury and the requirement for unanimous conviction, invidious racial discrimination, and other assaults on fundamental American values.[29]

Biddle's brief "hearing" with Roosevelt was destined for failure: the president had already decided to accept the advice of the army and Assistant Secretary of War John J. McCloy, who had persuaded FDR of an urgent military necessity for internment.[30]

"In the tug-of-war between war and justice . . . , war pulled by far the heavier weight."[31] Biddle left FDR convinced "that the constitutional difficulty [never] plagued him."[32] For his vigorous championing of civil liberties, Biddle was rewarded with denunciations in the national media. The attorney general was variously condemned as "weak, timid, effeminate, devoid of the tough (manly) warrior virtues that the times demanded."[33]

Biddle's defeat on internment had profound implications, leading to measures that went beyond the unprecedented suppression of constitutional rights. Historically, in matters of internal security, the Justice Department and its Federal Bureau of Investigation, not the military, had plenary authority. With Executive Order 9066, Roosevelt transferred from the Justice Department to the War Department authority over the suspected Japanese American subversives.[34] Now the army would have sole jurisdiction over the lives of 117,000 civilians living within the nation's borders.

But after the news from Amagansett, Biddle was determined that the Justice Department would not lose its authority over the apprehension of these Nazi terrorists.

Chapter 7

Mr. Dasch Goes to Washington

As the alarm spread from Amagansett to New York to Washington, D.C., Dasch and his men arrived in Jamaica, Queens, around 9:30 a.m. Jamaica had a sizable population of German immigrants. While pleased that they apparently blended in with everyone, the team still went to a nearby clothing store on Jamaica Avenue to buy some underwear, socks, shirts, and fancy suits. After they changed out of their fishermen's clothes and got a shave, they agreed to split up: Dasch with Burger, Heinck with Quirin. They scheduled a rendezvous for three o'clock at the Automat located at Thirty-fourth street and Eighth Avenue in Manhattan.

After the initial adrenaline rush of landing and near disaster, the fact that they were now totally on their own in a hostile country gave rise to conflicting feelings. Their superiors were no longer controlling every aspect of their lives, but they now had to think for themselves and carry out their orders without any help. They took the Long Island Rail Road again, this time directly into New York City. Arriving at bustling Pennsylvania Station, Dasch and Burger noticed a sign advertising the upscale Governor Clinton Hotel. Burger registered there under his real name, and Dasch registered under the name George John Davis, the same one he had given Cullen.

Shortly after they checked into separate rooms on the fourteenth floor, it was time to meet the others at the Automat, where they enjoyed a pleasant late lunch. Feeling comfortable and relaxed in their new surroundings, dressed in their new outfits and amply provided with money, they could look forward to staying in nice hotels, eating in fine restaurants (at least better ones than the Automat with its simple food and low prices), and perhaps get around to a little casual sex. They were now enjoying a wonderful life compared to that in the cramped and grungy quarters on the U-boat, much less in concentration camps or the Russian front!

Contrary to Dasch's suggestion, Heinck and Quirin had registered at the Hotel Martinique, instead of the Hotel Chesterfield. Heinck signed under the name Henry Kaynor, and Quirin became Richard Quintas. The Germans settled in, easily assuming the roles of tourists or even New York residents.

While they sat around enjoying the good life, a huge patriotic celebration called New York at War—a parade featuring half a million men and women from labor and management joined by thousands of armed forces members and hundreds of military vehicles, guns, and tanks—was under way. Millions of exuberant Americans lined Fifth Avenue from Washington Square to Seventy-third Street to commemorate the war effort, while four would-be saboteurs tried to figure out just what they were going to blow up.

Meanwhile, Kerling and his men were still on their way to Florida. On the day after they left the French coast, Commander Deecke decided to surface—and paid the price for it. They were immediately seen by British aircraft (which could still manage some coverage of the Bay of Biscay and the western approaches to the UK) and came under attack. U-584 was forced to crash-dive. Kerling, Thiel, Neubauer, and Haupt were thoroughly shaken by the attack.

After the bombing on the second day, Kerling's group became accustomed to the life of a submarine crew member. These men were very close to each other, and they enjoyed one another's company, much more so than Dasch's group. This made the three-week trip pass a little faster for them, and before they knew it, they were coming up on Ponte Vedra on Florida's east coast, their scheduled landing site.

Back in New York, Dasch and Burger were having a soul-searching conversation. Burger bluntly told Dasch that he questioned Dasch's ability to be an effective leader. He pointedly referred to Dasch's lackadaisical attitude during their training at Quenz Lake and reproached him for carelessly leaving his wallet behind on the train. Burger also resented Dasch because he felt that Dasch received special privileges from Kappe, while the rest of the men were treated strictly.

After Burger voiced his criticism, Dasch took a calculated risk, though he was not at all sure that he could trust Burger. Dasch told Burger that he wanted to turn the team and himself in to the FBI. He confided that this was a plan he had been mulling over for some time. The mission already had been compromised, and in any event, Dasch did not feel he could proceed. If they came forward on their own, he asserted, they would be treated leniently.

Burger listened attentively; what Dasch said made sense. Burger finally agreed that he would assist Dasch in sabotaging their sabotage mission. It would be a momentous pact for Burger.

It is not exactly clear when Dasch decided to abort the operation. If it was from the very beginning, as he claimed, Dasch certainly had deceived some of the top officers in Germany's High Command. Dasch's motives for scuttling Operation Pastorius were unclear. He would later claim that his decision was influenced by his strong anti-Nazi feelings. Yet he could also have been thinking of the favorable treatment and rewards granted William G. Sebold in 1941 when he helped the FBI arrest so many German spies.

It is equally plausible that Dasch realized after the unfortunate confrontation with Cullen that the mission was doomed. The likelihood now was that every cop, soldier, and FBI agent in the country must be looking for him. At that point, he might have calculated that if he confessed and turned himself and the others in, he would be much better off than if they were eventually captured.

Whatever the reason, Kappe's trusted recruit turned out to be a traitor. That he entertained delusions of grandeur is certain. That he misjudged the probable response of the enemy would cost his men dearly.

So, in room 1421 at the Governor Clinton Hotel, Dasch told Burger that he was going to call the FBI. This put Burger in a predicament. If Dasch did implicate all the men, Burger had to appear as though he was eager to do the same. On the other hand, if Dasch split with all the money, Burger would have to play the part of the loyal Nazi saboteur and be able to convince the others that he had tried to kill Dasch.[1]

Dasch told Burger that he had been an anti-Nazi even before they went to Quenz Lake. Burger then confessed that he, too, was not an avid Nazi. Burger's conversion was all the more curious given his early Nazi activism and work for the head of the SA. Perhaps, as he confided to Dasch, his readiness to betray the mission was motivated by his mistreatment by the Gestapo and seventeen months in a concentration camp.

Both felt profoundly relieved that they had expressed their reluctance to go through with the operation. Repressing their misgivings for too long, they had been forced to go through the motions of being Nazi loyalists. Each assured the other that Operation Pastorius was his way of getting back to America to join in the fight against Hitler and Nazism.

That night, after making their fateful decision, they celebrated by having dinner in the elegant Coral Room at their hotel. Like old friends, they talked of their pasts, former jobs, and families. Then Dasch revealed what he believed was his well-thought-out plan to scuttle their mission.

After they talked it over, Burger seemed satisfied. They took a stroll through the city, visiting Rockefeller Center and viewing a collection of murals by Jose Maria Sert, whose paintings depicted slavery from its beginnings up to the present. Both said later that any uncertainties about their plan melted away as they looked at the murals and identified with victims of slavery.

Dasch and Burger then went to a coffeehouse frequented by waiters with German backgrounds. Burger remained outside, while Dasch chatted with some former acquaintances. Burger overheard Dasch bragging: "I'm going to Washington, and I'm going to hit Hitler where it counts." As they were leaving, Dasch added: "You'll be reading all about it in the papers pretty soon."[2]

After Dasch finished boasting that he was about to become a national hero, he joined Burger outside, and the two men walked back to their hotel. Burger went to bed feeling reasonably content with Dasch's plan. Still, he could not quite get rid of a foreboding that something was wrong. Maybe Dasch was trying to trick him or set him up. He also recalled that Kappe had always said that there would be no reprisals against any member of the sabotage team who killed another attempting to expose the plan.[3] Burger had always felt that Dasch was a peculiar fellow, yet he desperately wanted to believe Dasch. For the most part he did, but he still harbored some doubts.

The next morning, Dasch and Burger were a little uneasy. Their mutual trust was still shaky. Realizing that their plan would work only if they were fully in agreement about their commitment to abort the mission, Dasch staged a melodramatic confrontation.

Pushing the breakfast cart into the hall, Dasch locked it outside, tossed the key into the bathtub, and closed the bathroom door. Then he threw open the windows and looked down on the street, fourteen floors below. Burger was watching apprehensively, waiting for an explanation of this strange behavior.

"We are going to have a talk and if we [don't] agree with each other, only one of us [will] leave the room alive," Dasch told him.

Eventually, the two settled on a plan. Dasch would go to the FBI and turn in everyone. Before he did this, however, Dasch and Burger had to meet with Quirin and Heinck. They figured that they should keep track of the whereabouts of Heinck and Quirin but not let them in on the plan.

On Sunday, June 14, the four met at Grant's Tomb on the Upper West Side of Manhattan. The meeting did not go well. Quirin was very antagonistic. Burger and Dasch did their best to allay any suspicions on the part of Quirin and Heinck. Time was running out.

The meeting concluded, Dasch and Burger went back toward their hotel. On the way, they stopped at another hotel, and Dasch glanced over at the phone booths. They exchanged glances; it was now or never.

Dasch went into the phone booth to call the FBI in New York. Burger waited anxiously outside, chain-smoking one cigarette after another. Both men were nervous. Dasch could barely dial the number. As they stood there, they recalled that Kappe had once told them that they would all be safe in America since the Gestapo had infiltrated the FBI.

Eventually, Dasch reached Agent Dean F. McWhorter.

"Hello, my name is Franz Daniel Pastorius," Dasch told him. "I have just come from Germany, and I need to give some information to J. Edgar Hoover."

Believing that this was another crank call like all the others that the FBI had received in several cities ever since Pearl Harbor, McWhorter responded with understandable skepticism. But Dasch plunged ahead.

"You should inform Washington that this information will be given on Thursday or Friday this week."

"Why don't you just come down here to our office and deliver your information in person?" McWhorter asked.

"No. This is a matter for Washington only."

"Where are you located, sir?" McWhorter inquired.

"That is not important. Please just make a record of this call and tell Washington to be expecting something in the next few days," Dasch pleaded.

"Okay, sir, but why won't you—"

Dasch abruptly hung up the phone, cutting off McWhorter.

Agent McWhorter routinely made a memorandum about the call, but he did not consider it very important. Nor did he connect it to the news about the German spy hunt currently under way. His report read as follows:

Re: F.D. Postorius, Memorandum for the file. Please be advised that at 7:51 P.M. on this date, Frank Daniel Postorius called this office by telephone, and advised the writer that he had made the call for the purpose of having a record of it, in this office. Postorius advises that he had arrived in New York City two days ago from Germany. He would not reveal his present address in the city, and remained uncommunicative concerning any information that he might be able to furnish this office. He stated that he was going to Washington D.C., on Thursday or Friday of this week, and would talk to Mr. Hoover or his secretary. He refused to come to this office and report his information and said that he had to see a certain person in Washington first, but he wanted this office to make a record of his call and to notify our Washington office that he was coming there. This memo is being prepared only for the purpose of recording the call made by Postorius.

Filed without any follow-up action, the memo never made its way to FBI headquarters in Washington.[4] As Dasch would later learn, it is not that easy for a German terrorist to surrender to the FBI. More ominously, this bureaucratic snafu would loom large in later government decisions affecting the lives of the German saboteurs and the course of constitutional law in America.

Confident that he had done the right thing, Dasch accompanied Burger back to their hotel. He realized that he must go to Washington, D.C., as soon as possible, but a part of him wanted to remain in New York for a while. He wanted to prepare himself, to make sure he was in the right frame of mind to surrender to the FBI. He also wanted to have a good time. So later that night, he returned to the coffeehouse and joined a pinochle game that would become a day-and-a-half-long marathon. It served as a means of temporary escape from all his anxieties.[5]

Members of the club came over and greeted him and asked him questions, but he did not answer directly. Dasch merely said, "Boys, don't ask me nothing. I cannot tell you the truth anyway."

Dasch cleaned up—he won about $250 and paid the bills of everyone in the house, giving a Polish boy named John $10 because he was busted and handing $5 to a Jewish boy. Dead tired, Dasch took a taxi back to the Governor Clinton Hotel, where he rested for three entire days.

Awakening from his slumber around noon on Wednesday, the seventeenth of June, Dasch was reenergized, convinced that he had to go to Washington, D.C., if he was to extricate himself from his predicament. While he went out to shop for some things he might need in Washington, Burger met with Heinck and Quirin.

This meeting did not go well, either. The other two were uneasy, perhaps suspicious, he felt. Burger believed that he could not keep them at bay too much longer, even though he told them he was traveling to Chicago soon. Burger's report made Dasch nervous; he paced around the hotel room while Burger tried to calm him down, reassuring him that it would all be over soon.

Dasch realized that Burger was right, and that night they went out for a final dinner together. Dasch was in the mood for corned beef and cabbage, so they went to an Irish joint called Dinty Moore's. After dinner, Dasch thought it best to go back to the hotel and get some more rest to prepare for the big day ahead of him. Burger instead went out to the Swing Club to rendezvous with Heinck and Quirin, hoping to reassure them and dispel any suspicion about the progress of the operation.

The next morning, June 18, Dasch and Burger enjoyed one last meal together, during which Dasch gave some final instructions to Burger. "Stay here. Stay at this hotel. Don't let Heinck and Quirin know that I'm in Washington, and for Godsakes, keep them happy."

"Okay, George. Good luck. This will all be over soon."

Dasch wondered what to do with all the money that Kappe had given him. At first, he considered putting it in a safe-deposit box, but his stash was too big. So he purchased a leather briefcase along with three manila envelopes and rubber bands. Returning to his room, he made reservations at the first-class Mayflower Hotel in Washington, D.C. Nothing but the best for George Dasch.

Dasch then packed, taking the money from the original moneybag and putting it in the three envelopes wrapped with a rubber band. He then wrote a note: "Content $82,350. Money from German Government for their purpose but to be used to fight them Nazis. George J. Dasch, alias George J. Davis, alias Franz Pastorius."[6]

Dasch put this note on top of the envelopes in his new briefcase. He went down and paid Burger's and his bill—and then decided to write a farewell note to Burger.

> Dear Pete, Sorry for not having been able to see you before I left. I came to the realization to go to Washington and finish that which we have started so far. I'm leaving you, believing that you take good care of yourself and also of the other boys. You may rest assured that I shall try to straighten everything out to the very best possibility. My bag and clothes I'll put into your room. Your hotel bill is paid by me, including this day. If anything extraordinary should happen, I'll get in touch with you directly. Until later, I'm your sincere friend, George.

As he made his way down to Washington on an overcrowded train full of soldiers and sailors, Dasch was made acutely uncomfortable at the thought of holding in his arms a suitcase with more money than he had earned his entire life. He kept asking himself questions about how he should handle his approach to the FBI.

Should I simply go to the FBI office like William Sebold? That might not be the best idea, he reasoned, especially since he was not familiar with the government offices and bureaus. *And do I just walk straight into J. Edgar Hoover's office?* That seemed to be a bit too far-fetched. Even George John Dasch, American hero in waiting, might not be able to pull that off.

Still, he reassured himself, he had now been in the United States for six days. Even though his landing had been discovered and he had called the FBI, he remained free. The FBI was clueless about his whereabouts. *If I had not decided to turn myself in, they might never find me,* he concluded.

Roughly a thousand miles south, Kerling and his group had been in the United States for two days, totally undetected. Committed to their mission, they were dutifully carrying out their orders, while Dasch was about to betray them.

Arriving at Union Station toward the end of the day on June 18, Dasch went straight to the Mayflower Hotel and, like the proverbial condemned man, ate a hearty meal. The next morning, June 19, Dasch decided to go through with his plans and got the numbers for the FBI as well as the U.S. Army. He first called a Colonel Kramer and left a message with his secretary. Not receiving a prompt return call, Dasch telephoned FBI headquarters.

He was put through to Agent Duane L. Traynor.

"Hello, my name is Frank Pastorius, you should know who I am," Dasch asserted.

"I'm sorry," replied Traynor, figuring it was just some nut.

"Yes, I was in touch with your offices in New York, and they said they would notify you that I would be getting in touch with you."

"Uh, I, um, there is no record of that, sir," Traynor said.

Frustrated, Dasch replied: "Well, I have some very important information that you may benefit from. It is a matter of military importance."

Traynor now realized that this call might be connected to the ongoing Amagansett investigation being conducted by the FBI. "Okay, why don't you come down to our offices and deliver it."

"I'm not sure where the FBI office is. Will you please send someone over here to get me?" Dasch retorted.

"Okay, pal, where are you at?"

"I'm at the Mayflower Hotel, room 435."

"Okay, someone will be over shortly. Don't move."

By now Dasch was almost jumping out of his skin with anxiety. Just to make matters more complicated, Colonel Kramer returned his call.

"Hello."

"Uh, hello, is this George Dasch?" Kramer inquired.

"Yes, yes it is. What do you want?"

"Hello, this is Colonel Kramer. I got your message. Please tell me what this is all about," replied Kramer.

"Well, sir, I am the leader of German saboteurs who landed by submarine on Long Island, and I was just reporting the matter to the government."

"No, no, you must come see me right away," Kramer insisted. "This is a military matter."

"I'm sorry, sir, you were not there; the FBI is already on its way to get me," Dasch said.

"Very well, you must contact me with further details," Kramer demanded, the frustration in his voice evident.

"Yes, sir," Dasch politely replied.

As he waited to be picked up by a federal agent, Dasch contemplated his future. What would happen to him? Would the FBI believe him? Could he cut a deal for his freedom?

Meanwhile, when Burger came back to the Governor Clinton Hotel on June 18, he read Dasch's note. He then knew that he had no options—he was irrevocably committed to Dasch, no matter what either of them might say later.

How did it happen that my fate is being determined by the likes of George Dasch? Burger kept asking himself.

The next night, Heinck and Quirin came over to Burger's hotel room because they were going to go out with some girls they had met at the Swing Club. While Burger was in the bathroom, he noticed Heinrich Heinck open up the drawer of his writing desk and take out the letter that Dasch had written. Heinck appeared to read the letter and then handed it to Quirin. They then returned the letter to the drawer. Heinck also took the paid bill from the Governor Clinton Hotel from the right-hand desk drawer and looked at it. In order to avoid any possible bodily harm to himself and prevent his confederates from asking awkward questions, Burger hurriedly dressed, and the three men left the hotel.[7]

Burger was worried that Heinck and Quirin would start interrogating him about Dasch's note. But Heinck and Quirin were either biding their time or distracted by the women at the club, and apparently they forgot about it completely. They never did confront Burger.

After two days, Burger's anxieties shifted to Dasch. He had not heard from him, and now he had serious doubts that Dasch was following through with the plan. After all, the FBI would not take so long to act on Dasch's information. *Did George skip town with all that money?* Burger kept asking himself. *And leave me here? Bastard!*

Chapter 8

True Believer

Shortly after midnight on June 17, four days after the Dasch team had landed, Kerling and his group, wearing German marine infantry caps and swimming suits, made a successful landing at Ponte Vedra near Jacksonville, Florida. They quickly unloaded and buried their four crates of explosives and other materials. The entire operation went smoothly and, unlike their counterparts, they went undetected.

Kerling was very satisfied with himself. A true believer, this committed Nazi was thoroughly convinced of the significance of his mission and eager to carry it out as swiftly and effectively as possible. He gathered his team and moved out. Dressed in civilian clothes, the men dined together in Jacksonville the next evening. Kerling then ordered Haupt and Neubauer to go to Chicago, but separately; Kerling and Thiel would go to New York City.

Kerling understood the importance of keeping his men separated and dispersed until Dasch and he met to make specific sabotage plans. They were scheduled to rendezvous on July 4—Kappe had savored the irony when he chose the date.[1] Once Dasch and Kerling had agreed upon a plan of action, Kerling would summon Haupt and Neubauer from Chicago.

After their arrival, several of the men sought out the people with whom they had become very close when they lived in the United States, including their families, old friends, and mistresses. Secrecy is hard to maintain for a sustained period of time—especially by men not used to maintaining the discipline necessary for a clandestine operation. These men needed to confide in someone, if only to relieve the pressure that had been building up inside them as training gave way to stark—and scary—reality.

This insecurity (in both senses) highlighted an obvious fact: none of the eight Germans was really qualified for their assignment. They had no prior experience in espionage, spying, or commando operations. Their training had been highly abbreviated compared to that given to many of the resourceful spies and terrorists ordinarily used by the Third Reich. Undoubtedly, that is why experienced military leaders such as Admiral Canaris believed that these amateurs were being sent on a senseless, impossible mission—and to their deaths.

Nor did the German eight fit the profile of effective terrorists. None was a professional spy. None was sophisticated or well-educated. And with the possible exception of Kerling, none seemed all that prepared to die for the cause.

In fact, men such as Haupt were a spymaster's worst nightmare. Following Kerling's order, Haupt went to Chicago via train. Proud of himself, he was looking forward to his triumphant return to his pro-Nazi neighborhood, where he could tell everyone that he was on a special assignment from the German government.

When Haupt reached Chicago on June 19, he decided to visit his uncle, Walter Froehling, an avid Nazi sympathizer. Kappe was aware of this fact, and just to make sure he was taking every precaution necessary, Kappe had told Haupt to remind Froehling that his brother, Otto, was in a concentration camp in Germany. Otto's release would come only at the price of Froehling's cooperation.

Kerling and Thiel traveled to New York via Cincinnati on June 20. Thanks to Hoover's news embargo, they had no knowledge of Dasch's perfidy or the ongoing FBI manhunt. If he had had the slightest inkling of Dasch's intentions to betray his country, Kerling would have killed him on the spot in France.

Putting his limited training to good use, Kerling had purposely gone through Cincinnati to get to New York. While it would have been a shorter trip to take a direct route, Kerling feared that the passenger lists were checked on trains traveling northbound on the East Coast route. Kerling figured that he had come this far, and he was not about to get caught because of some careless error on his part. When Kerling bought two tickets for New York, he gave one to Thiel and made him inconspicuously board the train by himself.

Much to Kerling's chagrin, when they reached New York and checked into the Hotel Commodore on June 20, they were forced to take a double room. But he remained calm. After all, it was a large and busy hotel next to subway and bus lines, easily accessible directly from Grand Central Station.

The next afternoon, June 21, Kerling decided that he should visit his friend Helmut Leiner in Astoria, Queens. With Thiel in tow, he took a subway ride out to see Leiner; Thiel had first met him several years earlier when both men were active in the American Bund in the United States. The reunion was a happy occasion for all. Leiner had not seen Kerling since Kerling went back to Germany at the beginning of the war. After a friendly embrace, Leiner agreed to go out to dinner with Kerling and Thiel.

The three compatriots dined at the Blue Ribbon, a popular German restaurant on the fringe of Times Square. Kerling shared some of his privileged information with Leiner, explaining to him how and why he had come back into the United States. Leiner agreed to assist in any way possible.

Leiner specifically promised to make it possible for Kerling to meet with the two most important women in his life before he returned to Germany—his wife, Marie Kerling, and his mistress, Hedwig Engemann. The former was working as a cook in a New York apartment, while the latter helped out in her family's grocery store in Yorkville.

After the men finished dinner, they walked to a nearby bar and chatted over drinks for nearly three hours. Made less cautious than he should have been after a few drinks, Thiel decided that Leiner also could help him. Before the men retired for the night, Leiner agreed to deliver a message to Anthony Cramer, Thiel's closest friend in America. The message was in code: " 'Franz from Detroit' wanted to meet him Monday evening at nine at the Grand Central Terminal Information Desk."[2]

Leiner did his job. Thiel and Cramer later met at the rendezvous and walked to a bar located on the corner of Forty-fourth and Lexington. Thiel was uncertain about how much information he wanted to divulge to his good friend and thereby put him in danger. Thiel suspected that Cramer had guessed exactly what he was doing back in America.

Thiel's hunch was reinforced the next morning when a newspaper column carried a headline reading: "F.B.I. agents are swarming through the Florida swamps because of stories that Nazi submarine crews in civilian clothes are at large in that state."[3] Overcome with anxiety, Thiel decided that it was urgent to meet Cramer again at the same bar.

During the meeting, Thiel insisted that Cramer take his money belt; Cramer acquiesced. The two friends then decided that they were in the mood for some pie and coffee, so they went over to Thompson's Cafeteria, located near the Commodore Hotel. Calling it a night, they made arrangements to meet the next day, and Cramer mentioned that he would attempt to locate Norma Kopp, Thiel's former girlfriend, who was believed to be still in the United States and working in Connecticut.

As Thiel walked back to his hotel, he pondered his situation. He was happy to have gotten rid of the money belt, and although he wanted to see Norma and Cramer, he was also happy to be going to Cincinnati, as Kerling indicated that they would be doing soon. They had been in the United States for all of six days.

It was Tuesday, June 23. Thiel was anxious about hanging around New York. He hoped that Kerling shared his anxiety.

While Thiel was turning in for the night, Kerling was trying to sort out what to do about his wife and his mistress. On Monday, June 22, Kerling had met with Hedy in Central Park, eager to learn how she felt about him after their long separation. He could not have been happier with her response. She loved him as passionately as she ever had, and she wanted to go wherever he went, whether Chicago, Cincinnati, or Florida.

Kerling felt guilty. All he told Hedy about his situation was that he had come over on a German submarine. He could not bring himself to tell her that he was a saboteur on a secret, dangerous mission. All that mattered was that they were still in love and that Kerling finally felt human again, especially after the months of virtual confinement during his training and preparation.

Hedy knew that although she was ready to run off with the man she loved desperately, she had to settle some things with Kerling's wife. So she took it upon herself to meet with Marie, and they agreed that Kerling belonged with Hedy. Kerling's wife explained that her relationship with him was more that of a brother and sister than that of a husband and wife. For Hedy's sake, Marie agreed to divorce him. Hedy was beside herself with joy.

Before Kerling met with Hedy, he went with his friend Leiner to Newark, New Jersey, in order to select a hiding spot for all the explosives that had been cached in Florida. While in Newark, the two men tried to locate a minister whose name was on the handkerchief (with U.S. contacts) that Kappe had given Kerling. They could not find him, and Kerling surmised that this man was deliberately staying out of the public eye. Just the past Saturday, he had read a newspaper article recounting how a pro-Nazi minister had been arrested in Philadelphia.

Kerling was somewhat disappointed, but he had come to realize that he was going to have to carry out a great many of the sabotage operations on his own. He had little confidence in Dasch and his group—and for good reason. Thanks to Dasch's treachery, Thiel and Kerling were arrested that very night in New York. The handkerchief that Dasch gave to the FBI enabled agents to locate them.

Once the lab figured out a way to bring out the writing in invisible ink, agents were dispatched to watch all the contacts named on the handkerchief. Leiner's name was one of the first ones. After a couple days of surveillance, the FBI spotted Kerling talking to Leiner. They followed Kerling to a bar, where he met with Thiel. Both men were arrested that night, Tuesday, June 23.

Ten days after the first landing on Long Island, three of the eight German saboteurs were in custody.

Chapter 9

Citizen Haupt

Following Kerling's order, Herbert Haupt arrived in Chicago on Friday, June 19. Bold and brash, Haupt acted like a conquering hero without a care in the world. But then, he had no reason to suspect that Dasch had already disclosed his identity to the FBI.[1]

As the train pulled into the station, all Haupt wanted to do was pick up where he had left off before he went back to Germany. Most of all, he wanted to reunite with his girlfriend, Gerda Melind. Now Haupt was returning with money in his pocket. This pleased him greatly because he believed that enough money could open any door. Indeed, at some point before they left Germany, Burger had remarked: "[I]f Haupt got a chance to double-cross the group . . . he might do so purely for money."[2] True to form, one of the very first things Haupt did after landing in Florida was to buy a flashy gold wristwatch, while the others spent money only on civilian clothes and food.

Kerling had ordered Haupt to resume his American life as a cover until instructed to join Kerling. By prearrangement, communication with Haupt in Chicago would be made through Walter Froehling, Haupt's uncle. Froehling's address was written with invisible ink on Kerling's handkerchief.

Alighting from a taxi in his old neighborhood, Haupt held his head high. Having lived in this pro-Nazi community, he was expecting lavish praise from his friends and relatives when they learned the truth about his return. Arriving at his uncle's house, Haupt warmly hugged his uncle, aunt, and two young cousins. Froehling called Haupt's mother and told her to come over without telling her why. Haupt hid while his uncle prepared his mother for the surprise. Seeing her son, she was overjoyed. She became "nearly paralyzed seeing him," she recalled, "and still I was happy to see him."[3]

Haupt gave the family a brief account of what exactly he had been doing over the past year or so. No one believed him when he said he had lived in Germany for a while, until he mentioned seeing his grandparents in Stettin. Then his family started to believe what he was telling them—even the incredible fact that he had come over on a German U-boat.

Haupt decided to pull out all the stops. So he opened his new suitcase in front of everyone and took out Kerling's canvas bag full of money. "This is proof of Germany's faith in me!" he exclaimed. His relatives were momentarily speechless.

"You all must promise me to keep this a secret," Haupt insisted.

"Okay . . . okay," they all replied.

"Uncle Froehling, here is my bag. Don't give it to anybody, no matter what they say," Haupt firmly instructed him.

"Okay, I won't, Herbert," his uncle promised.

"And here is my money belt with $4,000 in it. Don't let anything happen to it."

"Okay, Herbert, I promise you."

"Also, you should know that there are three other men on the same mission as me, and I am expecting a telephone call here on Sunday, the twenty-first."

"Yes, okay."

"Oh, and I am to remind you that Uncle Otto's chances of release depend on your cooperation."

Froehling's expression turned sour, and he became depressed as he thought about his brother, imprisoned in a concentration camp in Germany.

Haupt returned home with his mother, who tried to ignore his strange behavior. As far as he was concerned, he was acting quite normally. He slept soundly, believing that he was doing a good job so far.

One little problem, however, had cropped up while he was in Germany. His mother reported that the FBI had questioned her the previous December about his failure to register for the draft since he was a naturalized citizen. She told the agents that he had left the country. Haupt decided to register for the draft on Monday in order to avoid any more questioning.

Possible prosecution for draft dodging did not worry Haupt too much—not nearly as much as he fretted about his girlfriend. He had left her pregnant, but he had recently heard that she had had a miscarriage soon after he left for Mexico. Now he looked forward to seeing Gerda again—and was relieved that he had avoided the responsibility of paternity.

Haupt relaxed on Saturday, but later that night he met up with an old friend of his, Otto Wergin, who had accompanied him to Mexico. Haupt had to wait to see Wergin until after three o'clock in the morning because Wergin was a drummer in a band that played at Haus Vaterland, a German American social center in the Chicago suburbs. They caught up on old times, and when he met Wergin's mother later that morning, Haupt gave her $50 because he could tell she was hard up.

Saturday night, Haupt went to sleep at his uncle's because he had told Neubauer to call him there on Sunday. Around noon on June 21, the call came.

"Herbert?"

"Yes, hello, Hermann?"

"Yes, this is he. Listen, I just arrived from Cincinnati, and I am eager to meet up with you."

"Okay, well, why don't we meet at the Chicago Theater."

"Okay, when do you want to meet?"

"How does eight o'clock sound?"

"Sure, that sounds fine, I will meet you there at eight."

They met at the theater at the designated time and decided to see a movie. The movie playing at the theater was *The Invaders*, starring Laurence Olivier, Leslie Howard, Raymond Massey, and Eric Portman. The movie told the story of six survivors of a bombed German submarine making their way across Canada.

After the movie, the two men decided to go to a restaurant. Neubauer confessed that he was worried, and he feared Kerling and Thiel were also concerned. Young and foolish, Haupt downplayed these fears and tried to ease Neubauer's mind.

"Everything is going to be fine," he reassured Neubauer. "We're in great shape."

Neubauer had met with Kerling in Cincinnati briefly before he came to Chicago, and he relayed the message that Kerling wanted to meet with Dasch in Chicago on July 6. As they parted, Haupt again tried to reassure Neubauer that everything had gone perfectly so far.

"We'll meet here again on Wednesday, June 24," Haupt suggested. Neubauer nodded his agreement and disappeared into the warm Chicago night.

The next morning, Haupt reported to the local draft board, registering with minimal difficulty. With his new draft card, Haupt nonchalantly walked into the local FBI office. Calmly, he explained to a couple of agents that he understood they had questioned his mother about his absence from the United States. He endeavored to clear his name, explaining why he had left the country. The story had a ring of truth to it: he had fled to Mexico not to evade the draft, but merely to get away from his girlfriend. "[I] had been wrongfully accused of causing the pregnancy of a woman who was a habitual drunkard and who had slept with some ten or twelve men."[4]

The agents seemed satisfied—especially since he had registered for the draft. They did, however, ask him if he would fight for the United States if called to military service. Haupt said that he would rather not fight against the Germans, but if in fact he was called, he would go. He was free to leave, they told him.

Haupt was amazed at how well he had performed for the FBI. It was time to find Gerda and make amends. *Could things be going any better?* he wondered as he hopped a taxi to his mother's house.

His mother arranged for the reunion. They all met up together, and then Haupt's mother and Gerda ate lunch by themselves while Haupt went to a movie so that his mother could find out how Gerda was feeling about Haupt. Returning to his mother's house after the movie, Haupt learned from his beaming mother that Gerda was just as eager to see him.

That evening, he went out with Gerda. As part of his celebration of a new life, he had decided to buy a new car with some of the money supplied by the Nazis. Kerling had sternly advised Haupt not to buy a car until Kerling gave approval. With his taste for the high life, however, Haupt could not resist the temptation of a brand-new Pontiac convertible. Given the shortage of new cars in the country, he was lucky to find one.

Caught up in this magical moment, Haupt spontaneously dropped down on one knee and proposed to Gerda. She thought he was just simply pulling her leg at first, but then he made a gesture that changed her mind. Haupt gave her $10, which he told her would be used to pay for the blood tests required by law before a couple could obtain a marriage license.

Gerda was flustered by Haupt's proposal. "I couldn't understand why he wanted to marry me all of a sudden, after not hearing from him a whole year. So I thought, well, I would agree to have [the test] taken, and maybe by that time he would tell me a little more why he wanted to marry me all of a sudden, what the reason was."

Haupt did not mention anything to her about his mission, telling her only that he had been to Mexico. The only reason that Gerda could imagine for Haupt's marriage proposal was that he felt guilty for abandoning her when he learned that he was going to be a father.

The next day, Wednesday, June 24, Haupt planned to go to the car dealer to make the down payment. He had intended to use the money from his money belt, but his mother knew better. She had read that the United States government was on the lookout for large bills coming into the United States from Axis countries. So she took out $150 from her own savings account and gave her son the money in bills of small denomination. She intended to hold on to the large bills and not deposit them.

Later on that day, he called Gerda and lied about taking the blood test. He then met with Neubauer at the theater. Haupt next focused on evading the draft—this time for real.

Haupt met with a young man by the name of William Wernecke, who was a pro-Nazi volunteer worker for several isolationist societies in Chicago. Draft dodging was his specialty, and he would help out Haupt by taking him to a pro-Nazi doctor. Wernecke told Haupt to tell the man that he suffered from "coronary thrombosis, rheumatic pains, swelling of . . . [the] ankles, pain in [the] upper left arm, dizzy spells now and then, headaches every week, indigestion, pains in [the] chest and pains in [the] back."[5]

It seemed excessive, but he played along. The doctor tested Haupt's blood pressure and found it was unusually high for a man his age. The doctor mentioned that it might be the cause of his nervousness. Haupt could not imagine anything that would make him nervous at that time.

The doctor also noted that Haupt's heart was not fully functioning, and so the doctor advised that he get a cardiogram. Eventually, the doctor wrote a note that Haupt could show his boss at Simpson's, the place where he once worked, that would ask for Haupt to be held back from any physical exertion until a definite diagnosis was made. Haupt needed this note from the doctor because Simpson's had military contracts, including for the famed Norden bombsight that was critical to winning the air war over Europe. He had decided to seek employment there and needed to show that he was exempt from the draft for medical reasons.

Two nights later, Haupt met up with several of his old co-workers from Simpson's for dinner and drinks. It was his night for celebration. After all, in one week, he had taken care of all that he needed to do: his family and friends, Gerda, the draft, his job, and a car. Plus he still had a great deal of money left. He was very proud of himself.

What Haupt did not know was that the FBI had followed him to the Blue Danube Tavern and then to the Tip Top Tap at the Allerton Hotel that night. They had been tracking him ever since he came into their office to clear up his draft-dodging accusation. Agents trailed Haupt for nearly three days, hoping that he would lead them to Neubauer, but no such luck.

The next morning, Haupt drove his new Pontiac to the Loop and turned onto Webster Avenue. He was on his way to get his job back. A car was unobtrusively following him. Finally, on Saturday, June 27, the FBI agents decided to arrest Haupt.

Haupt was taken to the FBI office in downtown Chicago, where he was strip-searched and given other clothes. He was practically forced to sign papers giving agents a warrant to search his home, and he simultaneously allowed them to keep him in custody and prevent him from being arraigned. Over the next couple of days, Haupt signed two confessions of his involvement in the sabotage mission. Before being transported to the FBI offices in New York, he gave them Neubauer's location at the Sheridan Plaza.

Neubauer was the most uncomfortable of all the men in his group when he was in the United States. Since he had not lived in the city since the World's Fair during the 1930s, he had no friends or even mere acquaintances. He visited a couple in Chicago whom he barely knew, telling them about his situation and leaving most of his money with them. Although they were very friendly and Neubauer trusted them, he still felt forlorn.

Haupt could not really be considered a friend, but it did help ease Neubauer's feelings of loneliness when he met with him to see *The Invaders*. (The film shows that the trek across Canada was harrowing—and the ending is not at all a happy one.) Neubauer stayed in Chicago after he met Haupt for the first time, moving around from hotel to hotel: the LaSalle to the Sherman to the Sheridan Plaza. Yet he was still unsatisfied.

Neubauer spent most of his time going to the movies and smoking cigars, since he did not find solace in drinking. He counted the days until Kerling would come to meet him in Chicago. He heard on the radio that Germans were being landed in the United States by submarine, and he grew very weary and even lonelier, as he was virtually all by himself.

But not for long.

On Saturday, June 27, Neubauer left the Sheridan Plaza for a matinee. It would be the last time that he ever saw a movie. When he returned that evening, three FBI agents were waiting for him. This was the last arrest made of a member of the original group of eight saboteurs—two weeks after the first landing.

While the German commandos were infiltrating the United States, President Roosevelt was hosting British prime minister Churchill, who had arrived in Washington, D.C., on June 18 following a twenty-seven-hour flight in the Boeing seaplane *Bristol*. Over the weeklong visit at FDR's home in Hyde Park, New York, and the White House, the two friends discussed wartime strategy. One weighty topic was the priority of shared development of an atomic bomb.[6]

On the evening of June 25, Churchill was spirited out of the White House via an underground tunnel and driven to the British Overseas Airways seaplane facilities at Baltimore's municipal airport. Arriving just before midnight, his car stopped near the pier where the *Bristol* was waiting. Secret Service Agent Mike Reilly told Churchill to stay in the car for a moment while he checked out security.

That precaution may have saved Churchill's life.

As Reilly approached the seaplane, another Secret Service agent,

John Chandler, was "wrestling with a pistol-toting BOA employee who had been overheard muttering to himself, 'I'm going to kill that [expletive] Churchill. I'm going to kill him.' "[7] Reilly and Chandler subdued the would-be assassin, who turned out to be an insane American of Irish extraction. Churchill arrived safely in London on June 27, unaware that he had come close to being assassinated.

Chapter 10

Double Cross

Growing increasingly anxious, Dasch waited for about thirty minutes before he heard a rap on his door at the Mayflower Hotel. Standing there was a young agent who ordered Dasch to come with him.

It was June 19—six days after landing on Long Island and four days after he had first called the FBI.

When he arrived at FBI headquarters, Dasch insisted on seeing J. Edgar Hoover himself. Instead, he was escorted to an office to speak to Agents D.M. "Mickey" Ladd and Duane L. Traynor. Dasch was assured that Ladd was an aide to Mr. Hoover and the highest person in the organization he would be allowed to see without disclosing his information.[1]

Hoover had assigned Ladd to the German spy case. When Dasch mentioned the phone call that he had placed on Sunday to the FBI's New York office, Ladd was dumbfounded. Dasch repeated what he had said to the agent in the New York office, embellishing as he went along:

> I [told him I] was the leader of the Pastorius mission, that we had landed on Long Island and that our efforts were supposedly directed towards crippling the light metals plants in the Tennessee Valley. I ended by saying that instead of doing this, I considered it my duty as a former soldier of the United States Army to do everything I could to prevent the attack and had come to report the matter to Mr. Hoover.[2]

Ladd was convinced that Dasch was some kind of nutcase or con man. He thought that despite Hoover's news blackout, Dasch had somehow heard about the manhunt and was trying to cash in on it—how exactly was not clear. Dasch sensed that neither agent was taking him seriously, and he did not know what to do at first.

Here was the moment I had been waiting for, the supreme climax of eighteen long years of hard, determined grinding away to make a better life for myself, my wife and my principles. I had left New York at six o'clock in the morning just about a year ago. I had crept across the ocean on an overcrowded ship, rumbled across the endless wastes of Russia, and schemed and prayed my way through a dangerous maze of bureaucratic suspicion and favoritism in order eventually to face these two men before me. I suppose that after the terrible battle I expected a bit too much—I suppose I thought I would hear the national anthem being played or buttons being pressed with squads being formed to round up the saboteurs at my slightest instruction. Maybe so, but I certainly didn't anticipate the cold, impassive expressions before me. Here was a cruel and bitter end indeed! The table between us was about three feet wide, no more, but it seemed as if every quarter inch of the smooth, polished surface stood for months of anguished hopes that were about to be blown up by an explosion that always occurs when skepticism tangles with the naked truth.[3]

There was a long, awkward moment of silence. Dasch was at a loss—and so were the agents. They were waiting for something but were not exactly sure what that something was.

Then Ladd turned and glanced at Traynor, who shifted in his chair and returned a blank stare. Dasch began to sweat. He knew he had to do something now or all his efforts would be in vain—and he would be in big trouble.

"Sebold, William G. Sebold . . . like me . . . landed in 1940 . . . ," Dasch said in a low voice.

"What do you know about Sebold?" Ladd asked sharply.

"Everything, Mr. Ladd, everything," Dasch shouted. "And right out of the files of the Abwehr II in the German High Command!"

Ladd and Traynor leaned in closer to Dasch as he grew more animated.

"Here Mr. Traynor, here Mr. Ladd, have a present, a green present, from the black of the Nazi swastika, from the black of the party's heart and soul."

Dasch grabbed his briefcase and dumped everything in it on the table between Dasch and his interrogators. "Three feet of polished wood [of the table's top] were too narrow to hold eighty-four thousand dollars in cash. Packets of bills cascaded over the sides to create the illusion of a miniature waterfall."

This got the attention of Ladd and Traynor, who jumped out of their chairs.

"Is this stuff real?" Ladd asked, while Traynor stood there flabbergasted.

"Yes, yes, examine it and see for yourself," Dasch calmly replied. "And the note, look for the note."

Traynor finally looked for Dasch's note. Finding it buried under the pile of cold hard cash, he pulled it out and began to read it aloud. "Content $82,350. Money from German Government for their purpose but to be used to fight them Nazis. George J. Dasch, alias George J. Davis, alias Franz Pastorius."

Dasch grinned from ear to ear. His confidence restored, he was again convinced that this would make him an American folk hero. Ladd and Traynor were now taking Dasch very seriously.

"Lock that door, man," Ladd said to Traynor. "We've got something real here."

Dasch did eventually get to see Hoover, but it was only a brief audience. Over the next several days, he told his entire story to Ladd and Traynor. Dasch was questioned intensively by a variety of people in the FBI and various branches of military intelligence. In total, Dasch's thirteen hours of interviews generated over 250 pages recorded by stenographers. Dasch revealed everything, beginning with where Burger was staying.

FBI agents then staked out Burger's hotel room, where he was waiting for them. Burger was very cooperative, leading the agents to a nearby clothing store where he met with Heinck and Quirin. The agents arrested all three men that day, June 20. Burger made it clear to the FBI that he knew about Dasch's surrender and had also agreed to betray the mission. He assured the agents that he was eager to assist them in any way possible.

With the entire first team now in custody, Hoover considered it appropriate to notify President Roosevelt. On June 22, Hoover wrote Roosevelt a letter reporting that his agents had already apprehended all members of the Long Island group and expected to arrest the Florida contingent very soon. Although he probably told Dasch otherwise, Hoover neglected to inform FDR that Dasch's surrender and confession had led to all the arrests. Roosevelt assumed from this letter that Hoover and his men had been successful in their manhunt and had captured the spies entirely through their unaided efforts. The president commended Hoover and the FBI on a job well done.

The team from Florida was still unaccounted for, however, and the FBI was having trouble locating them. Dasch and Burger helped out. Dasch offered a silk handkerchief on which the High Command had used invisible ink to list several German contacts in the United States. He was unable to recall the method for exposing the writing and was surprised that the experts in the FBI could not initially figure it out either. Dasch, Ladd, Traynor, and various laboratory technicians wrestled with the problem.

Dasch was accused of delaying the investigation by refusing to reveal the formula. Dasch cursed himself for not paying better attention during the lessons at the training school outside of Berlin. Eventually, the FBI laboratory called to report that they had found the solution that brought out the invisible ink. FBI agents fanned out to keep under surveillance all of the contacts listed on the handkerchief.

Dasch was in an unenviable situation, and he did not even know the worst of it yet. Before the news of the other Germans' capture was made public, Traynor, Ladd, and Dasch had a number of conversations that were not made part of the record. They discussed the problem of how to handle things so that the Nazis would not learn of his treacherous role in the mission's failure.

Dasch professed to be concerned about protecting his family and associates still in Germany. The FBI's interest was to let the Nazis think that a vigilant United States had nipped the sabotage mission in the bud and that it would be useless to waste any more men and time on similar missions against such an alert country. Dasch and the FBI discussed the trial of the seven men. The FBI said no decision had been made about how Dasch would fit into the picture, but at no time did they suggest that he would have to be charged and tried as a criminal.

Dasch wrote: "They did assure me, though, that when the final story came out, my name or picture would not appear in the newspapers."

Dasch also entertained the notion that the FBI and he would soon get around to working out plans for striking at the Nazis through the anti-Nazi resistance in Germany. "Consequently I felt no concern when the FBI suggested that I allow myself to be returned to New York to show the other Pastorius men that I was also in the hands of the authorities." The FBI had kept him posted on their success in rounding up all the others and reported that some of them, apparently thinking Dasch was still at large and able to do Hitler's dirty work, refused to talk. If he then showed up in prison where his men could see him, they would know there was no one left and the mission was dead. "It made sense to me and I agreed to go along."[4]

While FBI agents were interrogating Dasch and the other Germans as they were apprehended, they assumed that these men would be arraigned before a federal district court judge and tried in civil court on federal criminal charges. The agents, whom Dasch now considered friends, encouraged him to go before a judge and plead guilty. Dasch was originally willing to do so, but then he stubbornly decided that he wanted to go into court to tell the whole story, ending with his turning himself in and terminating the mission. That, however, was the very last thing Hoover wanted.

Dasch met with Hoover, who explicitly promised Dasch that he would receive a full presidential pardon in roughly three to six months, but only if he pled guilty. Dasch agreed. He would be indicted before a federal court, and he would plead guilty so long as everything was kept under wraps.

The next day, Dasch went off with agents Frank Johnstone and Norval D. Wills to New York, having been assured by Ladd and Traynor that everything would be all right. At the federal court building in New York, he was finally placed under arrest, but actually no one ever told him that he was being arrested. They took his civilian clothes, photographed him holding a prison number in front of his chest, and put him through the arrest routine—all the while explaining this was part of the act to deceive the other men. Dasch was led past the cells of all the men except Burger so they could get a good look at him. Finally, he was stuck in a cell and left there. As time passed, Dasch began to sense that something was wrong.

* * *

Hoover did not keep his word. On the evening of June 27, the press was summoned to the New York office of the FBI in the United States Courthouse at Foley Square. It was now fourteen days after the first landing on Long Island. Traveling from Washington for this rare personal press conference, Hoover told reporters of the plot and the subsequent arrests. The master of PR and self-promotion was at his best, selectively recounting the story so that it would appear to the reporters that the FBI had cracked the case all on its own using its highly sophisticated investigative and counterintelligence techniques. The key events—Dasch turning himself in and Cullen's discovery of the landing party—were omitted from the story.

Hoover gave the press a brief overview of the men's profiles and handed out their photographs. He listed the weapons they had brought with them, described their targets, and revealed how they landed. He did not tell the press much more. Surprisingly, the reporters had few questions.

Not surprisingly, however, the news of the saboteurs' capture made the headlines in all the major newspapers the next day. Recognizing that this victory would be a major boost in Americans' confidence in their government's ability to protect the homeland, the press trumpeted the arrests in blazing headlines: "Axis Agents Landed from Submarines; FBI Announces Seizure of Eight Men, One American Citizen." "Churchill, F.D.R. Pledge Attack; U.S. Nips Big Nazi Sabotage Plot."[5] (This *L.A. Times* headline was above the one describing Jimmy Doolittle watching his Tokyo air raiders being awarded medals.) The *New York Times* headline read: "FBI Seizes 8 Saboteurs Landed by U-Boats Here and in Florida to Blow Up War Plants; Allies Pledge Moves to Relieve Russians."[6] The *Chicago Sunday Tribune* boasted: "U-Boats Land Spies; 8 Seized: Capture Saboteurs with Bombs, TNT and $150,000; Spy Suspect Once Chicago ROTC Officer."[7] The ROTC officer was, of course, one of Chicago's own. Citizen Haupt even had an article written about him in the *New York Times*, describing his planned marriage to Gerda Melind. According to the account, they were to have been married the following week. Gerda was interviewed after her fiancé's arrest.

> I knew he liked Hitler's policies, but that was a couple of years ago and we weren't in the war. . . . I saw him at dinner that night in his parents'

home, and he was very nervous. I thought maybe it was because he hadn't registered for the draft. . . . I asked him how he came back and he didn't say anything. . . . He had mentioned marriage Tuesday, and we'd agreed to be married this week. When I accepted [his proposal], he told me he wanted to right the "wrong he had done his country," but I didn't understand the meaning of "wrong to his country" until I heard of his arrest.[8]

The general public—as Roosevelt predicted—was bent on revenge. The terrorists deserved no mercy. Across a still jittery nation, the cry was "death to the spies."

The American public was understandably impressed with the FBI and J. Edgar Hoover. They felt safe knowing that Hoover was capable of meeting any threat of subversion, but they had been given only a rosy version of how the Nazi saboteurs had been rolled up. After the initial news of the arrests, President Roosevelt received hundreds of letters and telegrams recommending that Hoover be awarded the Congressional Medal of Honor. The president did not think his performance merited this distinction, but Hoover did receive a congratulatory message.

The media campaign orchestrated by Hoover and the administration was "the beginning of government control on information about the Saboteurs' Case and the government's successful use of the case for propaganda purposes."[9] Hoover's press conference—and later "orchestrated press extravaganzas" about the capture of the Nazi saboteurs—generated favorable worldwide publicity for the FBI and its director.

Not everyone, however, was pleased with the public disclosure of the FBI's allegedly brilliant and swift capture of the German spies.[10] The War Department was furious with Hoover. In violation of "every principle of counterespionage and sabotage," as McCloy bitterly complained to Stimson, the names of the saboteurs had been made public, thereby alerting the German High Command "who was apprehended, and . . . how they were apprehended."[11] In the ongoing turf battle over internal security, the departmental rivalry between War and Justice again erupted. The military was livid that the FBI was given all the credit for the Germans' apprehension.

Someone else was also apoplectic about the news of the mission's failure. Upon hearing of the capture of his terrorists, Adolf Hitler angrily lashed out at Canaris and Lahousen: "Why didn't you use Jews for that?"[12]

Peering through the peephole in his wooden cell door, Dasch saw a guard sitting on a chair reading a copy of the New York *Daily News*. On the front page was a huge headline, "Captured Nazi Spy"—and underneath was a full-page picture of Dasch.[13]

Dasch felt betrayed. As he sat in his gloomy cell, he kept asking himself why Hoover had double-crossed him. At that moment, he resolved not to go down without a fight.

So he withdrew his offer to plead guilty. Now Dasch's main objective was to go to court and tell the world everything, even if it meant putting at risk his family back home in Germany. Dasch's surprise move caused consternation in Washington. At least one German agent was not prepared to "go gentle into that good night."

Chapter 11

Prisoners of War

A few weeks before George Dasch's surprise visit, Colonel Kenneth C. Royall arrived in Washington, D.C. He had never spent a lot of time there, but the city made the handsome native of North Carolina feel as though he had never left the South. By the summer of 1942, Washington was rapidly being transformed from a sleepy southern city (John Kennedy would later describe it as "a city of Southern efficiency and Northern charm") into a booming military-political center. Its population had almost doubled since 1940. Housing was scarce, buses were overcrowded, and the cost of living was skyrocketing.[1] The federal government was rapidly expanding into any available space, including schools, apartments, skating rinks, gyms, storefronts, and rickety "temporary" buildings that would be used for decades.

In Washington, D.C., like the rest of a nation recently dragged into a global war for which it was conspicuously unprepared, life was anything but normal. The changes began at the White House. The war had a swift and dramatic effect on presidential security. The social season for 1941–42 had been canceled, blackout curtains were hung at each window (depressing Eleanor Roosevelt), and new dim external lighting was installed.[2] In addition, the police detail was doubled, personal identity cards were issued, and the Oval Office was outfitted with bulletproof glass windows on the south side. The net result of all these changes in White House arrangements and regimen was a radical alteration in "the easy informality of Roosevelt's preferred lifestyle while also abolishing certain formalities that Roosevelt was quite willing to do without."[3]

Daily life was also dramatically impacted—from the way people greeted each other to living arrangements among single men and women. Feeling tension in the air, Royall was struck by the apprehension in the somber faces of ordinary people. Every American knew that war was no longer something that took place "over there." The nation's survival—and freedom itself—would be decided not just "over there" but also right here and now.

The powerful Wall Street lawyers and corporate executives recruited by Roosevelt to administer the U.S. military buildup—men such as Stimson and McCloy—found life in Washington very different from what they had left. The capital city—a most unlikely place to become the epicenter of the Allies' efforts to defeat totalitarianism—was provincial, suffering from being at once a small town and an overcrowded city.[4] Unlike other nations' capitals, Washington was a "one-industry, one-company town . . . much less metropolitan" than New York City or Boston.[5] Newcomers such as Attorney General Biddle "found themselves suddenly deprived of theater, opera . . . fashion houses, nightclubs, and a galaxy of restaurants."[6]

Besides serving as the nerve center of war planning, Washington, D.C., was also a symbol of American democracy. Royall vividly recalled his first visit, as a young man, to Washington, and seeing only its public face—the imposing marble monuments of the Lincoln Memorial, the Supreme Court, and the Jefferson Memorial. He never forgot the thrill of reading the originals of the Declaration of Independence, the Constitution, and the Bill of Rights at the National Archives.

As a young Harvard law student and then as an army officer who fought in World War I, Royall cherished the fundamental principles of American democracy—the nation's devotion to liberty and due process of law, the dignity of the individual and human life, equal protection under the law, and a government of laws, not men. Now Royall had made another journey to Washington to defend those fundamental and "self-evident" values—which were the core justification of FDR's social revolution, dedicated to helping millions who were "ill-housed, ill-clothed, ill-nourished"—derived from the Declaration of Independence's revolutionary assertion that "all men are created equal."

But what Royall saw there this time distressed him—the disconnect between those lofty ideals and the reality of daily life in the nation's capital. The three Civil War amendments to the constitution outlawed slavery, guaranteed equal protection of the laws, and prohibited denial of the right to vote on the basis of race, color, or previous condition of servitude.[7] Yet Royall could not help noticing that the "other" Washington exemplified not only outright violations of those prohibitions but also a wide gap between rich and poor, African Americans and whites. The Washington that had *not* been transformed by the war was a racially segregated city where far too many were "ill-housed" in a place that was "expensive, crime-ridden, intolerant, with inadequate transportation, schools, and health facilities."[8]

Royall had seen firsthand grinding poverty in his native North Carolina, but he was appalled by the hidden poverty and open discrimination he witnessed around him. African Americans who had come to Washington (mainly from the poor rural South) in search of better lives and greater opportunity found themselves confined to slums such as the already overpopulated alleys behind row houses. These converted stables and tiny, mostly dilapidated shacks—with no electricity, running water, or indoor bathrooms—were owned by whites who charged exorbitant rents. With fifteen thousand privies consisting of open barrels over holes in the ground, the squalid alleys posed a serious health problem.[9]

Washington at war, with new jobs and housing, offered a glimmer of hope to these dispossessed families whose grandparents had been slaves. Few found a better life, however. The established but small black middle class greeted the uneducated, often unskilled new arrivals with disdain and trepidation, while the entrenched white power structure was egalitarian in one sense: it discriminated against *all* African Americans. The failure of the American dream was all too evident: within a few blocks of the White House, black children regularly died from malnutrition, disease, and neglect.[10]

Three-quarters of a century after the end of the Civil War, slavery's legacy of racial prejudice—reinforced by de jure and de facto segregation in all aspects of life—remained the Achilles' heel of American democracy. A country supposedly united in a struggle to defend basic human rights was, in reality, two nations, not one "indivisible." Nowhere was this polarization more evident than in the nation's capital.

The pall of racism hung over the city like a blanket on a muggy

June day. Public amenities—hotels, restaurants, movie theaters, taxi-cabs, and even libraries—refused to serve blacks, who constituted one-third of the population. Nor could these citizens buy homes in white neighborhoods or even be hired to work in stores catering to black customers. At the D.C.-Virginia line, they suffered the indignity of having to move from the front to the back of the public bus.

Consistent with the reality of "two nations," good jobs for blacks in the federal government were scarce. Most decent-paying jobs went to the two hundred thousand white employees of the federal bureau-cracy, which was under the effective control of southern whites. Be-yond the enclave of Washington and despite FDR's and Eleanor's efforts, defense contractors were also reluctant to break the color bar, particularly in the aircraft industry. (This discrimination was also per-vasive in the armed forces and even in labor unions.) Even a world war could do little to eradicate three centuries of intolerance and discrim-ination.[11] Kenneth Royall was one of those southerners who knew, through hard experience, just how difficult it was to cope with what Gunnar Myrdal would later term "the American dilemma."

Royall was a decent man who loved his family, God, and country. Pub-lic service was a family tradition. He was a third-generation south-erner. His grandfather came from Chesterfield County, Virginia, to Goldsboro, North Carolina, about the time it became a town in 1847. When the South went to war against the North, he served as a first sergeant in the Goldsboro Rifles and was injured at Fort Macon, leav-ing him lame.[12]

Born on July 24, 1894, in Goldsboro to George Claiborne and Clara Howard Royall, Royall grew up with his father because his par-ents divorced when he was a young child and his mother moved to New York City, where she later married an Englishman. His father was a leading Goldsboro citizen—a merchant, a manufacturer, and chair-man of the school board. The organizer of the local chamber of com-merce, he was active in the Episcopal Church. Royall's father believed in giving back. His philanthropic activities—ranging from the local hospital to a girls' school in Raleigh—left an indelible impression on his son. "My father was my all-time hero," he would tell everyone. "His example inspired me greatly."

Royall was highly intelligent and skipped several grades in public school. At age fourteen, he graduated at the top of his class at Episcopal

High School in Alexandria, Virginia. While he eventually grew to six feet five inches and 230 pounds, Royall was the smallest boy in his boarding school class. Royall had the benefit of a classical education but came to realize that in education, as in life, "really what you learn is training of the mind."

Taking only two and a half years and excelling in math, Royall graduated Phi Beta Kappa from the University of North Carolina at Chapel Hill in 1914. Instead of pursuing a science career, Royall opted for law because of his interest in debating. Royall loved to argue— a passion that would serve him well as a brilliant trial lawyer both in county courthouses and in the corridors of power in Washington, D.C. A champion high school and college debater and honors student, Royall was one of the youngest students ever to be admitted to Harvard Law School.

At the end of his second year, he was near the top of his class and an editor of the *Harvard Law Review.* In his third year, World War I intervened, and he joined the army in the spring of 1917. Later, while he was at boot camp, he received his law degree.

As a second lieutenant in artillery, he got to use his math skills, leading his class at Fort Sill. Promoted to first lieutenant, he fought overseas in 1918 in an artillery brigade, the Wildcat Division, that was part of the 81st Infantry Division. Like so many southerners, Royall excelled as a soldier. "Southerners learn, in small towns—particularly— to fight with their fists," Royall recalled years later. "If a boy won't fight, he's not respected much. . . . [T]he tradition of the Civil War still lives there much more than it does up [in the North]."[13]

After the war, Royall returned home to Goldsboro, where he quickly made his mark as an up-and-coming trial lawyer and, like his father, a respected civic leader who presided over the Rotary Club and Chamber of Commerce. As a sideline, he did some contract work and became a banking expert when he served in the North Carolina Senate beginning in 1927.

Royall was a staunch Democrat. His party loyalty was tested in the 1928 presidential election. While he opposed Al Smith's nomination because he did not think a Roman Catholic could carry North Carolina in the election, the Protestant Royall nevertheless supported him as "a regular Democrat" in the November election. "But there was a great division of the state, and a great and intense religious feeling, particularly among the Methodists and the Baptists, the leading denominations in the state. A lot of Democratic candidates running for local office would not support Smith for the Democratic ticket. They wouldn't say anything—but many of them voted for Hoover."[14]

When Hoover won, a lot of North Carolina Democrats—including Royall, who was seeking reelection to the state senate—went down to defeat. When Roosevelt ran in 1932, Royall was an enthusiastic supporter and a presidential elector for FDR in 1940. More than anything else, Royall considered himself a son of Goldsboro. "I was really just a small town man and loved it."

Royall may have lived and practiced in a small town, but his skills as an advocate enabled him to win many jury trials throughout the state. He also handled several cases before the United States Supreme Court—his first one in 1926, when he was only thirty-one.

Royall and his wife, Margaret Pierce Best from nearby Warsaw, were married in 1917 before he went off to war. She was only eighteen—"by northern standards she was quite young." They had two children— one born in 1918 while he was in France and a second two years later. Royall was devoted to Margaret, whom he regularly praised as "wise, efficient and thoughtful."

Royall's legal skills were first forged at Harvard Law School— a hard-driving, ruthless place where a third of the first-year law students flunked out. His provincial rough edges were largely rubbed smooth in his encounters with more sophisticated young men from all over the country. It was, he admitted, "a very broadening experience for a small town boy."

The education of Kenneth Royall in race relations began the very first day of class with famed progressive professor Felix Frankfurter— a Jew who would befriend and train a generation of gifted lawyers such as Royall. Classroom seats were assigned according to a chart so that the professor could learn the names of his students. As Royall later recalled, his seat "was about five or six rows back, and when I came in and sat down, there was a Negro in the seat next to me. So, I just got up and moved to a vacant seat at the back of the room."

After class, Frankfurter summoned Royall and instructed him to remain in his assigned seat.

"Yes, sir. There was a nigger sitting by me," Royall replied.

"Don't you think that's rather narrow-minded?" Frankfurter fired back.

Yes, Royall admitted, he might be narrow-minded—but he still wasn't going to sit next to a black man.[15] As a Jew, Frankfurter had suffered the pain of discrimination, but he allowed Royall to change his seat—and never let him forget it. In time, Royall realized Frankfurter was right and he was wrong, so he went back to his assigned seat and befriended the two blacks in his class, one of whom graduated. "I knew them and respected them. They were not trying to force anything on people. That began my racial education, . . . which grew as time passed."[16]

Even though he lived in rural North Carolina, between the wars Royall kept up his friendship with Frankfurter, a man who had influenced him more than any other teacher in his life. "I first put him down in my book as a sort of crank [teaching new fields of law in their initial stages—such as public utilities, municipal government, and interstate commerce]. . . . [E]verybody said he was a socialist. . . . [H]e went way beyond what the law was then. . . . Then it got through to me that he was teaching us to think more than just teach[ing] [us] the law . . . teaching us how to reason."[17]

The lessons he learned then, combined with his innate ability and fierce competitive spirit, made Royall one of the most highly respected trial lawyers in North Carolina and beyond. His peers elected him president of the North Carolina Bar Association when he was only thirty-five. Tenacious, strategic, and aggressive, he was much sought after in all kinds of civil litigation. In Kenneth Royall, a client had an indefatigable champion. And an opponent faced a fierce, wily antagonist—something the country and its president would soon learn when the worlds of law and politics collided in the prosecution of the German saboteurs.

FDR was personally sympathetic to the plight of African Americans and their distinctively second-class citizenship. A significant component of his winning Democratic Party coalition, they enthusiastically supported him in each of his elections.[18] In his first presidential campaign in 1932, Roosevelt had proclaimed that "the Presidency . . . is pre-eminently a place of moral leadership." When it came to his African American supporters, however, he had failed them in many critical ways.

By mid-1942, FDR had been president for a decade—two years longer than any predecessor. Public housing was not fairly allocated to African Americans. Racial discrimination was rampant in the federal government and private workplace. And thirteen million African Americans as a class remained the poorest of the poor.

While 1.2 million African Americans fought bravely in the army and served in the navy, they were relegated to segregated units led by white officers. "We are suffering from the persistent legacy of the original crime of slavery," Secretary of War Stimson wrote in his diary on January 17, 1942.[19] Segregation was the tradition of the military, except in its officer candidate schools. Impressed by his inspection tours of African Americans in training, Stimson wanted to accelerate the glacial pace of integrating white and black combat soldiers in the army. Whenever he learned of racial injustice to African American soldiers, he took decisive steps to stop such "blatant unfairness."[20] Stimson did not, however, recommend to President Roosevelt that the military be fully integrated. (It took Harry Truman to make a concerted effort to end discrimination in the armed forces by issuing Executive Order 9981 on July 26, 1948.)

Roosevelt's gradualism reflected his political pragmatism: the coalition that had elected him three times included not only the poor, union members, farmers, urban Jews, Irish, Italians, and Germans, but also the Democrats of the "Solid South," who were critical to his string of electoral successes. Roosevelt's allies in the Congress—who promoted his New Deal programs and then supported his war efforts— were southern racists who controlled the major committees. (It was no accident that FDR's first Supreme Court appointment in 1937 was U.S. Senator Hugo L. Black of Alabama, a former member of the Ku Klux Klan but a man who, like Royall, later overcame the prejudices of youth to help overturn segregation and became a close friend of the first African American justice, Thurgood Marshall.) Sensitive to his need for southern support, FDR the pragmatist was timid in pushing for reforms that would end or even mitigate segregation in government and society at large. Civil rights were important to FDR, but not at the expense of creating any distractions that would impede governing the nation and winning the war. In one sense, blacks yearning for true economic, social, and political freedom were prisoners of war.

Despite his reluctance to stir up animosity in what was already becoming a not-so-solid South, Roosevelt developed a reputation for caring about blacks. As much as anything, Eleanor Roosevelt's aggressive championing of civil rights—and her influence in getting her husband to appoint blacks to his administration—significantly boosted

FDR's popularity among blacks. Mrs. Roosevelt fervently believed civil rights constituted the true litmus test for American democracy.[21] Throughout the war, Eleanor proclaimed that democracy in America must include democracy for blacks. Fighting a war against racism and fascism while maintaining a racially segregated society was sheer hypocrisy. Racial prejudice enslaved blacks as much as the institution of slavery itself.[22] "One of the main destroyers of freedom is our attitude toward the colored race," she wrote in a 1942 article in the *New Republic*.[23]

Demographic trends rather than moral imperatives put FDR in an increasingly difficult situation with respect to discrimination. During the 1940s, one million African Americans moved from the South to the North. These new northern city residents became a solid voting bloc. As they increasingly asserted themselves politically, white politicians courted their vote. With blacks now dispersed throughout the country, a national civil rights movement blossomed, with new organizations such as the Congress of Racial Equality (CORE) joining the venerable National Association for the Advancement of Colored People (NAACP). Segregation and discrimination were no longer uniquely southern problems.

Black civil rights leaders—including A. Philip Randolph, president of the Brotherhood of Sleeping Car Porters—expected favorable action from President Roosevelt. Adopting a new civil rights strategy, Randolph advocated an innovative tactic—a massive march on Washington, D.C., by blacks and sympathetic whites to demand an immediate halt to discrimination against blacks in employment and the armed forces. War or no war, the time to end three hundred years of racial injustice in America was long overdue.

FDR, while sympathetic, opposed Randolph's confrontational tactics. More than anything, he feared that his administration would be embarrassed by unwanted attention focused on widespread discrimination against blacks in the United States at the same time that he was trying to rally support for America entering a war against Adolf Hitler and his persecution of religious and ethnic minorities.[24] FDR summoned Randolph to the White House, where the impatient human rights advocate and deal-making politician reached a compromise. On June 25, 1941, Roosevelt, in exchange for Randolph canceling the march on Washington, issued Executive Order 8802, creating the Fair Employment Practices Committee (FEPC) to enforce a new ban on discriminatory hiring by the federal government and federal contractors.

The FEPC reform was vintage FDR crisis management. A grand gesture, the agency in practice was largely a paper tiger.[25] Roosevelt was unwilling to unleash the FEPC to undertake vigorous antidiscrimination enforcement in wartime. Civil rights for black Americans, like the civil liberties of Japanese Americans, must take a backseat to winning the war and preserving his southern Democratic governing coalition.

"I don't think, quite frankly, that we can bring about the millennium just yet," he convinced himself.

Part II

THE RULE OF LAW

The Constitution of the United States is a law for rulers and people, equally in war and in peace, and covers with the shield of its protection all classes of men, at all times, and under all circumstances.

— *EX PARTE MILLIGAN,* 71 U.S. (4 WALL.) 2, 120–21 (1866)

[W]e are fighting a war here. We realize that. We also realize that the Constitution is not made for peace alone, that it is made for war as well as peace. It is not merely for fair weather. The real test of its power and authority, the real test of its strength to protect the minority, arises only when it has to be construed in times of stress.

— KENNETH C. ROYALL, ORAL ARGUMENT IN *EX PARTE QUIRIN*
(JULY 30, 1942)

It is a bitter pill to swallow for those who have seen and experienced the devastation that results from terrorist outrages to see systems established to protect the legal rights of those they believe responsible for them. And those who are responsible, let it be admitted, do not have a single shred of concern for the legal or human rights of those they would kill, maim and

terrorise. So why should we care, some would say, about
theirs? The answer to this is that the rule of law is the heart of
our democratic systems.

—LORD PETER GOLDSMITH, QC, ATTORNEY GENERAL OF GREAT

BRITAIN (JUNE 25, 2004)

Chapter 12

Military Justice

On the morning of June 28, President Roosevelt had to make a decision about what to do with the German saboteurs. The question had become more complicated after Dasch had threatened to demand a public trial and tell his story to the world. That, the president vowed, was not to be allowed under any circumstances.

Roosevelt saw trials as a means to an end. When Winston Churchill later proposed at Yalta that Nazi leaders should be shot after the war as soon as they were apprehended, Joseph Stalin suggested a show trial and then execution. FDR supported a trial, but only so long as, in his words, it was "not too judicial."

Roosevelt recalled the precedent of a military commission trying and sentencing to death Abraham Lincoln's assassins. Secretary of War Edwin M. Stanton had arrested eight suspects, who were prosecuted before a special military tribunal of nine officers. Following a trial, all were convicted. Four defendants, including boardinghouse owner Mary Surratt, were sentenced to death by hanging, while three were given life sentences and one a six-year sentence. The trial lasted two months, no appeal to civilian courts was allowed, and the public's thirst for retribution for the wartime assassination of a president was satisfied.[1] All in all, from apprehension to execution, the process took less than three months.[2] A civil trial in federal court, Roosevelt knew, could take on a life of its own; a military proceeding would be far more likely to stay on track—and impose the death penalty.

Military tribunals had "a long and dark history" in America.[3] During the American Revolution, both sides used military tribunals to try those suspected of treason and espionage. The case of Major John André—a British spy captured wearing civilian clothing and carrying the defensive schematics for West Point given to him by General Benedict Arnold—was the most famous. A military court of inquiry convened by General George Washington convicted André of spying and sentenced him to death by hanging—the same fate as Nathan Hale, tried for spying and executed by the British.[4]

In the War of 1812, General Andrew Jackson used military tribunals to imprison lawyers, judges, and journalists in New Orleans who had been critical of his autocratic measures. The term "military commission" is thought to have been first used during the Mexican-American War. U.S. Army general Winfield Scott issued an order convening these tribunals to try crimes committed by Mexicans against the occupying American forces that were not covered by the Articles of War. They were used to convict ordinary criminals as well as unlawful combatants (guerrilla fighters) for violations of the law of war such as "threatening the lives of soldiers" and "riotous conduct."[5] The military commissions were used where martial law had been declared, but few executions were reported.

President Abraham Lincoln employed military tribunals to silence his press and political opponents. In the Dakota War Trials of 1862, more than three hundred Native Americans were condemned to death by military courts.[6] And during the Spanish-American War, military tribunals in Cuba were used by occupying American forces to punish law of war violations not covered by the Articles of War.

Roosevelt expected conflicting advice on how to treat the Nazis. It all came down to which side—the military or the civilian—won the struggle for jurisdiction. The German saboteurs had been "captured" by the FBI, not the military, and thus were subject to criminal prosecution by the Justice Department for violation of various federal laws. Yet the military had a keen interest in taking charge of their prosecution and execution because they were enemy combatants who had come to wage war. But what, exactly, was the status of these "combatants" according to precedents in the law of war?

On Sunday afternoon, June 28, Attorney General Biddle telephoned

Secretary of War Stimson to arrange a meeting to determine whether these prisoners should be prosecuted in a military or a civilian court. When they met the following day, Stimson, aware of how seriously Biddle took the imperative of due process, fully expected another contentious discussion of fundamental legal and constitutional questions similar to those raised in the debate over Japanese American internment just a few months earlier.

Knowing the president's predisposition, Biddle argued that a military court but not a court-martial—he wanted an appointed special military commission—would, through swiftness and secrecy, best serve the government's interests. Stimson was shocked that Biddle, the government's most senior civilian legal officer, "instead of straining every nerve to retain civil jurisdiction of these saboteurs, was quite ready to turn them over to a military court."[7] What Stimson may not have known is that Biddle had already been advised by Assistant Solicitor General Oscar Cox that the two most preferable charges against the defendants that allowed for the death penalty were for offenses subject to military jurisdiction.[8]

Biddle also realized that a military trial could be held in secrecy. He insisted on absolute secrecy in his discussions with Stimson. Biddle told Stimson that Dasch's statement "was especially dangerous" if it came out that he had essentially been double-crossed by the Bureau. What Biddle did not tell the secretary of war, however, was that he did not want the press and public to know that both German teams had found it so easy to penetrate America's defenses, much less that the FBI had ignored Dasch's initial call and the Coast Guard had not reported the landing to the FBI for twelve hours.[9]

Biddle further recommended that Stimson serve as the military commission's chairman. Stimson demurred, believing it unwise for him as secretary of war both to appoint the commission and to serve as the presiding officer. He thought it would be prudent, however, to appoint a civilian to chair the commission. But his candidate, Undersecretary of War Robert Patterson, insisted that the tribunal be totally military.[10]

On Sunday evening, June 29, Stimson dined with Supreme Court justice Felix Frankfurter, Kenneth Royall's professor at Harvard Law School. The legally (though not socially) conservative justice—appointed in 1938 by President Roosevelt to replace Justice Benjamin Cardozo—was no stranger to giving informal advice to the Roosevelt administration. A philosophical mentor to the New Deal, Frankfurter had conferred with FDR over the Japanese Americans' internment.[11] With many friends like Stimson in the government, it was difficult for the superpatriotic Frankfurter—an Austrian-born Jew who despised Hitler and the Nazis—not to get caught up in the urgent issues of wartime. This evening, Frankfurter agreed with Patterson that "the court should be entirely composed of soldiers."[12]

These sensitive negotiations between the Justice and War Departments were leaked to the press. Thus, a *New York Times* article the morning of June 30 reported that Attorney General Biddle had indicated that the eight captured Germans would probably be prosecuted by the War Department. He further acknowledged that he had been in constant contact with Stimson and army judge advocate general Myron C. Cramer on these matters.[13]

On June 30, three days after the Germans were all in custody, FDR weighed in with his thinking on the subject. Sending Attorney General Biddle a blunt memo, he left no room for doubt about his expectations:

> 1. [T]he two Americans [Burger and Haupt] are guilty of treason. This being war-time, it is my inclination to try them by court-martial. I do not see how they can offer any adequate defense. Surely they are as guilty as it is possible to be and it seems to me that the death penalty is almost obligatory.
> 2. [The six German citizens] were apprehended in civilian clothes. This is an absolute parallel of the Case of Major [John] André in the Revolution and of Nathan Hale. Both of them were hanged [as spies]. The death penalty is called for by usage and by the extreme gravity of the war aim and the very existence of our American government.[14]

FDR took a firm line with Biddle: "Offenses such as these are probably more serious than any offense in criminal law."

Roosevelt's predilections were not based on some abstract notions about crime and punishment or customary international law. Instead, the president was reflecting broad public sentiment as reported by the *New York Times*. "Americans everywhere were demanding [the death penalty] for the audacious criminals. Americans wanted to hear the roar of rifles in the hands of a firing squad."[15] *Life* magazine's headline read: "The Eight Nazi Saboteurs Should Be Put to Death."

Not surprisingly, the general public—still fearful of enemy sabotage and invasions—favored the death penalty by a ten-to-one margin. Indeed, given public demands for their swift trial and execution, it was not always clear which event should come first.[16]

Biddle was profoundly troubled by FDR's insistence on executing the German saboteurs. Though enormously fond of Roosevelt and totally loyal to him, Biddle found himself caught uncomfortably in the middle between "the President's questionable pressure and his own reverence for the law."[17] It had not escaped the attorney general's notice that FDR had ended his memo to him by implying that this was not the time for "splitting hairs" between the cases of the German saboteurs and the Revolutionary War spies André and Hale.[18]

Biddle had devoted his professional life to fine moral and legal distinctions. Such hair splitting went to the very heart of the rule of law in a democratic society. That is why he fought so hard against the Japanese American internment. Roosevelt's stubborn defiance of what were arguably constitutional limits on his presidential powers—like Abraham Lincoln's suspension of the writ of habeas corpus, arresting civilians and trying them before military commissions, and seizing newspapers and withdrawing their mailing privileges during the Civil War[19]—"did not make things any easier for his Attorney General who was under a very special obligation to obey the law," Biddle stoically noted. Upholding the rule of law remained his duty "even if the [president's] words had the historical echo of some of his obstinate predecessors, who, in times of crisis, had resisted what they considered judicial interference with the President's duty to act."[20]

Biddle had learned the hard way that it was not easy to be the lawyer for Franklin Delano Roosevelt. Besides the obvious fact that Biddle's client was president, Roosevelt himself had been a lawyer early in his career. After graduating from Harvard College in 1903, he attended Columbia Law School until the spring of 1907, when he dropped out, forgoing a formal degree, after passing the New York state bar examination. FDR joined the venerable Wall Street firm of Carter, Ledyard & Milburn, where he practiced corporate law for a few years. (Founded in 1854, the law firm was one of the nation's oldest and most elite, representing some of the city's wealthiest families.)[21] Finding the routine of legal practice tedious and unfulfilling, the future president ran for (and won) his first election in 1910 as a state senator in a historically Republican district in Dutchess County.

The high-level government uncertainty over how to prosecute the

Nazis continued to be played out in the press. Hoover deftly dodged the issue, claiming that this was Biddle's problem.[22] After all, the FBI had been "working at top speed and didn't have time to look into the legal aspects of the situation."[23]

Biddle defensively responded that the Justice Department "will proceed swiftly and thoroughly" in prosecuting the Germans. The government's apparent indecision was mocked in a *Washington Evening Star* political cartoon depicting Hoover firmly guarding the eight prisoners with Biddle perched on a ladder in front of a shelf of law books. "You hold on to them, Edgar," shouts Biddle, "and I'll find something here that we can punish them under."[24]

Biddle knew that there were essentially three options: treat the Germans as prisoners of war and imprison them for the duration of hostilities; try them in a civilian federal court for sabotage-related offenses and perhaps treason, but likely without any prospect of execution; or establish a special military tribunal that could impose the death penalty, as the president wanted.

The first approach—treating the Germans as POWs—was not legally required under the conventions of international law and custom because the Germans had been caught in civilian clothes and were not identifiable as enemy soldiers. The United States, along with its allies and Germany, were signatories to the various treaties that defined the rules for treatment of combatants and noncombatants in time of war. This body of international common law—referred to as the law of war—was expressed in several Geneva Conventions since 1864.[25] Under the law of war, the German captives were not uniformed, lawful combatants entitled to POW status but rather unlawful combatants—in this case spies and saboteurs—subject to summary punishment.

Early in the war, Germany largely adhered to the Geneva Convention in its treatment of uniformed Allied soldiers captured behind enemy lines.[26] Treated as POWs, they were locked up and generally treated humanely.[27] The British, on the other hand, were less lenient with German military personnel (not in uniform) caught behind the lines. In the early days of the war, "the British had imposed the customary penalty on captured spies and saboteurs, execution." In fact, shortly after the war started, seven arrested German agents were hanged. Numerous others were waiting their turn at the gallows.[28]

The POW approach for the German eight—while not legally

required but accorded as a matter of "grace"—was unsatisfactory for several reasons. FDR needed a showcase trial to demonstrate to the American people and Hitler that the United States could protect itself from enemy spies and saboteurs. Imprisoning the Nazi spies until the war ended appeared to be a weak, inadequate response to a situation that demanded a rapid, forceful demonstration of American strength and resolve. After all, this was the bold president who had defied his military advisors (who had serious reservations about the operation's risk/reward ratio) by insisting on the morale-boosting Doolittle Raid on Tokyo only months after Pearl Harbor.

Roosevelt was particularly concerned about how easily the German U-boats could approach America's coasts and insert operatives on American soil, and how Germany and her Axis allies would perceive America's coastal defenses. By sending a message that the executive branch of the United States had the capacity to intercept and execute enemy saboteurs, the United States would deter any future German sabotage attempts. (After all, Dasch had claimed that Hitler planned to launch similar terrorist attacks every four to six weeks.) "Their deaths were to serve notice to the Nazis of the certain fate of any other spies and saboteurs sent to America."[29]

The president also wanted to send a wake-up message to his fellow Americans. As one junior member of the defense team, Boris Bittker, later noted: "According to gossip in the corridors of the Justice Department, the White House hoped that the drama of a military trial would help to convince the public that we were really at war, and to end the civilian complacency that prevailed even in 1942, six months after the debacle at Pearl Harbor."[30]

The second option of a public civilian trial was conspicuously inadequate. Only one charge carried the death penalty, but treason applied only to the two U.S. citizens. Treason—the act of "levying war against [the United States], or in adhering to their enemies, giving them aid and comfort"—was punishable by death, but the Constitution raised a high barrier for conviction, requiring a confession in open court or testimony by two witnesses to the same overt act.[31] Beside the strict problems of proof,[32] Biddle feared that charging Haupt and Burger with treason[33]—the only crime defined in the Constitution—"might give rise to the implication that we should accord to [these] two enemies the privilege of habeas corpus proceedings against the Military Commission."[34]

Government lawyers had also concluded that a prosecution under the federal statute on spying and sabotage (the Espionage Act of 1917), while not as hard to prove as treason, carried a maximum punishment of only thirty years in prison, since Congress had not prescribed the death penalty for espionage. With lengthy pretrial, trial, and appellate proceedings, a prosecution in federal court would also frustrate the president's and the public's desire for a speedy trial and swift punishment. And it was unlikely that the government could get away with a secret trial in a public courthouse—the truth about the saboteurs' capture and FBI miscues would trigger a media feeding frenzy.

Worse yet, Biddle had to advise the president that it was by no means certain that a sabotage prosecution could be won in a civilian court. No actual acts of sabotage had ever been committed. A charge of attempted sabotage, the attorney general concluded, would probably not be successful in federal court "on the ground that the preparations and landings were not close enough to the planned act of sabotage to constitute attempt. If a man buys a pistol, intending murder, that is not an attempt at murder." And an attempted act of sabotage "carried a penalty grossly disproportionate to their acts—three years."[35]

Judge Advocate General of the Army Cramer had similar misgivings about the likely effectiveness of pursuing a conventional prosecution: "[A] district court 'would be unable to impose an adequate sentence.' . . . [T]he 'maximum permissible punishment for these offenses would be less than it is desirable to impose.'"[36] Cramer also feared that a civil court might be able to imprison the Germans only for a maximum of two or three years combined with a fine of $10,000 for the conspiracy to commit a crime.[37] Cramer's opinion greatly upset Secretary of War Stimson.

And then there was the bloodlust factor—an eye for an eye. Americans were being killed in ships sunk by German U-boats. The country was at war with the Nazis, who had boldly sent terrorists to attack America. Those who had attempted to bring death and destruction to America deserved nothing less than death.

The third and by far most attractive option—the one instinctively favored by FDR—was a trial before a specially constituted military tribunal. For Roosevelt, this was as about as close to a perfect choice as could be imagined. Among the points in its favor: (1) The president could appoint reliable generals under his command and authorize imposition of the death penalty. (2) Military justice would be swift, the tribunal would not be handcuffed by having to abide by the traditional rules of evidence, and the death penalty could be imposed by only a two-thirds (instead of unanimous) vote. (3) The bungling, belated arrests of the saboteurs would be neatly covered up because the military trial would be held in secret.

That there might be considerable questions about the constitutionality of a military tribunal, imposition of the death penalty, and trial secrecy did not arouse much concern in the White House. FDR was clear that Hitler's terrorists had forfeited any right to a civilian court or POW status. "These men had penetrated battlelines strung on land along our two coasts and guarded on the sea by our destroyers, and were waging battle within our country." Thus, the president confidently reasoned, the Germans fell under the law of war and could be summarily tried and executed, as spies and saboteurs had been handled for centuries.

Biddle relented, knowing that nothing he said would change FDR's mind. The attorney general had seen the same steely resolve over the Japanese American internment decision. If anything, however, FDR was even more adamant in the case of the German eight.[38] Bowing to the pressure, Biddle rationalized that the military trial was justified because the Nazis could be charged "with penetrating in disguise our line of defense for the purpose of waging war by destruction of life and property, for which under the law of war the death penalty could be inflicted."[39] And, he wrote to the president on June 30, a military commission was preferable to a traditional court-martial—with all of its legal protections for the defendant, requirement of a unanimous verdict for death, and appeals—"because of greater flexibility, its traditional use in cases of this character and its clear power to impose the death penalty."[40]

Roosevelt readily accepted the recommendation of a military commission. After all, that was precisely what he had wanted from day one. It was always convenient when his advisors saw it his way. But Roosevelt wanted to be certain that the military would never lose jurisdiction over the prisoners. "I want one thing clearly understood, Francis," Roosevelt told Biddle. "I won't give them up. . . . I won't hand them over to any United States Marshal armed with a writ of habeas corpus. Understand!"

Biddle assured FDR that conviction would be swift and certain.

"[T]he major violation of the Law of War," he told the pleased president, "is crossing behind the lines of a belligerent to commit hostile acts without being in a uniform."[41] This augured "a big victory," the prosecution team confidently expected.[42] So, as far as the president and his attorney general were concerned, the eight German defendants were doomed men who would be sped on their way to execution in an expedient, preordained process masquerading as a fair trial.[43]

On June 30, Stimson selected the members of the military commission. The next day, the entire country was aware that FDR would appoint a seven-man military tribunal to try the eight Germans and that Biddle and Judge Advocate General Cramer would jointly conduct the prosecution. It was an unorthodox move, to say the least, for a civilian lawyer to prosecute (as opposed to defend) someone before a military proceeding.

Stimson could not understand why the attorney general—with an important department to run and plenty of competent prosecutors—would want to devote himself to a case that Stimson deemed "of such little national importance."[44] The only reason, Stimson surmised, was that Biddle "seemed to have the bug of publicity in his mind."[45] In fact, it was FDR, leaving nothing to chance, who insisted that Biddle join Cramer in prosecuting the eight men because the army's top lawyer "was rusty and had not tried a case for over twenty years. FDR wanted his own man before the bar," one he could trust not to botch the trial.[46]

Biddle wanted to lead the government's legal team for a good reason unrelated to publicity or interdepartmental rivalry. When he acquiesced in the president's desire to circumvent civil jurisdiction, he knew that the constitutionality of the president's authority to decree a military commission should be decided by the United States Supreme Court. Cramer had never argued up there. The former solicitor general—who had won key cases before the high court—would argue for his country.

"We have to win in the Supreme Court," Biddle told Roosevelt, "or there will be a hell of a mess."

"You're damned right there will be, Mr. Attorney General," a grinning FDR riposted.[47]

* * *

On July 2, 1942, less than a week after the eight had been apprehended, President Roosevelt issued Proclamation 2561, entitled "Denying Certain Enemies Access to the Courts of the United States." Under this decree, the Germans "shall be subject to the law of war and to the jurisdiction of military tribunals" and would not be "privileged" to seek relief from confinement in any court by means of a writ of habeas corpus or any other judicial remedy "except under such regulations as the Attorney General, with the approval of the Secretary of War, may from time to time prescribe." The president offered a succinct rationale for his drastic action:

> [T]he safety of the United States demands that all enemies who have entered upon the territory of the United States as part of an invasion or predatory incursion, or who have entered in order to commit sabotage, espionage, or other hostile or warlike acts, should be promptly tried in accordance with the Law of War.[48]

Biddle had recommended that the president close the civil courts to enemy saboteurs as a class rather than naming the specific defendants. Curiously, he advised the president that this phrasing of his proclamation would have the effect of denying these Germans access to the courts without suspending habeas corpus. It would remain to be seen whether the attorney general was "splitting hairs."

At the same time, Roosevelt issued a military order creating a military commission of seven generals to try the Germans "for offenses against the Law of War and the Articles of War." The same order appointed Attorney General Biddle and Judge Advocate General Cramer as the prosecutors. In addition, a career army lawyer, Colonel Cassius M. Dowell, and a volunteer, Colonel Kenneth C. Royall, were ordered to serve as defense counsel.

Under the military order, Roosevelt, acting under "the authority vested in me as President and as Commander in Chief of the Army and Navy, under the Constitution and statutes of the United States," also empowered the military commission to establish its own rules for the conduct of the proceedings "consistent with the powers of Military Commissions under the Articles of War . . . for a full and fair trial." The normal rules of evidence were relaxed, the president prescribing admissibility if the evidence had "probative value to a reasonable man."

In accord with earlier discussions, only a two-thirds vote of the military commission would be needed for a conviction and sentence.[49] Finally, bypassing the normal appellate review within the military justice system, the president would approve any judgment or sentence based on the record of the trial.[50] Roosevelt retained the sole authority to execute the German terrorists.

The president's allusion to trying the accused in accordance with the law of war was talismanic. The law of war—undefined by statute—represented a body of principles and customs developed over centuries in the field of international law. Unlike trials under the congressionally enacted Articles of War, requiring statutory procedures for court-martial that adhere to the *Manual for Court-Martial*, the military tribunal, guided by the uncodified but widely accepted common law of war, "would thus have greater latitude in selecting principles and procedures that it found compatible with the overall theme of Roosevelt's proclamation."[51]

Roosevelt knew exactly what he was doing. The president's announcement that a military commission composed of stern army generals would try the saboteurs was popular. Washington insiders were pleased with his decisive move, while Americans generally applauded avoiding "the delays and technicalities incident to civil trials."[52] The American people needed a boost of confidence. A speedy trial and execution of Hitler's terrorists was just the thing that could give it to them.

Chapter 13

"Sentence First, Verdict Afterward"

"Mr. Royall, wait! I have something for you," exclaimed the young black messenger from the White House. Colonel Kenneth C. Royall was just on his way out of his Pentagon office after a long day reading government contracts.[1] Royall opened the envelope and looked at the papers inside. Momentarily stunned, he collected himself and headed back to his office. His day would be a little longer than he had anticipated.

Royall was holding the proclamation and military order that had just been issued. To his utter amazement, his commander in chief had ordered him to defend the eight German saboteurs whom he had been reading about in the newspapers. This was not a request to defend the men, but an *order*—from the commander in chief. This was no ordinary military trial, Royall immediately discerned, since a military commission would try the accused, with no appeal to the civil courts.

Royall was not pleased. *What the hell have I done to deserve this treatment?* he kept asking himself. *I'm a damn volunteer!*

When his son had joined the marines, Royall figured that he could not let his generation fight the war alone. He was forty-seven years old with a comfortable trial practice back in Goldsboro, North Carolina. Ehringhaus, Royall, Gosney & Smith was one of the state's leading firms. Life was good, with a couple of golf rounds and a regular card game every week.

Using his legendary powers of persuasion, Secretary Stimson had persuaded Royall to come to Washington, D.C., to break the war production contracting logjam. Royall's old friend and teacher Felix Frankfurter told him that Roosevelt needed someone with his intelligence and experience to help mobilize American industry. Royall suspected that Justice Frankfurter's invisible hand had tapped him for this new and decidedly unwelcome assignment to defend a bunch of detested Nazi saboteurs.

Royall had to have been struck by the parallels to the story of *Alice in Wonderland,* in which Alice found herself in a kangaroo-style trial where the Red Queen famously intoned, "Sentence first, verdict afterward," and then pronounced, "Off with her head!"[2] It would be a whole lot easier to get a black man acquitted of almost any crime by a southern white jury than to secure an acquittal—or even something less than the death penalty—for these defendants.

But for some reason fate had cast him in this role, and he was determined to make the best of it.

Royall read the charges carefully. His clients were accused of four crimes: one against the law of war, two against the Articles of War (Articles 81 and 82), and one involving conspiracy. It was a curious mix of offenses—nonstatutory (law of war) and statutory (congressionally enacted Articles of War dating back to 1777). While he was hardly an expert on these issues, Royall instantly perceived that Roosevelt, by including violations of the unwritten law of war, had shifted the balance of power from Congress to the executive by charging violations of the law of war and ordering a military trial without explicit congressional approval.[3]

The linchpin of the charges was the fact that the eight Germans had entered the United States in German military uniforms, changed into civilian dress, and used fake names for the purpose of war-related industrial espionage and sabotage. From what Royall knew from the newspapers, that seemed to be the case. Unless he could find a legal defect in the charges, his clients appeared guilty.

Royall conferred with the other defense counsel, Colonel Cassius Dowell, a highly capable, forty-year career army man who had been wounded in World War I. His particular expertise was court-martial procedure—an esoteric subject on which he had written a book, *Military Aid to the Civil Power.* After discussing the case, the two agreed that the proclamation should not rule out an appeal to the civil courts.

To deny this fundamental right, they concurred, would constitute denial of a fair trial.

"What shall we do about it?" asked Colonel Dowell.

"The first thing I can think of is to write a letter to the president and send it to him by a messenger from the Justice Department, and ask him to eliminate from the order and from the proclamation the restriction now imposed," Royall replied slowly, picking his words carefully as he formed his plan.

Royall already realized that the only hope of his clients avoiding the death penalty lay in the highest civilian court in the land.[4] There would come a time when he would have to seek Supreme Court review of the constitutionality of the president's actions. But he could not even file a petition for writ of habeas corpus—the jurisdictional prerequisite for initiating federal court judicial review—because his superior officer had summarily denied access to the courts to his clients.

Knowing that Dowell was a regular army officer, Royall did not want to get him in hot water with Roosevelt and the top army brass. "I wouldn't want you to do anything that would endanger your standing in the Army," Royall sympathetically told Dowell. "I am not of the Regular Army and in my case it is immaterial." Resorting to his sense of humor that had served him well as a trial lawyer in North Carolina, Royall wryly added: "If I were asked to get out of the Army for defending a client, no matter who the client was, it would be about the best advertisement I could get, and so there is no reason why I should not write the letter alone, if there is any danger to your career."

Shaking his head, Dowell insisted that he wanted to sign as well.

So, after conducting some legal research and conferring with Secretary of War Stimson and others, they sent off the letter to the president, asking him in a courteous but very firm manner to change the proclamation.

There has been delivered to us your Order of July 2, 1942 which provides for a Military Commission for the trial of Ernest Peter Burger, George John Dasch, Herbert Haupt, Heinrich Harm Heinck, Edward John Kerling, Herman Neubauer, Richard Quirin, and Werner Thiel, and which further designates us as defense counsel for these persons.

There has also been delivered to us a copy of your Proclamation of the same date, which Proclamation provides that a military tribunal shall have sole jurisdiction of persons charged with committing classes of acts set forth in the Proclamation and that such persons shall not have the right to seek any civil remedy.

Our investigation convinces us that there is a serious legal doubt as to the constitutionality and validity of the Proclamation and as to the constitutionality and validity of the Order. It is our opinion that the above named individuals should have an opportunity to institute an appropriate proceeding to test the constitutionality and validity of the Proclamation and of the Order.

In view of the fact that our appointment is made in the same Order which appoints the Military Commission, the question arises as to whether we are authorized to institute the proceeding suggested above. We respectfully suggest that you issue to us or to someone else appropriate authority to that end.

We have advised the Attorney General, the Judge Advocate General, General McCoy, General Winship and Secretary Stimson of our intention to present this matter to you.

The next day Royall and Dowell received a call from FDR's aide Louis Howe and Marvin McIntyre, secretary to the president, telling the defense team that they should "come to the White House" immediately. When Royall and Dowell arrived, Howe and McIntyre told them only that "the president may want to see you, or he may want you to discuss it with us." After waiting around for the president to grant them an audience that never came, the two lawyers discussed the matter in full with McIntyre, who then went into Roosevelt's office and stayed for some time with the president. Royall and Dowell cooled their heels for what seemed like an eternity until McIntyre finally returned.

"The President does not wish to discuss the matter with you," he curtly informed them. "He will not change the proclamation."

FDR's only piece of advice, as conveyed by McIntyre, was hardly helpful: "You should act in accordance with your own judgment." The two army lawyers, standing outside the Oval Office in their uniforms, were dumbstruck.

What the hell are we supposed to do? they asked themselves.

Their commander in chief forbade them to test his authority. Yet their ethical duties as defense lawyers for clients on trial for their lives demanded that they zealously advocate their cause and pursue all lawful means to defend them. No self-respecting lawyer would shrink from contesting the validity of Roosevelt's suspension of habeas corpus and denying trial by jury. But they were officers of the army and officers of the court. To whom did they owe the highest duty? And in serving one master, would they be in dereliction of duty to the other?

Royall expressed his strong displeasure about their predicament to McIntyre, while Dowell walked away, mute with anger. The secretary to the president had nothing more to tell him. They were on their own.[5] What McIntyre did not tell them was that the president expected his officers to obey his orders as commander in chief.

The two lawyers went back to the Pentagon and sat in Royall's office. Colonel Dowell asked: "Is there anything else we can do?"

"I don't know but one thing," replied Royall.

"What is it?"

"Write another letter."

"What?"

"Well," Royall said, "let me write the letter, and then you look it over. I don't believe it would be wise for you to sign this letter."

So Royall went ahead and dictated the second letter to his secretary. This letter, dated July 7, stated they had received word via the president's secretary to "make our own decisions as to our duties and authority under the Order of July 2." The crux of Royall's message to his commander in chief was expressed in the remainder of the brief letter:

> I have considered carefully this Order and the Proclamation of the same date and am of the opinion that we are authorized, and our duty requires us, first, to try to arrange for civil counsel to institute the proceedings necessary to determine the constitutionality and validity of the Proclamation and Order of July 2 and, second, if such arrangements cannot be made, to institute such proceedings ourselves at the appropriate time.

Royall did not want to waste any more time trying to persuade Roosevelt to sanction a challenge to his own authority. So he made sure to end his curt letter with an unambiguous message: "I will so proceed unless specifically ordered otherwise."

Royall had been searching his conscience over the past five days since his appointment. His mind was made up. He knew what he would have to do.

Dowell studied the letter carefully, weighing his options. On the one hand, he knew that it was not a career-advancing move for a regular army officer to defy his commander in chief. On the other hand, he was a trial lawyer with clients facing the death penalty. Finally, he turned to Royall. "I'm going to sign it, too, whatever happens to me."

Amazed but impressed with his co-counsel's courage, Royall agreed. The two of them changed the *I*'s to *we*'s and sent the letter off by messenger to the White House. This time Roosevelt did not respond.[6]

While Royall, Dowell, and Roosevelt were engaged in their tug-of-war, the man who had precipitated this looming constitutional confrontation was not a happy fellow. Dasch sat alone in his cell, tired and confused, wondering about the delay in punishing the accused saboteurs and rewarding their leader turned informant. He had just gone through eight grueling days of interviews and interrogations in Washington, during which he dictated 254 typewritten pages to Agents Ladd and Traynor. After his statement was finished, the FBI had transferred him to New York, where he would stay in a jail cell down the hall from the rest of his apprehended henchmen in order to lead them to believe he was not on the U.S. government's side.

Hell, those fellows should be coming to get me out of here soon, Dasch thought. *What's the point in keeping me here? All the other prisoners have seen me now. All but Burger, anyway, and he knows what the situation is.*

Dasch paced back and forth in his cell, unsure of what to do. Had the FBI forgotten about its deal with him? Was the government going to keep him in jail even though he had been promised a pardon? Though they had a deal, the government had gone forward with the whole routine of officially placing him under arrest, taking his photo, replacing his suit with jailhouse clothes.

Dasch was beginning to believe he had been played for a fool. That the FBI had released his photo for all the newspapers was proof that they were not trustworthy. His intention to withdraw his guilty plea was his only leverage. But what was taking them so long?

The next day Dasch was taken to a room full of FBI agents. Agent Traynor, the one from the Washington office who had been on the case all along, was also there.

"How can the newspaper use my picture and call me a Nazi spy when the FBI had promised me that no pictures would be used?" Dasch demanded of the group.

"How the hell do you know that?" Agent Thomas Donegan yelled back.

"Don't try to bluff me," Dasch replied. "You know and I know full well my picture has been used."

Agent Donegan did not appreciate Dasch's tone, and he aggressively approached the German but was held back by Traynor. Traynor then explained to Dasch that the trial would be held in open federal court. In order to protect the secrecy of Dasch's involvement and to discourage the Nazis from sending any more agents through the porous U.S. coastline, Dasch would need to plead guilty to all the charges.

"For this reason," Traynor said, "you must become an actor, and a damn good one. . . . After the excitement has blown over and not more than six months after the trial, you will be freed with full presidential pardon and complete exoneration of all the charges on which you will be tried."[7]

Dasch reluctantly agreed.

Over the next few days, numerous FBI agents came to talk to Dasch. They worked out a cover story to back up the guilty plea and tried to prep Dasch by suggesting answers to any questions the court might put to him. Dasch, while uneasy about lying under oath in a federal court, thought that cooperation was the only road leading to his freedom.

A few days later, an FBI agent Dasch did not recognize came to his cell and tossed Proclamation 2561 toward him. It was titled "Denying Certain Enemies Access to the Courts of the United States."

"Say, what's this all about anyway?" Dasch asked.

"What the hell did you expect, something different?"

Dasch read through the stack of papers. He was now going to be tried by a secret military tribunal, and the list of charges included spying, planned sabotage, conspiracy, and breaking into a U.S. defense zone.

What is this all about? Traynor said a federal court, not a military one. Dasch demanded to see Agent Traynor or Donegan.

After a while, Donegan walked up to Dasch in his cell.

"What is this tribunal business all about?" Dasch asked.

"The army has taken the case out of our hands," replied Donegan. "It'll come before a military tribunal conducted in secret."

"You surely know enough about my part in the case to know that these charges are ridiculous. What's the point in pleading guilty if the trial is done in secret?"

"I have nothing to do with that," Donegan replied coldly. "And that goes for the agreement you have reached with Mr. Traynor."

"What do you mean?" Dasch asked. "Is the FBI turning against me?"

"Take it any way you want," Donegan replied.

As Donegan started walking out of the cell, Dasch yelled to him, "If that's the case, I'd better see a lawyer. If you people want a fight, you'll have it!"

Donegan's only reply was to slam the cell door. Dasch now made up his mind to fight the charges.

The eight prisoners sat in the jailhouse room under the attentive watch of army guards, waiting for their defense team. None of the exhausted and agitated men expected much help from lawyers employed by the government prosecuting them. The trial would start in a few days, and they had not yet even met the men who would defend them.

Soon the door swung open, and two men walked in, one obviously a respectful step behind the other. The leader loomed above the seated defendants. Colonel Royall was an imposing figure. His partner, Colonel Dowell, looked and played the part of the sidekick.

Royall and Dowell questioned the men for some time, learning all the facts of the case. It was apparent that the prisoners did not trust the two army lawyers, but Royall and Dowell worked tirelessly to gain their confidence. After extensive questioning, the two colonels left the room.

Two things were clear to Royall. First, his clients were just normal guys with regular jobs, and some had families. They hardly looked or talked like cold-blooded saboteurs or the pride of the Third Reich.

Second, Dowell and Royall could not represent Dasch.

"We need to have Dasch represented separately," Royall told Dowell. "His testimony could be damaging to the others."

"He'll probably turn government witness," replied Dowell.[8]

As the two lawyers left their clients, Royall pondered their predicament. *This whole thing is a publicity stunt,* he thought. *All they want is to make a show of this trial, and I am just an actor in this spectacle.*

The government did not have any choice but to furnish lawyers to these German soldiers. The appointment of counsel for defendants accused of capital crimes accorded with the practice in federal courts and military trials. Writing for the Supreme Court in a 1938 federal criminal case, Justice Hugo Black declared that the assistance of counsel is "necessary to insure fundamental human rights to life and liberty."[9] The Nazi saboteurs would thus have "the guiding hand" of experienced counsel to defend them.[10] Realistically, however, the Herculean task of defending before a military tribunal eight enemy spies—who had already confessed, and with less than a week to prepare—rendered the "effective" assistance of counsel a platitude.

The last thing Roosevelt wanted was a fair fight, Royall concluded.

A day later, Dasch was led down the corridor by the guards to another cell. He sat down at a table across from another army officer whom he had never seen before, but he was getting used to being trotted out before strange people to tell his story. So this was nothing new to him.

"My name is Colonel Carl L. Ristine, I work for the Judge Advocate General's Office, and I'm going to defend you separately from the rest of the men."[11]

Great, Dasch thought, *this guy's going to defend me all alone! He doesn't sound all that intelligent, doesn't speak that well . . . and the trial starts tomorrow!*

"Well," Ristine started tentatively, "I should say that I will defend you as the facts of the case allow."

"And what are those facts as you see them?" Dasch fired back.

"Now now," Ristine stuttered, "you've been arrested by the FBI, haven't you? You came here on a Nazi submarine, and boxes of explosives that you buried on the beach have been found."

Ristine went on and on, describing the case as the FBI depicted it, making a hero out of John Cullen, and basically relaying the story straight from the sensational radio and newspaper accounts.

"Let me make a few things more clear," Dasch said, and then he told the account of the story as he wanted it portrayed, shifting the hero worship from Cullen to himself. Ristine then spent the rest of the day going over Dasch's rambling story, from the journey back to Germany to Quenz Lake to the Long Island landing. Ristine now had to figure out which of these divergent accounts was reality. This assignment was going to be a lot more difficult than he had thought.[12]

A guard came to fetch Dasch, leading him downstairs to a meeting room. Once inside, the list of names of those present read like a who's who of government officials: Attorney General Francis B. Biddle, FBI director J. Edgar Hoover, Judge Advocate General Major General Myron C. Cramer, Brigadier General Albert L. Cox, who was the army provost marshal of the District of Washington, and others.

"I understand you have changed your mind about pleading guilty," Biddle stated to Dasch.

"In a secret trial, I can plead in an honest way without Hitler or the High Command ever knowing about it," Dasch replied.

"Yes, you're right," Biddle agreed. "But I ask you now to plead guilty even before the tribunal."

"Gentlemen, do you feel I am guilty as the charges say?"

"We want you to plead guilty to speed up the trial," replied Biddle.

"Does the agreement I made with Traynor still stand?" Dasch asked Hoover, referring to his deal for a six-month sentence and full presidential pardon recommended by both Biddle and Hoover.[13]

Surprised, Hoover stumbled for an answer. "Oh yes, it all stands."

"Can you be more specific about the government's side of the bargain?" Dasch pointedly asked.

"I know what you mean, Dasch, and it all stands!" Hoover replied, quickly and forcefully. "That is all I can tell you."

"I still want you to plead guilty," Biddle again insisted.

"The trial is in secret; I plan to tell the truth."

And with that, Dasch was led back to his cell.[14]

It was going to be harder to convict and execute these Nazis than Biddle had assured Roosevelt.

Chapter 14

Kangaroo Court

On the fifth floor of the Justice Department, workers scurried in and out of Room 5235 to get to adjoining Assembly Hall 1. The small, air-conditioned room—formerly used as an FBI lecture hall for training special agents—was set up with tables and chairs for a makeshift courtroom, but it was so cluttered with furniture that there was little room to move around. The windows were covered with black curtains, the clear glass doors of the entrance were painted black, and green velvet covered the motion picture screen.[1] The pseudo-courtroom was a virtual black hole: nobody could see into, and no one could hear a sound from, the dreary room.

It was July 8—the day set by President Roosevelt for the start of the trial of the accused saboteurs, and only eleven days since the last defendant had been arrested.

The news of the day was also gloomy. In the Arctic Ocean, a British convoy en route to Murmansk had lost eight ships to U-boats. The Germans continued to advance on the Eastern Front, crossing the Donets River in the Soviet Union. And in the Pacific, the Allied counteroffensive had not yet begun.

Military guards escorted the somber prisoners from their cells in the D.C. Jail, one by one, to be readied for their first day in court. Each was dressed in civilian clothes and shaved by a prison barber to prevent any last-minute suicide attempts. The men were then taken to two heavily guarded, black U.S. Marshals Service vans surrounded by military police. In an impressive display of military might, the two vehicles—with armed, steel-helmeted soldiers standing on the rear platform—then left in a procession with Washington, D.C., police on motorcycles escorting them to the Department of Justice. In the lead was a car full of FBI agents, followed by an army jeep with mounted machine guns and soldiers brandishing tommy guns.

Outside the Department of Justice gates, a large crowd gathered to watch the arrival of the saboteurs. Vendors hawking everything from newspapers to hot dogs and ice cream were doing a brisk business. The media were everywhere. Newspapers from around the country sent correspondents to the scene. Yet they all received the same answer to their requests for information: the trial would be held in secret, and the only information to leave the courtroom would be dictated by the military commission's president, Major General Frank R. McCoy.

One person not kept in the dark was Justice Felix Frankfurter. The opening day, he spoke with his friend Henry Stimson, who briefed him "about the situation in the saboteur trial."[2]

The press, while complaining about the curtain of "extraordinary secrecy" dropped on the German saboteurs' trial, had become accustomed to wartime news blackouts.[3] Arthur Krock of the *New York Times* dismissed calls for open press coverage as "thoughtless."[4] Despite a strong tradition of open criminal proceedings dating back to the colonial trial of the British soldiers charged with murder during the Boston Massacre, no one even considered filing a First Amendment lawsuit challenging the decision, since military trials had historically been closed to the public and press.[5] Instead, the journalists—undernourished by the terse, uninformative daily communiqués—would eagerly wait for the droplets of information leaking out of Room 5235—often reports casting the prosecution in a favorable light.[6]

The one day that reporters were allowed into the courtroom—July 11—the staged visit lasted only fifteen minutes. Yet it was enough time for Lewis Wood of the *New York Times* to observe that Haupt looked "like any petty defendant in a police court" and not "a burly, booted Storm Trooper, a brutal U-boat captain," or anyone resembling the "ruthless, blond German glorified by Hitler." Instead, these were "merely a group of most ordinary looking individuals."[7]

Led to the "courtroom" under heavy guard and seated in the hallway in alphabetical order, the prisoners anxiously waited to be ordered into the room. On one side of the chamber sat the prosecution team of Attorney General Biddle, Judge Advocate General Cramer, and their numerous assistants. Next to Biddle was J. Edgar Hoover, though his presence was never officially recognized or recorded. Other than lending moral support, Hoover performed one useful service—he fed pages of evidence to Biddle throughout the proceedings. While his agents had botched the apprehension of the saboteurs, the FBI did an impressive job organizing the prosecution's case and preparing blue books summarizing each witness' testimony for the government's lawyers.[8]

Hoover bristled at the military taking over the saboteurs' prosecution. He firmly maintained that it was up to the civilian authority to prosecute espionage. One day during a recess, Brigadier General Albert L. Cox, the provost marshal, refused to give a prisoner a cigarette, claiming there was no army appropriation for such a purpose. Standing nearby, Hoover—who Biddle found "was easily and often irritated by the unaccountable ways of the Army—whipped out a package and offered it to the young man."[9]

At the head of the hall, with the defense and prosecution tables at their right- and left-hand sides, sat the all-star commission—a distinguished collection of some of the nation's best-known, most decorated army generals.[10] The generals wore their summer khakis and not their full-dress uniforms with swords. General McCoy—a longtime friend of Secretary of War Stimson—anchored the center of three long wooden tables, flanked by three major generals on one side and three brigadier generals on the other. General McCoy, who had retired in 1938 after a career as a skillful administrator and negotiator, had served as Teddy Roosevelt's aide during the Spanish-American War and while he was president. No stranger to legal investigations and military trials, the World War I veteran had served on the infamous 1925 court-martial that tried Brigadier General William "Billy" Mitchell for what was allegedly insubordination but was actually for his outspoken advocacy of airpower. More recently, Roosevelt had tapped McCoy for the high-level official investigation of events leading up to the Pearl Harbor attack.

The other "jurors" were Major General Blanton Winship (former judge advocate general), Major General Lorenzo D. Gasser (formerly deputy chief of the army), Major General Walter S. Grant (former Third Corps commander), Brigadier General John T. Lewis (career artillery officer), Brigadier General Guy V. Henry (renowned cavalry officer), and Brigadier General John T. Kennedy (Congressional Medal of Honor winner). The combined years of service of the commission members approached three hundred—from the Spanish-American War through World War I to the present global conflagration.

"The Commission will come to order," General McCoy announced in his best command voice. "The Commission is now open for the trial of such persons as may be brought before it."

"Bring in the prisoners," Provost Marshal Cox ordered.[11]

The defendants were escorted from the hallway into the courtroom and again seated alphabetically behind Colonels Royall, Dowell, and Ristine, with a guard seated between each pair of prisoners. As soon as they were seated, the court reporter was sworn in, and the commission recognized the assistant trial judge advocates who would help prosecute the case.[12] Before the commission could proceed any further, however, Colonel Royall slowly rose to make a statement. He was about to begin the process by which he would defy the unambiguous order of his commander in chief and lay a foundation for possible Supreme Court intervention. It was a long shot, but it was the only chance to save his clients' lives.

"In deference to the Commission and in order that we may not waive for our clients any rights which may belong to them," he began softly, "we desire to state that, in our opinion, the order of the President of the United States creating this Court is invalid and unconstitutional. I do not think it necessary or appropriate to argue that question unless I am so requested," Royall stated in his most respectful tone, deliberately lowering his trademark booming voice.

Drawing upon the Supreme Court precedent of *Ex parte Milligan*, he added: "It is perhaps sufficient to state that our view is based, first, on the fact that the civil courts are open in the territory in which we are now located and that, in our opinion, there are civil statutes governing the matters to be investigated.

"In the second place, we question the jurisdiction of any court except a civil court over the persons of these defendants.

"In the third place, we think that the order itself violates in several specific particulars congressional enactments as reflected in the Articles of War."[13]

"Are there any remarks on the part of the prosecution?" McCoy asked, turning toward chief prosecutor Biddle, who had been surprised by Royall striking the first legal blow.

"I do not want to argue the case, but if at the appropriate time you wish to hear argument on it, I should like to be heard," Biddle confidently replied. "May I simply make a very brief statement in answer to Colonel Royall's remarks?"

McCoy nodded in agreement.

Biddle then argued that the high military rank of the members on the commission—and the fact that the president had issued the proclamation authorizing the military tribunal—trumped any question as to whether it had any authority. Surely, he noted, the president of the United States has the power. This was not a trial of civil matters, but one of the law of war, and therefore the army should settle the German saboteurs' guilt or innocence. As for the question of law, he declared that it was for the civil courts to determine, quickly adding, "should it be presented to the civil courts."

This was not, Biddle maintained, "the trial of offenses of the law of courts. . . . It is the trial of . . . certain enemies who crossed our . . . boundaries . . . in disguise in enemy vessels and landed here [like] armed forces invading this country. I cannot think it conceivable that any Commission would listen to an argument that armed forces entering this country should not be met by the resistance of the Army itself under the Commander-in-Chief or that they have any civil rights that you can listen to in this proceeding."

Royall swiftly parried Biddle's thrust. Using all of his considerable powers of self-restraint to keep a straight face, he reminded the commission that the defense argument had nothing to do with the rank of the officers or a "lack of confidence" in any way in the commission.

At this point, Colonel Ristine decided to make his presence felt.

"If the Commission please, on behalf of the one prisoner—" Ristine started haltingly.

"I take it you are Colonel Ristine?" the president stated coolly, interrupting Ristine in midsentence.

"Yes, sir."

"Representing the one prisoner by name?"

"Representing the one, may I request that the objections urged by defense counsel be equally applicable to that prisoner, George John Dasch?" Ristine said sheepishly, hoping to ride Royall's coattails.

"Does the prosecution care to remark on these statements of the defense counsel?" asked the president.

"No, sir," replied Judge Advocate General Cramer.

"Before any decision . . . the Commission shall be sworn and organized," stated McCoy.

The proclamation authorizing and organizing the commission was then read. When asked if the defense had any challenges to the commission, Royall requested that he be allowed to question the commission members for cause—the equivalent of voir dire of a jury.

"I would like to say that, in view of the great newspaper publicity that has been given to this matter, in spite of efforts to suppress it, I wish to inquire whether any member of the Commission has to any degree the feeling that the circumstances under which the Commission is appointed would make it difficult or embarrassing for him to reach a judgment in favor of the defendants in the event the evidence should so indicate," Royall inquired, knowing that he was hitting a raw nerve.[14] In light of the pretrial public clamoring for the defendants' swift execution and the commission's appointment by their commander in chief, Royall had genuine cause for concern.

Royall paused. "I hear no answer, and I assume there is no such—"

"Well, we are just considering the question," the president barked at him.

"I see, sir," Royall replied calmly.

"I will give you the answer."

"Yes, I see."

"There seems to be unanimity of opinion in the answer NO to your question," said the president defiantly.

Royall then asked if the commission found it hard to try the case fairly. After all, "the trial is being conducted in a time of war," and harsher punishments were to be expected than during peacetime.

"I do not consider it a proper question," McCoy snapped. "The Commission does not consider that a proper question to consider."

"We have no other questions to ask. The defense has no challenges for cause," finished Royall. His brief bias inquiry of the seven "jurors" was over before it had really begun. Nevertheless, Royall had preserved in the record that the defense did not recognize the commission's jurisdiction.

Relying upon the Eighteenth Article of War for a court-martial, Colonel Dowell then motioned for one peremptory challenge to the commission—a legal gambit to remove a juror for no cause at all. Predictably, after a brief debate with Biddle and an extended recess by the commission long enough to smoke a good cigar, this motion was denied.

With completion of the initial legal skirmishing, the seven generals took an oath that each "will well and truly try and determine according to the evidence" the case and "will duly administer justice, without partiality, favor or affection." The prosecution and defense teams were sworn in next, followed by an oath of secrecy that everyone in the courtroom had to take in order to be involved in the proceedings. A gag order was in place until the "proper authority" allowed them to speak openly about the trial outside of the courtroom. The "proper authority" was widely accepted to be President Roosevelt alone.

Royall informed the commission that he might not be able to respect the secrecy oath. "It is possible that some limited disclosure would have to be made," he explained, "if someone sought to assert the civil rights of these defendants." Royall could not depend on FDR to give him a dispensation from a secrecy oath in order to file a writ of habeas corpus. A compromise was struck allowing "proper authority" to possibly include a federal judge or the Supreme Court.[15]

Royall's stomach was churning. In all his years as a trial lawyer, he had never faced such a biased jury. Not only was the deck stacked against him and his clients, but Royall could see that General McCoy seemed to have a particularly strong personal dislike for him.

Great, a kangaroo court! a frustrated Royall thought.

In this case, that pejorative did not seem like an exaggeration. After all, Texas courts in the mid-nineteenth century, where the term originated, were known to bounce defendants swiftly from the courtroom to the gallows in a mockery of justice. Royall was reminded of a Reconstruction-era saying: "Give the nigger a fair trial and hang him quick."[16]

The commission was not even a jury. Their role was to take testimony and forward the record and recommendation on guilt and punishment to the commander in chief. Roosevelt alone was the ultimate jury, but he would never see the defendants, assess their demeanor and credibility, or make a judgment based on personal observations about their criminal intent. FDR was also the only judge. There would be no appeal to any higher authority—unless Royall could get the Supreme Court to intervene.

When it came time to enter pleas on behalf of the defendants, Royall chose to plead "lack of jurisdiction over the person of the defendants." His clients were not persons covered by Article of War 2, and they were not found in any military facility or vicinity, thereby negating Articles of War 81 and 82.

"We further desire to enter a plea to the jurisdiction of this court over the offenses charged," stated Royall.

"I would like defense counsel to take cognizance of the fact that this is not a court in the usually accepted term or as referred to in the *Court-Martial Manual.* This is a Military Commission, and please use that term," McCoy testily demanded.

"I will try to do so, sir," Royall said, with a slight hint of sarcasm.

"I know it is an easy habit for us all to speak of a court," explained McCoy, "but we have felt that we should emphasize the word 'Commission.'"

"I will make every effort to do that. From force of habit, I may lapse every now and then into the use of the word 'court,' but I will try not to do so," Royall said, feigning an apology.

"The second plea to the jurisdiction is that the *court* does not have jurisdiction of the subject matter of these charges," Royall continued, glancing at McCoy to see if he had paid attention to his defiant word choice. Royall then finished entering the pleas, and having made his point, never mentioned the word *court* again throughout the rest of the trial.

After Royall finished his objections to entering pleas, Biddle arose and briefly attacked his position. Returning to safe, familiar ground, he asserted "the basic power of the President to approve a Commission to try enemies of the country in time of war." Swept away by his own argument, the attorney general at one point advocated that these "soldiers not only invaded this country, but they have changed themselves into civilians and, as such, have absolutely no rights." But even under the law of war, the German saboteurs enjoyed some basic protections against torture and inhumane treatment.

Colonel Dowell—the authority on military law and procedure—could no longer abide the attorney general's exaggeration of the president's powers. "[W]e base the right of the defendant[s] to go into civil courts upon the broad policy that this country is dominantly one in which government is exercised by civil authority, and that the military authority comes to their assistance only in cases of necessity, where it is impracticable or impossible for the civil authorities to function in the manner prescribed by Congress."

Dowell knew that his argument was like throwing sand in the commission's eyes. So he went to higher ground. "[T]hat is one of the points upon which we fought the Revolutionary War, to get away from military domination, to make the civil authority ascendant and operative at such times as the civil authority is able and capable of operating."

Dowell then delivered a brilliant, scholarly summary of the American usage of military courts. Even General Andrew Jackson, the hero of the Battle of New Orleans in the War of 1812, was cited for contempt and fined $1,000 for continuing martial law after the civil courts had reopened. In a footnote to history, Dowell noted that Jackson did not get back his $1,000 for thirty years—"and then only by special Act of Congress and after being twice President of the United States, and only in the year before his death."[17]

Biddle could not resist displaying his erudition on military law. The defense's argument was predicated on "an entire misconception of the law of war," he claimed. "We are not confined to the Articles of War. We are charging offenses against the law of war, which is common law. . . . It is not necessary to find a statutory defined offense before a commission either in the Articles of War or elsewhere."

Biddle then illustrated his point with "a famous example of . . . the case of [British] Major Andre, which was not an espionage case, though espionage was involved, but it was passing through the enemy lines with the purpose and intent of bribing an officer of the United States Army." Biddle did not have to remind the seven generals that the officer was General Benedict Arnold.

Ironically, Biddle occasionally slipped up, referring to the "war of law" instead of "law of war."[18] Royall could not help being grimly amused by his opponent's gaffe.

This whole proceeding is an undeclared war on the rule of law, Royall thought.

When the commission reconvened after taking enough time for another long cigar break, the defense objections were quickly overruled.[19] A defense motion to strike certain charges was also rejected. Royall would have to enter pleas for each defendant, and the trial would proceed.

The clerk, Colonel F. Granville Munson, arose and went about his duty. One by one, each prisoner stood while Munson asked, "How do you plead to Specification 1 of Charge 1?" The question was repeated for each charge and specification for each prisoner, eliciting replies of "not guilty" each time, for each plea, for each prisoner. The process was ritualistic, running as smoothly as a perfectly choreographed play, with each defendant rising and sitting on cue.

With pretrial legal sparring and the entering of pleas out of the way, it was time for the prosecution's opening statements. Biddle launched into his presentation, patiently laying the groundwork of the government's case. He summarized War Department documents proclaiming the eastern United States as a war zone, showed a map of active Coast Guard stations, and told of forged draft registration and social security cards possessed by the accused.[20]

Biddle then detailed the actions of the group as they proceeded through Europe and how they split into two smaller landing parties. Dasch's group was assigned to blow up aluminum plants and Ohio River locks, while Kerling's team focused on various railroads. Biddle's perfunctory opening lasted only a few minutes.

Traditionally, the defense would now deliver its opening statements. But Royall and Ristine declined to make a statement at this time. It was hardly in their best interest to give away any surprises too early. *After all, when playing with a stacked deck, you don't show your cards until you absolutely have to*, Royall reasoned.

For an Ivy League–trained lawyer, Royall was a bit of a maverick. He was a triple threat: keen intellect, bruising cross-examination style tempered by a southern gentleman's graciousness, and fierce determination to win for his client.[21] Competitive, at times to a fault, Royall gave his clients 110 percent effort. If you were Kenneth Royall's client, you had a fiercely committed advocate—a take-no-prisoners trial lawyer.[22] He prepared meticulously so that he could perform with a seemingly effortless mastery of the facts and law. Royall was one of the breed of trial lawyers who had learned the hard way that brilliance in the courtroom was the result of 90 percent perspiration and only 10 percent inspiration.[23]

Even though he was a tough competitor, Royall was admired by friend and foe alike. Using his height and strength, he had once picked up an opposing counsel and carried him across the room to show him a piece of evidence. After a trial, he would drink with his adversary or take him out for a round of golf. In time, as Royall doggedly fought to limit the government's damning evidence, Biddle, like so many other foes, would come to greatly admire this remarkable man.

Before calling any witnesses, Biddle offered several exhibits, one of which was Public Proclamation 1, dated May 16, 1942, establishing the Eastern Defense Command, embracing the entire Atlantic Coast and portions of the Gulf Coast. Royall promptly objected to Biddle's attempt to bootstrap the entire eastern seaboard into a combat zone. Biddle countered that this was clearly an area "under the control of the Army." Royall replied that the area specified was woefully too broad, covering areas "even to and through the mountains." Not surprisingly, Royall's objection was overruled.

Biddle first called Matthias R. Griffin, the FBI agent who had served the charges and specifications on the defendants. Like every witness to follow, he was given two oaths: one to maintain secrecy and the other to tell the truth. The only reason for Griffin's testimony was procedural. Once he certified that the charges had been served on the date documented, and after answering a few questions, Griffin was excused.

The next witness was John C. Cullen, the young Coast Guardsman who accidentally stumbled upon Dasch's landing team on the beach at Amagansett. But for Hoover's grandstanding and lies to the press, Cullen would indeed have been the only real hero in the case. Biddle asked Cullen all about the night of June 13, 1942, when he had encountered Dasch and his team on the beach. Cullen described the dark, foggy night, the distance (almost a half mile) from the Coast Guard lifeboat station, and finally the man with whom he spoke on the beach.

"I asked these men who they were. I hollered out. One of the men walked toward me," started Cullen.

"Do you recognize the man in court who walked towards you?" asked Biddle.

"I think so, sir," replied Cullen.

"Will you stand up and identify him, if you see him in court? Stand up, please. Now, do you see the man?"

"Yes, sir."

"Which is he?"

"Right here . . . , sir." Cullen was pointing to Dasch.

"Is that the man that you remember seeing?"

"Would he mind saying a few words?" asked Cullen.

"Do you want to identify him by his voice? Is that what you mean?" replied Biddle.

"Yes, sir."

"What is your name?" Dasch asked Cullen.

"Yes, sir," Cullen replied meekly.

"What do you mean by 'Yes, sir'?" asked Biddle.

"That's the man," replied Cullen.

Biddle now had what he wanted—a positive identification that Dasch was the stranger on the beach to whom Cullen had spoken. Cullen then recounted the entire conversation, the death threat by Dasch to tell no one, the $260 bribe that Dasch offered to silence Cullen, and the boxes of explosives found on the beach.[24] Cullen was the perfect witness: credible, informative, and, best of all for Biddle, irrefutable.

At one point, Royall objected on the grounds of hearsay to Cullen's testimony about the equipment that other Coast Guard personnel dug up in the sand. While Biddle was prepared to concede the point, General McCoy used the occasion to highlight the fact that the president's proclamation established its own relaxed admissibility standard of "probative value for a reasonable man"—a critical difference between a federal court and a military commission.

"I want to make it perfectly clear the rulings will be to give full and free presentation of evidence," McCoy ruled.[25]

Royall cross-examined first, only to ask if Cullen had been harmed by the men or threatened violently in any way. After a couple of quick nos, Cullen was cross-examined by Dowell, who asked only if he had seen anything else in the water. Again, Cullen answered no.

Like the other defense lawyers, Ristine had little to ask Cullen except to prove that Dasch wanted to be identified by showing his face up close to Cullen with a flashlight. Dasch had succeeded, Cullen conceded, since Cullen had been able to identify Dasch in the courtroom but not the other German who approached Cullen on the beach. This was the only positive testimony for the defense so far.

Biddle methodically presented his case, now calling Chief Boatswain's Mate Warren Barnes to the stand, who identified the contents of the boxes found on the beach about six inches under the sand. Dramatically, boxes of TNT explosives, the trench shovels, cigarettes, the duffel bag, and a single white shoe were all trotted out before Barnes, who dutifully verified finding all these items on the beach. This positive identification was key evidence of sabotage against the accused, and the first day of the trial ended with the highly incriminating evidence arrayed before the seven American generals sitting in judgment of eight German saboteurs.

Besides being the first day of the German saboteurs' trial, July 8 was auspicious for another noteworthy reason. Believing FBI agents were the heroes in the interdiction and apprehension of the Nazi espionage team, the Senate Judiciary Committee voted unanimously to authorize President Roosevelt to bestow on J. Edgar Hoover an "appropriate medal" for this patriotic accomplishment.[26] While everyone inside Room 5235 knew the truth, the American people would be the last to learn of Hoover's dirty little secret.

Chapter 15

An Improbable Life

As the second day of the trial began on July 9, Biddle—concerned that Royall might discredit his best evidence—wanted to document the official chain of custody of the evidence found on the beach on Long Island. Several witnesses told of its transfer from the beach to the Coast Guard office at the Port of New York to the FBI. At the risk of proving the obvious, an FBI explosives expert, D.J. Parsons, confirmed the dangerous capabilities of TNT.

One fascinating item of evidence was a detonator disguised as a fountain pen. Parsons explained that it had delays of between seven and thirteen hours. "The force of the explosion from this," he elaborated, "would simply be the explosion of the detonator, which would be sufficient to set off any high explosive such as the TNT demolition blocks."[1]

Parsons also revealed that the Germans had a detonator in the form of an alarm clock with a fourteen-day mechanism. This testimony prompted one of the few questions from commission members other than President McCoy.

"Is the operation of the mechanism audible?" asked Major General Gasser. He was "old army" and had served under General Pershing pursuing Pancho Villa down in Mexico prior to World War I.

"No, sir. It is very quiet. The sound is no more than that of a fine watch. It must be held closely to the ear. It is now running, if you care to listen to it."

Discretion being the better part of valor, Major General Gasser passed on Parsons' invitation to put a ticking time bomb to his ear.

On the third day of the trial, July 10, Biddle tried to introduce evidence gathered by the FBI from Peter Burger's room at the Governor Clinton Hotel on June 20. Biddle offered a "waiver of arrest, removal, and search" Burger had signed, authorizing the FBI to search his room. The only problem with this offer was that it had been signed on the twenty-second of June. Shocked at the government's duplicity, Royall sprang to his feet to object.

"Without seeking to argue it at any length, our position is that the Constitution of the United States contains a guarantee against unlawful search and seizure, and we think that that law is applicable to any tribunal; but whether or not it is, it was certainly applicable to the FBI at the time of this search and seizure. . . . We, therefore, object on the grounds which I have stated to the Commission," Royall said, assuming that General McCoy could not cavalierly disregard the Constitution.

"It seems to me that the search was perfectly legal. I know of no constitutional right against the search," Biddle countered, apparently forgetting about the Fourth Amendment. "It would be like saying that when you arrested a man in the midst of his committing a crime, you could not search him afterward."

After much wrangling by counsel, the commission took a five-minute break to consider the matter. Royall thought he had made an excellent, irrefutable argument. The members of the commission soon reentered the courtroom, with McCoy taking his usual seat in the middle of the panel.

"Subject to objections from any member of the Commission, the objections of the defense counsel are not sustained," stated General McCoy, to the evident relief of Hoover, who had anxiously awaited the ruling as to whether his G-men had violated Burger's constitutional rights.

"May I proceed?" Biddle asked, clearly gratified by McCoy's brushing aside of Royall's objection.

A pattern was being set that would persist throughout the proceeding: the commission would side with Biddle on almost every objection raised by the defense. Biddle then proceeded to call a parade of witnesses in a relentless assault clearly intended to nail down the lids on the defendants' coffins.

*   *   *

Sitting with his aide William Hassett on July 12, President Roosevelt mulled over all the pressing decisions he had to make: the two-front war, development of the atomic bomb—and this Nazi spy trial.

"What should be done with them?" Roosevelt asked. "Should they be shot or hanged?"

"Hanged by all means," replied Hassett. "Shooting is too honorable a death."

"What about pictures?" FDR inquired.

"By all means," Hassett quickly replied. "Anyone who has ever looked at the photographs in old Ford's Theater of the hanging of the Lincoln conspirators is not likely to forget it."

The picture of Mary Surratt and the rest of them swinging in midair was forever burned into his memory.

"I know I'll never forget those pictures—especially since Mrs. Surratt was probably innocent," Hassett added.

"I always thought her guilt had been proved," noted Roosevelt. "Anyway, I hope the finding will be unanimous."[2]

The trial dragged on as Biddle took an entire week to present the prosecution's proof in mind-numbing detail. Biddle trotted out every FBI agent who had come in contact with the eight men, as well as their superior officers. More explosives experts described in repetitive detail the obvious lethal capability of the weapons found buried on the beaches. If a trial is good theater, this was a story with little drama and a predictable plot. Those sitting in the courtroom struggled to stay awake at times.

The only respite from the monotony of the government's overkill was the intermittent evidentiary battle over the admission of evidence. True to his word, President McCoy admitted every bit of prosecution testimony and all of the exhibits Biddle and Cramer introduced. One pitched fight involved the admissibility of the confessions of Dasch and Burger against the other defendants. Royall argued passionately his "firm conviction" that this would violate his clients' basic constitutional rights. "[W]ith all deference to the Commission, . . . the confession should not be considered as [evidence] against a man who did not make it," Royall asserted.[3]

Both confessions—highly damaging to the other six defendants—were admitted.

Nor was there much in the way of comic relief as the days faded into each other. Royall had to be amused, however, on the morning of July 13. Ristine was cross-examining FBI agent Norvel Wills about the circumstances surrounding Dasch's extensive cross-examination while he was in "protective custody." Specifically, Ristine was trying to get him to admit that Dasch's cooperation led to the apprehension of the other defendants. "Do you know whether following that information [from Dasch] the F.B.I. agents went to New York and apprehended Mr. Burger?" Ristine inquired.

"I was told—"

"I object to anything you were told," Biddle interrupted, "just answer of your own knowledge."[4]

Biddle's hearsay objection to his own witness's answer was swiftly sustained by President McCoy, who had no trouble admitting rank hearsay when offered by the government.

On July 13, J. Edgar Hoover announced that the FBI had arrested fourteen people who had assisted the German saboteurs. They were charged with treason, conspiracy to commit espionage and sabotage, and other serious offenses. Eight were taken into custody in Chicago and six in New York City. The defendants included Haupt's parents, Hans and Erna Haupt; Kerling's wife, Marie; Kerling's mistress, Hedy Engemann; Haupt's uncle and aunt, Walter and Lucille Froehling; Neubauer's friends Harry and Emma Jaques; Heinck's friend Hermann Faje; Thiel's close friend Anthony Cramer; Haupt family friends Otto and Kate Wergin; Kerling's wife's close friend Ernest Kerkof; and Helmut Leiner, Kerling's confederate in New York. Unlike their friends and loved ones being tried by a military tribunal, these accused would be prosecuted in a federal court and afforded a jury trial.[5]

By July 14, the prosecution's case against Dasch and Burger had concluded. Two of Dasch's statements and one of Burger's had been admitted. The prosecution had spent five full days on only two of the eight defendants.

Now Biddle quickly unfurled the evidence against Heinck and Quirin. Each defendant's statement was read, and everything brought from the submarine was entered into evidence. It was obvious that while the dedication of Dasch and Burger to the mission may have been in doubt, Biddle's evidence against Heink and Quirin showed they were committed saboteurs.

On July 15, Biddle called to the stand B. Downey Rice, the FBI agent who had retrieved the two letters that Dasch sent to Burger at the Governor Clinton Hotel while Dasch was in protective custody. After Rice positively identified the letters, Biddle proceeded to ask him to comment on one but not the other. Both Ristine and Royall strenuously objected that if one letter was read, the companion letter must also be read.

Biddle countered that the prosecution had to present only what was relevant to its case, while the defense could offer the other letter when it was their turn to call witnesses. The commission recessed to decide the matter. President McCoy quickly decided against the defense, ruling that the second letter should be put into evidence when the defense started its case. They lost that skirmish, but Ristine had a plan to surprise the prosecution and successfully admit Dasch's third, 254-page statement, which Biddle had not introduced, into evidence during the government's case.

"Are there any questions by the Commission? There seem to be none. The witness is excused," President McCoy said to Rice, who quietly left the witness stand.

"We will recall Mr. Wills," Biddle stated.

"I believe Mr. Wills has been recalled for cross-examination by the defense," President McCoy said.

"That is correct, sir," replied Ristine. He knew that FBI Agent Wills, present during the Dasch confession, was the perfect witness to use to get Dasch's statement read in its entirety. "I wish you would look at page 129 of Defendants' Exhibit A and see if the last question on that page and the answer contained on page 130 was asked and answered in your presence by Mr. Dasch," Ristine started, setting the trap for the unsuspecting Wills.

"The first paragraph on page 130?" asked Wills.

"That is correct."

"I recall the substance of that reply made by Dasch, but whether Traynor was in the room or not at that time I do not have any recollection," replied Wills, unsure of his own memory.

"I did not ask you whether Traynor was in the room or not," Ristine shot back. "I asked you whether that question was asked and that answer given while you were present."

"The substance of it. Whether it was word for word, I do not recall."

That was all Ristine needed. He had now shown that the memory of the agent present while the statement was taken was shaky. For that reason, the entire statement should be read in full, not just the excerpts that helped the prosecution's case. During the government's presentation, Ristine wanted to dispel doubts about Dasch's intentions, while the other defendants looked like true saboteurs.

"If the Commission please, in order that there be no misunderstanding about the position of the defendant Dasch, we now offer in evidence the entire document marked Defense Exhibit A which contains a stenographic transcript of the statements made by Dasch and all of the questions asked and the answers given by him from June 19, 1942 to, and including, I believe, June 25, 1942, at which time Mr. Dasch signed each page thereof and the certificate, so to speak, which is attached. The document, I believe, contains, in all, 254 pages," explained Ristine, confident that his logic could not fail.[6] "This is offered because the *Court-Martial Manual* states that if the prosecution only elects to go into a part of what is said, the defense may offer the entire document itself."

"If the Commission please, I object," Biddle announced. "I take it that the Commission does not wish me to argue the point, since you have already ruled that the defense should put in their evidence when the time comes. I do not think I need to belabor the case. . . . [W]e have never offered any part of the statement and we simply say it seems to us appropriate that the defendant should offer this evidence when he is putting in his case."[7]

"May it please the Commission, under the present rules of the Commission, I would be entitled to read every question, every statement and every answer in that document and thereby get the entire document before the Commission," Ristine replied. "The only thing I would be required to do, under the previous ruling, would be to get one of the agents who was personally present when the various statements in that document were made to state that he was present when the statement was made. . . . It is true the prosecution did not refer to this confession or offer it in evidence, but the questions they asked their witnesses related to the isolated parts contained in this document."

Ristine sensed that he was close to finally winning a battle—however small—with Biddle and the commission members. "There was not but one interrogation of Dasch during that period of time. And the testimony they gave orally from the stand is contained, in my opinion, more accurately in this document. Certainly it is all contained in the document, because there is no showing here that there were separate questions and answers, one for this confession and another one that they testified to orally."

Ristine now delivered his clinching line, reading directly from the *Manual for Court-Martial*, which Biddle and Cramer were so fond of quoting: "Evidence of a confession or supposed confession cannot be restricted to evidence of only a part thereof. Where a part only is shown, the defense by cross-examination or otherwise may show the remainder so that the full and actual meaning of the confession or supposed confession may appear."

Biddle sat back in his chair, perfectly aware that there was no logical refutation of Ristine's point. He could only hope that President McCoy would rule in the prosecution's favor for some reason or another—as he had so far throughout the entire trial.

Judge Advocate General Cramer now tried to clarify a technical point, pointing out that " 'by cross-examination or otherwise' means he may bring it out by cross examination or otherwise as a part of his defense. That is what that means."

"That is the rule, a rule that is promulgated against the side that is attempting to use a confession and the rule is written because of the dangers involved," Ristine countered, hoping that President McCoy would not find a loophole to prevent admitting Dasch's confession—all 254 single-spaced pages.

"My remembrance was, though—and I will state it to you—that the prosecution had not attempted to use this confession, that it was the defense that used it," President McCoy replied, grasping for something that would overcome the defense's position.

"Now when they offer part of it—and when I say part of it I do not mean that they read from it, because they did not, but they offered testimony respecting the same answers and statements made by Dasch that are contained in that statement, but they only went into a small part of it, and we say that when they fail to go into the whole of it, then we are entitled to go into the rest," Ristine replied, confident that his position was airtight.

After mulling over the issue carefully for a moment, President McCoy decided that a quick judgment might be viewed as biased. So he opted instead for another recess to contemplate the matter.

* * *

When the afternoon session resumed, the anticipation of the ruling could be felt in the air. The lawyers all knew that the reading of the entire Dasch confession could take two days. Ristine hoped that something in Dasch's rambling statement would engender doubt in the commission members' minds about whether the would-be leader really had planned to carry out the sabotage mission. Royall, on the other hand, feared that the document might hurt his seven defendants.

So much for collegiality! Royall thought, surprised that Ristine, who had ridden his coattails during every argument from day one of the trial, would turn against him in such a flourish and without notice.

Having already read Dasch's statement, Biddle and Cramer must have dreaded the thought of having to listen to it read out loud in its entirety for several days.

President McCoy got the ball rolling. "I first want to get all the facts."

"With due deference, I think counsel for the defendant offered it as part of the record. Am I correct?" asked Biddle, hoping to avert a public reading. If the document was simply put into the record of the trial, the commission would likely not take the time to read through the entire "novel" of Dasch's life. If the statement were read aloud, however, there would be no way to avoid the entire commission hearing every self-serving piece of evidence that Dasch had conjured up during his six days of FBI questioning—unless, of course, they fell asleep during the reading.

"That is correct," Ristine replied.

"I should like to have read the purpose for which he offered it," one commission member said.

"Just pardon me a moment until we get a little further along with this thing," President McCoy snapped, obviously irritated.

Biddle now saw that his opportunity had come to avoid the reading.

"First, I think we would like to have clarified the ruling as to whether it goes in as part of the record; then after that perhaps counsel could make some suggestions which might be approved by the Commission as to whether all of it or portions of it by agreement should be read."

Biddle obviously hoped that if he could stall a decision as long as possible, he might block the statement being read in full. "I think we all agree that large portions of it are irrelevant and that all of us want to preserve the Commission's time and get to the relevant material."

Ristine's strategy became clear: it was better to have the entire statement read rather than just selective portions. It seemed that President McCoy was leaning toward reading the whole document or waiting until later in the trial, so both Ristine and Royall were now pushing for the reading in full.

"May it please the Commission, I think they should hear it when it is introduced. All the other confessions have been read at the time they were introduced," Dowell stated, knowing that this point was irrefutable.

"I think they should hear it in order to enable themselves and defense counsel to proceed with reference to continuing evidence based upon that document."

President McCoy had now heard enough of the sparring, and it was time for a decision. "The Commission will close," he stated firmly.

Fifteen minutes later, McCoy reopened the proceedings. "The paper concerned, the so-called confession of the defendant Dasch," McCoy concluded indignantly, "will now be read."

Ristine had succeeded in his battle to get Dasch's confession read aloud in court. The defense had finally outmaneuvered Biddle. Even though it was a procedural victory, it provided the defense lawyers a glimmer of hope that the commission might be swayed in their favor on more momentous issues.

So, late in the afternoon of Wednesday, July 15, Dasch's long-winded statement—more like an apology for his life—was read aloud to the commission. Ristine, along with a few of Royall's assistants, read the entire document over the next day and a half, covering every imaginable aspect of Dasch's improbable life, including Dasch's ruminations about the mission, Walter Kappe, and Nazism itself. The statement also covered subjects as diverse as Dasch's studying to become a priest, his ambitious plan to become a pilot, his childhood with twelve siblings, and his training at Quenz Lake. The reading—with many points repeated several times—seemed endless.

The marathon continued all of July 16. Biddle and Cramer wisely decided not to sit through the entire statement, showing up at one-thirty instead of the customary nine-thirty. Royall, Dowell, and Ristine were present for the entire day's reading, even though not one objection was made by either the prosecution or the defense. Over time Dasch's self-serving ramblings grated on the listeners' nerves.

Royall must have seen the irony in this turn of events. *Ristine might be missing a golden opportunity!* he playfully speculated. *At any point, a motion for acquittal of Dasch—in exchange for halting the reading of his pathetic statement—might have mustered at least four votes!*

The next day started out the same way. Biddle again decided to skip the actual reading of the confession, showing up at twelve-fifteen. When he finally did appear, it was miraculously at the end of Dasch's confession. Biddle sat through the questioning of Norval Wills, an FBI agent who had stayed with Dasch at the Mayflower Hotel before he was put behind bars. Biddle then added a few questions of his own. The court adjourned for an hour at twelve-thirty, and when it reopened, Biddle was again absent, turning the prosecution over to Assistant Solicitor General Oscar Cox. A few more FBI agents and an hour later, the prosecution's full attention shifted to the Florida landing.

The rest of the afternoon of July 17 was designed by the prosecution to incriminate Edward Kerling, the leader of the Florida landing. Cox brought in several FBI agents who had interrogated Kerling as well as those who had accompanied him to the beach in Florida to recover the buried explosives. Toward the end of the day, Biddle once again rejoined his prosecution team, just in time to participate in yet another confrontation with Royall.

When Biddle called D.J. Parsons to the witness stand to testify about the explosives found on the beach, Royall saw an opportune time to object.

"May it please the Commission, it is our intention to object to this evidence on behalf of all the defendants, solely on the ground that it was obtained by illegal search." Royall protested. "I think the Commission has passed on that adversely to our position. Therefore there is no necessity for me to argue it to the Commission. I make it because we think it is a sound objection."

Again, Royall thought that it would be hard for the commission to blatantly disregard testimony in the record that proved a flagrant constitutional violation.

"I am not cognizant of your making that particular objection before," President McCoy said, aware that he was about to fight a tough battle with Royall.

Royall took a deep breath to collect his thoughts. "Well, sir, the reason I said I had was that I did object to the questions asked the preceding witness as to what happened on the trip to Florida. The ground . . . was

an illegal search and seizure and I might add the additional ground of requiring the witness to incriminate himself. I do not desire to press the
point to the Commission. If the Commission has made up its mind, I do
not want to argue further."

Royall made sure to emphasize "made up its mind" to let the commission members know that he was aware of their bias.

"We would, however, like to have it understood in the record if the
Commission does overrule our objection that we have an objection to
each of these articles, without repeating it. If the Commission will
make a ruling on that, I have one more remark to make about it," Royall stated.

"I have no remarks to make," Biddle quipped, already certain that
the commission would quickly brush aside Royall's objection.

"I understand the Commission has already ruled on a similar matter, and I should assume that they would rule on this the same way.
There is no particular reason to argue it again," Biddle added, sound-
ing like an annoyed parent who keeps giving a child the same answer
to a repeated question.

"They are offered in evidence now?" a commission member asked,
referring to the articles found on the Florida beach.

"I am about to offer them," Biddle replied.

"You are about to?" the member repeated, unsure of how an objection could be raised to something that had yet to be stated.

"Yes," the exasperated Biddle replied, eager to admit his incriminating evidence.

"I take it that you are objecting to all of the articles that were found
on the beach in Florida?" President McCoy asked Royall.

"That is correct," Royall replied.

"Without objection on the part of any member of the Commission, the objection is not sustained," the president quickly ruled.

Even before a kangaroo court, Royall could not believe he had
again lost such an obviously valid legal objection.

"May it please the Commission, I desire to make this further statement without waiving in any way my objection. It is not my desire to
require any undue delay in the development of this evidence, and to
the extent that the Attorney General desires to do so it is agreeable
with the defendants to shorten this testimony, either by reference to
the previous testimony of this witness in the description of the explosives or in any other manner that will save time," Royall said.

"I appreciate that very much and I certainly will avail myself of that very generous offer," Biddle responded, a touch of sarcasm in his tone. "I will ask the reporter to mark these photographs for identification."

Biddle then proceeded with his questioning of FBI agent Parsons. Parsons told the commission how he had accompanied Kerling to the Florida beach, took the photographs of the articles retrieved that were now in evidence, and then opened and inventoried the boxes after they were transported to Jacksonville. Biddle deliberately prodded Parsons until he had explained the significance of each item found in the cache, and he had also linked the boxes to the Long Island landing, confirming that the markings as well as the contents of the boxes were nearly identical. With no ammunition, Royall let Parsons go without cross-examination.

Biddle next called FBI agent Charles Stanley to the witness stand. Stanley had seen the clothing left behind on the beach at Long Island and questioned Kerling as to whether or not this was the same type of clothing Kerling had worn when he landed with his compatriots on the Florida beach. Royall shot up like a rocket.

"May it please the Commission, I should like to ask the witness a question or two."

"Is there any objection at this time?" President McCoy asked Biddle.

"No," Biddle replied curtly.

"When was your conversation with Kerling?" Royall asked Stanley.

"July 1."

"Who was present?"

"Agent Duke."

"May it please the Commission, I myself have serious doubts whether my objection is well taken in this instance, but because of the fact that we have objected to the other declarations and confessions of Kerling on the ground of duress and of their not being voluntary, we desire to enter an objection to this, realizing that the Commission's same ruling will apply," Royall said, conceding his defeat on the matter, yet making sure his objection was preserved. Royall was making a record for a future day in what he hoped would be a more hospitable forum.

"Unless there is an objection on the part of any member of the Commission, the objection of counsel is not sustained," President McCoy ruled.[8]

Biddle continued his questioning, linking the Florida landing team to its Long Island counterpart. With the conclusion of the questioning of Agent Stanley, Biddle's case against Kerling was finished. And Kerling's fate was very nearly sealed.

The prosecution's case was winding down. On Saturday, July 18, the commission heard testimony against, as well as the statements of, defendants Haupt, Neubauer, and Thiel. Biddle introduced into evidence their waivers of search and custody, confessions, and any articles of clothing belonging to each man. The statements were relatively short but covered the movements of each man once he landed and how he spent his time and money. Haupt's statement included everything from his decision to marry Gerda Melind to his purchase of a car with the German High Command's money and his going to see *The Invaders* with Neubauer at the Chicago Theater.

Following his earlier pattern, Biddle then brought forward every FBI agent who had come into contact with the men. There was little that Royall could refute. He was too seasoned a trial lawyer to think he could change the damning facts, and Biddle's case was centered upon the facts.

With the prosecution's evidence against each of the individual defendants presented, the prosecution officially rested its case. Biddle leaned back in his chair, confident that the evidence against the defendants was overwhelming. They were trained enemy saboteurs caught on United States soil who had confessed their guilt. Even before the prosecution had rested, Biddle was predicting victory and advising Roosevelt how it might be exploited for propaganda purposes at home and abroad.

Looking at the row of prisoners, Biddle saw just ordinary-looking men, hardly the pride of the Aryan race. Confined in sunless cells, they "looked pale under the glaring artificial light."[9] Except for Burger and Dasch, the defendants were "a sorry-looking lot, their eyes dim with the certainty of death . . . the dark circles beneath their lids a little heavier each morning."[10]

Biddle actually had some sympathy for the defendants other than Dasch. They were merely pawns in Hitler's murderous game of chess. They honestly thought that they were waging "war for their country, not without pluck," Biddle thought. "It must have required skill and courage to undertake their desperate and dangerous adventure."[11]

Soon they would be casualties of war.

Royall knew that his clients sensed the tribunal was going to recommend to President Roosevelt a conviction and the death penalty. Besides filing a perfunctory motion for acquittal, what was Royall to do? How could he ever begin to climb the mountain of evidence proving them guilty as charged? Royall had one shot—a long shot—and it was less than a mile north of the Department of Justice building. So while Biddle was counting his chickens, Royall was hatching his plan to get to the Supreme Court.

Chapter 16

A Lion in Summer

After ten days of the prosecution's case, the defense opened on Monday, July 20. Royall's first order of business was to try to limit the devastating effect of each confession so that it would pertain only to the individual who made it.

"Now, may it please the Commission . . . confessions are not under any circumstances admissible as to any charge except the last [conspiracy] charge made against these defendants. A confession or a declaration made by one person relating to another person is nothing but hearsay, and I do not suppose it is necessary to argue at any length the reasons against convicting people upon hearsay," Royall argued.[1]

"Take the statement, for instance, of the defendant Dasch. Contained in there are hundreds of statements which Dasch could not be asked about if he were on the witness stand. . . . Yet the effect of admitting these confessions is to put in evidence without the benefit of any cross-examination evidence that one of these defendants could not himself have given if he had been put on the witness stand and sworn."[2]

Admitting into evidence all the statements, Royall added, was "not doing much more, on that feature of the case, than trying them on common gossip." By this time, Royall had cited the *Manual for Court-Martial* as well as five federal court cases squarely supporting his argument.

"If the Commission please . . . if an accused confessedly makes a statement after he is apprehended and then says it is not a true statement, but then says he desires to make a true statement, I say, [w]ould it be safe for us to accept either statement under those circumstances and use it for the purpose of depriving a person of his liberty or his life?" Colonel Ristine argued, hoping to discredit the confessions for their lack of accuracy.[3]

President McCoy then acknowledged Biddle.

"With due deference to my learned opponents in the common law," Biddle began, "I think their argument has tended to complicate the issue before the Commission rather than simplify it." Biddle launched into a long-winded explanation about how each defendant had freely given a statement without having any interaction with any other defendant. In spite of this lack of communication, Biddle argued, each statement was interlocked with the same facts. "Dasch supports Burger, Burger supports Kerling, and so on, right down the line. Right down the line they are alike. You have got each one of them. You have got all eight," Biddle stressed. "The whole thing is completely interlocked, each one being tied in with the confession of the other."[4]

By this point in the trial, Royall was distinctly aware of Biddle's knack for flipping arguments around and turning the focus away from specific rules of law favoring the defendants. It was time to call him on it.

"It seems to me that the Attorney General has illustrated very concretely the reason why these confessions should not be admitted. . . . It is only to the extent that they differ that it is material to the defendants to exclude them. It is only where one defendant says something about the other's mental processes or acts that the other one did not say that it is essential to exclude them. As to the other features of the confessions, the argument advanced by the Attorney General does not apply. . . . [T]he Attorney General has cited no authority of any court anywhere to sustain the position taken," Royall argued, his message clear.

With nothing to refute Royall's argument, Biddle lamely stated: "May I remind the Commission that you were kind enough to say that you might adjourn just before 11? That is just a reminder."

It was already 11:20, and the arguments on the matter had been running for a solid two hours.

"The Commission will recess for fifteen minutes," President McCoy stated, and the courtroom emptied.

*   *   *

When the commission reconvened at 11:40, the defense arguments were quickly shot down with President McCoy's pithy statement that the commission "will admit the confessions and admissions for all purposes."

Royall had made an impressive, seemingly irrefutable argument citing controlling precedents, the *Manual for Court-Martial*, and elementary logic why the confessions should not be allowed. Any lingering doubts about the commission's bias were forever dispelled. It was time to begin planning his exit strategy.

Royall's first move was to make a perfunctory motion. "Now, we first, on behalf of all the defendants whom we represent except the defendant Burger, with whom we will deal separately, desire to make a motion for a verdict of not guilty on certain of the counts."[5]

Royall began to go through the charges like a surgeon. He first lanced the second charge of relieving or attempting to relieve the enemy. It was impossible for five of the defendants—Heinck, Kerling, Neubauer, Quirin, and Thiel—to assist the enemy for the obvious reason that they were all German citizens.

"If that meant that it was a crime for a German citizen to help Germany, then every German soldier, if there were an invasion of this country, in uniform, would be guilty under that section and be punished by death. That cannot be the meaning of it," Royall argued. "We think, therefore, that Charge No. 2 should be dismissed as to the five defendants whom I have named."

Royall then proceeded to move to strike all the charges against these defendants. This was clearly for the record only, since the commission had already rejected the defense objection to its jurisdiction at the outset of the trial.

"Now, as to all six of these defendants, we do move to dismiss the third charge, which is a violation of the 82nd Article of War," Royall continued.[6] This accusation dealt with lurking around military fortifications and spying. After noting that the charge dealt specifically with the word *spying*, Royall defined *spying* as understood by the tribunal in The Hague Convention and the Rules of Land Warfare—two respected sources for the law of war. There must be clandestine conduct, operation in a military zone, and intent to communicate military information to the enemy, Royall argued. Although the first prerequisite—clandestine conduct—had been proven, the other two elements of spying were missing. Royall noted the absence of any zone of operations, asserting that an unarmed beach patrol hardly constituted a military fortification on Long Island. In Florida, there was no military presence at all.

Royall then shifted to the third prerequisite: giving military information to the enemy. "I do not believe that this evidence remotely shows that. These people came over here, according to the prosecution's testimony, for the purpose of sabotage, and not spying. The FBI recognized that to be the fact, because they used the word 'sabotage,' both on the witness stand and in every question that they asked the defendants in taking their statements; and you will not find in all these voluminous statements any other descriptive term used, so far as I recall," Royall concluded.[7]

Colonel Dowell now spoke at length to the commission about the intricacies found in the *Manual for Court-Martial.* His argument prompted Judge Advocate General Cramer—his rival in terms of knowledge of military law—to put his spin on the law. Having heard all the arguments, the commission recessed for a short time. When the judges returned, Royall got the ruling he fully expected—all motions were denied.

At this point, Colonel Ristine motioned for a verdict of not guilty on all counts for Dasch. He relied heavily upon the admittance into evidence of the entire Dasch statement as well as the fact that Burger's statement backed up Dasch on nearly every detail, including Dasch's mind-set and attitude. The judge advocate general quickly responded: Ristine had advanced no grounds why the case against Dasch should be thrown out now. His argument was better suited as a closing argument, Cramer noted.

Before the commission could close and decide on the Dasch matter, Royall arose and asked the commission to delay judgment on Dasch until the next morning, at which point he would present the case for Burger.

"It is quite a thankless task to address this Commission on so many subjects, as to none of which we seem to be very successful. . . . I should like very much to defer the presentation of the Burger argument until tomorrow morning. I do not want it split in two. It is impractical to finish it this afternoon, since it is almost the closing hour," Royall observed.[8]

Royall reasoned that since the two defendants were so similar in their defenses, the commission could save time ruling on the matter at the same point in time. What Royall really wanted to do was associate Burger as much as possible with Dasch, who had the best chance of escaping the death penalty. For the first time in the trial, Royall prevailed—although on only a small point. The commission decided to delay ruling on the Dasch motion until the next morning, at which point the Burger and Dasch motions would be decided together.

On the morning of Tuesday, July 21, the commission resumed the business postponed the previous afternoon.

"May it please the Commission, is it in order for me now to bring up the motion of the defendant Burger for a verdict of not guilty?" Royall asked.

"Yes, it is in order," President McCoy responded.

"As was stated to the Commission yesterday, counsel for the defendants, and particularly counsel for the seven defendants other than Dasch, dislike very much to impose upon the time of the Commission in matters that apparently do not accomplish anything," Royall began, looking each general squarely in the eyes as he made his points.

"It has not been our purpose during this case to present any contention that is not thoroughly consistent with the law under which we are accustomed to practice; in fact, I think in most instances that has been admitted by the prosecution. Our various positions have been overruled because of a variation from the ordinary and generally accepted methods of procedure," continued Royall, who clearly could not suppress his strong disapproval of the commission's blatant disrespect for the rule of law. No one knew better than this veteran trial lawyer that Burger's motion for a not guilty plea was a loser, but it was his duty to preserve the legal issues for another day.

"May it please the Commission," Royall elaborated, "the prosecution in this case—and I use that term broadly to include the FBI also—has seemed to us to take the position—I may be charging them improperly; if so, they can correct me at the proper time—that the only solution of this case is for all the defendants to be adjudged guilty, leaving any relief which might be afforded them to the question of Presidential discretion."[9]

Royall's belief was based on the fact that several FBI agents testified that they actually believed Dasch was telling the truth in his confession, yet had urged him to plead guilty anyway.

"If that is equally applicable to the trial of this case, we are just going through wasteful motions," Royall concluded, hoping to forestall the commission from rushing to judgment. "We are not interested— I am sure the Commission is not interested—in doing what somebody said in a case down in my country: 'Just give him a fair trial and then convict him.' We are not interested in going through motions." Royall was unusually blunt. Here was a junior officer lecturing seven of his superiors. If his objective was to make the commission pay attention, it seemed to work. Dasch looked admiringly at Royall as he battled fearlessly for his clients.

"[H]e . . . [fights] like a lion and a true American, putting up a spirited defense for his men," Dasch felt.[10] The German often wished he had Royall as a lawyer instead of Ristine. "He could . . . easily upset the crazy case that was concocted by the prosecution."[11]

Royall started the case for Burger's acquittal by mentioning his FBI statement: "It was the confession upon which the prosecution relied to lay the basis of its case; and no none can doubt the fact that if that confession is true, Burger is guilty of nothing under these charges."[12]

Royall argued that each subsequent confession by each of the defendants, "taken at different times, without knowledge by one that the other had been given,"[13] supported every detail in Burger's confession— from his hatred of the Gestapo while at Quenz Lake to the other defendants' mistrust of him. Upon his arrest, Haupt, who was the first to be apprehended, said, "Burger turned us in . . . Burger is the man that must have turned us in."[14]

Royall now shifted his attention to the charges against Burger.

"In each of these offenses there must be a criminal intent," Royall asserted. "In the absence of an intent to carry out any criminal plan, each of these charges would fall. . . . In other words, if Burger came here with the intention merely of getting back to the United States because of his mistreatment in Germany, and not with the intention of committing any act against the United States, he is not guilty of any charge. Now, that is the milk in the coconut as far as his case is concerned."[15]

Royall then described the concentration camp where Burger had been confined for seventeen months, and how his only choice was either to embark on this sabotage mission to the United States or to return to being tortured.

"Let us apply the doctrine of reasonable men. How would any reasonable man have reacted to that situation?" Royall asked. His point was exquisitely clear: Burger had used the mission for the sole purpose of escaping Germany. The confessions, Royall continued, further substantiated this point.

"I would like to say this, parenthetically. We cannot try a man here, as reasonable men, on doubts as to what he might have intended or what he might have done. We are trying a man for a serious offense; and when the evidence shows, corroborated by other circumstances, that he was telling the truth, the matter ought to be dismissed as to him," Royall urged, his voice rising to a crescendo as he completed his passionate, hour-long argument.[16]

Judge Advocate General Cramer rose to refute Royall's motion.

"Counsel for the defendant Burger has made a very excellent argument if it were made at the close of the entire case," Cramer stated. "The prosecution still insists that according to the *Manual for Court-Martial,* to which counsel has referred, the question of the balancing of the evidence, the weight of the evidence, or anything of that kind, is not for the consideration of this Commission at this time."[17]

Cramer further argued that the prosecution had ample evidence to convict Burger, and that throwing out the case against the defendant was not an option available to them at that time.

"Going back, I think that after this long conversation—perhaps not a conversation but a dissertation on the part of Colonel Royall—we should consider just what this motion is," Cramer said, making a pointed criticism of Royall's lengthy exposition. "It is not a motion for the convenience of the Commission, to reduce the time of the trial, or for the convenience of counsel for the accused in the conduct of their case or cases of the various defendants. It is simply a motion on the strict legal principle whether or not there is any reasonable construction or inference from the testimony that has been admitted here that points toward the guilt of this particular defendant. The same argument applies to the defendant Dasch," Cramer asserted.[18]

It was Royall's turn at rebuttal. "Of course, if the Commission is going to take the view that a motion for a verdict of not guilty cannot be made at this point of the case—and I do not believe it will—the Judge Advocate General's argument is sound," he conceded halfheartedly. Then he turned defiant. "But unless this provision of the *Manual for Court-Martial* is to be utterly disregarded, we are entitled to have this motion considered as outlined in this *Manual.* Of course, the answer of the Judge Advocate General is the easiest one to make, because it would have been exceedingly difficult for him to have answered our argument upon the evidence before the Commission; we think it is unanswerable."

"We shall answer that at the proper time, Colonel Royall," General Cramer interrupted indignantly. Royall had at least succeeded in getting Cramer's goat.

"I have no apologies to make for that remark, because I do not believe that this argument can be answered on these facts," Royall explained. He then quoted the *Manual*, at the conclusion of which he stated: "That is the provision under which we are proceeding. It does not say 'at the end of all the evidence'; it says 'at the end of the prosecution's evidence,'" Royall pressed. "We are relegated to whether the prosecution by reasonable inferences has proven a criminal purpose on the part of the defendant Burger."[19]

President McCoy adjourned the commission to consider the matter. It did not take long. The generals returned to make quick work of Royall's hard-fought argument. Royall's attempt to dismiss certain charges against each of his clients, as well as Dasch's motion, were totally rejected. This was an ominous sign auguring the inevitable outcome of the trial. Royall could not afford the luxury of wallowing in self-pity; he had a job to do. It was time to start presenting the defense's case.

Over the next several days, the testimony of each defendant—to no one's surprise—would be essentially similar: he had no intention to conduct sabotage when he arrived in the United States. While some had to admit that they were enthusiastic saboteurs in training at Quenz Lake, they all experienced a submarine conversion as they crossed the North Atlantic. Dasch and Burger were more audacious— they had accepted Lieutenant Kappe's "invitation" to join the team as a means to flee Germany and get to America.

Royall had no illusions about his clients' "defense." He well knew that their stories—related in detail to the FBI before any defense lawyers were appointed—would be sorely tested in the crucible of cross-examination. Their fate before the commission had been sealed the day they were apprehended.

Royall's first order of business was to call the youngest defendant, Herbert Haupt, to the witness stand. One of the two American citizens on trial, Haupt answered over two hours of questions by Royall, the majority of them dealing with his state of mind while in Germany and his intentions on whether he would go through with the plot. Haupt spoke clearly and confidently when Royall led him through the questioning.

But then it was Biddle's turn.

The attorney general's plan was very clear: confuse Haupt through a series of fast-paced questions, jumping back and forth between totally different points in time. Royall quickly grew irritated with Biddle's tactics and let the attorney general know it.

"What was his name?" Biddle asked Haupt, referring to the man Haupt had met in Mexico City.

"That I can't tell you. . . . He had his wife and children sitting near—"

"You have answered the question," Biddle snapped, cutting off Haupt in midsentence.

"Wait a minute," Royall protested.

"He has answered the question," Biddle shot back at Royall.

"I do not know whether or not he has. I think the witness is the best judge of whether or not he has answered the question," Royall explained.

"I shall be glad to have you object whenever you wish to," Biddle replied.

"I am objecting to your interrupting the witness right now, because he did not sound as though he had finished his answer," Royall stated.[20]

President McCoy allowed the question to be restated, and Haupt was now given time to respond fully to the question. But it was hardly the last time that Royall would have to stop Biddle from interrupting, badgering, or berating the witness.

Biddle was soon back at it. "You did not care about the other men, whether they were turned in or not, did you?" he asked Haupt, still on the stand after two hours of intense, rapid-fire questions from the crafty attorney general.

"I didn't know the other men as well as I knew the men in this group, and I knew that I was with this group in Jacksonville, and I knew the way they acted in Jacksonville."

"Whom were you afraid of in that group?" Biddle asked, again cutting off the witness.

"Let the witness finish," Royall insisted. Now addressing Haupt, he said, "Have you finished?"

"No, I have not," Haupt replied.

"The witness is so seldom responsive to the question that it is a little bit difficult—"

Now Royall cut off Biddle.

"We object to that comment."

"I make it again," replied the defiant Biddle.

"I do not think so," Royall fired back. "I think the reason he is not responsive is that he is continuously interrupted before he finishes his answers."[21]

President McCoy again allowed Haupt to finish, and then the attorney general went right back to his karate-chop style of questioning. Only a few minutes later, Royall and Biddle were counterpunching once more. There was an electrifying air of tension in the courtroom.

"Did you talk to Wergin about methods of damaging power lines?" Biddle asked the defendant.

"I cannot recall," Haupt answered.

"You cannot recall about talking or not talking to Wergin about methods of damaging power lines? Do you want the Commission to believe that you cannot remember that?" Biddle asked rhetorically, belittling Haupt's credibility.

"I cannot recall," Haupt again replied.

"We object to that form of cross-examination. It is not proper in the case of any witness in any court, as far as I know," Royall asserted.

"I think it is perfectly proper, but I will be guided by what the Commission wants me to do," Biddle stated, holding his ground.[22] But Royall's objection was not even considered, and with a wave of his hand, President McCoy allowed Biddle to proceed in the manner he saw fit.

Biddle continued roughing up Haupt for another half hour. At 4:30, the commission was ready to close. More than ever before, Royall was painfully aware that the commission would convict his clients. The only way he could derail the express train that was speeding his clients to their deaths was to seek relief from the Supreme Court. Now was the moment to inform the commission of his decision to try to take the case to the civil courts—and defy the explicit orders in his commander in chief's proclamation establishing the military commission.

Waiting for the defendants to be removed from the courtroom, Royall began his "announcement"—essentially committing the military's equivalent of civil disobedience.

"May it please the Commission, there is a matter that we wanted to call to your attention. At any time it is convenient to the Commission, it will be satisfactory to us, but that matter may take ten or fifteen minutes. I thought you ought to have that in view, possibly," Royall stated respectfully. Little did he know that the estimated fifteen minutes would turn into over an hour of a seminar on duty and honor.

Royall quoted from the *Manual for Court-Martial*: an officer appointed to defend an accused in a military proceeding is obligated to perform "such duties as usually devolve upon the counsel for a defendant before civil courts in a criminal case." As such, Royall continued, he must protect his clients' interests "by all honorable and legitimate means known to the law."[23]

Royall went on to explain that, as counsel for the seven defendants, he and Dowell "thought it was our duty, first, to make an investigation of the law relating to the Presidential Order and the Presidential Proclamation, and Colonel Dowell himself made that investigation." Royall now made it clear that "before the opening of this case we called to your attention the fact that we thought there was doubt as to the validity of the order creating this Commission." Royall then produced copies of the two letters that Dowell and he had signed and sent to President Roosevelt, stating that they believed a civil court process was appropriate under the circumstances.

Royall informed the commission that he had not been able to obtain civilian counsel to bring a court challenge. "Accordingly, we have prepared papers for an application for a writ of habeas corpus, the purpose of which is to test the constitutionality and validity of the President's Order and of the President's Proclamation," Royall explained. "Those papers have been drawn with a view to disclosing nothing more about the proceedings here than is absolutely necessary for the assertion of the rights which we think ought to be asserted."[24]

Royall now answered questions from confused members of the commission. The generals did not understand whether they were being asked to rule on the application or if they were merely being informed of the matter.

"What I do wish to make clear is that we do not want to ask the Commission to take any course that might be construed as asking you inferentially to approve or disapprove either the fact that we are going to resort to a writ of habeas corpus or, second, that Colonel Dowell and I are going to present it," Royall hastened to explain.

The other members of the defense team then isolated themselves from Royall.

"I do not want to dissent from anything, but I do want to add a few words," started Dowell, standing almost at attention. Although he was fully aware of why Royall ethically felt it was essential to turn to the Supreme Court, he had to decline to support that approach for reasons he was about to explain. The pain caused by his dilemma was clear from his address to the commission.

"Colonel Royall has been trained in the law, and I have been trained as a soldier for over forty years. I cannot get it out of my mind, probably because of my training, that my duty as a soldier is circumscribed by the orders I receive from our Commander, in this case the Commander-in-Chief of the Army of the United States, who has detailed me to come here to act as defense counsel before this Commission.

"I am in the embarrassing situation of feeling that way about my military duty. The moment this Commission has ended, I am under orders to return to my proper station and go on with my duties as a soldier. I have to do that because I do not know of any other way to be a soldier than to obey the orders I receive.

"On the other hand, a duty has been imposed upon us as defense counsel to do everything legitimate and honorable in the interest of our clients; and we see something here, of course, that seems to be honorable and correct, but not legitimate, as far as I am concerned. That is my viewpoint," Dowell explained. As a soldier, he could not bring himself to file a public challenge to his commander in chief's authority that would generate publicity and thereby "injure our national cause, our war effort."[25]

Colonel Ristine then stood to present his view on the subject with a very brief explanation. Ristine believed that he could not honorably "construe those orders as authorizing me to file in any other tribunal any application for a writ of habeas corpus or other proceeding, and therefore I stand on that interpretation of my orders."[26]

Royall was all alone—the only defense lawyer willing to challenge the presidential proclamation. Respectfully, he made clear that he was not criticizing Colonel Ristine for deciding not to pursue the challenge, and that he was certainly "not critical of Colonel Dowell, for whom I have just about as sincere admiration as I have for any man I have ever met, when he decides that he cannot go ahead."

Royall made his position clear: "I am not trying to throw the burden on the Commission or anybody else. I am going to do what I told the President [of the United States] I was going to do in this memorandum, unless somebody orders me specifically not to do it, because that is what I conceive my duty to be."

After a few more questions by the commission members and a pass by the attorney general on any comment except to say he would like to see the papers, Royall concluded his statement to the commission: "I am not asking anybody to take any part of my responsibility. I will do that and suffer the consequences."[27]

With the habeas corpus petition sitting on the table, the commission adjourned to discuss the matter. When the panel returned, President McCoy stated: "[T]he Commission does not care to pass on that question," again leaving the agonizing decision up to counsel. That sweltering afternoon, Kenneth Claiborne Royall had to be the loneliest soldier in the United States Army.

Chapter 17

They Don't Shoot Saboteurs in America

While Royall moved quickly to make arrangements for his Supreme Court challenge, the military commission resumed the next morning, July 22. In his absence, Haupt's cross-examination was postponed, and Colonel Dowell called another witness to stall until Royall returned. James Eagen, Haupt's employer before he initially left the United States, was called to testify. Eagen was dismissed almost as quickly as he had arrived.

With Royall back at the defense table, Biddle resumed Haupt's grilling with the same fast-paced interrogation that fringed on being abusive. At one point, Biddle asked Haupt to refer to one of Burger's statements, drawing Royall's immediate ire.

"If the Commission please, I think that it is sufficient for me to make another objection," Royall noted. "I do not think we are playing a game here; we are trying people for a serious offense."

Royall argued that Biddle was violating the most basic rule of cross-examination: a statement of another witness cannot be used in examining the current witness. Royall's objection was finally sustained—the first time Biddle had been overruled in days. Haupt's interrogation dragged on, with more questions being posed by Royall, Biddle, and President McCoy. At one point, President McCoy asked Haupt what would have happened if he had told Kappe that he would not undertake the mission.

"In the position that I was, not being a German citizen and having trouble with German officials—well . . . I would have probably went to a concentration camp."

Dasch felt sorry for Haupt. He realized that the other man's return to Germany "had been something of a boyish lark and he had ended up trapped." Haupt had come back to America, Dasch believed, because he was homesick for his family in Chicago.

At nearly 11:30, Haupt's ordeal on the stand—nearly six total hours over two days—finally ended.

Haupt's mother, Erna Haupt, next took the stand, but only for a few questions to confirm her residence and acknowledge she talked with her son when he came home. Agnes Jordan, a neighbor, then Gerda Melind, the girl Haupt had impregnated and abandoned, took the stand. Both were asked only a few questions and then dismissed. The defense's case for Herbert Haupt was now finished.

Hermann Neubauer was next.

The nervous thirty-two-year-old former clerk stammered through a brisk line of questioning by Royall as well as Biddle. He testified that he was a Nazi Party member and had been ordered by the army to take part in the sabotage mission. Neubauer also explained why he was visibly shaking on the stand. Badly wounded in action by the Russians in occupied Polish territory, he had twice been put in a sanitarium back in Germany for the condition. His nerves were completely shot, and he jumped at the sound of sudden noises. Soon Neubauer was dismissed, almost as quickly as he had been called.

Werner Thiel took the witness stand.

Unlike Neubauer, who shook nervously and spoke slowly, Thiel was so excited on the stand that he talked too fast—so fast, in fact, that Royall had to calm him down and ask him to speak slower. Royall fed the former machinist the same line of questions given to Neubauer. The only difference was that Royall made sure to dwell on the fact that FBI agent Donegan had mistreated Thiel when he was first taken into custody.

"Tell exactly what happened," Royall asked. "Do not exaggerate it in any way, but tell exactly what happened."

"He took me to his office, and I don't know exactly what he asked me, and I didn't answer, and he pulled my hair and slapped me," Thiel replied.

"Was anybody there with you at that time?"

"No."

"What was done after that?"

"Nothing," replied Thiel.[1]

As with all his clients, Royall sought to bring out any sympathetic facts bearing on their lack of criminal intent. Thiel tried to portray himself as a reluctant recruit for the sabotage mission. When he agreed to go to Quenz Lake, he had not recovered from the shock of one brother being killed in battle and another blinded in one eye fighting for the Third Reich.

After a quick round of questioning by Biddle, Thiel was excused from the witness stand. The thirteenth day of the commission now came to a close, and President McCoy officially adjourned until Friday, July 24. There would be no proceedings the next day. Royall and Biddle had the matter of the Supreme Court appeal to handle.

When the commission reopened on Friday, July 24, Royall continued to call the accused saboteurs to the stand. Lack of sleep, not to mention the stress of defending seven clients, should have taken a heavy toll on a man half his age. But Royall seemed indefatigable, physically and psychologically; he thrived on pressure. Somehow he had found a place inside himself that gave him the fortitude to carry on—occasionally brilliantly—in the face of overwhelming odds. In fact, Royall was so consumed with his work that he might have forgotten that he had turned forty-eight if Margaret had not wished him a happy birthday as he left their temporary home in Washington before sunrise.

Royall called Edward Kerling, leader of the Florida landing team. Early in Kerling's testimony, Royall made sure to bring out the fact that FBI agent Donegan had also pulled his hair and slapped him during the first night of questioning. Royall knew that showing this mistreatment would not help his case, but exposing the Bureau's cruelty might help him in the event of a credibility contest.

Kerling's testimony followed a now familiar pattern. Royall hoped to establish doubt in the commission members' minds that Kerling—while initially a true believer—would in fact execute the plan. But Kerling himself tripped over this line of questioning, changing his answers when cross-examined and giving contradictory statements. The best case made against Kerling came from his own testimony.

Of all the defendants, Kerling was the least apologetic about his role in the sabotage mission. He knew what he was doing when he entered the United States. To the end, he considered himself "a loyal German."[2]

It was now Heinrich Heinck's turn on the stand.

The former mechanic and chauffeur testified about his time in America, his jobs, and why he returned to Germany. Heinck "liked the liberty of this country, the freedom over here," which was lacking in Nazi Germany.[3] He related the same story as the rest of the defendants: the first meeting with Kappe, the school at Quenz Lake, the road to Lorient, the submarine voyage, and the events of the landing and subsequent days in America. His most ironic statement may have been more wishful thinking than anything else: "They told us nobody ever gets shot over here in America on account of doing sabotage work."[4]

Royall proceeded with the questioning of the sixth defendant, Richard Quirin. Like the defendants before him, the Nazi Party member spoke primarily about his experiences at the sabotage school as well as the landing in America and events leading up to his arrest. But when questioned about his loyalty to the mission and whether he intended to go through with the sabotage, Quirin was hesitant, wavering in his answers. Quirin's equivocal responses were damaging in the tribunal's eyes.

The commission resumed the next day, Saturday, July 25. The trial had been running for fourteen days, and the defense was nearing the end of its case. It was now time for the Germans' Benedict Arnold to take the stand.

Colonel Ristine started off the questioning, making it a point to remind Dasch not to go into great detail. But Dasch was the client from hell—he would escape death at any cost. What he accomplished, as his answers rambled on and on, was to bore the commission with irrelevant detail.

After only a few questions, Biddle obviously could not stand to hear Dasch pontificate any more. He found him "glib, vain, and essentially unsteady—hardly a man who could be counted on to take heroic risks."[5] Dasch may have convinced himself that he was a hero and may have fooled the usually "methodical" German High Command, but the prosecutor dismissed him as a mental defective.[6] Unlike Burger, who would not make a deal with the FBI to escape death if there was a risk of Nazi reprisals against his wife and parents, "Dasch, to save his skin, pleaded and begged and whined."[7]

Biddle interrupted, gently enough, "I think this witness is so unresponsive to the questions and is so wasting the time of the Commission that I do not think it would be inappropriate if the Commission directed him to be responsive and answer the questions. His own counsel is trying to control him. We will be here for a week if this kind of thing goes on. I have never heard any evidence like this in my life," proclaimed Biddle, who was not exaggerating.

Surprisingly, Royall concurred. It was one of the rare occasions that the attorney general and Royall seemed to agree. Royall also suspected that the unstable Dasch was mentally ill—the proverbial loose cannon that could blow up Royall's clients without warning.

"May it please the Commission, I would like to join in that request from the standpoint of the other defendants for this reason. It is impossible to tell from the question asked what the answer is going to be, and I do not know whether to object or not. I would have to object to every question. I do not know what he is going to say about these other defendants. That particular question, I think, if I recall, was, 'Did the defendant Thiel join in this?'"

"He answered that 'no,'" Ristine responded quickly.

"He answered that 'no,' but he did not stop there. He went on with something that did not have anything in the world to do with the question," Royall insisted.

"Well, proceed with your question," President McCoy interjected, "and I hope that the witness will follow the instructions of his own counsel and be responsive and direct insofar as he can be to the questions."

"I shall try to do so," Dasch replied.

Ristine continued with his examination. While Dasch's answers were considerably shorter, he still strayed from the point from time to time. Dasch mainly restated what had been previously read to the court in his voluminous statement/confession to the FBI. Royall and Biddle also questioned Dasch, but nothing new was elicited. Shortly before 12:30, the commission closed for the day.

The next day of the trial, Monday, July 27, began with an ominous distinction: it was the last day of testimony and the eve of Royall taking his case before the Supreme Court. There was an outside chance that the Supreme Court might order a civilian trial and that the commission would not meet again.

The day began with Colonel Ristine calling two FBI agents. Both restated their prior testimony. There seemed to be no real point in Ristine's line of questioning, which Biddle objected to, deprecating it as "just a waste of time."[8] The witnesses were excused, and Ristine's defense of Dasch was finished.

Ernest Peter Burger was the last defendant to take the stand. Depending on his performance, the commission would decide whether he lived or died. By now Royall knew that Burger was probably his only client with a slim chance to avoid execution.

Burger was quickly put through the same line of questioning as his co-defendants. In addition to the usual questions, however, Royall made sure to dwell on Burger's imprisonment by the Gestapo and the fact that there was no other realistic option for him. The only way out of Germany had been to cooperate with the Abwehr.

"Get out and get even," Burger testified.[9]

On cross-examination, Biddle hammered home the fact that Burger had been a card-carrying Nazi Party member before he went to America and as soon as he returned to Germany. The attorney general also got him to admit that he was instructed by Walter Kappe to run advertisements in the *Chicago Tribune* as a commercial artist "to be a communication to . . . [his superiors in Germany] that you had established your front in America."[10] Burger refused to assume an alias because he had U.S. citizenship papers and he "was supposed to tell anyone who asked me that I did not leave the United States."[11]

Biddle adopted a more congenial, familiar approach with Burger, several times calling him "Pete." He coaxed out of the witness damaging testimony about Dasch being close to Kappe and espousing "some Communist ideas." (Burger conveniently claimed he was an anti-Communist who had fought the Bolsheviks in the riots from 1923 to 1927.) Despite being pressed by Biddle, Burger clung tenaciously to his earlier testimony on direct examination that "as soon as I came out of the Gestapo [prison] . . . I would find a way to get even."

Under Colonel Ristine's questioning, Burger supported Dasch's defense that Dasch had expressed anti-Nazi sentiments to Burger back in Germany. Burger was convinced of Dasch's bona fides because

Dasch did not betray Burger when Burger confided in him about his bitterness against the Gestapo. The other saboteurs, Burger added, also thought that Dasch "did not act like a Nazi" and appeared disinterested in learning sabotage at Quenz Lake.[12]

President McCoy wanted to know if Kappe had instructed the saboteurs to confess if they were apprehended.

"No sir," Burger replied. "On the contrary, in case anyone got caught, we were not to tell anything. . . . That was understood from the beginning."

Royall pounced on this opening, eliciting from Burger that violation of "the pledge of secrecy" carried a harsh sanction.

"What was the penalty if you violated the secrecy?"

"Death," Burger responded as Royall quietly sat down.

Finished with the defendants' testimony, the defense had two final witnesses: Marie Kerling, Eddie Kerling's wife, would take the stand first, and then Hedy Engemann, Kerling's mistress, would testify. Royall was pulling out all the stops.

"Have you been happy with your husband?" Colonel Dowell asked Mrs. Kerling.

"Well, yes—yes and no," she replied.

Marie explained that when Eddie and she had worked in the same house as a cook and chauffeur team, they saw too much of each other and did not get along. Mrs. Kerling went on to tell of her friendship with Hedy Engemann, and how she knew that Eddie and Hedy spent a considerable amount of time together.

"I am requested to ask you one more question by the defendant. Did you ever express a desire for your husband to marry Hedy Engemann?" Dowell asked.

"Did I ever express that to my husband?" Marie asked back.

"A desire that he should do so?"

"I thought he was in love with her; but I don't know; maybe Hedy is in love with him. I don't know," Marie replied.

"Did you say any such thing to him or suggest to him that he should get a divorce and marry Hedy?" Dowell asked again.

"I asked him if he wanted to marry somebody else," Marie replied.

"That is all," Dowell stated. Mrs. Kerling was then excused from the courtroom, the purpose of her testimony unclear.

It was now Hedy's turn to take the stand. Dowell focused primarily on the two and a half years that Hedy had known Eddie and how they had grown to be extremely close friends.

"Did you know he was married?" Dowell asked.

"I didn't know right away but soon afterward."

"Did that make any difference?"

"No."

After a few questions about her occupation as a governess, Dowell asked bluntly: "What I am trying to find out is, had she [Mrs. Kerling] ceased to love her husband or not?"[13]

"I think so," Hedy replied.

Dowell finished up his round of questions, and Biddle then went to work. Instinctively, "the fighting attorney general" (as his colleages affectionately called him)—using trial techniques honed prosecuting Philadelphia bootleggers—attacked right away.

"When was the last time you stayed with him before he went to Germany?"

"Well, I would see him frequently before he left," Hedy replied innocently.

"Were you intimate before he left for Germany?" Biddle asked.

"Do I have to answer that?" Hedy asked, clearly embarrassed.

"I think you ought to answer that."

Hedy hesitated, not wanting to answer the question in open court for all to hear. She finally replied, "We were very good friends," again skirting the question.

Biddle let it pass. Everyone knew the truth.

Hedy then described her conversation with Eddie in New York's Central Park, and how he told her that he had come to the United States on a German submarine. This testimony directly conflicted with Kerling's, in which he had denied under oath telling anybody about the submarine. Hedy also told of how she changed large bills for Eddie.

The testimony of Kerling's wife and mistress were extremely damaging to his credibility—especially when they testified to his loyalty to the German government. But Royall had to take a calculated risk that he could humanize Kerling for the commission. Maybe the generals would accept in mitigation that Kerling had come back to America to be with Hedy.

After Hedy was excused from the witness stand, Colonel Dowell rose slowly. "If it please the Commission, the defense rests."

"The defendant Mr. Dasch rests his case," Colonel Ristine also announced.

Biddle's prosecution team called two rebuttal witnesses for brief testimony. The first, Colonel Stephen Sherrill, was on duty in the Operations Division of the General Staff in Washington, D.C., in charge of the North America Theater Group. He testified to the fact that, in essence, the eastern seaboard of the United States—called the Eastern Defense Command—was a theater of military operations, even if it was not specifically given that name. The second witness, FBI agent Donegan, testified that he had not struck Thiel, and that his "punching" Kerling was really more of a brush by the face.[14]

The taking of testimony from forty-two witnesses was now concluded. The closing arguments would be heard in a few days. But first it was time for Royall's Supreme Court challenge.

Chapter 18

The Great Writ

Royall walked into his cramped office across the hall from the court-room. The small workspaces were divided by a temporary wall into separate prosecution and defense sections. Making his way to the defense side, Royall plopped down in a chair next to Dowell.

"Looks like the Commission's getting ready to decide against us," Royall said. "I think we should start preparing the application to the Supreme Court."

"The quickest way to get before the Court is through action by a Justice, but they're in summer recess," Dowell advised his colleague. Although he had taken a position of conscience in open court, he was still determined to give every assistance to his colleague. "Do you know if any of the Justices are in the area?"

"Justice Black," replied Royall. Searching through several phone directories, he finally found a way to contact him. After a brief conversation, Royall bolted for the door.

"Take over for the afternoon," Royall told Dowell. "I'm going to talk to him right now." Royall was already halfway out the door when he finished his sentence.

Royall's appeal to the Supreme Court was admittedly a last-ditch maneuver to spare his clients from the firing squad or scaffold—the two methods of execution customarily used for military cases. While it was a long shot, Royall believed he was right on the law.

Royall and his meager staff had been burning the candle at both ends, defending their clients before the commission by day and researching the law by night. Royall had concluded that fundamental principles of civil rights guaranteed even enemy aliens—and certainly two United States citizens—a jury trial in federal court and the right to challenge its deprivation. While he did not consider himself a constitutional scholar, the former *Harvard Law Review* editor firmly believed that seven centuries of Anglo-American jurisprudence supported his position.

At the heart of Royall's constitutional challenge was a basic legal principle: a criminal defendant's right to trial by jury. By the time the Constitution (1789) and Bill of Rights (1791) had been adopted, the institution of trial by jury was universally revered—its origins had been traced back to the Magna Carta in 1215.[1] By the seventeenth century, the jury, as the trier of evidence, had become an established safeguard for the criminally accused in England and colonial America.[2] The noted English legal historian Blackstone celebrated trial by jury, along with indictment by grand jury, as a "strong and twofold barrier . . . between the liberties of the people and the prerogative of the crown" because the charges must be proven by a unanimous vote of twelve of the defendant's peers "indifferently chosen and superior to all suspicion."[3]

The British tradition was guaranteed in the constitutions of the thirteen original states, the body of the United States Constitution, and the Sixth Amendment. As Supreme Court justice Joseph Story, a legendary legal scholar, noted a century before Franklin Delano Roosevelt was elected president, those who colonized America brought from England the cherished privilege of trial by jury "as their birthright and inheritance, as a part of that admirable common law, which had fenced round and interposed barriers on every side against the approaches of arbitrary power."[4]

From his own firsthand experience, Royall had seen the wisdom of entrusting to the people, as the conscience of the community, the conviction of the guilty and the protection of the innocent. In a democratic society founded on right and not might, the jury was the cornerstone of an independent judicial system essential to curbing an overzealous prosecutor. But was Royall's challenge a hollow formalism? After all, why would German saboteurs fare better in front of a jury of ordinary citizens than a panel of generals?

The truth of the matter was that Royall was hoping to secure federal court jurisdiction over the charges because there was no federal death penalty for what his men had done. Moreover, Royall thought that he would have a better chance of persuading a jury of laymen of mitigating circumstances surrounding how at least some of his clients had become enemy agents. In fact, Royall recalled a colonial jury's acquittal of the British soldiers charged with murdering civilians during the Boston Massacre of 1770.

The other elementary principle underlying his assault on President Roosevelt's usurpation of power was the right of any person detained by government officials to challenge the lawfulness of his confinement in federal court. The writ of habeas corpus—the Great Writ—was another fundamental constitutional right originating in England. This common-law remedy originated as a means for testing in the courts the validity of arrests and convictions at the hands of the government.[5] This privilege was so well accepted in colonial America—and so highly regarded as an indispensable protection against official abuse of power—that it was guaranteed in all state constitutions, and the United States Constitution prohibited its suspension "unless when in Cases of Rebellion or Invasion the public Safety may require it."[6]

The Great Writ had long been considered "the most important right in the Constitution" and "the best and only sufficient defense of personal freedom."[7] It was not merely a procedural remedy.[8] As the Supreme Court declared:

> Although in form the Great Writ is simply a mode of procedure, its history is inextricably intertwined with the growth of fundamental rights of personal liberty. For its function has been to provide a prompt and efficacious remedy for whatever society deems to be intolerable restraints. Its root principle is that in a civilized society, government must always be accountable to the judiciary for a man's imprisonment: if the imprisonment cannot be shown to conform with the fundamental requirements of law, the individual is entitled to his immediate release.[9]

Royall's research indicated that the president, without congressional approval, could not unilaterally suspend habeas corpus.[10] President Abraham Lincoln had suspended the privilege on his own order early in the Civil War. Even with the nation ravaged by civil war, his "coup" was widely criticized—including by Chief Justice Roger Taney, who found, in *Ex parte Merryman*, the president's action unlawful.[11] A chastened Lincoln then obtained congressional authorization for dispensing with the Great Writ.[12]

Roosevelt had neither sought nor received Congress' blessing in the case of the German saboteurs. The president had unilaterally decreed that the federal courts were off-limits to this class of enemy saboteurs. Even in time of war, this was an audacious power grab that shifted the balance of power from Congress to the president.

Royall had one exceptional Supreme Court precedent on his side. In the opening moments of the trial, he had cited *Ex parte Milligan*—the 1866 decision invalidating the imposition of martial law and suspension of the writ of habeas corpus in Indiana because the civilian courts in that jurisdiction were functioning.[13] Royall was particularly struck by the lifeline that *Ex parte Milligan* offered his despised clients: "The Constitution of the United States is a law for rulers and people, equally in war and peace, and covers with the shield of its protection all classes of men, at all times, and under all circumstances."[14]

Given that the country had not been invaded, the federal courts were open, and the duly constituted civilian government did not need the military's assistance to protect the public safety, Royall felt he was on solid legal ground asserting the primacy of the seventy-six-year-old decision in *Ex parte Milligan*. In lawyer's parlance, the case was "on all fours." Royall would soon learn whether the current Supreme Court would endorse its continuing validity—or dismiss it as a legal fossil born of vastly different times and exigencies, as Biddle insisted.

Royall walked to the front door of Justice Black's home and knocked on the door. Soon the door swung open.

"Justice Black, how are you?" asked Royall, who was never considered shy.[15]

"Colonel Royall, please come in," Hugo Black replied slowly in his soft rural Alabama tones.[16]

This could be Royall's lucky day. Roosevelt's first appointee, the fifty-six-year-old Black was widely regarded as one of the Supreme Court's staunchest champions of the Bill of Rights.

Royall immediately launched into the purpose of his visit. "I'm here to tell you that within a few days I'm probably going to bring you a petition for a writ of certiorari in the saboteur case," he announced. "You are the only Justice available in this area."

"You mean this case of these German spies?" Black asked coldly, a distinct edge in his voice.

"We don't call them spies, but I suppose that's the case you're talking about," Royall replied, taken aback by Black's evident hostility.

"I don't want to have anything to do with that case," Black responded matter-of-factly.

"Mr. Justice, you shock me," Royall replied, his steely eyes fixed on Black. As the stern-faced jurist opened his front door in a clear demand that the unwelcome visitor leave at once, Royall added, "That's all I can say to you." Black made no response, and Royall quietly left without another word being spoken.

Royall was stunned and deeply disappointed. Justice Black was liberal and especially solicitous of the poor, downtrodden, and unpopular, but lending aid or comfort to the defense of eight suspected German spies was obviously not his idea of justice. If Black did not want to get involved, who would?

As Royall made his way back to the Justice Department office, he pondered how to get the case before the Supreme Court quickly. He knew all too well that the commission might try to convict—and President Roosevelt execute—his clients before the Supreme Court could even decide whether to hear the case. His best option was to persuade some other justice to bring the case before the Court, but they were scattered all across the United States. His mentor, Justice Frankfurter, was in Massachusetts, but he could not reach him by phone. Time was rapidly running out.

The next morning, July 22, as Royall sat in the defense office, he happened to come across a *Washington Post* article mentioning that Justice Owen Roberts would be in attendance at former justice George Sutherland's funeral.

"That's it!" he exclaimed, startling his co-counsel.

"What?" Dowell asked.

"You're in charge this morning," Royall replied.

When Roberts returned to his chambers from the funeral, Royall told him all about the case and his brief visit with Justice Black. Roberts listened attentively and then said: "I think you've got something here that ought to be reviewed, but I won't take any action on it until I've talked with Justice Black."

"Thank you very much," Royall replied.

"I have a suggestion to make, that you meet me at my farm, which is west of Philadelphia, tomorrow morning, say at 11 o'clock, and I will have Justice Black there, if he will come. I suggest you notify Francis Biddle, so that he can be in Philadelphia, too," Roberts said thoughtfully.

"All right, sir, I'll do that," Royall gratefully replied, hoping his bad luck might be changing. He immediately headed straight to Biddle's office, right next to his own in the Justice Department building. Royall told Biddle of his conversation with Roberts.

"I want you to go with me, so you can explain your views," Royall insisted. "I also want you to join me in asking the commission to adjourn for a day, without giving any reason for it. I don't want to prejudice my case."

"I have no authority to do anything about it," Biddle replied. "You know what the Proclamation said."

"I know what the Proclamation said. You probably know what I wrote the President."

"I do . . . you're going ahead with it anyway?"

"It doesn't make any difference what happens. I'm going ahead with it," Royall replied without hesitation.

"Well . . . give me an hour, and I'll let you have an answer," Biddle said reluctantly.

"Well, if you see the President within the hour—"

"I didn't say I was going to see the President," Biddle testily shot back, cutting Royall off.

"No, you didn't say so . . . but that'll be fine," Royall said, not wanting to push his luck. He was fortunate to get even this concession out of Biddle.

Royall anxiously waited in his office for any word from Biddle. It seemed like an eternity. Finally, the telephone rang.

"I'll go tomorrow to Mr. Justice Roberts' farm," the attorney general informed Royall. "Is there anything else?"

"Yes, my second request is we want you to have us flown up to Philadelphia—and with you."

"I'm going on the train," Biddle replied.

"But we want to be flown up there," Royall persisted. "There are plenty of planes."

"Fine," Biddle said disgustedly, and the conversation was over almost as quickly as it began.

Even if Biddle supported Royall, an appeal to the institutionally conservative Supreme Court was hardly a sure thing. Review was discretionary, and the justices were never eager to take on politically charged controversies. As Royall had already seen with Justice Black, the civil rights of Nazi saboteurs were hardly a sympathetic cause.

An even more daunting obstacle was the fact that Royall was challenging the constitutional authority of a popular wartime president. Undoubtedly, public sentiment would run heavily against Royall for "bothering" the high court with such a trivial matter. Worse yet, FDR had appointed eight of the nine justices. In many instances, he enjoyed a close personal and political relationship with his appointees.

Chief Justice Harlan Fiske Stone, first appointed to the Supreme Court by President Calvin Coolidge in 1925, had been elevated to chief justice in 1941 by President Roosevelt. In his early years on the Court, the former Columbia Law School dean and attorney general who hired J. Edgar Hoover sided with the dissenters Louis Brandeis, Oliver Wendell Holmes, and later Benjamin Cardozo in opposing the conservative majority's repeated invalidation of state and federal legislation regulating economic affairs. Eventually, in the wake of FDR's plan in 1937 to increase the number of justices from nine to fifteen, thus allowing the president to pack the court, Stone's judicial restraint jurisprudence—giving deference to executive and legislative judgments in social and economic reforms—commanded a majority.[17]

When Chief Justice Charles Evans Hughes retired in June 1941, President Roosevelt appointed the Republican Stone. Like the earlier selection of Republican Henry Stimson as secretary of war, FDR's choice was "widely viewed as an attempt to emphasize bipartisan unity in the face of a rapidly advancing world war."[18] As chief justice, Stone had his hands full trying to reign in, and forge majorities with, the "wild horses"—independent thinkers Hugo Black, William O. Douglas, and Felix Frankfurter.

Owen Josephus Roberts, appointed by President Herbert Hoover in 1930 to replace Justice Edward T. Sanford, had an illustrious career as a trial lawyer, prosecuting Espionage Act violations and convicting former secretary of the interior Albert B. Fall of bribery in the Teapot Dome scandal. Roberts generally sided with the ultraconservative "Four Horsemen"—James Clark McReynolds, George Sutherland, Pierce Butler, and Willis Van Devanter—who consistently invalidated President Roosevelt's New Deal programs. Following FDR's overwhelming reelection in 1936 and his controversial proposal to appoint up to six new justices, Roberts helped resolve the great constitutional crisis of the 1930s when the Four Horsemen "flouted the nation's voters by vetoing much of Franklin Roosevelt's New Deal."[19] A month after Roosevelt announced his threat "to seize political control of the Court by appointing justices disposed to sustain his policies," Roberts joined with Chief Justice Hughes and the Supreme Court's three liberal justices.[20]

Contemporaries derisively dubbed Roberts' dramatic conversion to the New Deal as the "switch in time that saved nine" from Roosevelt's heavy-handed threat. As a jurist, Roberts was widely viewed as inconsistent, confused, and intellectually second-rate.[21] But one thing about Roberts was clear: he could read the election returns. He was also respected enough by President Roosevelt to be appointed to head the high-level investigation of the Pearl Harbor debacle—the panel on which Major General Frank McCoy also served.[22]

Hugo Lafayette Black, appointed by President Roosevelt in 1937, was a dyed-in-the-wool Southern Baptist from Alabama. While he served in the military during World War I, he never saw combat overseas. Elected to the U.S. Senate in 1927, he was a passionate New Deal disciple, sponsoring the Fair Labor Standards Act and supporting FDR's court-packing plan.[23]

When Justice Willis Van Devanter accepted the enticing retirement package for justices over seventy passed by Congress at the president's request, Black was Roosevelt's first appointment in the summer of 1937. No appointment could have goaded the conservatives who had killed Roosevelt's court-packing plan more than the "militantly liberal" Hugo Black.[24] The nomination hit a speed bump, however, when the news media reported Black's two-year membership in the Ku Klux Klan in the 1920s. *Time* magazine sarcastically wrote: "Hugo won't have to buy a robe, he can dye his white one black." Already confirmed, Black made a brief radio address admitting the allegation but stressing his withdrawal from the racist organization. The firestorm over the racist issue passed, and Black strongly supported desegregation in the South in later years.[25]

Black forged an early reputation as an absolutist on the First Amendment who recognized no exceptions for government interference. He likewise championed application of the basic guarantees of the Bill of Rights to the states through the due process clause of the Fourteenth Amendment. While he served as a county prosecutor early in his legal career, Black promoted constitutional principles of fairness in the prosecution of criminal defendants.[26] His jurisprudential credo was eloquently expressed in his 1940 opinion in *Chambers v. Florida*:

> Under our constitutional system, courts stand against any winds that blow as havens of refuge for those who might otherwise suffer because they are helpless, weak, outnumbered, or because they are non-conforming victims of prejudice and public excitement. . . . No higher duty, no more solemn responsibility, rests upon this Court, than that of translating into living law and maintaining this constitutional shield . . . for the benefit of every human being subject to our Constitution—of whatever race, creed or persuasion.[27]

Stanley Forman Reed, appointed by President Roosevelt in 1938 to replace Justice George Sutherland, was also an ardent New Dealer. The Kentucky native, who served as a lieutenant in army intelligence in World War I, had toiled as a lawyer for railroad and tobacco interests. Appointed by FDR as solicitor general in 1935 after a stint as a New Deal lawyer, Reed defended the president's economic programs for three tumultuous years before the "nine old men" who frustrated Roosevelt's legislative proposals to put America back to work. Reed argued New Deal cases "with a patient passion that caused him once to faint in the course of argument."[28]

With Reed on the Supreme Court, Roosevelt had a proven ally to support his legislative agenda. While an economic liberal, Reed was a social conservative on civil rights and civil liberties issues. Above all, he had an abiding confidence that government acted wisely and benevolently.[29]

Felix Frankfurter, appointed by President Roosevelt in 1938 when Justice Benjamin Cardozo died, had been one of FDR's closest confidants for a long time. The celebrated Harvard Law School professor had sent a steady stream of his best and brightest graduates to staff significant positions within the Roosevelt administration. Advising the president privately on numerous issues, Frankfurter helped draft such landmark New Deal legislation as the Securities Act of 1933 and the Securities Exchange Act of 1934. His instrumental role in crafting new laws prompted Justice Louis Brandeis to dub him "the most useful lawyer in America."[30]

Frankfurter's utility as a close Roosevelt advisor did not end with his Supreme Court appointment. The justice, Roosevelt, and the president's top cabinet officers maintained close political and social ties.[31] Ironically, Frankfurter both helped recruit Royall to the War Department and gave Roosevelt pivotal advice on the structuring of the military commission trying the German saboteur case.

Justice Frankfurter generally supported government economic legislation based on his aversion to conservative judicial activism. Yet he also opposed liberal judicial activism, preferring what he considered a consistent philosophy of judicial restraint. Accordingly, in frequently opposing application of the Bill of Rights guarantees to invalidate state criminal procedures, he regularly aligned himself against "general libertarian views" and "writing [his] . . . private notions of policy into the Constitution."[32]

William Orville Douglas, appointed by President Roosevelt in 1941, replaced retiring Justice Louis Brandeis. A brilliant, progressive Columbia Law School and Yale Law School professor, the forty-year-old was one of the youngest appointees ever to sit on the Supreme Court. Brandeis remarked to his successor, who was less than half his age: "I wanted you to be here in my place."[33] Another devoted New Dealer, Douglas served as chairman of the Securities and Exchange Commission. Attracting FDR's interest, Douglas became one of the president's poker party pals and an informal economic advisor.

Douglas aligned himself with Black on most issues, particularly a passionate commitment to civil rights and individual liberties. Douglas was less interested, however, in developing a body of judicial opinions expressing a coherent legal philosophy. For years, the politically ambitious Douglas—unfulfilled by the cloistered life and deliberate pace of the Court, which passively reacted to events—aspired to the presidency and courted FDR and his advisors.[34]

Frank Murphy, appointed by President Roosevelt in 1940 to replace Justice Pierce Butler, had an illustrious public career. As an Irish

Catholic whose forebears had been hanged by the British for rebellion and jailed for promoting Irish nationalism, "[t]he blood of the outcast and the rebel ran in his veins."[35] In World War I, the army first lieutenant fought with the American Expeditionary Force in Europe.

Following distinguished stints as a criminal judge, Depression-era mayor of Detroit, and governor-general and high commissioner of the Philippines, Murphy was elected governor of Michigan in 1936, the same time FDR swept to his second-term victory. Following Murphy's defeat in his 1938 reelection bid, Roosevelt rewarded him with the post of attorney general. Disappointed that Henry L. Stimson was named secretary of war, Murphy later accepted Roosevelt's subsequent Supreme Court appointment.

A man of action, Murphy was an unrepentant champion of civil liberties and civil rights. In supporting the unpopular and unrepresented, he was willing to risk the ire of the Washington, D.C., political establishment and even his longtime ally Roosevelt. With the outbreak of World War II, Murphy relentlessly sought to reenlist in the army. In the summer of 1942, he swapped his judicial robe for an army uniform, serving as a lieutenant colonel at Fort Benning in Georgia.

James Francis Byrnes, appointed by President Roosevelt in 1941, replaced retiring justice James Clark McReynolds. He was descended from John Rutledge, one of the Supreme Court's first justices, appointed by President George Washington. Never having attended law school, he apprenticed by reading law with a local Charleston judge, eventually earning admission to the South Carolina bar.

After fourteen years in the House, Byrnes was elected to the Senate in his second attempt. His unwavering loyalty to FDR's New Deal earned him the title of "the senator from the White House." The winds of war also made him a staunch advocate of Roosevelt's foreign policy and rearmament efforts.

Byrnes took his seat on the Court in mid-June 1941. Writing sixteen opinions for the majority in the first Supreme Court term after his appointment, he spent a lot of his time "consumed with [the] president's business."[36] His one memorable opinion for the Court struck down an "anti-Okie" law that prohibited bringing indigents into California.[37]

Robert Houghwout Jackson, President Roosevelt's eighth appointment, filled the seat of Justice Stone, whom FDR nominated to replace Chief Justice Charles Evan Hughes when he resigned in mid-1941. Raised in western New York, Jackson was the last Supreme Court justice to get his legal education by reading law. He had served as a personal advisor when Roosevelt was governor of New York.

Like so many of his fellow justices, Jackson joined the Roosevelt administration early in the New Deal. His initial claim to fame was nailing former secretary of the treasury Andrew Mellon for almost half a million dollars in back taxes. Following several high-level Justice Department posts, Jackson was named by FDR as solicitor general in 1938. He was so impressive as an advocate that Justice Brandeis urged that Jackson be named solicitor general for life.[38] Instead, Roosevelt appointed him attorney general in 1940.

Philosophically, Jackson was aligned with Frankfurter as a staunch supporter of national power and judicial restraint. A world at war made him increasingly restless to serve his country. The day after Pearl Harbor, he chafed at sitting in the serene comfort of the Supreme Court hearing a case about taxation of country club green fees.[39]

It would be an understatement to say that the deck was stacked against Royall. By any definition, this was the "Roosevelt Court."[40] Eight of the nine justices owed their current positions to Roosevelt, and all nine were philosophically in tune with the president on numerous issues. The nation was fighting for its survival, and the justices were eager to support the war effort. They were all patriotic, many were veterans, and one was actually an active army officer.

But the close and often clandestine relationships between the president and certain members of the Court were not only inappropriate; they also had the odor of unconstitutionality since the executive and judicial branches were supposed to be separate. Unfortunately, such troubling relationships or affinities—particularly Frankfurter's intimate involvement in the German saboteurs' case from the very beginning—were more common in times of crisis and would certainly play a significant role in the resolution of Royall's appeal. This lowering of the wall of separation between the judicial and executive powers would cast a long shadow on the legitimacy of any Supreme Court rulings on President Roosevelt's authority and future challenges to President Roosevelt's wartime powers—especially Japanese American internment.

* * *

The next morning, July 23, Royall, Dowell, Biddle, and Cramer all boarded an army plane and headed to Philadelphia. They were met at the airport by FBI agents who escorted them to Justice Roberts' farm in Chester Springs. Justice Black, who had arrived in Philadelphia by train the night before, was also present.

Playing the role of gracious host, Justice Roberts set out cheese, crackers, and milk for his guests. Soon the informal gathering took up the serious topic of the saboteur case before the military commission. Royall and Dowell made a brief presentation of the case to Roberts and Black, followed by Biddle, who, surprisingly enough, supported the Supreme Court test. After Biddle, Justice Black spoke openly about his opposition to the justices' taking the controversial case.

At this point, the two justices excused themselves to discuss the matter privately. While the lawyers took a peaceful stroll around the farm, Justice Roberts succeeded in contacting and discussing the matter with all but two justices by telephone. Justice Douglas was in the mountains out west, and Justice Murphy's location was unknown since he had joined the army.

When the lawyers returned from their stroll, the justices had reached a decision. Justice Roberts looked at Royall and said simply: "The Supreme Court will meet and hear this case."

A jubilant Royall had won a key round in a historic battle, but the hard work had only just begun. He now had to backtrack and file habeas corpus petitions in the district court as well as in the court of appeals and then have them denied in a timely fashion. This procedural exercise was imperative. Because the Supreme Court's jurisdiction here was appellate and not original, a case had to originate in the lower courts before it could be heard by the high court.

Immediately after returning from Philadelphia, Royall began the process of applying to the federal courts. His first stop was the district court of Washington, D.C.[41] Royall filed seven petitions for writs of habeas corpus before Judge James W. Morris. Royall and Biddle both made short appearances in a secret hearing to argue their sides, but Royall did not put forth much of an effort. To ensure that the applications were promptly denied, he readily conceded that the petitioners had come to the United States with the mission of sabotage. Making a strong case before a lower court was useless. The legal and moral authority of the Supreme Court was needed for any possible success.

Judge Morris promptly rejected the petitions in a terse order:

> In view of this statement of fact [by counsel], it seems clear that the petitioner comes within the category of subjects, citizens or residents of a nation at war with the United States, who by proclamation of the President . . . are not privileged to seek any remedy or maintain any proceedings in the courts of the United States.[42]

Royall had now received the rejection he desperately needed.

Late in the afternoon of July 27, the clerk of the Supreme Court read a brief announcement from the chief justice that the Court would take up the German saboteurs' case on Wednesday, July 29.[43] This was a sensational development. "[T]he colonels struck a bold, desperate blow on their clients' behalf," the *Washington Post* reported, "challenging the authority of their Commander-in-Chief."[44] Royall had breathed momentary hope into a hopeless cause.[45]

The public reaction to the electrifying news was swift and mostly negative.[46] Congressmen complained that the military trial had already taken too long. The *Los Angeles Times* condemned dragging the Supreme Court into "this wartime military matter." The *Detroit Free Press* was less delicate: "Realism calls for a stone wall and a firing squad, and not a lot of holier-than-thou eyewash about extending the protection of civil rights to a group that came among us to blast, burn, and kill." Even the Communist *Daily Worker* decried this "unprecedented action" as "in itself a victory for the enemies of America."[47]

A few voices applauded this extraordinary moment in history. Arthur Krock of the *New York Times*, who had supported a secret military trial, praised the Supreme Court's intervention as "a fine service to democracy." The *Washington Post* also cheered Supreme Court review as demonstrating to the world that "here in this citadel of liberty law and justice still function"—even for enemy saboteurs.[48]

In anxious war times, defying one's commander in chief was clearly dangerous. Royall was personally attacked for being unpatriotic in defending the Nazis so vigorously.[49] In his home state, his popularity plummeted. The *Charlotte News* vilified Royall as "a braying ass," suggesting that he be "thrown in with the accused and made to stand trial himself."[50] Royall received hate mail, and even a friend advised him to "remain in Washington when the war is over."

While they were working under severe time constraints, the lawyers for both sides filed briefs in excess of 180 pages on the morning of July 29, the first day of argument. In essence, the defense's five arguments boiled down to their right to file a habeas corpus petition because the president alone could not suspend the Great Writ. The president's proclamation and the establishment of the military commission were unconstitutional because the tribunal lacked jurisdiction over the charges and the prisoners, the petitioners were being deprived of important civil rights, and the accused were entitled to a civil trial under *Ex parte Milligan* since the courts were open and functioning.

For the petitioners, the case presented "a real test of our Democratic form of Government and its judicial system." The courts were always available to citizens and aliens alike to protect precious constitutional and legal rights, except in rare situations not present in the America of 1942. Without an insurrection, armed rebellion, or actual and present invasion, a military substitute for the civil authority was not necessary to preserve the safety of the army and society. The Constitution— guaranteeing the right to indictment by a grand jury and trial by jury in a civil court—must reign supreme "equally in war and peace," as the Supreme Court held in *Ex parte Milligan.*

> It is trite but true to say that the soundness of any system of govern-
> ment proves itself in the hard cases where there is an element of pub-
> lic clamor. Such circumstances test the real ability of a government
> and its judicial system to protect the rights of an unpopular minority.[51]

In a hard-hitting, unapologetic counterattack, the government's brief contended that habeas corpus was not available in time of war to armed enemy invaders who "are paid agents, acting for and under the orders of the German Reich"; *Ex parte Milligan* did not apply to this case because Milligan had never worn an enemy uniform or crossed lines in a theater of operations; this was a total war where the theaters of operations were inherently different from those in the Civil War; the military commission had jurisdiction by a grant of authority from Congress to try violations of the law of war and the Articles of War;

and the president, as commander in chief, had the constitutional power to alter the customary procedural safeguards in a court-martial.[52]

At the heart of the government's argument was an unvarnished appeal to sanctioning the use of the legal process as a means of terrorizing the enemy. Military tribunals—which were "not part of the recognized judicial system"—were necessary "to deal swiftly and inexorably with spies and other war offenders" as opposed to "different, slower, and less certain punishment in the civil courts." After all, "in time of war the trial of spies and similar offenders is a form of combat."

In its conclusion, the prosecution pulled no punches about the stakes and what was expected of the justices in light of "the exigencies of a total and a global war."

> The United States and Nazi Germany are fighting a war to determine which of the two shall survive. This case is no more than a small skirmish, but on an important front. It is part of the business of war. . . . Military trial for the petitioners endangers no traditional civil liberty. These German soldiers have already been given rights which no American would receive in Germany, and now ask for "constitutional" privileges which we do not allow our own soldiers.[53]

The stage was set for an epic David and Goliath showdown in the Supreme Court.

Chapter 19

May It Please the Court

"Excuse me, Mr. Bittker. Mr. Cox would like to see you in his office at the Justice Department," the secretary informed Boris Bittker as he reported for work in Washington, D.C., on Tuesday, July 28. One year out of Yale Law School, Bittker had recently completed a clerkship for the prestigious United States Court of Appeals for the Second Circuit in New York. Bittker's boss was Oscar Cox, general counsel of the Lend-Lease Administration as well as assistant solicitor general. In the civilian-military power struggle a month earlier, Cox had been one of the few high-ranking Justice Department officials to support the military tribunal over a civilian trial. Now he was heavily involved in the prosecution of the eight Germans.

Bittker found it somewhat odd that Cox had summoned him because his boss was entirely focused on the trial of the saboteurs and was doing virtually no work on lend-lease matters. So why would he want to see Bittker, who had nothing to do with the trial? Upon reporting to Cox's office, Bittker was joined by Lloyd Cutler, a fellow Yale Law School alumnus who was also working on the German saboteurs' prosecution team.

"Boris," Cox began, "Colonel Royall, chief counsel for the saboteurs, needs some help with his habeas corpus applications to the Supreme Court. We'd like you to give him any assistance that he needs."

"Oh, well, sure," Bittker stammered, not sure why he was being given this assignment. The Justice Department had scores of experts who knew far more about the subject than Bittker—and Cox was well aware of that. In fact, it would be hard to find someone who knew less. It was a blatant setup.

"I'm sure that you are well versed in federal practice, having just completed that clerkship with Judge Frank on the court of appeals," Cox told him.

"Well, not rea—"

"Okay, then," Cox interrupted. "How about you head down to Colonel Royall's office and see what you can do for him?"

Bittker left the room quietly, not knowing how to react. He wanted to tell Cox or Cutler that he hardly remembered anything about federal habeas corpus, and he was hardly an expert. Not knowing what else to do, he went directly to Colonel Royall's office.

"Mr. Bittker, thank you for coming by." Royall shook his new helper's hand and expressed his gratitude for Bittker's willingness to help him on such short notice. "My prewar law practice in North Carolina seldom took cases into the federal courts," Royall said. "The help of an expert of your caliber is the best news I've received in days."

Cox had pulled a fast one on Royall, who had no clue that his "expert" was a rookie one year out of law school.

"I'm applying to the Supreme Court for writs of habeas corpus," Royall calmly explained. "I'm relying on the Court's power to issue extraordinary writs such as those issued in the Civil War cases."

Bittker sat there mute. Royall might as well have been speaking to him in German.

"My brief is being shepherded through the Government Printing Office, so I don't have a copy for you to read. I'll be focusing on my oral argument for tomorrow's hearing from now on, so I won't be around for any questions." Royall made it clear that time was of the essence. "What I need you to do is find a reference to the extraordinary writs power in the United States Code and get it to me as soon as possible," he said. "Basically, I want to find a statute that permits me to skip the court of appeals, as I'm doing."

As a Harvard Law School graduate, Royall recalled the tale of the trembling student arguing an unsupported point against Justice Frankfurter, only to have Frankfurter inquire: "Counselor, how did you get here?" One version of the story had the student responding, "By train, Your Honor," while the other version had the student embarrassingly silent. Royall wanted to be as thoroughly prepared as possible when he went before Frankfurter, who would almost certainly pose very tough questions. He did not want to humiliate himself in front of his former professor.

"Thanks so much for your willingness to help," Royall said, concluding their brief meeting. "I know it's not the popular thing to do right now. Hope to hear from you tomorrow."

Bittker stood and shook hands with the colonel, and the two men parted company. Royall was pleased to have an "expert" on his side, while Bittker was terrified at the thought of coming up empty for a man who had no one else to help him. He didn't have the heart to confess to Royall that he was even less conversant with the matter at issue than the colonel.

Not quite knowing what else to do, Boris went immediately to the Justice Department Library and worked late into Tuesday night. The opening arguments would start at noon the next day, and Boris knew he had to find something to help Royall present a strong jurisdictional argument before the Supreme Court. At the conclusion of his research, at nearly 2 a.m., Boris summarized his findings in a memo. Not knowing how else to contact Royall, he left it in Cox's office with a request that it be forwarded to Royall as soon as possible. There was nothing more for Boris to do except wait for the start of the oral arguments.[1]

As the day for the Supreme Court challenge finally arrived, the media circus reached new heights. On the morning of Wednesday, July 29, newspapers all over the country ran articles and editorials describing the events to come. By the time Royall and Dowell arrived at the Supreme Court, the press seemed to have mellowed, now understanding that the lawyers were doing their sworn duty.

This momentous appeal was not for the sake of German spies, the *Washington Post* noted, "but for the American ideal of justice under law."[2] "The case utterly transcends that of providing justice for the Nazi prisoners," Walter Karig of the Newark, New Jersey, *Evening News* wrote. "They are merely guinea pigs in a great laboratory of jurisprudence."[3] The Supreme Court's public proceedings also had the salutary benefit, as one journalist noted, of "dispel[ling] the uneasiness of those citizens who have been troubled by the ultra-secret military trial of the eight alleged German saboteurs."[4]

The stakes were high. While Royall cared about seven lives hanging in the balance, Biddle sought to bolster a wartime president's power to stop inflation, allocate labor, and control industry by decree and without further congressional action. It was widely reported that the basis of the case came down to Biddle's prosecution team arguing Justice Oliver Wendell Holmes Jr.'s maxim that "[p]ublic danger warrants the substitution of executive process for judicial process."[5] Royall's position, the press predicted, was that "all alien enemies, no matter what their status, are entitled to enter the courts to protect their liberty."[6]

The media characterized the rare summer session as "historic" and "unprecedented" in Supreme Court annals. In fact, it was the first special term since the Civil War, except for an April 1920 session when the justices reconvened to decide the Texas-Oklahoma oil dispute that was costing a million dollars a day. Ironically, the extraordinary Civil War sitting—arising out of President Lincoln's suspension of the writ of habeas corpus in 1863 and prosecution of a civilian southern sympathizer—was to decide *Ex parte Milligan*.

The summer session was not the only unique aspect of the proceeding. On Saturday night, the FBI had reportedly been conducting a nationwide search for "three dangerous German saboteurs" who had been seen in nearby Takoma Park, Maryland.[7] The usual security at the Supreme Court was augmented by more than a dozen FBI agents. The three German saboteurs turned out to be a figment of someone's overactive imagination or a deliberate fabrication.

As the Supreme Court met in extraordinary session, accused spies and saboteurs captured by Germany were reportedly receiving far different treatment. "[F]iring squads were busy all over Europe [executing] Frenchmen, Netherlanders, Yugoslavs, Norwegians, Russians and others . . . at the whim of the conquerors."[8] No one had reason to believe that Americans captured by Axis forces and deemed "unlawful combatants" would not receive the same treatment. The enemy would observe the law of war's humanitarian rules when it suited their purposes; its rights and protections were denied to even uniformed combatants who clearly deserved proper treatment as prisoners of war. Japanese treatment of Allied prisoners was often savage and appalling; many of the responsible commanders would face trial for war crimes at the end of the war. Hitler was so infuriated by British commando raids that he ordered that any captured members of that elite force be immediately executed.

* * *

His black shoes spit-shined, a determined-looking Royall wore his army dress uniform and brimmed hat. The press noticed his wound stripe from World War I combat service in the Argonne as a first lieutenant in the 317th Field Artillery Brigade, 81st Infantry Division. Tall and youthful, Royall was the embodiment of an American officer waging another great battle for democracy. While his son was fighting for his country as a marine lieutenant, Royall's field of battle was "at the bar of the Supreme Court, where Royall pleaded for two days for the doctrine that America's Bill of Rights is a law for rulers as well as for people, in war as in peace, and covers with the shield of its protection all classes of men, at all times, under all circumstances."[9]

Notwithstanding what he had told the commission, Dowell walked into the Supreme Court building to the right of his partner. Carrying their papers and wearing his service medals, Dowell looked straight ahead as he passed the crowd of reporters, photographers, and spectators. He had helped Royall write their petition for writ of habeas corpus and their Supreme Court brief. In conscience, he could not abandon Royall as their against-all-odds struggle approached its climax. Dowell shared Royall's "determination from the start to give their 'clients' a complete and not a shadow-boxing defense."[10]

As Royall and Dowell approached the Supreme Court, photographers snapped their picture and reporters shouted questions at the two military lawyers. The American people finally got to see two men who had withstood the public outcry against them, persevering against death threats and calls for their imprisonment along with the German clients. To the surprise of many, the two colonels did not look like the scoundrels portrayed in the press. Instead, Americans came to understand that the two men represented precisely what the United States was fighting for—to uphold the rule of law and fight against injustice. The strong, confident demeanor of Colonel Royall and the determination seen on Colonel Dowell's face showed the American people that these soldiers were involved in this legal battle for only the right moral reasons.

The Supreme Court—"a grandiose temple of white marble . . . symboliz[ing] the power and independence of the judicial branch"—loomed over Royall and Dowell as they approached the front entrance on East Capitol Street.[11] Behind them stood the Capitol, home of the Senate and House of Representatives. They were also fighting for the constitutional prerogative of Congress, arguing that the president needed the legislative branch's acquiescence to suspend the writ of habeas corpus and employ a military tribunal instead of a civilian court.

Occupying one square block and set back from the street, the four-story Supreme Court building had been completed in 1935 at a cost of $9,646,000.[12] At last the Court had an appropriate home, after decades of holding its proceedings first in New York City and Philadelphia and then in everything from a tavern near the Capitol in 1809 to the basement of the latter building. Before it finally secured its own permanent home, the high court had occupied the Old Senate Chamber for seventy-five years.[13]

As Royall climbed the fifty-three steps to the second-floor entrance, he noticed the motto "Equal Justice Under Law" emblazoned over the columns on the triangular pediment.

How fitting, Royall thought as he gathered his final thoughts for the argument of a lifetime, set to begin in a few minutes. *That's why we are here.*

Above the inscription was a frieze of allegorical figures and symbols from American history celebrating the concept of ordered liberty. In the center sat the enthroned goddess of liberty, the scales of justice resting on her lap. Flanking her on either side was a Roman soldier, representing order and authority.

Which one will prevail? Royall wondered as he quickened his pace.

Passing through the double row of Corinthian columns and massive bronze doors, Royall walked down the center of the cold, lofty marble Great Hall toward the courtroom. On either side of him were the busts of every chief justice since 1790. FBI agents were everywhere. Security was so tight that even Hoover and Biddle had to show their government passes.

Royall entered the high-ceilinged courtroom and found it filled to its three-hundred-person capacity. Like anyone else who rarely had occasion to be present during a session of the Court, Royall was impressed with the sheer grandeur of the chamber—the ineffable majesty of this uniquely American house of justice. Towering over him were the massive marble columns and red velvet hangings behind the bench and decorative friezes carved on the upper walls with scenes and personalities representing themes of law and justice. Even lawyers who argued before the Court on a regular basis felt some degree of awe.

Of the three coequal branches of the federal government, the Supreme Court is the only one that "depends for much of its immense influence on its prestige as a semi-sacred institution and preserves that prestige with the trappings and show of superficial dignity. . . . Under our otherwise democratic form of government, only [the Supreme Court] . . . uses ceremony and secrecy, robes and ritual, as instruments of its *official* policy, as wellsprings of its power."[14]

The mystique of the Supreme Court—nourished by the august scale and mighty splendor of its building—was that the justices were "a group of detached sages . . . impervious to popular pressures."[15] Royall knew better. The nine justices were "not judicial automatons but highly human and hence inevitably political men."[16] It was a myth that men who got to the Court because of their political connections and philosophy magically became high priests totally divorced from politics.[17] The Supreme Court was a political institution.[18] What Royall did not know, however, was that the fix was in on the German saboteurs' case.

On one side of the lectern that stood before the raised platform where the justices sat were Biddle, Cramer, and their team, while on the other side sat Dowell, nervously fidgeting with the goose quill pen in front of him. Behind counsel table, Hoover and a hundred members of the Supreme Court bar sat on straight-backed chairs with padded leather seats. The rest of the two hundred people in attendance were reporters, justices' wives, friends of the advocates, and members of the public. Some spectators, hoping to catch a glimpse of the German saboteurs, were disappointed to learn that the defendants would not be appearing before the Court.

Boris Bittker sat alone in the audience. He had arrived just as the argument began and was unable to speak with Royall. Little did he know that Cox had never transmitted to Royall his memo on the thorny jurisdictional question. (It was just another example of things slipping through the cracks in the rushed and frantic atmosphere in which the defense was forced to function.) Today would be like every other day for Royall over the past tumultuous month—he would be all alone.

In contrast to its august public image of impartiality, the Supreme Court that convened on July 29 was anything but impartial and independent, aloof from the protagonists, or even uninvolved with the issues to be adjudicated. Several of the justices were caught in a tangled web of conflicts of interest that should have disqualified them from sitting on the case. If the case was historically significant, as the New York *Daily News* wrote, because "it pits the authority of the Supreme Court directly against that of the President," it was not a fair fight.[19]

Justice Frank Murphy, a military reserve officer, was on active army duty. Justice Felix Frankfurter, a regular Roosevelt administration confidant on public policy matters, had actually advised Stimson to try the Nazis by a military commission. Indeed, over dinner before the president issued his proclamation, Frankfurter recommended to Stimson that the commission should be entirely military in composition.[20] Frankfurter went even further, secretly advising the president's men on how to structure the military tribunal in anticipation of a Supreme Court challenge.[21]

Justice James F. Byrnes "had been serving as a de facto member of the Roosevelt Administration for the previous seven months, working closely with Roosevelt and Biddle on the war effort."[22] Byrnes offered advice on a range of issues, including draft executive orders, war powers legislation, and other presidential initiatives. On a nearly full-time basis, he was so intimately involved in the day-to-day functioning of the government that he arranged for introduction—and lobbied legislative leaders for support—of administration bills.[23]

Behind the curtain separating the private and public chambers of the courtroom, the justices chatted among themselves as they prepared to open the special summer session. Several private communications from the Roosevelt administration to the justices had made it clear that the president expected unanimous approval of his war powers. Justice Owen Roberts reported to his colleagues that Biddle had expressed "concerns that Roosevelt would execute the Germans no matter what the Court did." Pausing for effect, Roberts added: "I believe FDR intends to have all eight men shot if we do not acknowledge his authority."[24]

"That would be a dreadful thing," came the understated reply of Chief Justice Harlan Fiske Stone.[25] What went unsaid at this critical time, however, spoke volumes. At least three of the justices had disqualifying conflicts, either in the actual development of the case, advising the Roosevelt administration, or serving in the military.[26]

The scene in and of itself was extraordinary. One-sided communications with the justices were ethically prohibited. But it seemed as though all the normal peacetime rules were being swept aside in the name of military necessity. This kind of presidential pressure on the Supreme Court made a mockery of impartial justice.

Royall was walking into a set trap, and everyone knew it except him.

* * *

The marshal sitting to the right of the bench called the proceedings to order promptly at noon.

"Oyez, oyez, oyez," he announced in Old French, meaning "hear, hear, hear." "God save the United States and this honorable Court," he added, rapping his gavel.

From behind the long, elevated mahogany justices' bench along the back wall, through the marble columns and heavy red curtains, the justices solemnly entered and proceeded to their high-backed leather swivel chairs.

Only seven black-robed jurists took the bench. Justice William O. Douglas was still en route to Washington, D.C., by train from Oregon. At the last minute, Justice Murphy had disqualified himself because he was on active duty. The colonel did take leave from the army, however, and, wearing his officer's uniform, he eavesdropped on the entire proceedings from a chair placed behind the back curtain of the courtroom.

"The court is now sitting," the court clerk cried out.[27] Royall took a deep breath to calm himself. This was the biggest case of his life, and he knew he had to be at the top of his game. Any slipup would be immediately pounced on, especially by Justice Frankfurter. The former law professor's keen mind could unravel the most complex legal argument and turn it into a mortifying defeat for any advocate who challenged him.

"The Court has ordered that it convene in Special Term in order that certain applications might be presented to the court, in open court, and argument be heard in respect thereto," Chief Justice Stone began.[28] "Mr. Justice Douglas is in the West and is on his way to attend, but he has not yet been able to arrive. He will be vouched in and participate in the decision of the Court.

"Mr. Attorney General, from the papers filed, we are aware that this proceeding is brought to contest the validity of the detention of certain persons now being tried by a military commission. I am informed that my son, who is an officer in the Army, was assigned to participate in the defense. Of course, if that fact were regarded as ground for my not participating in the case, I should at once disqualify myself. In order that I may be advised and that the Court may be advised whether he has participated in this proceeding and what his connection with the case is, I will ask you, if you are so advised, to state, so that it may become of record," Chief Justice Stone inquired.

At the point, Attorney General Biddle explained to the Court that Major Lauson Stone, the chief justice's son, had participated in the defense case before the military commission under orders, but had not in any way participated in their preparations for the Supreme Court. Biddle and Royall agreed that it was not necessary for the chief justice to disqualify himself. Major Stone was a very young assistant lawyer assigned to help Royall and Dowell, and he had done nothing substantive in the courtroom.

As counsel for the petitioners, Royall argued first. Standing at the small rostrum between the two counsel tables, he faced Chief Justice Stone only a few feet away. On either side were three justices, the most junior on the far wings. Royall was struck by the intimacy of the setting, the pomp and ceremony giving way to an informal conversation between Court and counsel. It was "as direct, unpretentious and focused a discussion as can be found anywhere in Washington."[29]

"May it please the Court," Royall began. "On behalf of the petitioners . . . Colonel Cassius M. Dowell and I present to the Court and ask leave to file a petition for a writ of habeas corpus."[30] Royall then explained that Judge Morris had refused to permit the filing of the petition in the district court. "We therefore ask the consideration of this present writ in the appellate jurisdiction of the Supreme Court."

Just as Royall had expected, Justice Frankfurter immediately started to question the constitutionality of the petition. Frankfurter was going to make it clear that just because Biddle and Royall had made an agreement to come to the Supreme Court, that pact did not confer jurisdiction. They would have to prove their legal path.

"Will either you, Colonel Royall, or the Attorney General state briefly the grounds on which you claim this Court has jurisdiction, how it has such jurisdiction over an order to review Justice Morris' denial of the petition?" Frankfurter asked.[31]

In the audience, Boris Bittker squirmed in his seat as he listened attentively.

"The Court is familiar with the statute which provides that the Supreme Court may issue a writ of habeas corpus." Royall responded. "That statute must, of course, be construed consistently with the Constitution of the United States, which limits the jurisdiction of this Court to an appellate jurisdiction. To give the statute any meaning at all, therefore, it must be construed as being a method of appeal or a method of review. The ordinary methods of review are not included within the writ of habeas corpus. Therefore the ordinary procedure—"

An irritated Frankfurter cut Royall off in midsentence.

"Why do you say that?" Justice Frankfurter asked.

"Because a writ of habeas corpus is, in and of itself, a different type of writ from a writ of certiorari or any other method of review with which I am familiar," Royall replied, not backing down.

This sparked an intense debate between Frankfurter and Royall over whether any writ could skip the court of appeals. The dispute was never settled. Mercifully, Justice Jackson intervened to propose that the defense be allowed to file any necessary papers to obviate the difficult question of jurisdiction at a later time and that the oral arguments begin.

Colonel Royall immediately set out to make sure the Court understood he was there not to ask for a determination of innocence or guilt, but rather to request a decision on the military commission's jurisdiction. Royall's first hurdle was whether the country was in a state of martial law.

"Under the Constitution, the President, either with or without the authority of Congress, may declare martial law and enforce martial law?" Chief Justice Stone asked.

Royall had to concede this point, but when Stone insisted that Roosevelt's order established martial law throughout the country, Royall had to disagree. He said that martial law "ordinarily is a territorial matter and not a matter dependent upon the character or conduct of the individual."[32]

Justice Jackson sarcastically likened Royall's argument to "the case of a criminal whom you might shoot at in order to stop the commission of a crime; but when he has committed it, he has a right to a trial?"[33]

The justices jumped on Royall when he contended that prisoners caught not wearing their military uniforms were entitled to a civilian trial. Immediately, Justice Byrnes questioned Royall's logic.

"Your contention is that if the Führer and seven generals of the Army of the Reich should land from a submarine on the banks of the Potomac, having discarded their uniforms, they are entitled to every right you have discussed in the application for a writ of habeas corpus and to require an indictment by a grand jury under the Constitution?"

"My argument would have to carry that fact, and does," Royall replied firmly.

Questioned whether his position would also apply to spies, Royall responded that it would not "because there is a specific statute which deals with spies." Again, he was hammering away at his major theme: that President Roosevelt had unconstitutionally bypassed established federal criminal statutes.

Frankfurter summed up the point: "What you are saying is that that which Congress can take out of the constitutional provisions by statute, the President as Commander-in-Chief cannot take out of civil statute by military proclamation?"

"That is correct," Royall agreed, grateful for Frankfurter's lobbing a softball.[34]

Now it was time for Royall to defend his contention that the eastern seaboard of the United States was not a zone of military operations. Justice Frankfurter went back on the attack, trying to pin down Royall with a tough line of questioning.

"Cannot the enemy determine what the theater of operations is by being the aggressor?" Justice Frankfurter asked. "If a parachutist should come into this building or near this building, would this not be a theater of operations?"

"I think it would be, sir," Royall conceded, not seeing any wiggle room.

"Well, why was not this made a theater of operations by the landing of the U-boats?" Justice Frankfurter logically followed up.

"Of course, the U-boats did not land; but you mean the men from the U-boats?" Royall asked, already knowing the answer, but wanting to buy a few moments to think over his response.

"Yes, the area of the U-boat landing," Justice Frankfurter replied.

Royall now knew that he needed to change the focus of his argument. "They came unarmed. They came with explosives, of course. . . ." Royall paused as laughter could be heard throughout the courtroom. Calling trained saboteurs armed with explosives "unarmed" was obviously a stretch. "But they did not engage in any actual combat operations," he quickly added.

The argument now focused on whether coming ashore with explosives was an act of combat. Royall asserted that it was only an act of preparation, lacking intent, while the justices seemed to equate the act with combat itself, though unopposed.

"Yet you would say that that is outside of the conflict or theater of operations?" Justice Frankfurter pressed.

"I would, sir, because that is, at the most, a preparatory stage and not a stage of actual combat," Royall contended, holding his ground.

"It is not your contention that the President should wait until these explosives are set off before we do anything with these persons, whatever they are, invaders or what-not?" Justice Jackson asked pointedly.

After an exchange over whether the spying charge was valid, Royall argued that Congress had already passed legislation that dealt expressly with charges of sabotage and attempted sabotage. This, Royall contended, demonstrated that the men should be tried in a civilian court. The only problem with Royall's argument, Chief Justice Stone observed, was that the charges and their penalties as specified by Congress could not be imposed in a time of martial law. The debate quickly returned to whether President Roosevelt's July 2 decree dealing with the men enacted martial law.[35]

"We will take a recess now," Chief Justice Stone announced at two o'clock. Having argued for two hours straight, Royall was now afforded the luxury of a half-hour break before resuming his marathon presentation.

"You may proceed," Chief Justice Stone told Royall, marking the beginning of the afternoon session.

During the recess, Royall and Dowell agreed that the focus must be shifted entirely to deal with the question of presidential authority and the conflicts with congressional statutes raised by Roosevelt's decree.

"I have tried to cover in one way or another the questions of the authority of the President to deprive the petitioners here of their rights in civil courts, and I would like to go back . . . long enough to mention two things which I did not get an opportunity to mention," Royall began.

Royall then explained that the recent Trading with the Enemy Act enacted by Congress did not deprive enemy aliens of their rights to go into civil court, as the government had contended. Therefore, the president did not technically have the powers he had usurped.

"That is the point I want to raise," Chief Justice Stone stated. "Here are men who are not entitled, by all the recognized laws of war, to the privileges of men wearing uniforms and engaged in combat. Assuming they came in bearing arms and were prepared to use them, has the President constitutional authority to appoint a commission to try and condemn them and, in connection with that, to suspend the writ?"[36]

"We do not think, sir, that he has any constitutional authority to suspend the writ of habeas corpus in the absence of an express statute. The Congress is the only one that can authorize the suspension of the writ under the first Article [of the Constitution] and under the Fifth Amendment," Royall replied, believing his argument unassailable.

Royall then launched into a lengthy explanation that the prosecution in the case against the saboteurs had relied on the law of war, but no such formal body of law applicable to the federal, civil, or military courts actually existed. Royall believed that there was a "serious question as to whether there is any such offense as the violation of the Law of War."[37] The proper course of action therefore would be to rely on the Articles of War and other acts of Congress rather than try to figure out the correct meaning of a body of law that had never been officially written down. This would in effect negate the first charge against the saboteurs.

But Justice Frankfurter sharply disagreed, suggesting that there must be some sort of discretion at the president's disposal to enact a special tribunal.

"Of course, you have to conceive that he had some element of discretion there," Royall replied, "but I do not believe his discretion goes far enough to disregard the absence of an essential element where that absence affirmatively appears on the record."[38]

Royall now turned his attention to the acts of Congress in the hope that he could discredit the presidential proclamation. "I would say that Congress could authorize him to determine it [the military commission] on his own account, but until it has done so, he has not that right, because the Constitution gives that right to Congress. Article I relates to the legislative power," Royall explained.

Royall then read from the congressional enactments entitled "Articles of War":

The President may, by regulations, which he may modify from time to time, prescribe the procedure, including modes of proof, in cases before courts martial, courts of inquiry, military commissions, and other military tribunals, which regulations shall, in so far as he shall deem practicable, apply the rules of evidence generally recognized in the trial of criminal cases in the district courts of the United States. . . . Provided, that nothing contrary to or inconsistent with these Articles shall be so prescribed.[39]

"It is our contention that if [even] we concede that the President had a right to appoint a commission, and if we concede that these men have committed offenses which might be tried by a commission, yet the order in this case is invalid and the commission illegal, because there has been an express violation of that Congressional enactment. That violation has occurred in three general ways," Royall asserted, again feeling that he was basing his argument on an irrefutable point.

"In the first place, the order of the President itself is absolutely inconsistent with three provisions of the Articles of War.

"In the second place, while the Article of War gives the President the right to prescribe rules, he has sought to delegate a portion of that right to the Military Commission, contrary to the provisions of the statute.

"In the third place, the Military Commission, assuming to act under that delegation, has itself prescribed rules which are contrary to law."[40]

Royall then described how the commission did not allow peremptory challenges and permitted only one challenge for cause, as well as how it did not require a unanimous conviction for a death sentence, only a two-thirds margin.

"But regardless of that, if they did not impose the death sentence, it would be valid," Chief Justice Stone asserted.

"No, sir. Three-fourths is required for ten years' imprisonment, and the president's order says two-thirds," Royall stated, relying on the federal statute.

"You have to have a fraction in either case, and I do not know how you could have a fraction of an officer," Justice Jackson quipped, trying to discredit Royall.

"You could not unless you dismembered him," Chief Justice Stone chimed in with a grin.

"You raise the question at this stage of the proceeding, in any event. Suppose you have a unanimous decision against you, no matter what the rule is that is applicable?" Justice Frankfurter asked in a serious tone.

"I think that is a fair inquiry, but I believe there are two good answers to it," Royall replied.

"Then, you are twice as well off as I thought you were," Justice Jackson playfully retorted.[41]

Royall next outlined his contention that the Articles of War

Hanging of American spy and patriot Nathan Hale by British soldiers on September 22, 1776 (CORBIS)

Execution of four Abraham Lincoln conspirators who were sentenced to death by a military commission in July 1865 (LIBRARY OF CONGRESS)

President Abraham Lincoln, who used military commissions to prosecute thousands of anti-Union judges, journalists, and legislators (LIBRARY OF CONGRESS)

Chief Justice Roger B. Taney, author of *Ex parte Milligan* decision declaring unconstitutional President Lincoln's unilateral suspension of habeas corpus in 1861 (LIBRARY OF CONGRESS)

Attorney General Alexander M. Palmer (1919–21) who arrested thousands of antiwar dissidents, socialists, and radicals during and after World War I
(LIBRARY OF CONGRESS)

February 7, 1920, cartoon mocking repressive climate in the Palmer era
(LITERARY DIGEST/RED SCARE COLLECTION, NEWMAN LIBRARY, BARUCH COLLEGE, CUNY)

SEDITION BILLS

HONEST OPINION
FREE SPEECH
FREE PRESS

AS GAG-RULERS WOULD HAVE IT.
—Satterfield in the Jersey City *Journal.*

Saboteur Heinrich Harm Heinck in courtroom corridor; at the far right is U.S. Coast Guardsman John C. Cullen (NATIONAL ARCHIVES)

Military commissioners at hearing with President General Frank R. McCoy (second from left) (ROYALL PAPERS #4651, SOUTHERN HISTORICAL COLLECTION, THE LIBRARY OF THE UNIVERSITY OF NORTH CAROLINA AT CHAPEL HILL)

President Franklin D. Roosevelt on the *U.S.S. Houston* reviewing the Fleet, July 14, 1938, in San Francisco (FDR LIBRARY/AP/ WIDE WORLD PHOTO)

Winston Churchill (left) and President Franklin D. Roosevelt, seated during 1942 meeting of Pacific War Council at the White House (LIBRARY OF CONGRESS/AP/ WIDE WORLD PHOTOS)

Segregated American soldiers during World War II (LIBRARY OF CONGRESS)

1943 Supreme Court with Chief Justice Harlan F. Stone (center front) and Justice Felix Frankfurter (right front row) (CORBIS)

Numbers on unmarked graves of six German saboteurs in Potter's Field (WASHINGTONIA DIVISION, D.C. PUBLIC LIBRARY)

Saboteur Heinrich Harm Heinck in courtroom corridor; at the far right is U.S. Coast Guardsman John C. Cullen (NATIONAL ARCHIVES)

Military commissioners at hearing with President General Frank R. McCoy (second from left) (ROYALL PAPERS #4651, SOUTHERN HISTORICAL COLLECTION, THE LIBRARY OF THE UNIVERSITY OF NORTH CAROLINA AT CHAPEL HILL)

Colonel Cassius M. Dowell (left) and
Colonel Kenneth C. Royall arriving at
Supreme Court for oral argument
(AP/WIDE WORLD PHOTO)

Chief Prosecutor Attorney General
Francis B. Biddle (ROYALL PAPERS)

Chief Defense Counsel Colonel Kenneth C. Royall wearing his Brigadier General star awarded after the German saboteurs' trial (ROYALL PAPERS #4651, SOUTHERN HISTORICAL COLLECTION, THE LIBRARY OF THE UNIVERSITY OF NORTH CAROLINA AT CHAPEL HILL)

Boxes of explosives on the beach at Ponte Vedra, Florida (NATIONAL ARCHIVES)

Contents of explosives box: blasting caps, pen and pencil delay mechanisms, and other time-delay devices (NATIONAL ARCHIVES)

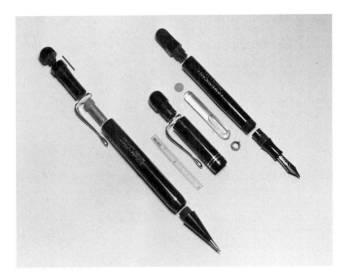

Pen and pencil set detonator disassembled, showing component parts (NATIONAL ARCHIVES)

Cartoon praising J. Edgar Hoover and his FBI
(NATIONAL ARCHIVES)

Cartoon showing FBI netting German saboteurs
(NATIONAL ARCHIVES)

Cartoon depicting FBI
rounding up spies and
saboteurs (NATIONAL ARCHIVES)

EIGHT GERMAN SABOTEURS

GEORGE JOHN DASCH

EDWARD KERLING

ERNEST PETER BURGER

HERBERT HANS HAUPT

RICHARD QUIRIN

WERNER THIEL

HEINRICH HARM HEINCK

HERMANN OTTO NEUBAUER

(NATIONAL ARCHIVES)

Newspaper headline of Japanese American relocation (FDR LIBRARY)

Housing in a Japanese American relocation camp at Manzanar (FDR LIBRARY)

Eleanor Roosevelt with Dillon S. Myer of the War Relocation Authority at the Japanese Internment Camp (FDR LIBRARY)

Attorney General Alexander M. Palmer (1919–21) who arrested thousands of antiwar dissidents, socialists, and radicals during and after World War I
(LIBRARY OF CONGRESS)

February 7, 1920, cartoon mocking repressive climate in the Palmer era
(LITERARY DIGEST/RED SCARE COLLECTION, NEWMAN LIBRARY, BARUCH COLLEGE, CUNY)

SEDITION BILLS

FREE PRESS
FREE SPEECH
HONEST OPINION

AS GAG-RULERS WOULD HAVE IT.

—Satterfield in the Jersey City *Journal*.

2004 Supreme Court that decided *Hamdi*, *Padilla*, and *Rasul* (CORBIS)

Taliban and al-Qaeda
detainees at Guantánamo
Bay (CORBIS)

Lieutenant Commander Charles Swift,
counsel for Salim Ahmed Hamdan, during
preliminary hearing at Guantánamo
Bay (CORBIS)

Frank Dunham, court-appointed counsel for Zacarias Moussaoui and Yaser Hamdi (CORBIS)

Yaser Esam Hamdi (AP/WIDE WORLD PHOTOS)

Shafiq Rasul, former Guantánamo Bay detainee whose Supreme Court case established habeas corpus jurisdiction to challenge unlawful military detention of so-called enemy combatants (CORBIS)

Donna Newman, court-appointed counsel for Jose Padilla (NINA BORMAN/AURORA)

Jose Padilla (AP/WIDE WORLD PHOTOS)

specifically stated that a unanimous vote was required for a death sentence conviction and a three-quarters vote for a sentence of over ten years. Since the commission was said to be under the Articles of War, it was expressly violating them and therefore illegal. Moreover, the transmission of the verdict directly to the president—without informing the defendants of the outcome or how the commission voted—was a violation of their rights. Another procedural defect with the commission was that the president had placed the judge advocate general in a prosecution role with the attorney general instead of his rightful place as an independent counsel to review the adequacy of the trial.

By this point, it was already four o'clock on the first day of oral argument. Royall was finally finishing up his opening argument amid intense grilling by the justices. By any objective measure, it was a tour de force of appellate advocacy. Royall's presentation—focused and thematic with occasional flashes of brilliance—was the epitome of fearless representation and a grace note in the symphony of American justice.

It was now Biddle's turn to take the hot seat.

"May it please the Court," the former solicitor general began, his white linen suit starkly contrasting with the khaki uniforms of the military lawyers and the justices' black robes. "The United States and the German Reich are now at war. That seems to be the essential fact on which this case turns and to which all of our arguments will be addressed." Whenever pressed by Justices as to why the commission was necessary, Biddle would simply return to the United States' wartime status for justification. His path was far less steep and perilous than Royall's.

"The great bulwarks of our civil liberties—and the writ of habeas corpus is one of the most important—were never intended to apply in favor of armed invaders sent here by the enemy in time of war. A jealous regard for this . . . writ has been and should be maintained to prevent prosecutions for political opinions and possible abuses of military power in periods of great stress and high emotional feeling," Biddle shrewdly conceded. No one would ever be able to claim that liberal Francis Biddle—who had stoutly resisted FDR's insistence on prosecuting antiwar agitators—was not a champion of civil liberties. "But no such inroads will result from denying the privilege to belligerent enemies charged with breaking through our lines to commit hostile acts."[42]

Biddle concentrated his argument primarily on the nettlesome case of *Ex parte Milligan*, knowing full well that Royall's justification for bringing the case to the Supreme Court was premised on that decision. Biddle claimed that the doctrines established by the Civil War landmark decision could "by no stretch of the imagination" apply to the saboteurs' case in World War II.

"Milligan never wore the uniform of the armed forces at war with the United States. The petitioners did. Milligan was a resident of Indiana. He did not cross through the lines and enter into a theater of operations. The petitioners did," Biddle explained. "Milligan was charged with the commission of military offenses at a time when invasions gave their slow forewarning months in advance."

"The mere absence of uniforms makes a difference?" Justice Reed asked.

"All the difference in the world; and that runs especially through all the law of war," Biddle responded.

This was by far Biddle's most compelling argument on the law and facts. Under well-settled principles of international law, the Germans had forfeited their lawful combatant status (and thereby entitlement to POW treatment) by adopting a civilian disguise. The law of war contemplated a military trial of their guilt and punishment.

Biddle next dealt with Royall's position that the commission itself was an illegal body. In perhaps his weakest argument of all, he quoted from the Alien Enemies Act of 1798, which was still in force 144 years later: "Whenever there is a declared war, and the President makes public proclamation of the event, all natives, citizens, denizens, or subjects of the hostile nation . . . shall be liable to be apprehended, restrained, secured and removed as alien enemies."[43]

Biddle concluded that this law—highly unpopular when enacted by the Federalists—formally permitted the president, with the consent of Congress, to close the civil courts to aliens such as these Germans. A legal stretch to say the least, Biddle's argument was based on infamous legislation enacted early in the nation's history as a response to hysteria and prejudice. The Alien Enemies Act was one of four statutes narrowly passed by the Federalist Congress as part of the Alien and Sedition Acts at the urging of President John Adams and in the war fever following the XYZ Affair.[44] The four acts were directed against aliens—especially the "wild Irish," who were notoriously pro-French and anti-British—and Republican editors.[45]

The other three repressive laws—the Naturalization Act, the Alien Act, and the Sedition Act—all expired by 1801.[46] The Alien Enemies Act, however, became a permanent statute and authorized the president in time of war to imprison or deport alien subjects of an enemy power whom he considered dangerous. That the liberal Biddle would reach back to this less than stellar chapter in the nation's history and invoke a discredited law of doubtful applicability to the petitioners that accorded no due process protections for its targets reflected his blind ambition to win for Roosevelt at any cost.

At this point, it was 6 p.m., marking one of the longest oral argument sessions in modern Supreme Court history. Though Biddle was not finished with his argument, the Court adjourned to reconvene at noon the following day.

As Royall and Dowell gathered up their belongings to leave the Supreme Court chamber, Royall motioned for Boris Bittker to speak to him. Bittker immediately went to Royall's side.

"I need you to take care of that extra 'piece of paper,'" Royall said quickly, referring to Justice Jackson's proposal that "an additional piece of paper" should be filed to alleviate the jurisdictional difficulties.

"I'll do that right away, sir," Bittker replied. Before Royall could even thank him, Boris Bittker was out of the chambers on his way to filing the petition in the Court of Appeals. But the petition would be slightly more troublesome that Bittker had thought.

Bittker's first step was to organize the paperwork for the appeal. The most serious problem was a logistical one: the filing needed to include a copy of the commission's transcript, which was unavailable, and even if it had been, it would not be handed out because it was a classified document. Bittker had to reach Oscar Cox and Lloyd Cutler to correct this problem, which he was not able to do until shortly before the Court was supposed to reconvene.

In that final hour, Bittker had to draft another pleading—this time a petition for a writ of certiorari for the Supreme Court to bring the case up from the Court of Appeals. This would have been a challenging assignment for a veteran appellate advocate, much less a rookie. At last, Bittker finalized all the papers as the Court was about to commence the second day of oral argument. In a real sense, "the Court's jurisdiction caught up with the Court just at the finish line."[47]

* * *

At noon on Thursday, July 30, the justices (including Justice Douglas) once again proceeded into the Supreme Court chamber, this time with far less fanfare than the previous day. While the house had been packed the first day, attendance was sparse.

"Mr. Attorney General, you may proceed," Chief Justice Stone announced.

Biddle wasted no time launching a frontal assault to discredit Royall's crucial *Milligan* case, asserting: "I think that the case of *Ex parte Milligan* is very bad law and that its effect not only on the courts but on the Army is harmful. I hope very definitely that even should you decide that the proclamation stands in the way of further action, you may think it advisable to consider whether now you shall not, at least, overrule that portion of the opinion of the majority in *Ex parte Milligan* which says that where civil courts are sitting under the circumstances in the *Milligan* case, there can be no trial by military commission."

It was classic overstatement by the savvy veteran appellate advocate. His exaggeration did not go unchallenged for very long. Justice Jackson reminded Biddle that during the previous day's argument, he had asserted that *Milligan* had no bearing whatsoever on the current case.

"You can satisfy all the requirements of this case without touching a hair of the *Milligan* case," Biddle replied, "but this petition would not have been in this Court except for the *Milligan* case."[48]

"You want to touch the head as well as the hair?" Justice Frankfurter asked, a mischievous twinkle in his eye.

A smiling Biddle simply replied: "Yes." Of course, Frankfurter and Biddle had already discussed *Milligan* and how to distinguish the case in their private strategy discussions before the military commission was even constituted.

Biddle then addressed Royall's claims about the Articles of War, but he could not resist wandering back to take another shot at the *Milligan* case. Biddle's final exclamation point was a quotable sound bite: "[T]he Commander-in-Chief, in time of war and to repel an invasion, is not bound by a statute."

Royall aimed his rebuttal directly at the technical questions raised by the Court about Articles of War 46 and 50½. He was quickly derailed, however. The justices bombarded him with penetrating questions about the military zone of operations.

"If they came within the theater of war for the purpose of committing sabotage—if that was the fact—would you say they were subject to a military commission?" Justice Reed inquired.

"No, sir; we would not concede so unless you overruled *Ex parte Milligan*. We would not say so if the civil courts were functioning in the area," Royall responded, quick to point out the similarity between the current case and *Milligan*.

"Even though it was a theater of war?" Justice Reed pressed on.

"Was there a theater of war in the case of *Ex parte Milligan*?" Chief Justice Stone asked.

Royall responded: "No, there was not; but I think the principle of that case—"

Justice Reed interrupted. "So, even if it was a theater of war, the purpose of sabotage is distinct from—"

Royall in turn interrupted the justice. "If the purpose was to commit an act of sabotage outside a theater of war, I would say no."

Later, Royall would explain that "if they invaded the coast with a view to using those explosives immediately in connection with a military campaign or operation, I think it would. Of course, Article 81 is broad enough by its language to cover a very wide range, but it must be construed in connection with the constitutional provisions."[49]

"I still do not quite get your distinction there," Justice Black commented. "What about the planes that fly over foreign countries and drop bombs and destroy property far removed from the scene of battle?"

"If it was a military plane, that is generally accepted as a means of fighting or of combat," Royall replied.

"A submarine, too," Justice Black shot back, trying to equate the two events.

"A submarine is, but these submarines in this case did not do anything but transport," Royall noted.

"But all the plane does is transport a bomb," Justice Black retorted.

"Yes, but the submarines just transported men. A plane would be an instrument by which bombs immediately would be put into operation. The submarine transported men so that in the future they could put something into operation," patiently explained Royall, who was tired of playing games with Justice Black.

"Your distinction is one of time?" Justice Black asked again.

"Well, there has got to be a line drawn somewhere on everything,"

Royall responded, wanting to make one of his most salient points. "And the question is this: if you take the theory that everything that was done that might aid the enemy makes it a theater of operations, you reduce the thing to an absurdity. If that were true, a strike in a war plant could be tried by a military commission sitting in judgment over the strikers, if there was any pretense that they did it in violation of any law with any ulterior intent."

Royall was pressing a fundamental point of constitutional law. Judges were frequently called upon to draw lines—to make reasoned distinctions based on common sense. The core problem with Biddle's argument was the lack of any apparent limitation on the elastic notion of "a theater of operations." If the justices accepted Biddle's contention, *Ex parte Milligan* offered no assistance to the German saboteurs.

Royall next debated with several justices over the effects of a zone of operations as well as the difference between a citizen caught in such a zone and a foreigner found there. Soon, the debate was over, and Royall outlined his case one more time in his closing remarks. It was his last, best chance as counsel for the damned.

"Suggestion was made by the Attorney General in his opening re-marks that we are fighting a war here. We realize that. We also realize that the Constitution is not made for peace alone, that it is made for war as well as peace. It is not merely for fair weather. The real test of its power and authority—the real test of its strength to protect the minority—arises only when it has to be construed in times of stress."

Royall paused at this point, and a tense silence prevailed in the courtroom. You could hear a pin drop in the cavernous chamber.[50] Re-gardless of their feelings about the merits of his argument, the justices were impressed by his sincerity and eloquence as he championed the cause of his unpopular clients. It was a bright, shining moment in the noble tradition of championing the rights of the underdog in a demo-cratic society in troubled times.

"Thank you," Royall concluded, his last-ditch effort to spare the lives of the German saboteurs completed.[51]

No one who was there that day would ever forget the image of an army colonel in uniform standing at ramrod attention in the Supreme Court chambers, fulfilling his duty as a lawyer and honoring his coun-try at the same time by vigorously defending Nazi terrorists. Patrio-tism takes many forms. That day, in that hallowed place, Kenneth Claiborne Royall was an American patriot.

"The Court stands adjourned until twelve noon tomorrow," Chief Justice Stone announced. With one swift smack of the gavel, nearly nine hours of argument to save the terrorists' lives was finished. The justices processed out of the room, and all Royall could do now was wait.

Chapter 20

Total Wipeout

On Friday, July 31, Room 5235 was once again bustling as the members of the commission, prosecution and defense teams, and attendants took their seats. Guards once more escorted the defendants to their seats, in alphabetical order, behind their defense counsel. Because the trial had been adjourned to allow for the Supreme Court challenge, the men had been confined to their cells for the past three days.

It was time for the closing arguments—a process that could consume a day or more. The defendants knew that a decision would be rendered very shortly after the arguments finished, and that once President Roosevelt reviewed and confirmed the verdicts and sentences, the punishments would be swift and severe. If death was their fate, they surely had only a few days to live.

The judge advocate general spoke first for the prosecution.

"Members of the Commission: This has been a most unusual case," General Cramer began, in one of the great understatements of the century. He then mentioned how unusual it was for eight defendants to be on trial in one case and to have the confessions made by the defendants constitute the bulk of the prosecution's evidence. "I will make it unusual in one other sense . . . my opening statement will be very brief," Cramer promised in a rare attempt at humor.[1]

Cramer now laid out the basic facts of the government's airtight case: the accused had lived in America for varying periods of time, went back to Germany, were recruited for a sabotage mission, and trained at a school for the purpose of sabotage.

"The prosecution has shown that they came over here in two submarines, through a theater of operations, through the Atlantic Ocean, which we all know at the present time is a theater of operations at sea, where ships are being sunk, frequently, 5 and 10 miles off the shores of the United States," Cramer stated, his voice slightly rising for emphasis.

"They came and landed at night, in the darkness of night, on our shores at Long Island and Florida, through our naval sea defenses.

"We have shown that in that school they were taught the various places that should be particularly taken care of and sabotaged, like bridges and aluminum plants, and how to get at them. We have shown that since they have been here they have had communication between themselves in aid of this whole conspiracy," Cramer noted. Listing the charges against the defendants, he explained how the specifications of each charge and the unrebutted evidence squarely applied to the prisoners.

"The prosecution submits upon that evidence that we have made out a case for which we ask on each of these charges and specifications a finding of guilt and a sentence in these cases of death," Cramer demanded.

In a workmanlike presentation devoid of any rhetorical flourishes, Cramer had sketched the basic architecture of the prosecution's case without going into great detail. But the government's strategy was not to close this case with one argument. Instead, they would listen to Royall's points in defense and reply to them in their rebuttal statement.

Three decades of training and countless trials had prepared Royall for the most important argument of his career. He had one goal: to save as many of his clients' lives as possible. An acquittal before this military tribunal was unthinkable. Saving any of their lives would be a miracle.

A resort to sympathy would be unpersuasive, if not counterproductive. Somehow he had to find some theme, some appeal to logic, that would resonate with seven tough-minded generals. As soon as he began arguing, Royall once again displayed his formidable intelligence and ability to respond at a moment's notice to anything the prosecution argued.

"May it please the Commission, the function of an opening statement—and, of course, the method of making that statement is entirely a matter of choice for the prosecuting officer, and what I say is in no sense a criticism—is to cover fully in the argument the contentions which are to be made by the prosecution. I assume that procedure will be followed in this case." Struck by the brevity of Cramer's initial closing argument, Royall wanted to make sure that Biddle would not try to end this trial with any surprises to which he could not respond. "It is not permissible, under any procedure I know, to retain the right to make the principal contentions until after the defense has spoken. If that is done, and I do not assume it will be done in this case, of course we would have an opportunity to reply to that; and I say that merely in order that the Commission may know that in case there is an extended argument, broader in scope than that which the Judge Advocate General has now presented, we may wish an opportunity to argue again in reply thereto."[2]

Royall first had to deal with the resentment probably felt by members of the commission because of his attempt to challenge the legitimacy of their proceedings by appealing to the Supreme Court. He deferentially explained that his appearance before the Supreme Court was in no way meant to disrespect the judgment and fairness that he was sure the Commission would display in the upcoming verdicts. Rather, he wanted only to challenge what he thought was an unconstitutional appropriation of jurisdiction to a military commission when the civil courts were open and functioning.

Royall now moved on to the topic of possible punishment. He knew the odds were stacked against his clients, but he wanted to try to make sure that when they were convicted, they would not be sentenced to death, as Roosevelt had authorized—and likely expected—the commission to order.

"The very excellent preventive work which has been done by the Federal Bureau of Investigation and . . . [others] makes it improbable, if not impossible, for any similar plan to succeed in the future," Royall asserted, exploiting J. Edgar Hoover's big lie about the arrest of the Germans and the military commission's ignorance about Dasch's role in the saboteurs' apprehension. "Therefore, it is not necessary to punish these men as a preventive measure for any probable repetition of this offense."[3]

The impassive faces of the commission members told Royall that this contention was going nowhere. He moved to the best in an array of weak arguments.

"Let us get the proper perspective on this case. These men may have planned something, but they have not done any terrible thing. They prepared to do some things which, if accomplished, might have been terrible. But they have not done it. . . . Let us not let the fact of war absolutely change the character of what they have done. Give it weight, yes; but do not let it destroy our entire perspective of just exactly what has happened," Royall urged.[4]

"There is a criminal statute about committing sabotage which was enacted by Congress. . . . It imposed the maximum penalties in time of peace, and then it imposed the maximum penalties in time of war. That is the maximum. That was done after careful consideration. . . . It was considered by the authorities, civil and military, and it was prescribed that when a man in time of war actually committed sabotage and blew up a plant, the maximum penalty would be 30 years—the maximum; the most you could give him. These men have not done anywhere near that much—not anywhere near that much.

"I speak of sabotage, and I say that these men have not even attempted to commit sabotage because an attempt is distinguished from preparation. It is very seriously doubtful that they have gone far enough to constitute an attempt."

Then, as if he had read Biddle's memo to the president, Royall drove home his point. "Buying a gun to shoot somebody is not an attempt. It is a violation of law, but it is not an attempt to commit murder. . . . These men did not even go to the extent of an attempt," Royall explained, quoting the relevant statute.

Ignoring the irony of Abraham Lincoln's unilateral suspension of civil liberties and habeas corpus eight decades earlier, Royall then finished up his opening salvo with a cogent appeal to what the sixteenth president called "our better angels."

"Anybody can administer justice when the sun is shining, things are peaceful, and there is no stress or excitement," Royall asserted, pausing to look the generals squarely in the eye. "It takes a man to administer our system of government when that is not the case."[5]

Dowell next spoke at length about the statutes on military spying and espionage and how they differed. "I merely wished to point out that Congress has enacted two statutes, one on spying and the other on espionage, and that the espionage statute provides for punishment as between peace time and war time, and the maximum in war time is thirty years."[6] Dowell's presentation was clear, succinct, and erudite, but from the skeptical expressions on the seven generals' faces, he might as well have been whispering in a tornado.

The difference between espionage and spying, Royall further elaborated, was that espionage was reporting nonmilitary information to the enemy, while spying was reporting directly related military information to the enemy, such as the number of troops in an encampment. He then briefly explained that each man had testified to being instructed in the use of invisible ink, but that was to be used as a means of communicating among themselves, not as a way to communicate with Germany. Royall referred to the statements and testimony of the defendants that were unchallenged, stressing that only two of the men (Dasch and Kerling) were informed about ways to communicate to Germany. Both of these men also testified to the fact that they were told the spying would be taken care of by a separate branch of the German army, and they were to concern themselves only with sabotage.

It was now 11:40, and the commission recessed until 1:30 so that Royall, Dowell, and Biddle could attend the announcement of the Supreme Court decision. The accused could only hope that the high court would grant them a civilian trial. Otherwise, it seemed certain that the commission would unanimously condemn the Germans to death.

Just before the stroke of noon, Royall settled into his seat at the counsel table in the Supreme Court for the third day in a row. If nothing else, the serene, edifying atmosphere of the chamber was a welcome relief from the frenzied, depressing makeshift courtroom in the Justice Department building. While the justices had seemed unreceptive to his arguments, Royall at least felt that his forcefully asserted points were understood.

"Oyez, oyez, oyez," the marshal intoned as eight justices took the bench. Only minutes earlier, Royall's colleagues had succeeded in delivering to the Supreme Court the papers from the United States Court of Appeals for the District of Columbia Circuit, where an appeal from district judge Morris' order had been filed. The Supreme Court would now have authority to act on his petitions for writ of certiorari formally asking the justices to do what they had already done—allow him to leapfrog the federal appellate court and come straight to the high court.

Royall took a deep breath, trying to lower his heart rate and appear calm despite a flood tide of anxiety welling up inside of him. He knew that he had done his best in his first Supreme Court argument—especially with so little time to write his brief and prepare for oral argument. Ordinarily, a lawyer appearing in the highest court in the land would field a small army of colleagues and experts in the field to help him draft his brief over a leisurely month or more. He would then spend several days being mooted in mock court arguments, doing what amounted to a legal rehearsal on every conceivable question that the justices might pose. In Royall's case, however, he had had only Dowell to help him, a couple of days to draft his petitions, and no time or help to ready himself for two days of rigorous questioning by some of the best legal intellects ever to sit on the Court. Not a single private lawyer or law school professor had been willing to help him.

Royall's mind was churning with questions and gnawing doubts about the fate of his clients. Would the Court reject his petition out of hand, citing lack of jurisdiction because of the president's decree closing the courts to his clients? Or would the justices reach the merits of his claim that the petitioners were being deprived of their right to a civilian trial? And if they actually decided the issue, how would they rule and for what reasons?

It did not take long for Royall to get his answers. In fact, in the span of only four minutes, it was over. Reading from typewritten pages, Chief Justice Stone read the Court's unanimous *per curiam* opinion (a decision with no justice identified as the author). After discussing the procedural posture of the case and granting the petition for writ of certiorari before judgment, Stone got to the heart of the matter:

> The Court has fully considered the question raised in these cases and thoroughly argued at the bar, and has reached its conclusion upon them. It now announces its decision and enters its judgment in each case, in advance of the preparation of a full opinion which necessarily will require a considerable period of time for its preparation and which, when prepared, will be filed with the Clerk.
>
> The Court holds:
>
> (1) That the charges preferred against petitioners on which they are being tried by military commission appointed by order of the President of July 2, 1942, allege an offense or offenses which the President is authorized to order tried before a military commission.
>
> (2) That the military commission was lawfully constituted.
>
> (3) That petitioners are held in lawful custody for trial before the

military commission, and have not shown cause for being discharged by writ of habeas corpus.

The motions for leave to file petitions for writs of habeas corpus are denied. . . . The mandates are directed to issue forthwith.

Mr. Justice MURPHY took no part in the consideration or decision of these cases.[7]

A total wipeout, Royall thought as he quickly left the chamber.

An elated Biddle, who rarely displayed emotion in public, exulted with his team over what the *New York Times* called "the sweeping government victory."[8] Actually, having delivered on his promise to President Roosevelt, Biddle may have been more relieved than anything else.

When pressed by reporters to make a comment, Royall mastered his turbulent emotions sufficiently to state the obvious: "The Court has acted. I know of no other venues of relief available to my clients."[9]

In one-inch bold type, the *Washington Daily News* of July 31, 1942, summed up the Supreme Court's rulings: "Spies Denied Civil Trial: High Court Upholds F.D." The chief justice's announcement that a "full opinion" would follow after it had been prepared, the article noted, was a "procedure without recent precedent."[10]

A unanimous defeat, Royall mused. The only solace seemed to be the Court's acceptance of his argument that despite the president's proclamation, habeas corpus was available to his clients and the Court had jurisdiction to entertain the case.[11] But that was a lawyer's victory.

His clients were going to die.

With the saboteurs' last hope now dashed, Royall, Dowell, and Biddle returned to the fifth floor of the Justice Department building. The only thing between the German prisoners and certain death was their U.S. Army lawyers.

"The Commission will come to order," President McCoy announced as he gave his gavel two firm taps on the table in front of him.

Royall rose to speak. "As the Commission has perhaps learned, the Supreme Court acted during the recess and determined that this Commission does have jurisdiction to try these offenses. I thought that possibly some member of the Commission had not heard it; therefore, I made that announcement. The remarks which I made this morning, as the Commission must have gathered rather an assumption that [that] would be the action of the Court, are, of course, now appropriate," Royall explained.[12]

The *per curiam* decision of the Court was now quickly read into the record.

At this point, Royall faced the daunting task of trying to present some distinguishing, persuasive facts about each of his seven clients. If he had been afforded months and a dozen lawyers to prepare for this defense, the burden would be excruciatingly difficult. Under these extreme circumstances of little time and even less assistance, it would have been impossible for any lawyer to overcome the obstacles Royall faced. Nor was his job made any easier by the fact that he was emotionally devastated by the sharp kick to the stomach just administered by the Supreme Court.

But Royall did not flinch. An ingrained sense of duty to his clients sustained him as he pressed on. If a Medal of Honor were awarded for valor in the courtroom, Kenneth Royall would certainly have deserved it.

"I want to talk briefly about the individual cases. If I stood up here and told you everything that every witness said about every feature of the case, we would be here for a week, and I have no intention of doing that; but I do want to call your attention to a few highlights of what some of these defendants said about the intention with which they came here," Royall told the commission members. This was his only real hope—to persuade the tribunal that his clients had never really intended to commit heinous acts of sabotage.

"Kerling is the first one I wanted to discuss," Royall began. He then recalled how Kerling admitted he was not sure of whether he could go through with the plan, but that he also had other reasons for accepting the mission and venturing to America: he wanted to "straighten out in some way a triangular matrimonial difficulty," as Royall delicately put it. In other words, he wanted to sort out his relationship with his wife and his beloved mistress. It was a measure of this surreal "trial" that Royall felt compelled to advance adultery as a defense in a capital case.

"Then we have the defendant Heinck." Royall explained that Heinck was "a fellow who followed orders," and that without a leader to command him, he "was incapable of doing it." Royall said that Heinck's lack of personal motivation prevented him from having any intent to follow through with the orders to sabotage.

Royall now picked up the pace. He quickly argued that Quirin had been wavering in his dedication to the mission, and that Neubauer, the man who had been put in a sanitarium twice, was mentally incapable of going through with the plan. As for Thiel, he had been coaxed into accepting the mission by the smooth-talking pair of Dasch and Kappe. Thiel simply did not understand the gravity of his actions. "He was just being, as they call it in the mountains of North Carolina, chinking wood, to fill in between the chinks of log cabins. He just floats along. He had no initiative and no ability to carry out any criminal plan," Royall said of Thiel.

Royall reserved the cases of Haupt and Burger, the two American citizens, for later.[13]

"We think none of these men are guilty of spying for other reasons, but principally because the charge did not show it and the facts did not show that they ever endeavored to obtain information for the purpose of communicating with the enemy," Royall stated. His preliminary statement finished, he sat down, allowing Ristine to speak on behalf of Dasch.

"At the outset, I would like to state to the Commission that if I should make any unkind remarks about anybody, it is not in any way intended as personal. I consider myself as a member of this Commission, appointed by my superior [officer] to appear here, and anything I say will be said in an effort to be helpful to this Commission in arriving at a fair and just verdict, and not because I am employed as counsel or have any interest in the outcome," Ristine stated in the most deferential, if not sycophantic, tone possible.

Ristine asked that the commission keep in mind two things while listening to his argument. First, that without Dasch's voluntary cooperation with the FBI, the case would "in all probability be an unsolved problem today."[14] Second, Ristine wanted the panel to look at Dasch's actions as a method for escaping Germany and not as a way to cooperate voluntarily with the German High Command.

The whole of Ristine's argument focused not on the charges against the defendants but on Dasch's intentions throughout the ordeal. He first spoke about Dasch's mind-set while in Germany preparing for the mission. Ristine told of how Dasch had been looked upon unfavorably by the other men because of his apparent lack of interest in learning anything at the Quenz Lake training facility as well as his constant tardiness and refusal to wear the uniform given to him. These actions,

Ristine argued, were not consistent with the actions of a man who was going to lead a sabotage mission inside enemy territory.

Ristine then shifted his focus to the landing of the Long Island group. He highlighted Dasch's exculpatory conduct, how he had dealt kindly with the young Coast Guardsman Cullen, and how he had ordered the sailors back to the submarine prematurely. Ristine hammered home the point that Dasch had had specific instructions to overpower anybody the group encountered during the landing and send the person back to the submarine with the sailors. Ristine made sure to read into the record the exculpatory line of questioning while Burger was on the witness stand:

> "Would there have been any difficulty in overpowering that man?"
>
> "No."
>
> "And it would have been an easy matter to carry out the instructions of the captain of the submarine?"
>
> "Yes."

Ristine also pointed out that Dasch had made sure the Coast Guardsman could recognize him by shining the flashlight upon his face. Surely, Ristine argued, these were not the actions of a man who had any intention of executing the sabotage plan.

Ristine stressed his essential point about Dasch's actions after the landing. At the first meeting among Dasch, Burger, Heinck, and Quirin after they had split up in New York City, Dasch informed the group that they would not go back to retrieve the explosives buried on the beach. Once again, this was not the action of a man intending to carry out the sabotage mission.

Ristine's final and most compelling point was that Dasch was the reason why the FBI was able to round up all eight of the potential saboteurs. Dasch had traveled to Washington of his own free will, choosing to betray the plot before the other men could take any deadly action. According to Ristine, the FBI's refusal to express confidence in Dasch—even after they verified every fact they checked—was wrong.

"I think it is a shame that the FBI did not take the witness stand and say to this Commission candidly, 'we think, with respect to Dasch, that he is in a different category altogether. He came before us voluntarily. He spilled this whole thing in our lap, and we think that you should take that into consideration in this trial.'

"But not one word, except to conjure up reasons why they can tell this Commission; 'We do not have confidence in him.'

"And then the Judge Advocate General gets up and says to this Commission, 'You have heard all the evidence. Find them all guilty, and we want death for all eight of them.'

"Why, I submit, gentlemen of the Commission, that every one of these charges must fail, if that be true, and that there is but one just and fair finding that you can bring in, and that is: 'We find the defendant Dasch not guilty of every charge and every specification.' "[15]

Over two and a half hours after it began, Ristine's closing argument was finally finished. It was now nearly five o'clock, and the commission adjourned for the day. The defendants would have to wait one more day to find out if they had any hope of a reprieve from death.

The trial's final day had arrived. In keeping with the daily ritual, the defendants were brought from the D.C. Jail to Room 5235 of the Department of Justice. A verdict would likely be issued within a few days, but the defendants would not be present. They would be informed of the decision while in their cells.

Convening promptly at nine-thirty, the commission immediately continued with the defense argument.

"If the Commission please, I desire this morning to talk about the defendant Haupt and finally the defendant Burger, and then call your attention at the conclusion to some general principles, and my argument will be brief," Royall promised.

It was now or never—his last chance to spare the saboteurs' lives. Haupt and Burger—the two American citizens—had been reserved for last because Royall believed that they had the best chance of being saved. It is impossible to describe the knot in even a seasoned trial lawyer's stomach when he knows that his argument will literally spell the difference between preserving and forfeiting a human life.

"There have been some little inconsistencies between the statements of various of the defendants. We cannot run away from that fact. . . . But that is not confined to the defendants," Royall explained. "I have a list, which I would be glad to give to the Commission, of thirty-seven inconsistent statements made by members of the FBI in this trial."

Royall's point was that small, insignificant differences in details as related by the defendants should not discredit the fact that, on the whole, the statements of each defendant paralleled each other without the accused having any knowledge of what the others were saying. They had no opportunity to rehearse their statement. Royall then pointed out that FBI agent Wills testified to the fact that there was a "definite promise" of a presidential pardon for Dasch.[16]

Switching gears, Royall focused on the defendant Haupt. "He was subjected to the most thorough cross-examination of anyone who has been offered as a witness. . . . In that cross-examination, as I recall it, the prosecution did not develop a single inconsistent statement, either inconsistent with his direct examination or inconsistent with his statement given to the FBI upon apprehension," Royall insisted.

Royall also commented on the fact that the prosecution had made sure to show in detail Haupt's troubles with Gerda Stuckmann, his girlfriend, whom he had impregnated and left behind. "He said he left here because of some difficulty with a girl. We are not trying him for that. He has probably proved himself guilty of some unlawful or immoral conduct in connection with Miss Stuckmann. . . . That is a bad thing to do, but it happens every day. The girl, of course, deserves sympathy," remarked Royall, ever the southern gentleman.[17]

Royall finished up Haupt's defense after summarizing his unfortunate journey from the United States to Mexico, Japan, and Germany. "We can all remember, to some extent, when we were 21 years old. Some of us have children or friends of ours have children about the same age. Let us apply his story and test—we cannot apply it to anybody else—to that of a 21-year-old boy, raised in America, all his friends in America, his parents in America, and getting into trouble with a girl and running away, and getting to Europe the day Pearl Harbor occurred. That is the situation with him. It is a situation which differs radically from those situations of the other parties that I have discussed.

"That is the situation about Haupt. I think he is entitled to special consideration because of those facts." Royall was not merely Haupt's appointed lawyer doing his job. In every fiber of his body, he felt that Haupt did not deserve to die.

Turning to Burger's case, Royall declared, "We . . . had Burger on the stand, and, instead of weakening his case in any respect, we contend it has been immeasurably strengthened by your opportunity to observe him. . . . [His] answers, if you just sit down and read them— I think you recall it showed a frankness . . . the like of which I do not ever recall seeing on the witness stand in many days.

"Burger is in this situation. He is a proven man of character in this country. He served two enlistments in the National Guard in different States. Not only did each of his commanding officers give him a character of excellent, but they went out of their way to add a note, and one of them said, 'Exceedingly reliable and trustworthy,' or words to that effect, under 'remarks.' Not only is that true, but when he was leaving they wrote him a special letter commenting upon his integrity."[18] Royall wanted to establish that Burger was an honest man before getting into the facts of Burger's case.

"Burger had been terribly mistreated in Germany. You do not have to take his statement for that. He says that, but you have the statement of every witness on the stand who knew about it," Royall explained. "And I want to suggest to the Commission that his original statement, if there is any question in anybody's mind, ought to clear him, if there were nothing else."

Royall now played his trump card, hoping that Burger's horrific mistreatment in Germany would make clear his intentions—and save his life. "Burger had gotten into trouble . . . because he had said something about the treatment of the Poles, and they put him in jail, charging him with falsification of papers in a place in which he had never been—in Vienna. They investigated him three times and acquitted him, and finally the judiciary dismissed him, but the Gestapo would not let him go and put him in a concentration camp and kept him a year. They took away all of his medals and his decorations. They put him into a room with sixty persons, allowing one hour and a few minutes exercise every 14 days. They forced him to sign a pledge that he would not tell [anybody] about his treatment.

"And Burger, the soldier that he is—when he was on the witness stand, I tried to get him to magnify that a little. I thought maybe he would make it a little more graphic as to how they treated him and it would be more impressive. But I could not do anything with him. He just told it as it was; did not try to color it, did not try to exaggerate it, and he ended up by saying, 'I am not complaining about what they did to me; I am complaining about what they did to my wife.'

"That was somewhat like a courageous man, I think. I tried to get him to complain, but he would not do it," Royall added. "He said: 'They told my wife that I was going to be eight years in the chain gang. They knew she was pregnant, and they caused her to have a miscarriage and become terribly ill. They told her that she had to divorce me; made me write her a farewell letter.'"

Burger was a noble figure who simply wanted to get out of Germany, Royall asserted with all the vigor he could muster. "Who wouldn't? That is corroborated by every one of these defendants. They may not like Burger; they may feel that Burger has in part been responsible for their apprehension. The Commission may have observed in this trial some attitude of hostility to him; but in spite of that fact, every one of them corroborates him in every detail except some very minor ones," Royall noted.

Royall now explained how Burger had sabotaged the sabotage mission—how he had marked the place where the explosives were buried on the beach at Amagansett so the Coast Guard would easily find the explosives, and how he had patiently waited for the FBI in his hotel room, with all the evidence spread out in plain view and the door unlocked. Burger's actions were a product of his intentions, Royall concluded.

"May it please the Commission, we say in this case, in conclusion, that there is a varying situation as to these defendants. This being a judicial body, we say it must give consideration to this varying situation."

Royall pled one last time for the life of "this young boy Haupt, whose age in itself would justify a distinction, whose American citizenship would in itself justify a distinction, and the corroboration of whose story would justify you in accepting it, he ought to be acquitted. If he is not acquitted, we submit to the Commission, he ought to receive a very minor punishment.

"Now, it has been a difficult task to argue about all these defendants," Royall observed, making the greatest understatement of the entire trial. "It is difficult to be fair to all of them and present the case of one. We have sought to do it. We are convinced that they are different. We are convinced that none of them should receive the severe penalty. With that remark, we leave the matter to the Commission," Royall concluded.[19]

No one in that courtroom doubted Royall's sincerity or courage. Biddle, a decent man himself, was perhaps the most impressed. Royall had defended his clients, Biddle thought, "up to the hilt . . . with perseverance and skill." The attorney general particularly admired how Royall could be "as hard and sharp as steel, yet with admirable court manners and presence, warmed by a pleasant, deep-chested North Carolina drawl."[20]

Lloyd Cutler admired Royall's total and unreserved commitment to his unpopular clients. No defense had been left unasserted. Royall was a masterful trial lawyer. Regardless of the outcome, it was hard to imagine any trial lawyer doing a better job.[21]

The judge advocate general now presented the prosecution's concluding argument. Cramer went into great detail about the charges and specifications, citing military codes and the law of war.

"The whole proposition comes to this, that it is not a question of whether they actually go to the place where they could sabotage something, but they did come through the lines for that purpose; and the only reason they did not do it was because they were caught by the FBI before they could get to the place of the crime."

Cramer then spoke briefly about each of the defendants, disputing each one's alleged intention of never consummating the plot. He was determined to cast doubt on anything that Royall had argued. Cramer criticized Royall's case for Haupt, asserting that it was based only on a plea for sympathy. Burger may have been in a concentration camp, but he had never reported being mistreated or beaten. Dasch had worked for and with the German High Command for months before he helped organize the Quenz Lake school.

Making his best point of all, Cramer argued that Walter Kappe was a smart man who knew his men well. The handpicked team of saboteurs was in no way a group of "simply eight morons, as you might say, who had no intention of going through with this at all."[22]

Wrapping up his workmanlike but nonetheless effective argument, Cramer sternly asserted: "It seems to me that the prosecution has proved all the elements of all the specifications and that all these defendants should suffer punishment by death."

Before sitting down, Cramer added one more point on the topic of reducing sentences for those men who had cooperated with the government. "I respectfully urge the Commission to take into consideration the old maxim of courts: that clemency is a matter for the appointing authority and is not a matter for the court. It is for that reason that we do not think that those circumstances that have been brought up should be considered by the Commission in finding its sentence. For that reason, we ask for a finding of guilty under each specification and a sentence of death," Cramer chillingly concluded, handing over the final argument to his co-counsel.

"I had at first thought it would be unnecessary for me to say anything," Biddle began. "Even now I hesitate somewhat, in view of the admirable analysis of the case by the Judge Advocate General, and in view, also, of the fact that the facts speak for themselves, and speak loudly."

The attorney general then discussed the spying charge and explained that spying did not necessarily require successful communication to the enemy. Biddle read from the record testimony showing that the saboteurs did learn to write in invisible ink and that they did have an address in Lisbon to write to if necessary.

"I think it unnecessary to read more of this. There is quite a good deal more evidence on it, but my point is that they came with the means and the instructions to communicate and intended to do so," Biddle stated. "Lest it should be thought that I had not clearly expressed myself, I, of course, concur with the Judge Advocate General in asking for the death penalty. If you believe that these men were behind the lines for the purpose of sabotage and, in addition, for the purpose of spying, I think your obligation is to find that. I think that that is mandatory."

Biddle then concluded: "Perhaps they are soldiers. Perhaps they are young. Perhaps they are neurotic. But, nevertheless, they came over here and went behind our lines as spies and saboteurs."[23]

Biddle and Cramer had now concluded the long, exhausting prosecution of the German Eight.

"The prosecution and the defense having nothing further to offer, the Commission is closed," President McCoy stated.

At 2:25 p.m. on August 1, the military commission to try the eight Germans officially concluded. Beginning on July 8 and ending on August 1, the military tribunal had sat for nineteen days. Almost three thousand pages of testimony and argument had been heard. The verdict and record would be sent directly to President Roosevelt.

Chapter 21

Old Sparky

On Sunday, August 2, President Roosevelt was working in his Hyde Park bedroom with his secretary William Hassett. After some light paperwork, FDR indulged in one of his great daily pleasures—reading the newspapers. He noticed that after dragging on for so long, the military commission was finally deliberating on the German saboteurs' case.

"It's always hard for generals to act as judges," Roosevelt observed as he looked up from the *New York Times*. "I hope they don't string it out too long. They ought to bring in a verdict like a jury, and I don't see why their report should be a drawn-out one."

"One page should cover the case," Hassett noted. "It will make it easy for you to do your duty as the reviewing authority."

"It will likely be a wordy document," FDR sighed.

"Under military law, the Commander-in-Chief has to set the time and place of execution," Hassett reminded his boss.

"I still hope that they recommend hanging," Roosevelt replied.[1]

After the trial ended on Saturday, August 1, the seven generals deliberated throughout the weekend. They reviewed the evidence against each defendant on each charge, reducing their conclusions to written recommendations on guilt and punishment for President Roosevelt. After two days of deliberations, the commission reached a unanimous verdict.

At his home early Monday morning, August 3, Royall was awakened by a phone caller with a brief message: "The verdict is in; get to the Justice Department building." Donning his military uniform, Royall rushed off to his post. Once at the Justice Department, Royall went through the now familiar drill of passing through tight security. The barricades still prevented the press from intruding, the black drapes hung lifelessly on the windows, and the small offices across the hall remained partitioned between prosecution and defense.

As Royall and Dowell sat down at the defense table in Room 5235, however, they noticed one major difference.

That's strange, Royall thought. *Nearly the entire prosecution team is missing today.*

The prisoners—bleary-eyed from lack of sleep—marched more slowly than usual into the chamber. Dowell noted a restlessness in the room, a feeling of apprehension in everyone present.

General McCoy addressed the gathering. "The Commission is now open. The Commission has reached a verdict concerning the eight accused men, and this verdict will be transmitted to President Roosevelt for review and approval. The President will announce the verdict once it has been finalized. The Commission is now closed," McCoy concluded in a flat, emotionless tone.

A minute after they entered, the generals quietly exited the room. The prisoners—confused and anxious to know their fate—were escorted back to their cells. Royall wished he had something reassuring to tell them. In his heart, he feared the worst.

Once out the front door of the Justice Department, reporters trying to learn the saboteurs' fate besieged Royall and Dowell. Royall's parting comment was as brief as it was understated.

"We have no further rights or responsibilities in this case. We are leaving."

The truth of the matter was that the resourceful Royall had exhausted every possible legal means to save his clients. He had twice defied his commander in chief, first by filing a habeas corpus petition in the district court and then by petitioning the Supreme Court for relief.[2] Royall had run out of time and courts.

As soon as the commission closed on August 3, the three-thousand-page transcript, along with the commission's sealed verdicts, were transmitted by Cramer, McCoy, and Oscar Cox to the White House for the president to review. The only announcement came from the president's press secretary, Stephen Early, who said that an announcement that day was unlikely.[3] Early declined to mention that President Roosevelt was in Hyde Park and an army plane was bringing the record to him.

That same day, President Roosevelt signed legislation authorizing "an appropriate medal of honor" for J. Edgar Hoover for his stellar performance in apprehending the eight Nazi terrorists.

During his press conference the next day, President Roosevelt, looking relaxed in white shirt and trousers, tactfully circumvented the frequent questions about the German saboteurs' trial.

"I am now in the process of reviewing the evidence, which is voluminous," the president noted. "I will have finished within two or three days."

"What about the length of time that the trial has taken?" was the first question shouted FDR's way.

"The American process of justice operates that way," Roosevelt confidently replied. "I do not doubt that under similar circumstances Americans caught in Germany would have been summarily shot, but in the United States the preservation of society is carried out by legal means which take time."

"Who fixes the sentences?" another reporter wanted to know.

"I have a report and a verdict from the Commission," the president simply stated, dodging the question.

"Are you putting everything else aside to consider the case?"

"Oh my, no," FDR quickly responded with a dismissive chuckle.

In fact, Roosevelt saw only three visitors the following day, far fewer than his normal schedule. The commission's proceedings were undoubtedly interesting to FDR, a former lawyer and an avid reader of detective novels.[4] A master of symbolism, Roosevelt also probably did not want to appear to rush to judgment on such a weighty matter.

No one from the media reminded FDR that he had once campaigned to abolish the death penalty in America.

As each day passed, the press grew more frustrated with the news blackout concerning the saboteurs. Rumors and falsified reports were printed as if they were the gospel truth. Any tidbit of information was turned into an elaborate story.

Reports of lumber being delivered to Fort Myer in Virginia told of a gallows being constructed there so the executions could take place on government soil. Other stories claimed FDR was wavering between sparing the lives of three of the men and executing all of them. Dasch, Burger, and Haupt were the three defendants most frequently singled out as the ones who might escape execution.

The most widely printed speculation—which turned out to be true—was that the army had taken control of the D.C. Jail. This was supposedly an ideal place for an execution since it had ceilings high enough for a gallows, a concrete wall capable of providing the backdrop for a firing squad, and an electric chair.[5] Reporters staked out the jail around the clock, hoping to find anything at all to report.

On August 4, these inquiring minds missed their biggest chance—and their only clue. Brigadier General Albert Cox, jailor and custodian of the eight men, sneaked out of the jailhouse to boost the settings on the electrical transformer out on the street. He had just received official word from the president via Oscar Cox that six of the men would be electrocuted, instead of being hung or shot by a firing squad, in order to preserve secrecy. To carry out the execution, the transformer had to be adjusted days in advance.[6] Eluding the prying eyes of the press, Cox went about his duty unnoticed.

Meanwhile, the prisoners remained under heavy armed guard at the jail. To prevent suicide attempts, soldiers were placed in each defendant's cell, and the lights were kept on all night. As they anxiously awaited news of their fate, the defendants chain-smoked cigarettes that they rolled themselves.[7]

Early on the morning of Saturday, August 8, the D.C. Jail prepared itself for what would be its largest ever mass execution by electric chair. The dusty old death chamber was being ventilated with extra fans to clear away the nauseating smell of burnt human flesh, while two dozen witnesses' chairs were placed behind the one-way glass. Reporters were gathering outside the jailhouse grounds, tipped off by the alleged absence of the official New York state executioner from his home in Cairo, New York.[8] At exactly 6 a.m. and for the next six hours, key figures in the execution retinue began appearing at the jail entrance, including Cox, his deputy, Major Thomas Rives, Dr. A. Magruder MacDonald, the D.C. coroner, Father Daniel O'Connor, a Catholic priest from the nearby reformatory, several army chaplains and doctors, and a caravan of army vehicles said to be carrying six stretchers.[9]

General Cox made his way to the prisoners' cells, solemnly reading each his own verdict: "The military tribunal has found you guilty on all the crimes as charged and recommended to the President of the United States that you suffer death by the electric chair."[10] In Burger's case, this was followed by "The President has commuted your sentence to life imprisonment at hard labor." For Dasch, it was "The President has commuted your sentence to thirty years of imprisonment at hard labor." Cramer and Biddle had recommended the two commutations to Roosevelt in light of the pair's cooperation.

The six condemned men stood at attention as they learned of their fate. Resigned long ago to the inevitability of their sentences, they displayed little or no emotion. Their final human exchange would be prayers and last rites with prison chaplains.[11]

Irate at being double-crossed, Dasch babbled incoherently about the broken pardon deal with Hoover, his efforts to help America, and his hatred of Nazi Germany. Cox listened patiently for a while and then departed. Dasch would not talk his way out of his punishment.

At 7 a.m., all eight men were fed their normal breakfast of scrambled eggs, bacon, and toast. Dasch and Burger then returned to their cells, while the rest were taken to individual cells on death row, where their hair was cut short and one calf was shaved clean. The preparations for death were now complete.[12] It was only a matter of time before their fatal encounter with Old Sparky, the prison nickname for the eighteen-year-old electric chair, which had not been used for a year.

As they waited with a prison chaplain, the condemned men sent letters to their families.

"Where I am going I am with our friends—in Valhalla," Kerling wrote to his estranged wife. "Heil Hitler, your Eddy."

Neubauer's letter to his parents concluded: "So I shall walk down my last stretch proudly, firmly and courageously, as your son, as Germany's son."

A note accompanied each letter to the parents: "I want you to know your son was reconciled to his Church," wrote Father E.J. Gracey, a U.S. Army chaplain.[13]

At exactly noon, as a heavy rain drenched the city and General McCoy and J. Edgar Hoover sat among the subdued witnesses, the first man was led into the musty pastel yellow execution chamber. The procedure was the same for each man; he took his place in Old Sparky, and straps were secured around his waist, arms, and legs. A rubber mask was slipped over his face. Small sponges soaked in a salt solution were put on his head and calf at the places where the electricity would enter the body. A metal helmet was placed on his head. The anonymous executioner—who was paid $50 per electrocution—had to strike a gruesome balance: the prisoner had to get high enough voltage to be killed, but not so much that he would burst into flames.

Multiple executions usually take place in alphabetical order, and this day was no different. In rapid succession, Haupt, Heinck, Kerling, Neubauer, Quirin, and Thiel—each in a "stunned, confused, and trance-like state"—were electrocuted with two thousand volts of electricity.[14] At exactly 1:04 p.m., it was all over—six executions in sixty-four minutes.

Only Kerling was defiant in the face of death. Standing at attention, he declared his pride in being a German. His only regret, he told the spectators, was that Operation Pastorius had failed. Unrepentant to the very end, this loyal Nazi vowed he would undertake the mission if given another chance.[15]

As soon as the fastest mass execution in D.C. history had been concluded, the White House was immediately notified. The official statement from the White House came at 1:20 p.m., only moments after receiving word from D.C. coroner MacDonald that the executions had gone "smoothly, without a hitch."

The President has completed his review of the findings and sentences of the Military Commission . . . which tried the eight Nazi Saboteurs. The President approved the judgment of the Military Commission that all of the prisoners were guilty and that they be given the death sentence by electrocution. However, there was a unanimous recommendation by the Commission, concurred in by the Attorney General and the Judge Advocate General of the Army, that the sentence of two of the prisoners be commuted to life imprisonment because of their assistance to the government of the United States in the apprehension and conviction of the others. The commutation directed by the President in the case of Burger was to confinement at hard labor for life. In the case of Dasch, the President commuted the sentence to confinement at hard labor for thirty years. The electrocutions began at noon today. Six of the prisoners were electrocuted. The other two were confined to prison. The records in all eight cases will be sealed until the end of the war.

The six bodies were removed by two ambulances to Walter Reed Hospital's morgue. After being prepared for burial, each was placed in a plain pine box and secretly taken to Blue Plains, the potter's field for the District of Columbia. Each was buried with only a three-digit number on an unpainted wooden stake memorializing his presence.[16] Haupt's parents would not be able to visit his grave—they were in Cook County jail awaiting their trial for treason.

Later on August 8, President Roosevelt was staying at his presidential hideaway, Shangri-La, in the Catoctin Mountains of northwestern Maryland.[17] FDR was accompanied by a few of his closest friends, including Sam Rosenman, his lead speechwriter, and Rosenman's wife, Dorothy; FDR's cousin Margaret "Daisy" Suckley; his secretary Grace Tully; and the poet Archibald MacLeish. While mixing drinks and playing host, FDR started to tell stories from his days as governor of New York, most of them concerning last-minute appeals for clemency from inmates on death row. The president remembered everything from names to offenses, every little detail, and seemed to be quite pleased with his storytelling ability. While preparing his new favorite drink, gin and grapefruit juice, he recounted an Alexandre Dumas story about a Parisian barber during the 1870 siege of Paris who was able to supply beef for sale while some of his clients strangely turned up missing.

Dorothy Rosenman could not help but ask what brought about this dark sense of humor. FDR mentioned the executions earlier in the day, joking about how he had wished that the Nazis had been hanged instead of electrocuted because it would have boosted Americans' morale. Dorothy asked where the men would be buried, and the president replied that he did not know.

FDR then launched into a morbid story about an old American lady who had passed away while visiting Moscow. When the body was shipped back to the United States, the family discovered that it had accidentally been switched with the body of a dead Russian general. The family naturally complained, only to receive a cable from the Russian government: "Suggest you close the casket and proceed with the funeral. Your grandmother was buried in the Kremlin with full military honors." Roosevelt seemed to get quite a kick out of the story, while his audience was less amused.[18]

Roosevelt's keen political instincts had been right all along. The American people wholeheartedly endorsed the actions of the military commission as well as the president in imposing death sentences on six of the Germans. The White House was deluged with telegrams and letters of support from all over the country. Even the Victory Committee of German American Trade Unionists endorsed "the imposition of the death penalty on any saboteur or traitor. We know that no loyal German American need have the slightest fear providing he obeys the laws of the country."[19]

Other than some Nazi propaganda about American hypocrisy and a radio broadcast on Rome Radio condemning the suppression of habeas corpus,[20] the only noticeable dissent came from Ellis Island, where a meeting of interned Germans was held to announce the deaths of their countrymen. After a moment of silence, the congregation of internees joined together in the singing of the Nazi anthem, "Horst Wessel Lied."[21] The nation as a whole, however, was united behind its president, now more than ever.

The least they could have done was tell me directly, Royall thought as he unpacked his files after returning to his Pentagon office. *Why did I have to learn from the press that my clients had been executed?* Common professional courtesy would dictate a call from Biddle or Cramer. But nothing about this case had been ordinary or routine. He was less bitter than disappointed.

It was time to put this matter behind him and return to his duties as a soldier. Royall had a backlog of airplane production contracts to expedite—and a war to win. A round of golf and a good poker game, his favorite ways to relax, would be nice.

But Royall was tired, not so much physically but emotionally. The roller-coaster ride that had begun on July 2 was over, but he had not yet come to a full stop. His mind raced, overwhelmed by a kaleidoscope of rapidly moving scenes: the messenger delivering the president's order, cooling his heels outside the Oval Office, the first time he met his frightened clients in the lockup, Hoover stealing the hero's role from the brave young Coast Guardsmen Cullen, that blowhard Dasch pontificating on the witness stand, Biddle terrorizing his clients on cross-examination, Justice Frankfurter savaging his arguments in the Supreme Court as though he were a first-year law student again,

Major General McCoy relentlessly overruling his objections to inadmissible evidence, his clients walking one by one down a long, barren hallway to their electrocution.

God, what a month and a half! It feels like ten years.

A light knock at the door interrupted his reverie. It was a soldier with something for him. Royall looked down to see an envelope with his name handwritten on the front.

Great, he thought, *another piece of hate mail!*

Royall threw the letter into his briefcase and started for the door. He reached for the light switch, but something made him pause. Standing still for a moment, he reached into his briefcase.

Walking back to his desk, Royall lowered his angular frame into the chair. He opened and started to read the letter, hardly believing what was handwritten on the page: a letter from his six now dead clients.

> Being charged with serious offenses in wartime, we have been given a fair trial. . . . Before all we want to state that defense counsel . . . has represented our case as American officers unbiased, better than we could expect and probably risking the indignation of public opinion. We thank our defense counsel for giving its legal ability . . . in our behalf.[22]

Royall gently laid the letter down on his desk, lost in deep thought. Never would he have imagined such a sincere, touching expression of gratitude from six men who had been strangers six weeks earlier. In all his years of representing clients, he had never been so moved.

His spirits were heavy, and the late afternoon sun did not dispel the gloom. He had lost before, but nothing like this case. Six of his seven clients had paid the ultimate price for his failure to win in the Supreme Court. All the after-the-fact rationalizations were little solace for his feeling of profound disappointment.

Royall's eyes misted over. A solitary tear moved ever so slowly down his cheek, as if marching south to the distant sound of a funeral dirge. An ineffable sadness overcame him.

In his heart, he knew that he had done his duty as best as he knew how. He had not sought this appointment, and he would have gladly passed the burden to civilian counsel had he been able to find one. And yes, some were now generously praising his zealous advocacy when only a week earlier he had received death threats and been publicly vilified for defending despised Nazis. The letters of praise—from Justice

Frankfurter for his "admirable" handling of "the grim business" and from Justice Jackson for his "impressive" service as "an officer and a gentleman in a most difficult situation"—were gratifying.[23]

Still, Royall could not get out of his mind the thought of six young men buried in anonymous graves—victims of forces they little understood and could never overcome.

Blinking, he saw a water stain on the letter. His trembling hands gently picked up the letter and put it into his breast pocket, close to his heart. He knew then that, as long as he lived, he would cherish his clients' heartfelt appreciation for having defended them as best he could against insurmountable odds.

Chapter 22

Fait Accompli

As Royall's clients were being put to death, Chief Justice Stone was back in his summer retreat in New Hampshire struggling to write a unanimous opinion. While the Supreme Court's cryptic order had rejected the Germans' challenge to the president's authority to dispense with a civil trial (and implicitly sanctioned their execution), its reasoning remained shrouded in secrecy. Indeed, as the torturous three-month process of writing the promised full opinion unfolded, the justices struggled mightily to find common ground to rationalize a fait accompli. Eventually, an opinion commanding all eight justices' votes would be released, but the decision in *Ex parte Quirin* would raise more questions than it answered.

Assigning himself this historic opinion, the chief justice strived mightily to craft a unanimous decision following the unsigned opinion of July 31. Stone knew well that because the Germans were dead, any concurrences or dissents in the wake of a *per curiam* opinion would damage the Supreme Court's reputation. From the very first drafts in August, however, it was painfully obvious that holding the eight justices together in a coherent, intellectually defensible opinion would be a Herculean task.[1] Worse yet, the quest for unanimity necessarily "limited and conditioned what could be said."[2]

Even without the stress of such a momentous wartime decision, the

Court was an uncollegial collection of strong egos, sharp intellects, and petty jealousies. Stone was temperamentally ill-suited to preside "over one of the most fractious courts in American history."[3] Herding all these contentious "wild horses" was made all the more improbable because of the justices' jurisprudential differences over curtailment of civil liberties in wartime and the friction between abrasive Frankfurter and Black, Douglas, and Murphy.

As weeks passed into months, Stone's repeated redrafting of the opinion—and the frustration of being unable to harmonize his colleagues' antithetical positions—was an admitted "mortification of the flesh." The elusive search for consensus was further impeded by the high quality of Royall's written and oral argument and the inferior government brief.

"I hope," Stone wrote to his law clerk, "the military is better equipped to fight the war than it is to fight its legal battles."[4]

The chief justice had serious doubts about the government's construction of the Articles of War, particularly Roosevelt's bypassing the customary independent review by the judge advocate general. "The President's order probably conflicts with the Articles of War," he confided to his law clerk.[5] Remarkably, Stone even considered ruling in the dead petitioners' favor since

> counsel for the saboteurs had a more persuasive argument on this issue than did the government. The order creating the body that tried the German agents rather clearly did not comply with the requirements of these articles [46 and 50½]. If they applied to the saboteur case, then those six of the eight defendants who were already dead . . . had been executed illegally.[6]

But Stone could not bring himself to confess error, realizing that this "would leave the present court in the unenviable position of having stood by and allowed six men to go to their death."[7] Eventually, Stone punted on the "embarrassing" issue, preferring to save face than to do the right thing. Employing judicial legerdemain, the final opinion conveniently claimed that the secrecy surrounding the trial made it impossible to determine whether the president's proclamation and order were consistent with the Articles of War.[8]

Other justices—including Jackson, Black, and Frankfurter—weighed in with draft concurrences and memos debating the extent of the commander in chief's powers to override acts of Congress, the vagueness of the uncodified law of war, the excessive scope given to military tribunals, and other ticklish issues. It was a cacophony of divergent views that threatened to sharply divide the Court. Stone despaired of achieving a majority, much less unanimity.

The logjam appears to have been broken—at least in part—by Justice Frankfurter. Writing one of the most bizarre internal communications in Supreme Court history, Frankfurter revealed his deep-seated hatred of the German saboteurs and contempt for their audacity in petitioning the high court—something that this Machiavellian power broker may not have counted on in his plotting of the whole affair. In an October memo to his colleagues entitled "F.F.'s Soliloquy," the avenging justice depicts a fictional conversation between himself and the six dead terrorists. The ostensible legal issue is the divisive question of the president violating the Articles of War mandating appellate review by the judge advocate general of any convictions and sentences. But the intemperate memo reveals a dark side of the jurist that infected his objectivity about the case—and undoubtedly biased other justices against the Germans.

In Frankfurter's view, President Roosevelt clearly had the power to create the military commission—the very one Frankfurter himself had secretly proposed to Stimson before the trial started and the case came to the Supreme Court—"and all else was needless talk injurious to the country."[9] In his imaginary exchange with the saboteurs, who are pleading their case to him, Frankfurter blasts them as "damned scoundrels . . . just low-down, ordinary enemy spies who, as enemy soldiers, have invaded our country and therefore could immediately have been shot by the military when caught in the act of invasion." He quickly rules against them, declaring that "Congress specifically has authorized the President to establish such a Commission in the circumstances of your case and the President himself has purported to act under this authority of Congress as expressed by the Articles of War." Condemning them to their "just deserts with the military," Frankfurter seems to delight in the gruesome thought that the damned men's "bodies will be rotting in lime."[10]

Frankfurter ends his crude fantasy with a blatant appeal to unanimity in the name of patriotism as essential to winning the war. "Just relax and don't be too engrossed in your own interest in verbalistic conflicts," he lectures his fellow justices, "because the inroads on energy and national unity that such conflict inevitably produce, is a pastime we had better postpone until peacetime."[11] Whether it was "F.F.'s Soliloquy," Stone's jawboning, or both that carried the day is unclear. In the end, however, the members of the Court coalesced behind Stone's opinion and swept their differences under the rug.

On October 29, 1942, the Supreme Court finally issued a full opinion in the German saboteurs' case—eighty-two days after the executions. With Justice Murphy not participating, Chief Justice Stone wrote a forty-eight-page unanimous opinion holding that the trial by military commission, instead of a civil court with a jury, on the charges of violating the law of war and Articles of War conformed with the laws and Constitution.

After reciting the facts and procedural history of the case, the first order of business was to decide whether the Court could even entertain the dispute in light of the president's proclamation denying these enemy belligerents access to the courts. Dodging the constitutionality of Roosevelt's decree, Chief Justice Stone noted that the courts retained the power of "determining its applicability to the particular case." Furthermore, "neither the Proclamation nor the fact that they are enemy aliens forecloses consideration by the courts of petitioners' contentions that the Constitution and laws of the United States constitutionally enacted forbid their trial by military commission."[12] In other words, the Supreme Court was not going to allow the president, at least without congressional acquiescence, to close the courts to even the nation's mortal enemies.

The chief justice proceeded to lay the foundation for upholding the commander in chief's powers "in time of war and of grave public danger" to order a military trial of certain persons.[13] His authority derived directly from several grants of power in the Constitution, including the duty "to provide for the common defence" (Preamble), the "executive power" (Article II, Section 1, clause 1), the duty to "take care that the Laws be faithfully executed" (Article II, Section 3), his position of commander in chief of the army and navy (Article II, Section 2, clause 1), and the power to appoint and commission officers of the United States (Article II, Section 2, clause 1). "The Constitution thus invests the President as Commander in Chief with the power to wage war which Congress has declared, and to carry into effect all laws passed by Congress for the conduct of war and for the government and regulation of the Armed Forces, and all laws defining and punishing offenses against the law of nations, including those which pertain to the conduct of war."[14]

Stone then detailed the elaborate statutory scheme enacted by Congress in the Articles of War governing the trial and punishment by courts-martial of violations of the Articles of War by certain specified classes of persons. Articles 12 and 15 "recognize the 'military commission' appointed by military command as an appropriate tribunal for the trial and punishment of offenses against the law of war not ordinarily tried by court martial."[15] Articles 38 and 46 authorize the president to prescribe the procedure for military commissions; Articles 81 and 82 sanction trial, by either court-martial or commission, of those charged with relieving, harboring, or corresponding with the enemy and those charged with spying; and Article 15 makes clear that military commissions shall have "concurrent jurisdiction in respect of offenders or offenses that by statute or by the law of war may be triable by such military commissions . . . or other military tribunals." Similarly, Article 12 contains a catchall class of " 'any other person who by the law of war is subject to trial by military tribunals' and who under Article 12 may be tried by court martial or under Article 15 by military commission."[16]

In terms of the petitioners' attack on the uncodified law of war as an illegitimate basis for their prosecution, the chief justice gave a ringing endorsement to this common law dating back to the nation's founding. In Article 15, Congress included "that part of the law of nations which prescribes, for the conduct of war, the status, rights and duties of enemy nations as well as of enemy individuals." The president, as commander in chief, "by his Proclamation in time of war has invoked that law."[17]

Stone had no doubt that Congress had the constitutional power to authorize the president to try petitioners before a military tribunal if they are charged with transgressions under the law of war. These captured enemy military personnel were clearly subject to prosecution for long-accepted violations of the law of war.

> By universal agreement and practice, the law of war draws a distinction between the armed forces and the peaceful populations of belligerent nations and also between those who are lawful and unlawful combatants. Lawful combatants are subject to capture and detention as prisoners of

war by opposing military forces. Unlawful combatants are likewise subject to capture and detention, but in addition they are subject to trial and punishment by military tribunals for acts which render their belligerency unlawful. *The spy who secretly and without uniform passes the military lines of a belligerent in time of war, seeking to gather military information and communicate it to the enemy, or an enemy combatant who without uniform comes secretly through the lines for the purpose of waging war by destruction of life or property, are familiar examples of belligerents who are generally deemed not to be entitled to the status of prisoners of war, but to be offenders against the law of war subject to trial and punishment by military tribunals.* . . . Such was the practice of our own military authorities before the adoption of the Constitution, and during the Mexican and Civil Wars.[18]

The chief justice then determined that Specification 1 of the first charge sufficiently charged the petitioners with "the offense of unlawful belligerency, trial of which is within the jurisdiction of the Commission, and the admitted facts affirmatively show that the charge is not merely colorable or without foundation."[19] The petitioners' objective was to destroy war industries, war utilities, and war materials within the United States. They need not have intended to engage in combat with American armed forces or carried conventional weapons. Adopting the government's argument, Stone declared:

Modern warfare is directed at the destruction of enemy war supplies and the implements of their production and transportation, quite as much as at the armed forces. . . . By passing our boundaries for such purposes without uniform or other emblem signifying their belligerent status, or by discarding that means of identification after entry, such enemies become unlawful belligerents subject to trial and punishment.

Since the first charge was legally valid, the Court did not have to address the validity of the other three charges. The chief justice did reach the issue of whether Haupt's American citizenship changed the outcome. Assuming without deciding that Haupt had not forfeited his citizenship, as the government asserted, Stone nevertheless concluded that his citizenship did not relieve him of the consequences of being an enemy belligerent. "Citizens who associate themselves with the military arm of the enemy government, and with its aid, guidance and direction enter this country bent on hostile acts, are enemy belligerents within the meaning of the Hague Convention and the law of war."[20]

That the putative saboteurs did not actually carry out or even attempt their sabotage plan—or did not enter the theater or zone of active military operations—was irrelevant. Once they passed through the country's military and navy lines and defenses or went behind those lines "in civilian dress and with hostile purpose . . . [t]he offense was complete[d]."[21] And Haupt could be prosecuted for this violation of the law of war and not solely for the crime of treason, "since the absence of uniform essential to one is irrelevant to the other."[22]

The chief justice rejected the argument that the Fifth and Sixth Amendments required indictment by a grand jury and trial by jury in a civil court for prosecution of offenses against the law of war. While these two protections were widely accepted at the time of the Constitution's adoption, "they were procedures unknown to military tribunals, which are not courts in the sense of the Judiciary Article . . . and which in the natural course of events are usually called upon to function under conditions precluding resort to such procedures."[23] As early as the Continental Congress of 1776, the death penalty was imposed on alien spies (such as British Major John André and others) according to the law and usage of nations by sentence of a general court-martial. "[S]o far as we are advised, it has never been suggested in the very extensive literature of the subject that an alien spy, in time of war, could not be tried by military tribunal without a jury."[24]

Stone next attempted to distinguish *Ex parte Milligan*, where the Supreme Court repudiated the trial of a United States citizen—living in Indiana and suspected of supporting the southern cause—before a military tribunal. In *Milligan*, the Court proclaimed that the law of war "can never be applied to citizens in states which have upheld the authority of the government, and where the courts are open and their process unobstructed."[25] Chief Justice Stone stressed that this Civil War precedent must be construed in light of its peculiar facts and the critical differences between the circumstances of Milligan and Haupt. "Milligan, a citizen twenty years resident in Indiana, who had never been a resident of any of the states in rebellion, was not an enemy belligerent either entitled to the status of prisoner of war or subject to the penalties imposed upon unlawful belligerents."[26] In sharp contrast, Haupt and his German confederates were plainly within those boundaries [of the jurisdiction of military tribunals to try persons according to the law of war], and were held in good faith for trial by military commission, charged with being enemies who, with the purpose of destroying war materials and utilities, entered, or after entry remained in, our territory without uniform—an offense against the law of war.[27]

Finally, Stone made short shrift of the contention that the trial procedures specified by the president in his order (including lack of any independent appellate review by the judge advocate general) violated various provisions of the Articles of War. Without offering any explanation, he observed that "the Court is unanimous in its conclusion that the Articles in question could not at any stage of the proceedings afford any basis for issuing the writ." Noting a split among the divided justices as to the grounds, however, the chief justice stated:

> Some members of the Court are of the opinion that Congress did not intend the Articles of War to govern a Presidential military commission convened for the determination of questions relating to admitted enemy invaders, and that the context of the Articles makes clear that they should not be construed to apply in that class of cases. Others are of the view that—even though this trial is subject to whatever provisions of the Articles of War Congress has in terms made applicable to "commissions"—the particular articles in question, rightly construed, do not foreclose the procedure prescribed by the President or that shown to have been employed by the Commission in a trial of offenses against the law of war and the 81st and 82nd Articles of War, by a military commission appointed by the President.[28]

All the petitioners' arguments having been rejected, the Supreme Court affirmed the district court's denial of the petitions for writ of habeas corpus. The nation's highest court had spoken, but had justice been done?

A basic tenet of civilized jurisprudence holds that "justice delayed is justice denied." The treatment of the German saboteurs certainly satisfied at least one aspect of that goal. From apprehension to execution, the process took only seven weeks. Whether justice was done is another matter.

Constitutional scholars are divided over their assessment of the decision, but the majority criticize both the process and its reasoning. Some critics have castigated *Ex parte Quirin* as "a rush to judgment, an agonizing effort to justify a *fait accompli* . . . and even an appeal to patriotism in an effort to achieve a unanimous opinion."[29] Another commentator views Chief Justice Stone's opinion as more of a justification of "a dubious decision" than an intellectually honest elucidation of the law.[30] Shortly after the war, the eminent constitutional scholar Edward S. Corwin dismissed the opinion as "little more than a ceremonious detour to a predetermined goal."[31]

The decision's most glaring deficiency was upholding the charges against Haupt, a U.S. citizen. As one distinguished constitutional historian has concluded: "Stone realized Haupt should have been tried for treason in a civil court."[32] Equally suspect was Stone's attempt to distinguish the situations of Milligan and Haupt—both of whom were U.S. citizens and were prosecuted under the law of war at a time when the civil courts were capable of adjudicating the charges.[33] The Court's cavalier dismissal of *Ex parte Milligan*—and its eloquent message about the need for courts to vigilantly protect constitutional rights in wartime—supports the view that the opinion was more a political act than a judicial decision. And here lies the most pernicious legacy of *Ex parte Quirin*.

For decades, the unanimous decision in *Ex parte Milligan* had been viewed as "one of the great landmarks in defense of civil liberties."[34] Royall's instinct to construct his defense on the solid foundation of that opinion was legally sound. Indeed, J. Edgar Hoover himself had concluded that the German saboteurs had to be tried in a civilian court. Royall and Hoover both knew that the Supreme Court in *Ex parte Milligan* had rejected the notion that the entire nation was a theater of operations in wartime and that martial law could supplant civil law merely when an invasion was threatened.[35]

Haupt had been arrested by civilian law enforcement officials, not in any active battle zone but in Chicago. He was engaged in espionage, and federal law prescribed clear penalties for such conduct. Allowing the military to wrest authority from the civilian government was antithetical to "the very framework of the government and the fundamental principles of American liberty."[36]

Ex parte Milligan reiterated the credo of American democracy: "The Constitution of the United States is a law for rulers and people, equally in war and in peace, and covers with the shield of its protection all classes of men, at all times, and under all circumstances."[37] The justices also stressed the critical role entrusted to independent judges to preserve the principles of constitutional liberties in time of national crisis:

> By the protection of the law human rights are secured; withdraw that protection, and they are at the mercy of wicked rulers, or the clamor of an excited people. If there was law to justify this military trial, it is not our province to interfere; if there was not, it is our duty to declare the nullity of the whole proceedings.[38]

Ex parte Milligan concluded that the most egregious violation of civil liberties was the denial of the petitioner's right to a trial by jury. This fundamental right—"one of the most valuable in a free country— is preserved to every one accused of crime who is not attached to the army, or navy, or militia in actual service."[39]

In the case of the German saboteurs, the military trial itself "bore little resemblance to any legitimate criminal adjudication," even by the standards of 1942.[40] There had been no grand jury indictment, no jury of citizens, and no appeal to a civilian court—not to mention a substantial deviation from customary rules of evidence. Drawing a clear distinction between his clients' guilt and the process by which they were convicted, Kenneth Royall called the trial "a lynching."

"I am critical of the procedure, but not of the practical result of the trial before the Commission," Royall reflected twenty years later. "[A]ll these men had confessed before we got into the case, and the FBI had a couple of written statements from each of them."[41]

The constitutional confrontation was a litmus test of American democracy in perilous times.[42] Royall sharply criticized Roosevelt for his heavy-handed treatment of his clients. "President Roosevelt was a preacher of civil liberties, and here was the real test of whether he was just talking or believing 'liberty,' and he turned his back on what many thought were the requirements of 'liberty.' "[43]

Yet in the end, the colonel trumped his commander in chief's most audacious power grab. Royall won a major constitutional victory in the Supreme Court's final decision allowing his clients to file a petition for writ of habeas corpus: "A president cannot by simple executive order stop defendants—even foreign nationals bent on mayhem—from seeking review in the American court system."[44] The Great Writ retained its greatness even in a total global war.[45]

For the executive branch, the German saboteurs' case was "a constitutional and propaganda victory" expanding presidential power and allaying public fears of subversion.[46] Neither the Bill of Rights nor congressional prerogatives were weighty enough to overcome the commander in chief's policy judgments in time of war. As Biddle told FDR in a note transmitting the full opinion: "Practically . . . the *Milligan* case is out of the way and should not plague us again."[47] It was another step in the march toward an imperial presidency as Congress progressively lost its historical authority over war-making and punishment of wartime offenses—all in the name of national security.[48]

For the federal judiciary, *Ex parte Quirin* was an unmitigated disaster and an institutional defeat that would take decades to overcome.[49] As Chief Justice Stone himself realized, the judicial branch was "in danger of becoming part of an executive juggernaut."[50] By going to such extreme lengths to justify Roosevelt's actions, the Court preserved the "form" of judicial review while "gutt[ing] it of substance."[51] Ultimately, "the opinion did not dispel the thought that the civil safeguards of the Constitution were irrelevant to military affairs in the actual conduct of war."[52]

The frenzied pace of the proceedings and the Germans' execution without a full opinion gave the appearance that the Supreme Court was stampeded by Roosevelt. The justices heard argument without the benefit of reading the briefs ahead of time,[53] decided the case in less than a day with virtually no collective deliberation (much less reflection), and were in the dark about how the secret military trial had been conducted and how the military commission would rule.[54] In opting to draft an after-the-fact opinion that consciously sought to do the least damage to the judiciary at the expense of justice, Stone injudiciously gave short shrift to several issues on which the German saboteurs had the more persuasive legal argument. In the end, the Court felt it had no choice but to uphold the military tribunal's jurisdiction, casting itself as little more than "a private on sentry duty accosting a commanding general without his pass."[55]

The Court itself realized at the time the shortcomings of the process. As Justice Black's law clerk noted: "[I]f the judges are to run a court of law and not a butcher shop, the reasons for killing a man should be expressed before he is dead; otherwise the proceedings are purely military and not for [the] courts at all."[56] Justice Douglas agreed, citing the difficulty that Chief Justice Stone encountered in crafting a unanimous opinion after the petitioners had been executed.[57] Justice Frankfurter—the most complicitous in the whole affair—well knew that the decision was seriously flawed.[58]

Ex parte Quirin proves the adage of Justice Oliver Wendell Holmes Jr. that "[g]reat cases, like hard cases, make bad law . . . before which even well settled principles of law will bend."[59] The Court that uncritically upheld FDR's authority in the German saboteurs' case had succumbed to Biddle's argument that "total war" justified the suspension of fundamental legal rights traditionally accorded in peacetime. In deciding the case, concluded Michael R. Belknap, a distinguished historian, the Court—marching in lockstep to the drums of war—proved to be "an unreliable guardian of the Bill of Rights."[60]

The winds of war swept away the historical sympathies of judges for the underdog, who in this case were enemies of our nation as it was fighting for its survival. Justice Black's open hostility to Royall's request for his assistance is illustrative. Felix Frankfurter's troubling behavior is another unfortunate example. Ordinarily a staunch advocate of procedural fairness in federal criminal trials, he allowed his fierce commitment to crushing Nazi Germany to bias his judicial decision making. "To Frankfurter, a European-born Jew, Hitlerism seemed particularly menacing. He viewed it as a threat to the American democratic fellowship and to all civilized values. The fight against the Axis was for him 'a war to save civilization itself from submergence.'"[61]

Ex parte Quirin has been criticized not only for its uncritical acceptance of the government's claim of military necessity and the judicial "stamp of approval on military trials for a wide variety of wartime offenses,"[62] but also for some of the justices' egregious *ex parte* contacts and conflicts of interest and the Court's apparent bowing to presidential intimidation: "the private dealings within the U.S. Supreme Court raise troubling questions not only about the case but the Court's own susceptibility to bias and even threats in wartime."[63] Even by contemporary standards, these circumstances should have led Justices Frankfurter and Byrnes to recuse themselves.[64] Certainly, their conflicts of interest were as disqualifying as Justice Murphy's active military service.[65]

Ex parte Quirin has been praised by some scholars as a vindication of the American tradition of liberty.[66] At the time, the Supreme Court was applauded for intervening and expeditiously resolving the challenge to the government's authority in "a vigorous, impartial and learned presentation of the facts and the law."[67] What some condemn as haste others praise "as a model of military efficiency. . . . The total time it took from apprehension to completion of appeal was less than two months."[68]

> The Supreme Court stopped the military authorities and required them, as it were, to show their credentials. When this had been done to the Court's satisfaction they were allowed to proceed. . . . [The decision was] a wholesome and desirable safeguard to civil liberty in time of war.[69]

As Royall himself had to concede, the Germans' admitted violation of the law of war is indisputable. In debunking the evidence against the British soldiers who killed five of his fellow colonists in the Boston Massacre (and successfully arguing that his clients had been provoked by the riotous Bostonians), John Adams could have been talking about the German saboteurs' case. "Facts are stubborn things," he reminded the jury, "and whatever may be our wishes, our inclinations, or the dictums of our passions, they cannot alter the state of facts and evidence."[70]

Any negative assessment of *Ex parte Quirin* must be tempered by a stubborn fact in the historical record: the agents entered the country in German military attire and then changed into civilian clothes on the beach before embarking on their sabotage mission. "So long as they remained in uniform they were entitled to be treated as prisoners of war and could legally be neither tried nor executed."[71] By assuming a civilian disguise, however, they lost the protections of international law and were subject to summary punishment.

Lloyd Cutler—the youngest prosecutor, who later became one of the nation's most influential lawyers and counselor to two presidents—has noted that *Ex parte Quirin* "is the most Delphic, inscrutable decision you have ever seen. But . . . it was the proper decision. These guys were spies, caught with explosives, disappearing ink, out of uniform, behind the lines."[72]

To be fair, the actions of President Roosevelt, Attorney General Biddle, Secretary of War Stimson, and the Supreme Court must be judged in the context of the times and the prevailing social and legal culture. As two astute modern commentators, Professors Jack Gold-smith and Cass R. Sunstein, have observed:

> The capture of the Nazi saboteurs was one of the first pieces of good news in an unprecedentedly large-scale war that had not gone well during the first half of 1942. The future of the Nation was at serious risk, and everyone was aware of that fact. World War II was a "total war" that mobilized the entire Nation. Nearly everyone had relatives or acquaintances involved in the fighting, and tens of thousands of Americans had been killed or captured by the summer of 1942. On the home front, there were daily reminders of the war, including rubber shortages, gas rationing, and wage and price controls. Most people had a genuine fear of invasion by the Japanese on the west coast; and on the east coast German submarines had sunk hundreds of ships. Every-thing was disrupted; all of life was changed. There was no ambiguity about whether the Nation was at war, or about whether the nation's survival was at stake.[73]

Yet in his *Korematsu* dissent two years after *Ex parte Quirin*, Justice Robert Jackson warned:

> If the people ever let command of the war power fall into irresponsible and unscrupulous hands, the courts wield no power equal to its re-straint. The chief restraint upon those who command the physical forces of the country, in the future as in the past, must be their re-sponsibility to the political judgments of their contemporaries and to the moral judgments of history.[74]

In his conduct of the war, President Roosevelt deservedly won the overwhelming approval of his grateful fellow Americans. He was a po-litically effective, inspirational wartime president and astute com-mander in chief. In suspending civil liberties, delaying the black civil rights agenda, and executing the German saboteurs, he did not faith-fully execute all of the laws. But Roosevelt, like Lincoln, did save the nation.

Contrary to his most profoundly held principles, President Lincoln suspended habeas corpus, arrested persons who threatened the Union army's performance, and restricted freedom of the press.[75] In defending his actions, he told Congress in the dark days of 1861: "[A]re all the laws, but one, to go unexecuted, and the government itself go to pieces, lest that one be violated?"[76] In the Civil War, a "rebellion" justified the suspension, while in World War II the government claimed that an "invasion" by the German saboteurs warranted blocking access to the courts, under Article 1, Section 9 of the Constitution. Whether Lincoln and Roosevelt were legally justified in their actions is a controversy that will long endure.

As for the verdict of history, Roosevelt's actions in ordering a military trial for the German saboteurs has largely escaped notice compared to the widespread condemnation of his indiscriminate internment of Japanese Americans citizens based on an unsubstantiated pretext of military necessity. (This issue is discussed in Chapter 23.) In *Ex parte Quirin*, the president's attempt to suspend the writ of habeas corpus without congressional consent was properly repulsed by the Supreme Court. FDR's authority to use a military commission was debatable, but not brazenly unlawful, in light of the Articles of War enacted by Congress. While Haupt was shortchanged by not being prosecuted for espionage or treason in a civilian court, he likely would have been convicted by a jury of ordinary citizens, as was his father.[77] That the whole process resembled a legalized "lynching," as Kenneth Royall claimed, is an exaggerated assessment. Yet the military trial and appeal of the otherwise guilty defendants did in fact yield a preordained result with a thin gloss of due process.

Part III

A CAUTIONARY TALE

He [the King of England] has affected to render the Military independent of and superior to the Civil power.

—DECLARATION OF INDEPENDENCE

We have long since made clear that a state of war is not a blank check for the President when it comes to the rights of the Nation's citizens.

—JUSTICE SANDRA DAY O'CONNOR, *HAMDI V. RUMSFELD* (2004)

[W]hen this war is over, the thing we call the constitutional Bill of Rights will look a little different than it has looked.

—DANIEL SCHORR

Chapter 23

"A Loaded Weapon"

Six months after deciding *Ex parte Quirin*, the Supreme Court heard oral argument in *Hirabayashi v. United States*,[1] the first challenge to internment to work its way through the federal judicial system.[2] While some justices were deeply troubled by President Roosevelt's extraordinary action, they nevertheless acquiesced. Once again, the deafening cry of "military necessity" drowned out a plea to honor America's commitment to civil liberties and the rule of law.

A loyal American citizen of Japanese ancestry attending the University of Washington, Gordon Kiyoshi Hirabayashi had been sentenced to three months in prison on a misdemeanor conviction for violating curfew and evacuation orders. Writing for a unanimous court in June 1943, Chief Justice Stone upheld the conviction for curfew violation but avoided deciding the validity of the detention camp confinement. Relying in part on *Ex parte Quirin*, he first concluded that the president and Congress had authority under the war powers granted by the Constitution to enact the curfew/evacuation measures given the perceived threat of imminent invasion, espionage, and sabotage.

> Where, as they did here, the conditions call for the exercise of judgment and discretion and for the choice of means by those branches of the Government on which the Constitution has placed the responsibility of

war-making, it is not for any court to sit in review of the wisdom of their action or substitute its judgment for theirs.[3]

Stone then tackled the more troublesome issue of discriminatory treatment of Japanese American citizens. Rejecting the argument that these drastic measures should be imposed on all persons in the area or none at all, he reasoned that "constitutional government, in time of war, is not so powerless and does not compel so hard a choice if those charged with the responsibility of our national defense have a reasonable ground for believing that the threat [posed by all Japanese Americans] is real."

In a controversial portion of the decision, the chief justice uncritically accepted the grounds advanced by the military for this invidious racial discrimination against loyal U.S. citizens. These reasons included Japanese Americans' alleged failure to assimilate with the white population, their children's attendance at separate Japanese-language schools, the association of influential Japanese residents with Japanese consulates, the dual citizenship of children born in the United States of Japanese alien parents, and the presence of some disloyal members in this population. In short, these citizens posed some unspecified fifth column threat to national security.

The denial of equal protection had been compounded by the failure to afford any due process of law. General DeWitt justified the exclusion of *all* citizens of Japanese ancestry on the grounds that individualized determinations of disloyalty or security risk were infeasible and too time-consuming.[4] Stone accepted this excuse hook, line, and sinker.

> We cannot say that the war-making branches of the Government did not have ground for believing that in a critical hour such persons could not readily be isolated and separately dealt with, and constituted a menace to the national defense and safety, which demanded that prompt and adequate measures be taken to guard against it.[5]

As for singling out Japanese Americans solely on the basis of their race, Stone admitted that ancestry-based distinctions between citizens "are by their very nature odious to a free people whose considerations are founded upon the doctrine of equality." Nevertheless, the Court sanctioned such invidious discrimination because the danger of espionage and sabotage, in time of war, and of threatened invasion, calls upon the military authorities to scrutinize every relevant fact bearing on the loyalty of populations in the danger areas . . . [and] place citizens of one ancestry in a different category from others. . . . The adoption by Government, in the crisis of war and of threatened invasion, of measures for the public safety, based upon the recognition of facts and circumstances which indicate that a group of one national extraction may menace that safety more than others, is not wholly beyond the limits of the Constitution and is not to be condemned merely because in other and in most circumstances racial distinctions are irrelevant.[6]

As he did in *Ex parte Quirin*, the chief justice pleaded with his colleagues that the opinion be unanimous. "Utilizing to the full his titular and symbolic powers as Chief Justice, Stone . . . confronted strong-minded men divided by personal conflicts and divergent views on the function of the judicial role."[7] During the month of drafting the opinion, no fewer than five justices—Roberts, Reed, Douglas, Rutledge, and Murphy—expressed strong reservations about the legality of General DeWitt's orders and their constitutional basis.[8] Despite his own serious qualms about the discriminatory treatment of Japanese American citizens on the basis of race, Stone promised his colleagues that he would base the decision on the narrowest possible ground and evade the evacuation issue. In the end, as in *Ex parte Quirin*, "[c]ompromise, cajolery, and their own concerns that the Court should maintain unity in wartime finally persuaded this potential majority for reversal to make Stone's opinion unanimous."[9]

With the benefit of hindsight, if any of these justices had publicly opposed the curfew and exclusion orders, public pressure—and internal debate within the Roosevelt administration—might very well have caused the president to terminate the program long before the end of the war. Putting aside their strong aversion to internment, three justices reluctantly issued concurring opinions.

Justice Douglas stressed the "narrow ground" of the decision. "[N]ational survival is at stake. . . . Peacetime procedures do not necessarily fit wartime needs." It was a question of a military assessment of loyalty, not ancestry—a determination that should not be second-guessed by judges.[10]

After heavy lobbying by Justice Frankfurter, Justice Murphy at the last minute converted his draft dissent into a concurrence, but it read more like a dissent.[11] Justice Murphy believed that discrimination against seventy thousand Japanese Americans and "a substantial restriction of the personal liberty of citizens of the United States based on the accident of race or ancestry . . . bears a melancholy resemblance to the treatment accorded to members of the Jewish race in Germany and in other parts of Europe." This military measure—which "goes to the very brink of constitutional power"—was justifiable only in light of the "great emergency" and "critical military situation" prevailing on the Pacific coast in the spring of 1942 "and the urgent necessity of taking prompt and effective action to secure defense installations and military operations against the risk of sabotage and espionage." Finally, the Supreme Court, Murphy insisted, had an "inescapable duty . . . in time of war as well as in time of peace" to protect essential liberties—especially since invasions of civil liberties have often been "accompanied by pleas of urgent necessity advanced in good faith by responsible men."[12]

Justice Rutledge's concurring opinion took exception with any suggestion in the majority opinion that courts are powerless to review the legality of a military officer's discretionary actions against civilian citizens in military zones.

A year and a half later, on December 18, 1944, a sharply divided Supreme Court upheld a criminal conviction of an American citizen of Japanese descent for disobeying the evacuation order and not relocating to a detention camp.[13] Fred Korematsu was a twenty-three-year-old American-born Nisei living in the San Francisco Bay area and working as a welder. Korematsu's Fifth Amendment attack on the internment program fell on six pairs of deaf ears.

Writing for the majority in *Korematsu v. United States*, Justice Black—joined by Chief Justice Stone and Justices Frankfurter, Douglas, Reed, and Rutledge—constructed the decision on the shaky foundation of *Hirabayashi*, arguing that the "exclusion from a threatened area, no less than a curfew, has a definite and close relationship to the prevention of espionage and sabotage." Refusing to scrutinize the military's grounds for "believing that in a critical hour such [disloyal] persons could not readily be isolated and separately dealt with," Black excused the great burdens imposed solely on such a large group of

American citizens—"most of whom . . . were loyal to this country"—as the inevitable hardships of war.[14]

The landmark civil liberties decision in *Ex parte Milligan*—and its ringing condemnation of the unlawful exercise of emergency wartime powers to deprive citizens of their civil rights—posed a serious impediment to upholding internment. The Justice Department lawyers preparing the government's *Korematsu* brief debated the potential dispositive effect of that celebrated opinion. Rather than attempt to distinguish the case, Black—one of the Court's staunchest believers in deference to military authority in time of war or national emergency—simply ignored it altogether. Even worse, the majority opinion overlooks *Ex parte Milligan*'s requirement that an emergency be real and not imagined and that the courts must ascertain the truth of the facts purportedly supporting the military exigency. As one distinguished legal scholar, Joel Grossman, stated: "It is unlikely the government could have prevailed if the *Milligan* precedent was embraced by the Supreme Court."[15]

Three justices vigorously dissented. Justice Roberts drew a clear distinction between a curfew and "convicting a citizen as a punishment for not submitting to imprisonment in a concentration camp, based on his ancestry, and solely because of his ancestry, without evidence or inquiry concerning his loyalty and good disposition toward the United States."[16]

Finding that this single largest forced relocation in U.S. history "goes over 'the very brink of constitutional power'" into "the ugly abyss of racism," Justice Murphy condemned Roosevelt's order as "legalization of racism." He could not countenance depriving any person of his or her "constitutional rights on a plea of military necessity that has neither substance nor support." The "very real fear of invasion of the Pacific Coast [in 1942], accompanied by fear of sabotage and espionage," justified decisive military action, but the exclusion of all persons of Japanese descent was not reasonable. In fact, the supposed reasons supporting the internment appeared to be "largely an accumulation of much of the misinformation, half-truths and insinuations that for years have been directed against Japanese Americans by people with racial and economic prejudices—the same people who have been among the foremost advocates of the evacuation."[17]

Justice Jackson lambasted the whole scheme of "indeterminate confinement in detention camps" based solely on ancestry. He could not accept "an attempt to make an otherwise innocent act a crime merely because this prisoner is the son of parents as to whom he had no choice, and belongs to a race from which there is no way to resign." More than anything else, Jackson feared the danger of declaring constitutional

> the principle of racial discrimination in criminal procedure and of transplanting American citizens. *The principle then lies about like a loaded weapon ready for the hand of any authority that can bring forward a plausible claim of an urgent need.* . . . [This] passing incident becomes the doctrine of the Constitution. There it has a generative power of its own, and all that it creates will be in its own image.[18]

The course of American constitutional history might very well have taken a dramatically different (and salutary) direction if the government had told the truth to the Supreme Court. As they were preparing their briefs in the *Korematsu* case, Justice Department lawyers reviewed a draft of the army's final report on the Japanese American evacuation from the West Coast. They were shocked by the outright falsehoods about the "military necessity" that the government had advanced to justify internment.[19] Still smarting over losing the turf battle to the War Department two years earlier, the Justice Department lawyers slipped an incendiary footnote into their brief disavowing the claims in the final report about Japanese American disloyalty. Believing that these "lies" were "highly unfair to this racial minority" and not willing to allow the military to falsify the historical record, the government lawyers knew that their footnote would "fatally undermine the factual basis for the argument that military necessity justified the violation of Fred Korematsu's constitutional right to live where he pleased."[20]

The War Department exploded when it read the brief. Assistant Secretary of War John J. McCloy—the Wall Street lawyer who had called the Constitution "just a scrap of paper" when he urged internment to FDR—instantly realized that the footnote would shatter the fragile consensus that Chief Justice Stone had cobbled together in *Hirabayashi* and result in a decision in *Korematsu* that the whole relocation program was unconstitutional. After two days of heated argument, the Justice Department "once again buckled under McCloy's pressure and deleted the offending footnote."[21] Unaware of the truth, the Supreme Court decided the case[22] on the basis of a big lie—the fabricated "evidence" of military necessity.[23]

* * *

The last of the 117,000 interned Japanese Americans did not leave the camps until 1946—long after any "military necessity" could conceivably justify the extraordinary suspension of constitutional rights. Indeed, as early as June 1942, with the United States' decisive victory over the Japanese at the Battle of Midway, "the threat of air raids, let alone a full-scale invasion of the West Coast, had practically vanished."[24] Yet no one in the War Department even considered rescinding Executive Order 9066.

President Roosevelt showed no interest in restoring the internees to their homes. His wife's April 1943 visit to Gila River Camp in Arizona left her heartsick over the squalid conditions, but she could not persuade her husband to end internment. Even when Harold Ickes, secretary of the interior and a close FDR advisor, told him that it was no longer necessary to intern these Japanese Americans, Roosevelt did not want to address the thorny issue until after the November 1944 election.[25]

The "emergency" posed by the presence of persons of Japanese descent on the West Coast was largely fabricated by the military itself by means of false reports and exaggeration. This "proof" of massive disloyalty among Japanese Americans was then used to arouse public antipathy to Japanese Americans as fifth columnists. The ensuing popular outcry for decisive action was in turn exploited by the military as another basis for the evacuation order. Whether President Roosevelt was aware of this deceit is unknown.

Surrounded by armed guards, watchtowers, and barbed wire, the detainees lived a bleak, humiliating life in tar-paper barracks, each family, regardless of size, assigned to one room twenty feet by twenty-five feet. During internment, 1,862 died in the camps, and 6,000 babies were born. The heroism of Japanese American soldiers during World War II is legendary. While their families were living under harsh conditions in camps, thirty-three thousand of their sons, brothers, and fathers served in the U.S. Army, including the 442nd Combat Infantry Regiment, which bravely fought the Germans in Italy. And more than sixteen thousand Nisei served in military intelligence in the Pacific theater, providing critical assistance in defeating the Japanese by translating captured documents.[26]

For the loyal interned citizens, "the entire episode had been a cruel torment. By one estimate, they suffered some $400 million in property losses as a result of evacuation"—a sum of $4–5 billion in today's values.[27] The loss in self-esteem and the residual effects of alienation are incalculable.[28]

About one hundred Americans of Japanese descent challenged Executive Order 9066 and the resulting curfew, evacuation, and incarceration.[29] No court, including the United States Supreme Court, granted them any relief until near the end of the war, when victory was in sight.[30] At no time was the program declared unconstitutional.

Justice Jackson—who would serve as the chief prosecutor at the Nuremberg war crimes trial—later reflected on the Supreme Court's improvident endorsement of the abrogation of fundamental civil liberties in the *Hirabayashi* and *Korematsu* decisions upholding a curfew and internment. The Court, he concluded, "can never quite escape consciousness of its own infirmities, a psychology which may explain its apparent yielding to expediency, especially during war time."[31]

Earl Warren came to deeply regret his support of internment of Japanese Americans and the judiciary's failure to act, frankly admitting that his advocacy of the program was "not in keeping with our American concept of freedom and the rights of citizens." In a 1962 law review article, the chief justice observed that merely because the Supreme Court declares "that a given program is constitutional, does not necessarily answer the question whether, in a broader sense, it actually is."[32] Thus, in his view, the Supreme Court's upholding of Roosevelt's order did not mean that its action was consonant with constitutional standards.

Shortly after World War II, noted constitutional scholar Edward S. Corwin condemned the forced evacuation of Japanese Americans from their farms, businesses, and homes as "the most drastic invasion of civil rights in the United States which this war has evoked, the most drastic invasion of the rights of citizens of the United States that has thus far occurred in the history of our nation."[33] Right after the war, Eugene V. Rostow, a renowned Yale legal scholar, lambasted internment as "a program which violate[d] every democratic social value."[34] This stain on America's collective honor caused by "one of the most shameful episodes of constitutional failure" in history[35]—a disgrace to the cherished democratic ideals for which World War II was fought—is indelible.[36] Fortunately, efforts have been made to address this gross injustice.[37]

The healing process began during the bicentennial year. President Gerald R. Ford—a World War II navy veteran of the Pacific who had helped heal the nation in 1974 with a full pardon of his predecessor Richard M. Nixon for any offenses committed in connection with the Watergate scandal—felt strongly that America needed to make amends to its Japanese American citizens for the "tragedy" of evacuation and internment. On February 19, 1976, President Ford formally rescinded the thirty-four-year-old Executive Order 9066, stating:

> An honest reckoning, however, must include a recognition of our national mistakes as well as our national achievements. Learning from our mistakes is not pleasant, but as a great philosopher once admonished, we must do so if we want to avoid repeating them.[38]

Acknowledging the heroism of Japanese Americans on the battlefield in World War II, President Ford forthrightly admitted that "we now know what we should have known then—not only that evacuation was wrong, but Japanese Americans were and are loyal Americans." His eloquent statement of regret was in keeping with his personal belief, expressed a few months earlier in Hawaii, that human progress depends on the "capacity to grow from fear to trust and from a tragedy of the past to a hopeful future."[39] President Ford's termination of this odious symbol of the unjust repression of civil liberties in wartime set in motion a series of measures to redeem the "American Promise . . . to treasure liberty and justice for each individual American."[40]

Eventually, the U.S. government conceded that the relocation program was based on racial bias rather than any genuine threat to national security posed by Japanese Americans living on the West Coast. In 1982, after two years of testimony from 720 witnesses, the congressionally established Commission on Wartime Relocation and Internment of Civilians issued a 359-page report entitled *Personal Justice Denied*. The commission unanimously concluded that the detentions had been driven not by military necessity but by "race prejudice, war hysteria and a failure of political leadership." As a result, "a grave personal injustice was done to the American citizens and resident aliens of Japanese ancestry who, without individual review or any probative evidence against them, were excluded, removed and detained by the United States during World War II." The invidious discrimination was all the more reprehensible because "no documented acts of espionage, sabotage or fifth column activity were shown to have been committed by any identifiable American citizen of Japanese ancestry or resident alien on the West Coast."[41] The commission also recommended that Congress pass a resolution apologizing for the injustice done to Japanese Americans, offer reparations of $20,000 to each of the sixty thousand prison camp survivors, and expunge the records of persons of Japanese ancestry convicted of violating the West Coast curfew in 1942.

In 1988, Congress passed, and President Ronald Reagan signed, the Civil Liberties Act of 1988, incorporating all of the commission's recommendations. In an eloquent speech at the signing ceremony, President Reagan paid tribute to a Japanese American World War II hero who had died in battle for his country:

> Blood that has soaked into the sands of a beach is all of one color. America stands unique in the world: the only country not founded on race, but on a way, an ideal. Not in spite of, but because of our polyglot background, we have had all the strength in the world. That is the American way.[42]

In 1989, President George H. W. Bush issued a formal apology from the U.S. government. Further atonement came in 1998 in the form of President Bill Clinton's bestowal of the Presidential Medal of Freedom, the nation's highest civilian honor, on Fred Korematsu.[43] While the court of history long ago overruled *Hirabayashi* and *Korematsu*, the Supreme Court itself has never taken any official action to remove those decisions from the books.[44]

Meanwhile, supported by extensive findings of fact regarding the violation of due process caused by the government's misconduct in falsifying claims of military necessity, federal courts in the 1980s vacated the convictions of Gordon Kiyoshi Hirabayashi and Fred Korematsu.[45] Ninth Circuit judge Mary M. Schroeder summarized the verdict of history:

> The *Hirabayashi* and *Korematsu* decisions have never occupied an honored place in our history. In the ensuing four and a half decades, journalists and researchers have stocked library shelves with studies of the

cases and surrounding events. These materials document historical judgments that the convictions were unjust. They demonstrate that there could have been no reasonable military assessment of an emergency at the time, that the orders were based upon racial stereotypes, and that the orders caused needless suffering and shame for thousands of American citizens.[46]

While the Supreme Court may have been misled by the government about the factual basis for General DeWitt's orders, the justices' endorsement of racist governmental action

> cannot be attributed to ignorance and deception. The conclusion is thus inescapable that the Court made the decisions it wanted (or felt it had) to make to preserve its institutional power and prestige, support the war effort, and maintain for future use, a broad capacity to support the government's use of its war and emergency powers. This exercise in judicial statesmanship was justified by selective renditions of fact and some dubious constitutional interpretations.[47]

While apologies and reparations were decent (and long overdue) gestures, the most meaningful, systemic reform in response to internment came from the branch of government that had been the most passive. In 1971, Congress passed the Non-Detention Act, declaring: "No citizen shall be imprisoned or otherwise detained by the United States except pursuant to an Act of Congress."[48] This law—applying to any confinement of an American citizen by the president during war and other times of national crisis—was passed to repeal the discredited Emergency Detention Act of 1950. That repressive measure had authorized detention by the attorney general during an invasion, declared war, or "insurrection within the Unites States in aid of a foreign enemy" of "each person as to whom there is reasonable ground to believe that such person probably will engage in, or probably will conspire with others to engage in, acts of espionage or sabotage."[49]

The Non-Detention Act was primarily motivated by the travesty of the detention of Japanese American citizens during World War II.[50] Congress intended to cover military as well as civilian detentions and to require its express authorization before the president could detain citizens.[51] In terms of strengthening legal protection of civil liberties in time of war, the Non-Detention Act was a welcome statutory initiative that (as discussed in Chapter 26) would figure prominently in the challenges to the detention of U.S. citizens by President George W. Bush in the war on terror.

After four centuries of the uniquely American experiment in democratic self-government, we have learned that constitutional liberties are most threatened by the exigencies of war and other national security crises. The undeclared war between the Justice and War Departments during World War II epitomizes the age-old tension in a free society between preserving civil rights and promoting national defense. The silver lining in the dark cloud of this regrettable chapter in U.S. history is that we may have learned some valuable lessons. "[T]he existing consensus that the internment of Japanese Americans during World War II was a nadir in the history of civil liberties in the United States, plus the time-hewn institutional constraints in the U.S. government, provide hope that the episode will not be repeated again."[52]

But history will repeat itself—in new and more insidious ways—unless an informed American citizenry cherishes and robustly defends its precious freedoms. Two decades ago, in her eloquent repudiation of the miscarriage of justice in *Korematsu*, district judge Marilyn Hall Patel noted that the decision

> stands as a constant caution that in times of war or declared military necessity our institutions must be vigilant in protecting constitutional guarantees. It stands as a caution that in times of distress the shield of military necessity and national security must not be used to protect governmental actions from close scrutiny and accountability. It stands as a caution that in times of international hostility and antagonisms our institutions, legislative, executive and judicial, must be prepared to exercise their authority to protect all citizens from the petty fears and prejudices that are so easily aroused.[53]

In our constitutional system, the one institution that the people have entrusted to repulse any abuse of power by the legislative and executive branches is the independent judiciary. But can federal judges be counted upon to stand up to "the inevitable external and internal pressures for conformity and loyalty, and disregard of individual or group rights, that arise in times of crises"?[54] Whether it is a president violating the due process rights of suspected terrorists or Congress enacting repressive or discriminatory law enforcement measures in the war on terror, the Supreme Court must ultimately have the courage to just say no.

Chapter 24

Winners and Losers

President Franklin Delano Roosevelt, who died only weeks before V-E Day, accomplished his goal of teaching Hitler a lesson and deterring future sabotage.[1] Operation Pastorius was the first and only German terrorist attack on the United States. Whether Hitler abandoned his plan to send over waves of trained saboteurs because of FDR's summary treatment of the captured terrorists or because of the sheer difficulty of carrying out successful sabotage so far from Germany is not known. Undoubtedly, however, Roosevelt's steely resolve and nononsense attitude were decisive factors.

The Abwehr was so shaken by the mission's failure—and execution of six agents only fifty-seven days after they first came ashore—that no similar sabotage effort was ever undertaken again. German military records reveal that a major reason for the failure to launch similar missions was the German Naval High Command's refusal to allow a valuable U-boat to be risked for another futile sabotage mission.[2]

In the waning months of the war, a German submarine brought two espionage agents to the Maine coast. Landing on Crabtree Point near Mount Desert Island on November 30, 1944, Erich Gimpel, a thirty-five-year-old German radio expert, and William Curtis Colepaugh, a twenty-six-year-old American from Connecticut, came to collect information on U.S. industry. Armed with revolvers and carrying $60,000 in cash, the spies intended to communicate with the Third Reich through radio transmissions and secret messages embedded in letters ostensibly written to American prisoners of war in Germany. They did not come to kill or blow up anything.

A month after the landing, the quixotic mission was sabotaged when Colepaugh got cold feet and, like George Dasch, went to the FBI in Manhattan and led them to Gimpel. Following an eight-day trial at Governor's Island, New York City, both were convicted by a seven-man military tribunal and sentenced to death by hanging on February 14, 1945.[3] Three days before their scheduled execution, President Harry Truman commuted their sentences to life imprisonment. Gimpel was deported in 1955, and Colepaugh was paroled in 1960.[4] Both are still alive.[5]

Winston S. Churchill, who shared FDR's apprehensions about "enemies within," was turned out of office by the British people on July 28, 1945, while attending the Potsdam Conference with Joseph Stalin and the new U.S. president, Harry Truman. He served a second term as prime minister from 1951 to 1955. Churchill died on January 24, 1965, at age ninety.

After more than a dozen years as First Lady, Eleanor Roosevelt, who had opposed Japanese internment, devoted the rest of her life to human rights, eradication of hunger, pestilence, and disease, and world peace. A strong supporter of the new United Nations launched in San Francisco in 1945, she was instrumental in that body's promulgation of the Declaration of Human Rights. Eleanor Roosevelt—beloved by Americans and people around the world for her indefatigable, outspoken championing of civil rights, improvement of the human condition, and peace on earth—died in 1962 at the age of seventy-eight.

Secretary of War Henry L. Stimson retired from public office in September 1945 because of his chilly relationship with President Truman. Toward the end of the war, when it was apparent the Allies were headed for victory, Stimson opposed on moral grounds the terror bombing of the cities of Japan that created firestorms calculated to induce surrender. This public servant also objected to the total destruction of the German economy with the relentless bombing of its cities; it was not, he believed, in the United States' best economic interests.

With the transfer of the atomic bomb development to the army in June 1942, Stimson was directly responsible to the president for the Manhattan Project. On April 25, 1945, he gave Truman his first full briefing on the A-bomb. After failing to persuade Truman to soften the demand for "unconditional surrender" and offer the Japanese the right to keep their emperor in return for immediate surrender, Stimson became one of the key supporters of the atomic bombing of Japan to force an end to the war and save American lives.[6]

Stimson died on October 20, 1950, at age eighty-three.

Francis B. Biddle served as attorney general until June 30, 1945. President Truman appointed him the senior American member of the International Military Tribunal at Nuremberg, convened for eleven months between November 1945 and October 1946 for the trial of senior German government officials for conspiracy, crimes against the peace, war crimes, and crimes against humanity.[7] The panel heard one hundred witnesses, reviewed thousands of documents, and received affidavits bearing hundreds of thousands of signatures. The tribunal convicted nineteen defendants on one or more charges, sentenced twelve of them to death by hanging, and acquitted three.[8] (Hermann Goering evaded the noose by committing suicide with cyanide in his cell.)

Following his distinguished service at Nuremberg, Biddle was active in many private organizations. He was national chairman of the liberal Americans for Democratic Action and the American Civil Liberties Union. Biddle died at the age of eighty-two in 1968.

J. Edgar Hoover continued to serve as FBI director for, and amass dossiers about the private lives of, Presidents Roosevelt, Truman, Eisenhower, Kennedy, Johnson, and Nixon. During the Cold War, Hoover enthusiastically investigated—and cooperated with notorious senator Joseph McCarthy in purging the federal government of—alleged communists and their sympathizers for compromising national security. For some unknown reason, Hoover never aggressively pursued organized crime. At the end of his life, his own personal sex life—and the suggestion of a homosexual relationship with his longtime friend and aide Clyde A. Tolson—became a topic of widespread speculation. Hoover died in 1972, having served forty-eight years as the head of the nation's premier law enforcement agency.

* * *

Major General Frank Ross McCoy died in Washington, D.C., on June 4, 1954, at the age of eighty. With forebears who had fought in the Revolutionary, Mexican, and Civil Wars, he was widely respected as a soldier-statesman whose real love was the military. President Theodore Roosevelt once praised him as "the best soldier I have ever laid eyes on."

Major General Myron C. Cramer retired on November 30, 1945. Recalled to active duty in July 1946, he was appointed to serve as the U.S. member of the International Military Tribunal for the Far East in Tokyo for the trial of major Japanese war criminals. Cramer died in 1966 at the age of eighty-five.

For his bravery and coolness in crisis, John Cullen was promoted to Petty Officer Second Class and awarded the Legion of Merit. Now eighty-three, he lives in Virginia.

George Dasch and Peter Burger were eventually incarcerated at the federal penitentiary in Atlanta. In 1945, Dasch was moved to the federal penitentiary at Leavenworth, Kansas. Their appeals for clemency—and the broken promise of a presidential pardon—were widely publicized in the media. The prison warden urged the FBI to secure a pardon for Burger as a model inmate who had done a "tremendous job . . . for our country" in turning in his fellow saboteurs, furnishing information about U-boat bases in South America and the Gulf of Mexico, and testifying in several court cases against other German espionage agents.

Dasch, on the other hand, did not testify in those cases, was perceived as a bitter communist malcontent, and was despised and shunned by the other inmates. Erich Gimpel, the German spy caught in late 1944, encountered Dasch in Leavenworth prison and seriously considered murdering the "Judas-friend" but decided that Dasch would suffer more living "on the martyr's pile of his own conscience, pilloried by his own crime" and forced to listen to "the last desperate cries of his [six] victims . . . [sounding] in his ears."[9] The prison authorities expected him to flee to the Soviet Union as soon as he was sent back to Germany. Dasch's old nemesis—J. Edgar Hoover—adamantly opposed any executive clemency.

Finally, on March 20, 1948, President Truman, acting on the joint recommendation of the attorney general and judge advocate general, commuted Dasch's and Burger's sentences. U.S. Army Chief of Staff Dwight D. Eisenhower ordered the pair's release from prison and deportation to Germany. The failed saboteurs had spent almost six years in captivity—a year for each of their comrades' lives they had helped end by sabotaging the mission.

Burger faded into the chaos of postwar Germany, living and dying in obscurity. In another twist of his improbable life, Dasch returned home to find himself regarded as a traitor. He received death threats after a 1953 series of *Der Stern* magazine articles revealing his cooperation with the FBI and the tragic fate of his men. While his 1959 book *Eight Spies Against America* offered his exculpatory version of his role in Operation Pastorius, Hoover's undying enmity prevented him from returning to America. "Late in his life Dasch befriended Charlie Chaplin, who was living in exile in nearby Switzerland, and the two often compared notes on how J. Edgar Hoover had ruined their lives."[10] The enigmatic Dasch—was he a patriot or an opportunist?— died a troubled, angry man in 1991 without ever receiving the pardon he fervently believed that he deserved for betraying one country for another.

The saboteurs' handlers survived the wrath of Hitler and the war. General Erwin von Lahousen, the Abwehr chief, testified for the Allies at the Nuremberg trials and claimed that throughout the war he was "a member of a small resistance group . . . opposed to Hitler's program of aggressive warfare . . . [and] protest[ed] against the orders directing the killing of British commandos."[11] Like so many other Nazi officials, Walter Kappe returned to civilian life, undoubtedly pondering for the rest of his life how he could have foolishly entrusted a military assignment so vital to the Third Reich to the likes of George Dasch. The unfortunate Admiral Canaris, who had never believed the sabotage mission would be successful, was imprisoned and ultimately executed for his association with those involved in the July 20, 1944, plot to kill Hitler.

Those charged with assisting the saboteurs were vigorously prosecuted. Largely on Burger's testimony, the Haupts, Froehlings, and Wergins were convicted in a high-profile Chicago trial of treason for meeting with and aiding the terrorists. The three men were sentenced to death, and their wives received twenty-five years in prison. Following appeals reversing all six convictions, the women were released, and Wergin and Froehling received five years on a guilty plea to misprision of (that is, concealing) treason.

On retrial for treason for aiding his son, Hans Haupt—branded a "fanatical Nazi" by the trial judge—was convicted and got life imprisonment. In an opinion written by Justice Robert Jackson, the Court had no doubt that the government had satisfied its difficult burden of proof with admissible evidence that "[h]is acts aided an enemy of the United States toward accomplishing his mission of sabotage."[12] Justice William O. Douglas dissented, arguing that Haupt's "act of providing shelter was of the type that might normally arise out of a . . . [father's] relationship with his son . . . [and] is therefore not an overt act of treason, regardless of how unlawful it might otherwise be."[13] After the war, Haupt was deported to Germany, where he joined his wife, Erna.

Anthony Cramer was convicted of treason for furnishing assistance to his friends Thiel and Kerling and was sentenced to forty-five years in prison. The Supreme Court reversed on a 5–4 vote, with Justice Jackson authoring a historic decision enforcing the high evidentiary burden for proving treason beyond a reasonable doubt.[14] Cramer was later convicted on his guilty plea to trading with the enemy and sentenced to six years beyond the three already spent incarcerated.

Pleading guilty to trading with the enemy by taking Heinck's money, Hermann Faje was sentenced to five years. Hedy Engemann and Helmut Leiner, Kerling's friend whose name was written in invisible ink on Dasch's handkerchief, entered guilty pleas to misprision of treason. Kerling's mistress served three years, while Leiner was paroled in 1954. Kerling's wife and Ernest Kerkhof—a close friend of Kerling's wife and a suspected contact of the saboteurs in New York—escaped prosecution for lack of evidence.[15] Mr. and Mrs. Harry Jaques—Neubauer's friends found with $3,600 of his Nazi money—were interned and then shipped back to Germany.

The bodies of the six executed Germans remained interred in potter's field at Blue Plains until the early 1960s, when their remains were returned to their relatives in Germany.

Old Sparky remained in service for another fifteen years, until 1957. After the District of Columbia abolished capital punishment in 1981, the electric chair, which had taken forty-six lives, was permanently re-located to the Lorton Correctional Complex in Virginia.

Earl Warren, who vigorously supported Japanese internment as California attorney general, was elected the Golden State's governor. In 1953, President Dwight D. Eisenhower, a fellow Republican, appointed Warren to be chief justice of the United States Supreme Court. His appointment ushered in an era of liberal decisions, epitomized by numerous cases expanding the rights of the criminally accused and sharply departing from the World War II Supreme Court's deference to the president on matters of national security.[16] The Warren Court also took the first giant step to end the racial discrimination that stained America's profession of democratic equality. Eisenhower later lamented Warren's appointment as one of the biggest mistakes of his presidency.

Whether the German saboteurs' case made a breach in the wall of the Constitution or represented a justified vindication of presidential authority to use military tribunals to prosecute unlawful belligerents in wartime will long be debated. What cannot be debated, however, is the bravery of Colonel Kenneth Claiborne Royall as defense counsel for the Germans. In the annals of American law, Royall will forever rank as the exemplar of a zealous champion of civil liberties in uncivil times.

At the conclusion of the trial, Royall and Dowell returned to the positions they had held prior to the trial. Colonel Royall's life in the army's Fiscal Division was so boring compared to the life of a trial lawyer that he called it "slavery." One of the first letters Royall received was from his former North Carolina law partner, Blucher Ehringhaus. The ex-governor of North Carolina claimed that to his knowledge it was "the first instance in history of a lawyer losing 6 murder cases at one time—and still come out of court smelling like a legal rose."[17]

Ironically, Kenneth Royall's dedicated defense of the German terrorists—and his unquestionable loyalty to his country at the same time—furthered his military career, earning him the admiration of Secretary Stimson, Attorney General Biddle, President Truman, Congress, and many others. Royall remained in the armed services until he retired from the army in 1949 with the rank of brigadier general. In those years of exceptional service to his country, he held several high-level positions, including undersecretary of war, secretary of war, and secretary of the army. Royall was the last secretary of war and the first secretary of the army.

In all of his posts, he combined his gifts of keen intelligence, perseverance, and compassion. His many achievements included an instrumental role in establishing the U.S. Air Force as a separate service, settling 480,000 delinquent military contracts, reducing twenty-four thousand court-martial sentences, and reforming the army's court-martial policy into a more humane system. Royall presided over the postwar rehabilitation of Germany, Austria, Japan, and Korea and played a key role in the Berlin Airlift. His most notable accomplishment was spearheading the racial integration of the army.

After retiring in 1949 with the Distinguished Service Award, the General, as he liked to be called, resumed his law practice in New York until 1968, when he retired from the prestigious law firm Dwight, Royall, Harris, Koegel & Caskey (now Clifford Chance LLP). Among the early southern proponents of desegregation in public schools, Royall urged North Carolinians not to abolish the public school system in the wake of the Supreme Court's landmark *Brown v. Board of Education* decision in 1954. President John F. Kennedy appointed him as a mediator between civil rights groups and local officials during the 1963 racial disturbances in Alabama. Royall supported Dwight Eisenhower as well as Lyndon Johnson for president. He died at the age of seventy-six in 1971 in Durham, North Carolina.

President Truman summed up Royall's lifelong commitment to public service on the occasion of his retirement:

> In war and peace, you have served your government faithfully and well. As an officer with overseas combat service in both wars . . . you gained rich experience before you were called on to serve in various civilian capacities. . . . For your part in . . . activities of paramount importance to the national security, I tender you this assurance of heartfelt gratitude and appreciation.[18]

In a 1961 interview, William Safire asked Royall which of all his impressive achievements gave him the greatest satisfaction. Without hesitating, the distinguished Wall Street lawyer, who had argued for prestigious clients such as Procter & Gamble before the Supreme Court, responded: "My unsuccessful defense of the German saboteurs."

Great events and great people sometimes converge to shape the course of history. Certainly, Roosevelt and Churchill were such men during World War II. But so, too, was Kenneth Royall, whose greatness, unlike that of the celebrated wartime leaders, was established in apparent defeat.

At a time when government policy was influenced by mass hysteria and military leaders lied to their commander in chief about the threat of espionage and sabotage, civil liberties were sacrificed to earnest claims of military necessity. At a time when the courts were deaf to the pleas of citizens that their constitutional rights were being violated, the rule of law was a dispensable relic of peacetime. And at a time when the defense of Nazi saboteurs was exceedingly unpopular, one man rose to defend the condemned.

Notwithstanding popular condemnation, his personal distaste for his clients' conduct, and the wrath of his commander in chief, Royall mounted a vigorous defense of his clients in the noblest tradition of the trial bar in American history. When he realized that the military tribunal was a showcase to reassure the jittery American people and a propaganda weapon against Hitler, he defied Roosevelt's order barring resort to civilian courts. Fortified by courage, personal integrity, and a profound devotion to the rule of law, he risked the ire of the Supreme Court by forcing the reluctant justices to decide the first constitutional showdown during World War II between the executive and judicial branches of the federal government over the extent of the president's wartime powers to abrogate fundamental freedoms.

Scott Silliman, director of the Center on Law, Ethics and National Security at Duke University Law School, believes that Royall's stout defense of the German saboteurs epitomized the best in military lawyers. "He set the example for military attorneys in uniform. . . . [H]e is the model—that devotion to the client comes above wearing one's uniform."

In losing his case, Royall won a larger victory for the cause of justice. In time of war, the laws may be silent and the courts unsympathetic to the unpopular and the damned. But the tradition of the right to counsel and fearless advocacy against the overwhelming forces of official power nonetheless triumphed. With the support of his co-counsel, Dowell, Royall gave his doomed clients the kind of defense that validates the promise of American justice—a cornerstone of liberty that, thanks to his advocacy, assumed "new meaning, depth, and reality."[19]

Royall's fidelity to his obligation as an officer of the court—regardless of the personal risks and in the face of great public hostility—can be compared to that of John Adams 172 years earlier. A popular pre-Revolutionary leader in the growing protest against tyrannical British rule over the American colonies, Adams took on the defense of the British soldiers implicated in the Boston Massacre of March 5, 1770. In his stirring argument to a jury of his fellow colonists, who acquitted his clients on the murder charge, the future second president of the United States intoned:

> Gentlemen of the Jury—I am for the prisoners at the bar; and shall apologize for it only in the words of the Marquis Beccaria: "If I can but be the instrument of preserving one life, his blessings and tears shall be sufficient consolation to me for the contempt of mankind!"[20]

Kenneth Royall, if nothing else, was unapologetically for the prisoners. With the hindsight of six decades, we can discern that he also served another client—the American ideal of due process of law. Royall's German clients may have been executed, but his robust defense of them and his enviable display of personal courage and integrity was itself a triumph, for all time, for the very democratic principles for which nearly one million Americans died or were wounded in World War II.

Chapter 25

Clear and Present Dangers

On September 11, 2001, life changed irrevocably for all of us. America was attacked for the first time since Pearl Harbor—and more lives were lost on that terrible day than "the day that will live in infamy" sixty years earlier. Whatever notion of invulnerability we once might have entertained was blown away in the dust and wind of the collapsing Twin Towers and devastated Pentagon. America once again had been dragged into a global struggle—this time an ongoing, complex, and incredibly challenging effort to stamp out a new and implacable form of terrorism, perpetuated by religious extremists who believe their cause justifies criminal, genocidal acts.

From airports protected by armed military personnel to inspections of car trunks when entering parking garages, from "orange alerts" to a seemingly endless struggle to deal with a virulent hatred directed at this country, we are constantly reminded that we *are* at risk, that we *are* terribly vulnerable. Once again, fear stalks the land, and a brooding feeling of anxiety and helplessness has taken hold of the American people. The parallels to America in 1942 are real and eerie.

While martial rhetoric is used to describe the unfamiliar peril in which we find ourselves, the fundamental problems we face are not reducible to only military solutions. There is no defined battlefield; the fanatics bent on inflicting enormous damage on this nation (and other nations, lest we forget) wear no uniforms and bear no allegiance to any state. We seek to confront them thousands of miles from our shores, yet they move, undetected and unimpaired, among us—a new, invisible "enemy within," using terror as their weapon of mass destruction and operating outside the law of civilized nations.

That fear, while understandable, and the threat, however insidious, must not be allowed to inflict even greater damage on our country than the terrorists themselves. As Kenneth Royall kept reminding his contemporaries, then and now we fight and die for a just cause—the defense of our freedoms and a democratic way of life. For two centuries, the American people—proud citizens in a free society founded on the sanctity of the rule of law—have collectively been a beacon of hope and the implacable foe of despotism in a world beset by war and yearning for freedom. Just as it was in World War II and the Cold War, America is once again engaged in a principled global struggle against international tyranny, and brave Americans are spilling their blood on foreign soil for a noble cause. Indeed, as *New York Times* columnist Thomas L. Friedman has noted: "What you are witnessing is why September 11 amounts to World War III—the third great totalitarian challenge to open societies in the last 100 years."[1]

Once again, America confronts enemies who loathe our profound commitment to individual liberty, respect for human life, and due process of law. As Paul Berman, the noted author of *Terror and Liberalism*, has observed: "The rhetoric of Islamism in its more radical version—a rhetoric of martyrdom and random slaughter—is scarcely to be believed. Venerable holy men speak of blood, charnel houses, and massacres."[2] Driven by anger and resentment, these latter-day fascists would prefer a world in which religious zealots forcibly impose their nihilistic, totalitarian ideology on society through violence and intimidation. Contemptuous of human life, these despots hate our fundamental values of freedom of conscience, political and religious pluralism, the plebiscite, and democracy, regard women as chattel rather than persons, and denounce nonbelievers as agents of the devil.[3]

That is precisely why this just struggle—characterized as a war on terror—should not be tainted by compromising our historic respect for justice, constitutional liberties, and international law. If we stoop to conquer, we dishonor the very democratic ideals that we are fighting to uphold, and we give aid and comfort to the enemies of law and liberty. While our national defense must be fully supported, the government's war powers do not "remove constitutional limitations safeguarding essential liberties."[4] As the Supreme Court reminded us in *United States v. Robel* at the height of the Cold War:

> "[N]ational defense" cannot be deemed an end in itself, justifying any exercise of . . . power designed to promote such a goal. Implicit in the term "national defense" is the notion of defending those values and ideals which set this Nation apart. For almost two centuries, our country has taken singular pride in the democratic ideals enshrined in its Constitution. . . . It would indeed be ironic if, in the name of national defense, we would sanction the subversion of . . . those liberties . . . which makes the defense of the Nation worthwhile.[5]

Yet that is exactly what is happening.

In the wake of 9/11, America and her allies, supported by a congressional resolution but not a conventional declaration of war, went to war in Afghanistan against the Taliban and al-Qaeda militants who were responsible for the attacks on our homeland. Under the banner of Operation Enduring Freedom, the alliance also simultaneously launched a coordinated campaign against international terrorists and their supporters around the globe, seeking to interdict their finances, training, and operations. Eventually, beginning in January 2002, some 680 enemy soldiers captured in Afghanistan—designated by the military as "unlawful combatants"—were shipped in chains to the U.S. marine base at Guantánamo Bay, Cuba. Others were held at U.S. military facilities in Afghanistan and the remote island base of Diego Garcia. For more than three years, they have been held in small cells, cut off from communication with legal counsel and family, and deprived of any of the rights afforded prisoners of war under the Geneva Conventions of 1949 and U.S. military law.

The Geneva Conventions—integral components of the law of war—set forth the rights and obligations governing the treatment of civilians and combatants during periods of armed conflict. More specifically, the Third Geneva Convention addresses the treatment of prisoners of war, while the Fourth Geneva Convention addresses the treatment of civilians. As the Independent Panel to Review Department of Defense Detention Operations (chaired by former secretary of defense James R. Schlesinger) stated in August 2004: "American military culture, training and operations are steeped in a long-held

commitment to the tenets of military and international law as traditionally codified by the world community."[6] By explicit Department of
Defense directives, "[t]he Armed Forces of the United States will
comply with the law of war during all armed conflicts, however such
conflicts are characterized."[7]

The purported legal basis for these indefinite detentions was a
sweeping military order issued by President Bush acting in his dual capacity as chief executive and commander in chief. In his November
13, 2001, decree governing the detention, treatment, and trial of certain noncitizens waging a war of terrorism against the United States,
President Bush ruled that such detainees were "enemy combatants" or
"unlawful combatants" who would be tried by a "military commission," not by a jury in a civilian court, and would be eligible for the
death penalty. While guaranteed "a full and fair trial," the defendants
could be convicted and sentenced to death by only a two-thirds vote
of the military tribunal. Normal rules of evidence in federal courts—
including exclusion of illegally obtained testimony or documents—
would not apply.[8] And these detainees, according to the president's
order, were not entitled to file a writ of habeas corpus in federal court
to challenge their confinement or conviction.

Claiming that "the war against terrorism ushers in a new paradigm
[that] requires new thinking in the law of war," President Bush—
against the strong advice of Secretary of State Colin Powell[9]—also
announced that the United States would not adhere to "the letter" of
the Third Geneva Convention, particularly the minimum legal requirements for the treatment of combatants captured on the battlefield.[10] Among the most fundamental, threshold rights—codified in
Article 5—is a speedy determination of their status at a hearing conducted by a "competent tribunal": are they not combatants at all
(who should be immediately sent home), are they "privileged combatants" (who are entitled to the full panoply of rights of prisoners
of war), or are they, as the U.S. government alleges, "unlawful" or
"unprivileged" combatants (who are subject to U.S. military justice
under the law of war)? While claiming that it would honor "the spirit"
of the Geneva Convention and treat detainees humanely, the U.S.
government insisted that any rights that these foreign nationals eventually might enjoy were solely a function of "executive grace" and
not compelled by the Constitution, laws, or international treaties.[11]
The Bush administration also asserted that no court—U.S., foreign,

or international—could entertain challenges to the legality of the captives' indefinite confinement by the United States.

Three U.S. citizens were also apprehended as terrorists—two in Afghanistan and one at Chicago's O'Hare Airport. The government's handling of these three cases has been inconsistent and controversial. The first, John Walker Lindh of California, was promptly prosecuted in federal court in Alexandria, and the so-called American Taliban was sentenced to twenty years' imprisonment on his plea of guilty to fighting with the Taliban in Afghanistan. The other two American citizens—labeled as "enemy combatants"—have been treated much more harshly.[12]

Yaser Esam Hamdi, who was born in Louisiana and apprehended on the battlefield in Afghanistan, was held incommunicado in military brigs in Norfolk, Virginia, and Charleston, South Carolina, for nearly three years without access to a lawyer, indictment, or trial—much less a speedy trial. Jose Padilla, who was born in New York City and apprehended on U.S. soil, was likewise held in solitary confinement by the military in the same Charleston prison without any due process of law whatsoever. When Hamdi and Padilla filed habeas corpus petitions challenging violations of their constitutional rights as American citizens, the government took the position that President Bush had the unilateral legal authority to hold them indefinitely and incommunicado and that the federal courts were powerless to interfere.[13] In other words, these U.S. citizens were extralegal persons without counsel, charges, or a courtroom, existing in an indeterminate state of suspended citizenship.[14]

On March 21, 2002, the secretary of defense, Donald H. Rumsfeld—after conferring with several distinguished lawyers and former federal judges[15]—issued Military Commission Order 1, establishing the military trial procedures for detainees in Guantánamo Bay. Among other things, the military panels would consist of three to seven members, the cases would be handled by a chief prosecutor and chief defense counsel, a statement of the charges would be furnished before trial, and the defense would be afforded resources to investigate and call witnesses. Significant procedural safeguards would also be guaranteed, including the presumption of innocence, proof beyond a reasonable doubt, no compulsory self-incrimination, pretrial disclosure of the prosecution's evidence, the defendant's right to be present at trial, no double jeopardy, and a right of appeal.

The proceedings shall generally be open to the public—but not always. Under certain circumstances requiring protection of classified information, intelligence and law enforcement sources, methods, and activities, or "other national security interests," the trial may be closed. The accused and his civilian counsel (but not appointed military defense counsel)—as well as the media—may be excluded during the trial's secret sessions.[16]

In July 2003, the Pentagon announced that after one and a half years, President Bush had finally identified six "enemy combatants" (out of over 680 terrorist suspects in American custody) as eligible for the first trials before the U.S. military commissions. While the government promised that the trials would start in the next few months, no trials of any detainees had commenced well after the second anniversary of their confinement, and none will have gone through the entire process of charges, pretrial hearings, trial, and appeal by the time the third anniversary rolls around.[17] Given this glacial pace, the need to try hundreds of potential defendants, and the government's failure to honor international law by holding prompt hearings on the detainees' status as POWs, the military proceedings could last for many years, intolerably delaying justice for many persons who may be innocent—or at least are deserving of the presumption of innocence.[18]

One feature of Bush's military justice was not delayed: an execution chamber was promptly constructed near the courtroom at Guantánamo Bay, Cuba.

This chain of extraconstitutional detention centers extends from Guantánamo Bay, Cuba, through Charleston, South Carolina, and on to the U.S. military facility at Diego Garcia and the U.S. air base at Bagram, Afghanistan. Since 9/11, the United States and cooperating countries have arrested over three thousand alleged al-Qaeda "operatives and associates," virtually all of whom have been held without counsel, charges, or an opportunity to challenge the basis of their imprisonment. Beside the more than 680 indefinite detainees from forty-two countries at the Guantánamo Bay prison, the United States has held dozens of detainees in Afghanistan, where they were subjected to CIA "stress and duress" techniques such as hooding, blindfolding, forced prolonged standing or kneeling, twenty-four-hour lighting, and sleep deprivation.[19] The military admits that at least one detainee was murdered.[20]

The prisoners include children between the ages of thirteen and sixteen, the very elderly (one over a hundred), mentally incompetent adults, and shopkeepers swept up in the fury of war, some sold by rival tribes into American captivity for the bounty. The vast majority of the actual military personnel were foot soldiers of the Taliban.[21] No ranking al-Qaeda or Taliban leaders were detained. Many detainees are innocent victims of circumstance, and the military itself admitted that hundreds of these prisoners should be repatriated.[22]

The conditions of confinement at Camp Delta at Guantánamo Bay are harsh, to say the least. The detainees are housed in minute cells (six feet by eight feet) for up to twenty-four hours a day, and they are constantly, rigorously interrogated. Lights are kept on all day and night. As one official admitted, it is "not quite torture, but as close as you can get."[23] Held incommunicado with no sense of when (if ever) they will be charged, much less freed to go home, the prisoners live in a law-free zone. The isolation from family and friends, coupled with the intensive interrogation, has led to at least thirty-two attempted suicides by twenty-seven prisoners as of early 2004.

Contrary to their religious tenets, the Muslim prisoners were compelled to shave off their beards. They get virtually no exercise and have no clue about their fate. They are confined at a U.S. prison operating entirely outside the law. As the lawyers for four detainees told the Supreme Court: "With no legal process, no opportunity to establish their innocence, no human contact with the outside world . . . and no apparent end to their incarceration, the prisoners 'drift[ ] through life rather than live[ ], the prey of aimless days and sterile memories.' "[24]

How many Guantánamo Bay detainees were in fact enemy combatants or terrorists has been sharply questioned. By late July 2004, most of the 139 terror suspects who had been released had not been charged upon return to their home countries.[25] Amnesty International has asserted that the steady stream of releases demonstrates that "detention without trial as part of an open-ended 'war on terror' is unjustified."[26]

Released prisoners have plausibly claimed that they were systematically abused by their American captors.[27] For example, three British subjects detailed the harrowing conditions at Camp Delta, alleging that "they were beaten, shackled in painful positions, deprived of sleep and subjected to continual humiliation."[28] "All of the techniques they describe are illegal and a violation of the Geneva Conventions, and cumulatively, they amount to torture," asserted Michael Ratner, president of the Center for Constitutional Rights.[29] In a rare public statement, the International Committee of the Red Cross stated that if the allegations were true, they indicated systematic abuse and inhuman treatment tantamount to torture and war crimes.[30] The U.S. military denied use of "any kind of coercive or physically harmful techniques,"[31] but, as discussed below, several official investigations documented prisoner abuse.

President Bush opened a second front in the war on terror with the controversial invasion of Iraq in March 2003. Overmatched Iraqi armed forces were quickly defeated. Thousands of prisoners of war were detained, bringing to a cumulative total of fifty thousand the detainees in the custody of U.S. officials in Afghanistan, Iraq, and Guantánamo Bay, Cuba.[32] In October 2003, the largest facility, Abu Ghraib in Baghdad, housed up to seven thousand detainees. At least fifty-five prisoners there were subjected to shocking torture, inhumane treatment, and even death during confinement and interrogations.[33] President Bush condemned these "abhorrent abuses." Some of the "persuasion" practices used at Abu Ghraib—including isolation, the use of dogs, stripping detainees naked, sleep deprivation, and subjecting them to stress positions—were imported from Guantánamo Bay,[34] confirming once again that al-Qaeda and Taliban prisoners in Cuba were being physically and psychologically abused in violation of the Geneva Conventions and the Convention Against Torture and Other Cruel, Inhuman or Degrading Treatment.

Prisoner abuse was not restricted to notorious Abu Ghraib. At least eight documented cases occurred in Guantánamo Bay and three in Afghanistan, bolstering the claims of those released detainees that they were abused and tortured. The Schlesinger investigation found that five detainees died "as a result of abuse by U.S. personnel during interrogations."[35]

An army investigation of the Abu Ghraib abuse scandal found "misconduct (ranging from inhumane to sadistic) by a small group of morally corrupt soldiers and civilians."[36] Responsibility for this "brutality and purposeless sadism" at the hands of both military police and military intelligence personnel reached far higher in the chain of command—indeed, all the way to the Pentagon's senior civilian and military leaders, including Secretary of Defense Donald H. Rumsfeld.[37] More than management failures, the evidence clearly showed a "relationship between Secretary Rumsfeld's approval of interrogation techniques designed to inflict pain and humiliation and the widespread mistreatment and torture of detainees in Iraq, Afghanistan and Guantánamo."[38]

It was equally clear that the president's ruling that the Geneva Conventions did not apply to prisoners captured in the Afghanistan conflict—coupled with the outrageous legal advice of the Bush administration's lawyers legitimizing the torture of terrorist suspects, documented in Anthony Lewis' introduction to this book[39]—created the toxic environment for this lawless conduct.[40] The buck starts and stops at President Bush's desk.

As Dahlia Lithwick wrote in the *New York Times*:

> Abu Ghraib can't be blamed solely on bad apples anymore. It was the direct consequence of an administration ready to bargain away the rule of law. That started with the suspension of basic prisoner protections because this was a "new kind of war." It led to the creation of a legal sinkhole in Guantánamo Bay. And it reached its zenith when high officials opined that torture isn't torture unless there's some attendant organ failure.[41]

This shameful treatment of prisoners—a blight on the nation's honor—was rightly condemned by the community of nations. As Fyodor Dostoyevsky observed: "The degree of civilization in a society can be judged by entering its prisons." The United States is viewed not only as an outlaw that terrorizes POWs but also as a hypocrite. Human rights advocates—as well as U.S. officials charged with promoting respect for humanitarian law abroad—have lamented that Abu Ghraib "was devastating for U.S. credibility" in promoting human rights in other nations.[42] Conservative Republicans have excoriated President Bush. "We won the war in three weeks," noted Patrick Buchanan, "and we may have lost the Islamic world for a generation."[43] The world is a far less safe place for Americans and all other terrorist targets as a result.

The president's unprecedented assertion of virtually unlimited war powers in general—and his decision to use military commissions in particular—sparked a fierce debate between civil libertarians and national security champions.

The Bush administration—while claiming inherent presidential authority to detain U.S. citizens as suspected but uncharged terrorists—defended military courts for foreign nationals on several grounds, including the need to protect lay jurors and judges from reprisals, national security, and efficiency during wartime.[44] Mindful of the media circus surrounding the televised murder trial of O.J. Simpson in the mid-1990s, the president's prime defender and Patriot Act champion, Attorney General John Ashcroft, offered another justification: "Can you imagine the spectacle of capturing a solder-terrorist in Afghanistan, bringing them back with a publicly paid, high profile, flamboyant defense lawyer on television, making it the Osama network?"[45]

Republican congressman Bob Barr, a House Judiciary Committee member, did not mince words: "We are not interested in reading [the terrorists and those harboring them] their rights. We are interested in taking them out, lock, stock, barrel, root, limb."[46] Responding to critics concerned about which suspects would be subject to the order, the president's lawyers hastened to stress that it covers only "foreign enemy war criminals" and not United States citizens or "even enemy soldiers abiding by the laws of war."[47] War criminals—like members or active supporters of al-Qaeda and other international terrorists targeting the United States—are "not entitled to the same procedural protections as people who violate our domestic laws."[48]

The government stoutly defended the president's authority to employ military and not civilian courts to try enemy belligerents who commit war crimes. Invoking Civil War and World War II precedents and the names of two of America's greatest presidents—Abraham Lincoln and Franklin D. Roosevelt—the president's chief lawyer noted:

> The language of the order is similar to the language of a military tribunal order issued by President Franklin Roosevelt. . . . Military commissions are consistent with American historical and constitutional traditions. Confederate agents disguised as civilians traveling to New York to set it afire were tried by military commission. Nazi saboteurs who came ashore on Long Island during WWII disguised as civilians and intending to attack American war industries were tried before military commissions. The use of such commissions has been consistently upheld by the Supreme Court.[49]

Not surprisingly, the most frequently cited precedent was the Supreme Court's 1942 unanimous opinion in *Ex parte Quirin* upholding a secret military trial of the eight German saboteurs and the execution of six of the defendants. As discussed in Chapter 22, the Supreme Court held that, notwithstanding President Roosevelt's order to the contrary, the petitioners could invoke the writ of habeas corpus to test the legality of the military trial. On the merits, however, the justices sided with the president, concluding that the constitutional jury trial guarantee did not extend to "alien or citizen offenders against the law of war."[50] These German soldiers (two still formally U.S. citizens), who wore civilian clothes, not uniforms, and made clandestine landings on America's shores from German submarines, were acting under orders to carry out sabotage and terrorist actions. Ample precedent, the U.S. government maintained, sanctioned their trial by a military court and, if convicted, execution on the grounds that they were "enemy combatants" historically considered "offenders against the law of war subject to trial and punishment by military tribunals."[51]

Whether the sixty-year-old decision's precedential value was limited by the fact that Congress had not formally declared war in the 2001 resolution (as it had in World War II) was an open question.[52] The fact that Congress had not made such a formal declaration of war on international terrorism did not undermine the president's authority, the administration claimed, for at least two reasons.

First, like Lincoln and FDR, Bush had inherent authority as president and commander in chief to issue the order. As the Supreme Court ruled in upholding a military court trial of a Japanese military commander for war crimes in *Application of Yamashita*, "[t]he trial and punishment of an enemy combatant who has committed violations of the law of war is not only a part of conduct of war, but also is an exercise of authority sanctioned by Congress [in the Articles of War] to administer a system of military justice."[53]

Second, according to the president, a formal declaration of war or new legislation authorizing military tribunals was not necessary. Formal declarations of war had become passé. Congress had formally declared war only four times—in 1812 against Britain, in 1898 against Spain, and in the First and Second World Wars. President Bush, supported by a congressional joint resolution authorizing use of "all necessary force" against those responsible for the September 11 attacks, was fighting the equivalent of a formally declared war—just as his predecessors did in Korea, Vietnam, and Kuwait. In their capacity as commander in chief, presidents often take decisive actions without explicit congressional approval *during* wartime.[54] According to this view, the president had to act promptly without a congressional mandate so that the military court apparatus would be in place in case Osama bin Laden or his compatriots were apprehended.[55]

Predictably, the American Civil Liberties Union blasted President Bush's plan. Conceding that Supreme Court precedent allowed military tribunals in a foreign war zone such as Afghanistan, the ACLU criticized "kangaroo courts" deciding the fate of accused terrorists arrested within the United States.[56] "Trying terrorists before military commissions is a violation of due process and a rejection of our own legal traditions. It also hands those terrorists' allies a powerful public relations weapon to use against the United States."[57]

Civil liberties advocates singled out the military tribunals' shortcut concepts of justice, including authority over closure of, and access to, proceedings.[58] Why is the government afraid to allow a jury of American citizens to sit in judgment of the accused foreign terrorists? the ACLU wondered. "If the government had a strong case, people will rightly ask, why didn't it make its arguments before a jury in an open courtroom?"[59] After all, is there any reason to think that a lay jury of average Americans will be any less fair—or more inclined to acquit the guilty—than a panel of senior military officers?[60]

Following the secretary of defense's issuance of regulations, the civil liberties community toned down the harshness of its rhetoric and actually praised the detailed procedures for offering "many of the essential safeguards of the existing legal system." Yet critics still wondered why special tribunals were necessary at all.[61] Even with the improved procedural protections, the ACLU and human rights organizations objected to the relaxed standards for admission of evidence (including allowing hearsay), authorization of secret proceedings, and the limited right of appeal to a three-member review panel but no access to the civilian courts.[62] This latter deficiency, the protesters warned, will put the defendants' lives solely in the president's hands, in contravention of "basic American, and international, ideals of fairness and justice."[63] Distilling the rhetoric, their fundamental point was clear:

> [J]udicial proceedings are not meant as a shortcut to punish the guilty, but as a means of determining whether the accused are guilty or innocent. Punishment comes only after guilt is proved beyond a reasonable doubt. Watering down protections for the accused and easing the burden

on the prosecution dilutes the value of guilty verdicts and increases the possibility that innocent people will be punished.[64]

The attack on the military trial of terrorists did not emanate solely from the left. Prominent conservatives lambasted what they saw as a seizure of dictatorial power by the president without a congressional declaration of war or express authorization.[65] Indeed, their tone was far more caustic than that of liberals, who undoubtedly feared being perceived as "soft on terrorism."

Former Nixon speechwriter and prominent *New York Times* columnist William Safire wasted no time targeting "military kangaroo courts." In a series of columns beginning on November 15, 2001, Safire ferociously attacked President Bush's coup d'état "betray[ing] our principles of justice" by replacing

the American rule of law with military kangaroo courts. . . . He seizes the power to circumvent the courts and set up his own drumhead tribunals—panels of officers who will sit in judgment of non-citizens who the president need only claim "reason to believe" are members of terrorist organizations. . . . His kangaroo court can conceal evidence by citing national security, make up its own rules, find a defendant guilty even if a third of the officers disagree, and execute the alien with no review of any civilian court. . . . No longer does the judicial branch and an independent jury stand between the government and the accused. In lieu of those checks and balances central to our legal system, non-citizens face an executive that is now investigator, prosecutor, judge, jury, and jailer or executioner. In an Orwellian twist, Bush's order calls this Soviet-style abomination "a full and fair trial."[66]

Safire blamed "our Caesar['s]" "blunderbuss order" to dispense with even the limited rights afforded by a court-martial on bad advice from "a frustrated and panic-stricken" attorney general, John Ashcroft.[67] The precedents cited for support—military courts trying President Abraham Lincoln's assassins after the Civil War ended and German saboteurs during World War II—failed to persuade Safire. In another column, he took direct aim at President Franklin D. Roosevelt's "mistake" being used as justification by President Bush "for his own dismaying departure from due process."[68] Safire pointed out that FDR wanted a secret trial not to protect national security but at least in part to cover up the embarrassing bungling of the arrest of the lead German saboteur, George Dasch, who had to call J. Edgar Hoover's Federal Bureau of Investigation twice before they would come to arrest him in his hotel room.[69]

Safire derided President Bush's after-the-fact justification that "civil courts cannot be trusted to protect military secrets"[70] and that he was "protecting jurors (by doing away with juries)."[71] He also slammed the president's suggestion that his "Star Chamber tribunals" are a faithful implementation of

> the lawful Uniform Code of Military Justice. Military attorneys are silently seething because they know that to be untrue. The U.C.M.J. demands a public trial, proof beyond reasonable doubt, an accused's voice in the selection of juries and right to choose counsel, unanimity in death sentencing and above all appellate review by civilians confirmed by the Senate. Not one of those fundamental rights can be found in Bush's . . . order[s]. . . . Bush's fiat turns back the clock on all advances in military justice, through three wars, in the past half-century.[72]

Defending himself and other editorialists who were standing up for "American values," Safire derided as "phony-tough" proposals for overriding basic civil liberties with "extraordinary security measures" during a terrorist emergency.[73] Why not give Osama bin Laden and his cohorts a proper trial just as Israel afforded Nazi Holocaust architect Adolph Eichmann?[74] Ultimately, a democratic society has to take the risk of giving "a global propaganda platform" to terrorists—and even the possibility of "widespread hostage-taking by . . . [bin Laden's] followers to protect him from the punishment he deserves."[75] The alternative under President Bush's illegitimate scheme, Safire concluded, is "to corrupt our judicial tradition by making bin Laden the star of a new Star Chamber."[76]

Critics of President Bush's order echoed the ACLU's mixed review of the Rumsfeld procedures. While pleased that the Pentagon's initiative sets "partly right a deeply-flawed executive order,"[77] Safire continued to condemn the lack of civilian judicial review of the convictions and sentences, indefinite detention without a trial, and the absence of congressional participation "in the making of what is undoubtedly law."[78] In the end, Safire continued to believe that President Bush had unconstitutionally usurped power in unilaterally establishing his military courts.

But ours is a government of laws, not of executive fiats. The Uniform Code of Military Justice and the Court of Appeals for the Armed Forces are creations of Congress and do not weaken the executive branch. Besides, the war on terror is supposed to be a unified effort—why go it contemptuously alone in setting up an extraordinary military judiciary?[79]

In a melancholy reminder of McCarthyism, those who criticized the president's military courts plan were denounced as unpatriotic. Attorney General Ashcroft attacked Safire and other dissenters as "voices of negativism"[80] who were "aiding terrorists."[81] Fellow conservative Jonah Goldberg found Safire to be "hysterical" in his "spleen-venting in the *New York Times*."[82]

With the notable exception of Senator Patrick J. Leahy, liberals and the Congress—whose prerogatives were being championed by Safire and others—maintained mostly a Sphinx-like silence on the civil liberties issues raised by the president's military courts.[83] Other than some limited hearings on the president's order shortly after it was issued and two years later, Congress exercised no effective legislative oversight with respect to the treatment of Hamdi, Padilla, or the Guantánamo Bay detainees.

President Bush's order was condemned by numerous prestigious American, British, and other foreign lawyers, retired judges, and bar leaders as well as many respected lawyers' and judges' organizations. Some of the leading jurists and scholars in the United States and Great Britain also issued scathing denunciations. In fact, it was difficult to find any respected lawyers or jurists who unqualifiedly endorsed the plan. Even some of the president's early supporters—including two senior lawyers in his own administration—later criticized the scheme. The marked erosion of support was attributable not only to the fatal legal flaws in the military tribunal program but also to the fact that nearly three years passed after the president's order in late 2001 before defense lawyers were appointed and charges were filed against a handful of detainees. It became clear that President Bush was more interested in detention than justice. Proving once again that slow-motion justice is no justice at all, not a single Guantánamo detainee had been brought to trial by late 2004.[84]

One of the most damaging critiques of the military tribunals came from the prestigious International Commission of Jurists (ICJ). An international organization of judges and lawyers dedicated to upholding the rule of law and protecting human rights, the ICJ condemned President Bush's order as posing a threat to "the most fundamental principles relating to the due process and separation of powers" in violation of international law and the U.S. Constitution.[85] Among many things, they were concerned about "no role whatsoever provided for the judiciary in any phase of the process" and the unavailability of habeas corpus—constitutional infirmities not cured by the secretary of defense's more detailed procedures.[86]

The ICJ cited the International Covenant on Civil and Political Rights and the Third Geneva Convention on the humane treatment of prisoners of war as authority for urging that courts of law, not military tribunals, try suspected terrorists even during armed conflict.[87] Invoking a commonly cited rationale for open civilian trials, the international jurists emphasized the resounding propaganda victory for the rule of law.

> On a policy level, it seems that the United States would well serve both its own national values and the world community by setting an example in conducting trials in view of the world. Such an undertaking [affords] . . . an opportunity to demonstrate the imperative of human society based on the rule of law, the very destruction of which the terrorists who conducted the 11 September attacks sought to achieve.[88]

Finally, in concluding its appeal to President Bush to try accused terrorists before civilian courts, the ICJ recalled the wisdom of Supreme Court Justice Robert H. Jackson, who took a leave from his judicial duties to prosecute the major Nazi war criminals at Nuremberg. Reporting on the outcome of the public trial conducted by distinguished jurists from the United States, England, France, and the Soviet Union, Jackson wrote to President Harry Truman on October 7, 1946:

> [The victors] have given the example of submitting their grievances against these men to a dispassionate inquiry on legal evidence . . . [and] of leaving punishment of individuals to the determination of independent judges, guided by principles of law, after hearing all of the evidence for the defense as well as the prosecution. It is not too much to hope that this example of full and fair hearing, and tranquil and discriminating judgment will do something toward strengthening the processes of justice in many countries.[89]

*   *   *

With his dogged insistence on using military courts and indeterminate incarceration of U.S. citizens without any due process of law, President Bush managed to squander a large measure of goodwill toward the United States in the world community. The nation that made an unequivocal commitment to the Geneva Conventions of 1949 is now seen as a state run by a unilateralist administration that regards international tribunals and accepted norms of international law with thinly veiled contempt and conspicuously violates the long-established rights of captured enemy combatants. As Yale Law School dean Harold Hongju Koh noted: "In a remarkably short time, the United States has moved from being the principal supporter of that system [of human rights and international law] to its most visible outlier."[90] The hypocritical violation of our own Constitution, laws, and international agreements while battling against the lawlessness of terrorism only served to further denigrate America's once unquestioned status as the "citadel of democracy."

Nowhere is the loss of respect for American justice more glaring than in Great Britain, the cradle of Anglo-American democracy. Like their American counterparts, foreign legal experts found numerous flaws in the American military justice scheme established by the Bush administration. Among other things, they castigated the anticipated secrecy surrounding some or all of the proceedings; the "flexibility" in the procedural rights accorded the accused because the military commissioners, in the interests of national security, can suspend or override normal trial protections (such as access to relevant evidence);[91] the lack of a guarantee of attorney-client confidentiality; the failure to hold prompt hearings on the detainees' status; and denial of the right of appeal of confinement or conviction to independent civilian courts.[92]

Even President Bush's staunchest ally in the global war on terrorism, British prime minister Tony Blair, criticized American military trials of Britons caught up in the American dragnet. "Justice must be seen to be done," he told an alarmed House of Commons on July 9, 2003.[93] Ultimately, the international legal community regards these U.S. proceedings as highly offensive to many fundamental principles guaranteeing due process and protection of the dignity of the human person established by the Third Geneva Convention and three basic documents constituting the International Bill of Human Rights—the

Universal Declaration of Human Rights, the International Convention on Social and Cultural Rights, and the International Convention on Civil and Political Rights.[94] Regrettably, "[o]n most measures of a defendant's guaranteed rights, the [American] military commissions are far more draconian than other terrorism courts—such as Britain's Diplock courts in Northern Ireland [and the South African apartheid tribunals.]"[95] As the chart below demonstrates, they are also far less protective of the accused's chances for a fair trial than U.S. criminal courts or military courts-martial under the Uniform Code of Military Justice.

COMPARING FAIRNESS PROTECTIONS

RIGHTS	U.S. CRIMINAL COURT	U.S. COURT-MARTIAL	MILITARY COMMISSION
Jury	Yes	No	No
Counsel of defendant's choice	Yes	Yes	No
Know all evidence against the defendant	Yes	Yes	No
Obtain all evidence in favor of the defense	Yes	Yes	No
Attorney-client confidentiality	Yes	Yes	No
Speedy trial	Yes	Yes	No
Appeal to an independent court	Yes	Yes	No
Remain silent	Yes	Yes	Yes
Proof beyond a reasonable doubt	Yes	Yes	Yes

Source: Human Rights First

The most stinging rebuke of all came like a lightning bolt from one of Britain's most senior judges and a longtime admirer of the ideals of American democracy and justice. Shattering the convention that law lords do not speak out on politically sensitive issues, Lord Johan Steyn did not mince words about what he regarded as "a monstrous failure of justice" in "[t]he most powerful democracy . . . detaining hundreds of suspected foot soldiers of the Taliban in a legal black hole at the United States naval base at Guantánamo Bay, where they await trial on capital charges by military tribunals."[96] In a November 25, 2003, speech to lawyers in London that garnered worldwide praise,[97] Lord Steyn, after wrestling with his conscience for weeks, felt duty bound to speak out against "the utter lawlessness" of secret military trials where "[t]he military will act as interrogators, prosecutors, defense counsel, judges, and when death sentences are imposed, as executioners. . . . [The accused] are deprived of any right to test the legality of their detention."[98]

One of twelve judges on Britain's equivalent of the U.S. Supreme Court, Lord Steyn lamented the deliberate evasion of judicial review of the detainees' fate. "The purpose of holding the prisoners at Guantánamo was and is to put them beyond the rule of law, beyond the protection of any courts, and at the mercy of the victors."[99] He dismissed the purported legal basis for the military courts—the Supreme Court decision in *Ex parte Quirin*—as "a sordid episode in United States history" and a "discredited precedent [that] ignores more than half a century of progress of humanitarian law, notably in response to prisoners captured during armed conflict."[100]

This ranking British jurist felt that it was a sad day for a nation with "a long and honourable commitment to Magna Carta and allegiance to the rule of law" when it became hostage to the recent trend of "extraordinary deference of the United States courts to the executive [that] has undermined those values and principles."[101] "By denying the prisoners the right to raise challenges in a court about their alleged status and treatment," he further noted, "the United States government is in breach of the minimum standards of customary international law."[102] Quoting renowned professor Ronald Dworkin of the New York University School of Law, he noted that these are "the type of trials one associates with utterly lawless totalitarian regimes."[103] Lord Steyn condemned these "kangaroo courts" as "a stain on United States justice. The only thing that could be worse is simply to leave the prisoners in their black hole indefinitely."[104]

Equally shocking, Lord Steyn added, was the indefinite detention of U.S. citizens Hamdi and Padilla by the military. The failure to respect the rights of aliens "was bound to erode the civil liberties of citizens in the United States." Lord Steyn quoted Anthony Lewis' review of David Cole's illuminating book *Enemy Aliens: Double Standards and Constitutional Freedoms in the War on Terrorism*: "We must respect the humanity of aliens lest we devalue our own. And because it is the right thing to do."[105]

The actions of nations, like those of individuals, have long-lasting consequences. In a chilling reminder that history will hold America responsible for its lawless acts, Lord Steyn observed: "What takes place there today in the name of the United States will assuredly, in due course, be judged at the bar of informed international opinion."[106] And, Lord Steyn wonders, will not the ill treatment of these prisoners invite similar punitive treatment of Americans captured in future armed conflicts? "It would have been prudent, for the sake of American soldiers, to respect humanitarian law."[107]

Republican Senator John McCain, a former POW during the Vietnam War, likewise urged that the United States honor its commitments to international humanitarian law if for no other reason than self-interest.

> It is critical to realize that the Red Cross and the Geneva Conventions do not endanger American soldiers, they protect them. Our soldiers enter battle with the knowledge that should they be taken prisoner, there are laws intended to protect them and impartial international observers to inquire after them.[108]

In light of the scathing worldwide denunciation of President Bush's treatment of suspected terrorists, one is forced to wonder why the U.S. government persists in this folly. The roots of this hard-line approach apparently are planted deep in the psyche of the president and advisors such as Vice President Dick Cheney, Secretary of Defense Donald Rumsfeld, and Attorney General John Ashcroft. The Bush administration's extreme tendencies and ends-justify-the-means mentality—coupled with a dismissive attitude toward civil liberties and international agreements and a stubborn preference for unilateralism—have all contributed to this human rights and foreign policy debacle.[109]

President Bush's extreme views about his unfettered power to detain indefinitely terror suspects have infected other decisions to the detriment of civil rights and the rule of law. As Anthony Lewis points out,

314 IN TIME OF WAR

Bush administration lawyers have advised the president that he has unlimited constitutional authority to disregard U.S. and international humanitarian law in the war on terror.[110] This clearly erroneous construction of the Constitution, separation of powers, and Supreme Court jurisprudence led to widespread civil liberties violations. Indeed, the indefinite detention of U.S. citizens and Guantánamo Bay detainees was only the tip of the iceberg. As discussed above, the documented torture and abuse of prisoners at Guantánamo Bay and Abu Ghraib are direct outgrowths of this mind-set of omnipotent presidential prerogatives. And in a direct assault on vital personal and civil liberties, the hastily enacted USA Patriot Act, drafted by the Justice Department, vastly broadened the government's powers to conduct warrantless searches and seizures and spy on innocent citizens and noncitizens.[111]

In a campaign reminiscent of the infamous Palmer Raids during the Red Scare of World War I, Attorney General John Ashcroft's Justice Department indiscriminately rounded up and secretly detained some five thousand Arab Americans and Muslim men in the wake of 9/11. The Justice Department's inspector general found the vast majority were never linked to terrorism. Indeed, only five were charged with crimes, and only one was convicted.[112]

The Bush administration has gone to unprecedented lengths to cloak its decision making in a shroud of secrecy.[113] Senator Patrick Leahy cogently articulated the debilitating consequences of excessive secrecy in terms of compounding the "inherent tension between government powers and privacy rights. . . . [U]ndue secrecy undermines the system's built-in checks and balances. And over time it corrodes the public's faith that their government is not crossing the line and treading on the rights and freedoms of the American people."[114]

Senator Robert C. Byrd, who has spent forty-five years in the Senate and written a four-volume history of the institution, condemned President Bush for his arrogant abuse of trust:

The now controversial Patriot Act passed in the Senate 96 to 1, in mid-October of 2001, a scant four weeks after 9/11. Incredible, far-reaching power swung suddenly to the nation's leader to fight the war on terror. Americans trusted a president to use the power of his office effectively to protect them. Yet as we have since learned, that trust has been abused. Bush's power has been wielded with arrogance, calculation, and disdain for dissenting views. The Constitution's careful separation of powers has been breached, and its checks and balances circumvented. Behind closed doors, schemes have been hatched, with information denied to the legislative branch and policy makers shielded from informing the people or Congress. In fact, there appears to be little respect for the role of the Congress.[115]

Like the widespread abuse of prisoners of war, the Bush administration's heavy-handed approach to civil liberties has actually harmed America's security since 9/11. Richard A. Clarke, former national coordinator for security, infrastructure protection, and counterterrorism under Presidents Clinton and Bush, has observed that the attorney general, by championing the repressive USA Patriot Act, by his insensitivity to civil liberties issues,[116] and by attacking his critics as unpatriotic, has

> so mismanaged the important perceptions component of the war on terrorism at home that he became a symbol to millions of Americans of someone attacking rather than protecting our civil liberties [and] has caused many Americans to trust their government even less. . . . To protect our civil liberties and defeat the terrorists, we need to be careful not to do things that create a popular backlash against security measures. . . . The Battle with the Librarians [over FBI seizure of reading records under the USA Patriot Act], the case of José Padilla, and the request for Patriot Act II make it very difficult to gain consensus to do things that are needed to improve security, because trust in the government's sensitivity to civil liberties is eroded.[117]

Taking the nation to war is a president's most awesome responsibility. In the case of the post-9/11 invasion of Afghanistan, a united country supported President Bush's declaration of war on terrorists.[118] The invasion of Iraq in 2003 by nearly three hundred thousand American, British, Australian, and Polish troops, however, was an entirely different matter.[119] As the 2004 presidential elections drew nearer, America was sharply divided over the wisdom and necessity of this decision.[120]

President Bush claimed that Saddam Hussein's regime was a state sponsor of terrorism with ties to al-Qaeda and "weapons of mass destruction." In his State of the Union address on January 28, 2003,

President Bush asserted that "[e]vidence from intelligence sources, secret communications, and statements by people now in custody reveal that Saddam Hussein aids and protects terrorists, including members of al Qaeda." He went further, warning that Hussein could "[s]ecretly, and without fingerprints, . . . provide one of his hidden weapons to terrorists, or help them develop their own."[121] Bush asserted that his claims were based upon "a thorough body of intelligence—good, solid, sound intelligence."[122] On that basis, a majority of the Congress and American people supported the preemptive invasion of Iraq.

While Hussein and his government were quickly defeated, Iraq was destabilized. Pockets of stiff resistance to American occupation as well as an influx of terrorists led to the deaths of hundreds of American and allied soldiers and contractors and the wounding in action of over six thousand U.S. troops by mid-January 2005.[123] In the Muslim world, Islamic extremists exploited the Iraqi invasion and occupation, making the United States a reviled symbol of aggression and arguably more vulnerable.[124] With the nominal turnover of power to Iraqis in mid-2004, it was clear that the United States would have to continue to provide armed forces and financial support to that war-torn country for a long time.

The Bush administration's justification for going to war has been sharply challenged. It is now widely accepted that Iraq did not have deployable weapons of mass destruction. Nor is there any credible evidence that Hussein's government had any operational connection to the al-Qaeda terrorists.[125]

Democrats criticized the Bush administration for failing to establish a diplomatic solution in Iraq. Senate minority leader Tom Daschle said he was "saddened that this President failed so miserably at diplomacy that we're now forced to war."[126] Republicans savagely attacked such outspoken Democratic critics, not so subtly suggesting that they were unpatriotic to criticize the president in wartime. Republican House Speaker Dennis Hastert reacted by saying that Daschle's criticisms "may not undermine the President as he leads us into war, and they may not give comfort to our adversaries, but they come mighty close."[127] Responding to Daschle's charges, a White House official said that "France has a better chance [than Daschle] of getting back in Bush's good graces."[128]

Critics of the Patriot Act and other repressive measures supposedly in aid of the war on terror—such as indefinite detention and deportation of thousands of noncitizens—also had their patriotism impugned. The ACLU charged that after 9/11 hundreds of war protesters—branded "enemies of the state" by conservative commentator Bill O'Reilly—have been arrested for exercising their constitutionally protected freedoms.[129] The president's men preemptively attempted "to couple disagreeing on civil liberties with abetting terrorists."[130] Shortly after 9/11, Attorney General John Ashcroft declared: "[T]o those who scare peace-loving people with phantoms of lost liberty, my message is this: Your tactics only aid terrorists."[131]

In fact, challenging abuse of power—especially in wartime—is the epitome of patriotism. Since when is criticizing government not "love for or devotion to one's country"?[132] As President Theodore Roosevelt stated during World War I: "To announce that there must be no criticism of the President, or that we are to stand by the President, right or wrong, is not only unpatriotic and servile, but is morally treasonable to the American public."[133] Passionate and informed political dissent is not terrorism—it is patriotism.

In fact, America's national security is weakened by undermining civil liberties. As Senator Patrick Leahy commented:

> Contrary to this Administration's instinct, protecting our country, our ideals and our citizens requires that we uphold, not assault, our civil liberties. Our long-term fight against terrorism hinges on promoting democracy and American values, particularly in nations like Iraq. We undermine our credibility and our efforts by failing to respect individual rights here at home.[134]

The present crisis in reconciling security and liberty in a free society raises several questions: Will this country find other individuals like Kenneth Royall in a time of fear and uncertainty? Have we learned anything of value and relevance from the German saboteurs' case about striking a proper balance between civil liberties and national security as the United States wages its current war on terror? Will our constitutional system of government fail to check a president's claim to unlimited authority to imprison indefinitely U.S. citizens suspected of terrorist activities in violation of the Constitution and laws and to ignore U.S. and international law in the treatment of foreign nationals captured in Afghanistan and elsewhere?

To their credit, numerous lawyers, law professors, and retired judges have rallied to the cause of the detainees. Unlike the lonely battle waged by Kenneth Royall on behalf of Hitler's terrorists and the limited legal assistance afforded Japanese Americans during World War II, hundreds of distinguished human rights advocates brought several federal court challenges to the Bush administration's indefinite confinement regime. Using the Great Writ, these experts alleged violations of the U.S. Constitution and laws as well as army military regulations and universal human rights principles.

The initial results were discouraging.[135] One federal appellate court in Los Angeles early on held that the petitioners—lawyers, professors, clergy, journalists, and family members—lacked standing to represent a class of prisoners.[136] Another lawsuit in the District of Columbia rejected a petition for writ of habeas corpus on behalf of citizens of foreign nations detained in Guantánamo Bay, holding that U.S. courts lacked jurisdiction over challenges to confinement because the United States does not exercise territorial jurisdiction over that area despite a virtual perpetual lease from Cuba.[137] The net result of these rulings was that the detainees were left in legal limbo—men without a country or court where they could challenge their detention.

The American citizens Hamdi and Padilla also suffered initial setbacks in their quest for judicial review of their indefinite confinement. An American citizen raised in Saudi Arabia, Yaser Hamdi was captured on the battlefield in Afghanistan by Northern Alliance forces in November 2001. Shipped off to Guantánamo Bay, he was then transferred in April 2002 to a U.S. military jail in Norfolk, Virginia, when his American citizenship was discovered. Detained indefinitely and incommunicado in military custody, Hamdi was denied due process of law, access to counsel, indictment by grand jury, and a jury trial. He was never charged with a crime, and a military hearing was never held. Instead, President Bush designated Hamdi an "enemy combatant."

In May 2002, a petition for writ of habeas corpus was filed on Hamdi's behalf in Norfolk federal court by Frank Dunham, the federal public defender for the Eastern District of Virginia. The petition precipitated a roller-coaster ride between Judge Robert G. Doumar's courtroom and the United States Court of Appeals for the Fourth Circuit. Every one of the trial court's orders seeking to afford Hamdi some modest relief was reversed or modified by the appellate court.[138]

On the government's appeal, the Fourth Circuit reversed the trial court's initial order that Hamdi be allowed to meet with his counsel in private, reasoning that neither the federal public defender nor another person who filed a habeas petition as Hamdi's "next friend" had standing because they had no prior relationship with the prisoner.[139]

Following the filing of another habeas petition on behalf of Hamdi by his father, the government again appealed a new trial court order that Hamdi be allowed to meet privately with his counsel. The Fourth Circuit reversed and remanded for further proceedings on the grounds that Judge Doumar had not adequately considered the implications of this action and had not given the government an opportunity to respond.[140]

Judge Doumar then insisted that Hamdi be afforded a modicum of due process, ordering on July 31, 2002, that in addition to a conclusory declaration filed by Michael Mobbs, special advisor to the undersecretary of defense for policy, the government must provide the court with several documents, including copies of all of Hamdi's statements, a list of all interrogators who questioned him, and copies of any statements related to Hamdi by members of the Northern Alliance. This evidence was to be provided only to the trial judge and not to Hamdi or his counsel. Nevertheless, the government refused to comply and made another successful appeal. This time the Fourth Circuit ordered the district court to "consider the sufficiency of the Mobbs declaration as an independent matter before proceeding further."

Following a hearing, Judge Doumar found that before he could rule on the habeas petition, he needed more facts about Hamdi's capture and detention than were contained in the Mobbs declaration. Declaring that he would not be a "rubber stamp" for the executive, the trial judge again ordered the military to furnish him with additional information for his review. On August 16, 2002, Judge Doumar stayed the proceedings and sought the Fourth Circuit's guidance on the question of whether the Mobbs declaration alone was sufficient to allow meaningful judicial review of Hamdi's classification as an enemy combatant.

On January 8, 2003, the Fourth Circuit once again reversed the trial court and ordered dismissal of Hamdi's habeas petition. "Because it is undisputed that Hamdi was captured in a zone of active combat in a foreign theater of conflict," the three-judge panel concluded, "we hold that the submitted [Mobbs] declaration is a sufficient basis upon which to conclude that the Commander in Chief has constitutionally detained Hamdi pursuant to the war powers entrusted to him by the United States Constitution. No further factual inquiry is necessary or proper."[141]

Hamdi's hopes for relief were dashed once and for all when a sharply divided Fourth Circuit denied his request for rehearing en banc (by the entire court) on July 9, 2003.[142] Several of the appellate judges harshly criticized the panel's factual premise. Judge Michael Luttig bluntly noted that in fact it was not conceded or undisputed that Hamdi was seized in a foreign combat zone "because Hamdi has not been permitted to speak for himself or even through counsel as to those circumstances."[143] Judge Diana Gribbon Motz went for the jugular in lambasting the conspicuous lack of due process afforded this U.S. citizen.

> For more than a year, a United States citizen, Yaser Esam Hamdi, has been labeled an enemy combatant and held in solitary confinement in a Norfolk, Virginia, naval brig. He has not been charged with a crime, let alone convicted of one. The Executive will not state when, if ever, he will be released. Nor has the Executive allowed Hamdi to appear in court, consult with counsel, or communicate in any way with the outside world.
>
> Precedent dictates that we must tolerate some abrogation of constitutional rights if Hamdi is, in fact, an enemy combatant. However, a panel of this court has held that a short hearsay declaration by Mr. Michael Mobbs—an unelected, otherwise unknown, government "advisor"—"standing alone" (subject to no challenge by Hamdi or court-ordered verification) is "sufficient as a matter of law to allow meaningful judicial review" and approval of the Executive's designation of Hamdi as an enemy combatant. *See Hamdi v. Rumsfeld,* 316 F.3d 450 (4th Cir. 2003). I cannot agree.
>
> To justify forfeiture of a citizen's constitutional rights, the Executive must establish enemy combatant status with more than hearsay. In holding to the contrary, the panel allows appropriate deference to the Executive's authority in matters of war to eradicate the Judiciary's own Constitutional role: protection of the individual freedoms guaranteed all citizens. . . . [This] marks the first time in our history that a federal court has approved the elimination of protections afforded a citizen by the Constitution solely on the basis of the Executive's designation of that citizen as an enemy combatant, without testing the accuracy of the designation.[144]

Over the course of a fourteen-month battle in the federal courts, Hamdi never got an evidentiary hearing on the factual and legal sufficiency of his designation as an enemy combatant and indefinite confinement by the military. His only hope was to petition the Supreme Court for relief.

Padilla is an American citizen who was apprehended at Chicago's O'Hare International Airport when he arrived from Pakistan via Switzerland on May 8, 2002. Arrested by the FBI on a material witness warrant in connection with a New York federal grand jury investigation of the 9/11 terrorist attacks, he was carrying no weapons or explosives. Padilla was confined in a federal prison facility in Manhattan under the control of the Department of Justice. A week after his arrest, he appeared before a federal judge, who appointed Donna R. Newman as his counsel.

When Padilla's lawyer moved to vacate the material witness warrant and thereby challenge her client's arrest, the government did an abrupt about-face. The prosecutors withdrew the material witness subpoena, and in a striking reprise of the transfer of the German saboteurs from Justice to War Department jurisdiction six decades earlier, the government abruptly transferred Padilla to military custody pursuant to President Bush's June 9, 2002, order designating him an "enemy combatant" and directing Secretary of Defense Donald Rumsfeld to detain him.[145] The president purported to rely on the Constitution and the laws of the United States, including Congress's Authorization for Use of Military Force Joint Resolution, enacted shortly after the 9/11 attacks.[146]

Whisked off to a high-security naval brig in Charleston, South Carolina, Padilla was detained incommunicado without access to counsel, family, or nonmilitary personnel and without any charges or bail hearing from that date forward. The government sought intelligence information from him about his suspected plan to build and detonate a "dirty bomb" and his involvement with al-Qaeda terrorist activities. As a "next friend," Donna Newman filed a habeas corpus petition in the New York federal court.[147] The government moved to dismiss Padilla's petition on technical grounds,[148] while Newman argued that the president lacked authority to detain an American citizen and that her client at a minimum was entitled to consult his lawyer.

Chief Judge Michael B. Mukasey rejected the government's objections to hearing the petition and ordered conditional access to counsel.

On the merits, however, the court largely sided with the government, particularly in concluding that the president had the authority to detain an American citizen as an enemy combatant and that Padilla could be held indefinitely upon a showing of only "some evidence" that he was in fact an enemy combatant.[149] Despite a court order that Newman be afforded access to her client, the military refused to obey. Following two more hearings and opinions,[150] the trial judge sought guidance from the United States Court of Appeals for the Second Circuit.[151]

In a strong rejection of each of the government's legal positions, a majority of the three-judge appellate panel held that "Padilla's detention was not authorized by Congress, and absent such authorization, the President does not have the power under Article II of the Constitution to detain as an enemy combatant an American citizen seized on American soil outside a combat zone."[152] Without deprecating "the threat al Qaeda poses to our country and . . . the responsibilities the President and law enforcement officials bear for protecting the nation," Judges Rosemary S. Pooler and Barrington D. Parker nevertheless ruled that "the President is obligated, in the circumstances presented here, to share [his responsibilities] with Congress" for the following reason:

> Where, as here, the President's power as Commander-in-Chief of the armed forces and the domestic rule of law intersect, we conclude that clear congressional authorization is required for detentions of American citizens on American soil because 18 U.S.C. § 4001(a)(2000) (the "Non-Detention Act") prohibits such detentions absent specific congressional Authorization. Congress' Authorization for Use of Military Force Joint Resolution, Pub. L. No. 107-40, 115 Stat. 224 (2001) ("Joint Resolution"), passed shortly after the attacks of September 11, 2001, is not such an authorization, and no exception to section 4001(a) otherwise exists. In light of this express prohibition, the government must undertake to show that Padilla's detention can nonetheless be grounded in the President's inherent constitutional powers. *See Youngstown Sheet & Tube Co. v. Sawyer*, 343 U.S. 579, 637-38 . . . (Jackson, J., concurring). We conclude that it has not made this showing.[153]

The court of appeals sent Padilla's case back to the district court for issuance of a writ of habeas corpus and release of Padilla from custody within thirty days unless the government brought criminal charges against him or held him as a material witness in connection with grand jury proceedings.[154] "Under any scenario," the appellate court stressed, "Padilla will be entitled to the constitutional protections extended to other citizens." With this unambiguous (and courageous) judicial repudiation of President Bush's abuse of power, the Second Circuit struck an emphatic blow for liberty and civilian control over the military.[155]

The legal battle on behalf of the Guantánamo Bay detainees led to conflicting results. Relying on a 1950 Supreme Court precedent that U.S. courts lack jurisdiction over habeas corpus claims by aliens detained outside of U.S. sovereign territory,[156] the federal appellate court in the District of Columbia held that U.S. courts lacked jurisdiction over a petition for writ of habeas corpus by sixteen captives challenging the violation of the U.S. Constitution and laws and international human rights conventions.[157] On the other side of the country, the federal appellate court in Los Angeles held that U.S. courts are not "entirely closed to detainees held at Guantánamo indefinitely—detainees who would appear to have no effective right to seek relief in the courts of any nation or before any international judicial body." Writing for the majority, Judge Stephen R. Reinhardt flatly rejected any notion of an omnipotent president in wartime.

> [E]ven in times of national emergency—indeed, particularly in such times—it is the obligation of the Judicial Branch to ensure the preservation of our constitutional values and to prevent the Executive Branch from running roughshod over the rights of citizens and aliens alike. Here, we simply cannot accept the government's position that the Executive Branch possesses the unchecked authority to imprison indefinitely any persons, foreign citizens included, on territory under the sole jurisdiction and control of the United States, without permitting such prisoners recourse of any kind to any judicial forum, or even access to counsel, regardless of the length or manner of their confinement. We hold that no lawful policy or precedent supports such a counter-intuitive and undemocratic procedure. . . . In our view, the government's position is inconsistent with fundamental tenets of American jurisprudence and raises most serious concerns under international law.[158]

In the spring of 2004, the Supreme Court agreed to decide the cases of Hamdi, Padilla, and the Guantánamo Bay detainees. As the justices were hearing arguments in those cases, a divided U.S. Court of Appeals for the Fourth Circuit ruled that in preparing his defense, Zacarias Moussaoui—the so-called twentieth hijacker, a Frenchman born in Morocco, and the only person indicted for the September 11 attacks—was entitled to access to detainees held at Guantánamo Bay.[159] Daniel Schorr, perhaps the most trenchant and respected reporter for National Public Radio, offered his sobering assessment of the impact of the judicial fallout of the war on terror on civil liberties in America:

> [I]t's another illustration of the tension between the war and the law. Yes, a court of appeals insists that Moussaoui should have access to three al-Qaeda prisoners who might be able to exonerate him. . . . Then there are the people who have been held in Guantánamo arguing their case. . . . It seems evident that when this war is over, the thing we call the constitutional Bill of Rights will look a little different than it has looked.[160]

Two months later, the Supreme Court would decide how different.

Chapter 26

Securing the Blessings of Liberty

On June 28, 2004, the Supreme Court ruled in the three war on terror detainee cases.[1] For the most part, it was a stunning defeat for the Bush administration's audacious claim of unlimited executive power to detain indefinitely anyone whom the president unilaterally declared to be an "enemy combatant."[2] While the Court was sharply divided over how much due process to accord the detainees, no fewer than eight justices repudiated the commander in chief's assertion that the judiciary was powerless to question his actions in wartime. It was "a major loss for the government to have the Court . . . push back the executive in time of war."[3] As Human Rights First observed: "Taken together, these cases represent the most important referendum in a generation reaffirming the balance of power in U.S. democracy."[4]

In the case of the Guantánamo Bay detainees, six justices "squashed . . . [President] Bush's argument that no court could question his detention of non-American prisoners overseas," ruling that United States courts have jurisdiction to consider habeas corpus challenges to the legality of their detention.[5] As for Hamdi, the U.S. citizen captured in Afghanistan, a majority of the justices ruled that he was entitled at least to a hearing before a neutral decision maker to challenge his designation as an enemy combatant. In Padilla's challenge, a five-member majority dismissed the U.S. citizen's claim on a technicality involving the proper district court for bringing the suit, requiring Padilla to start all over again in his quest for freedom.

The current Supreme Court includes seven justices appointed by Republican presidents—Chief Justice Rehnquist and Justices John Paul Stevens, Sandra Day O'Connor, Antonin Scalia, Anthony M. Kennedy, David H. Souter, and Clarence Thomas[6]—but its decisions did not break down along partisan lines. The lead opinions in the two most significant cases—*Rasul* and *Hamdi*—were written by Justice Stevens and Justice O'Connor, respectively. Six of the eight justices who rejected President Bush's indeterminate detention of American citizens without due process were Republican appointees. Not surprisingly, the administration's lone supporter was Justice Thomas, the high court's most conservative jurist.[7]

Since the 1980s, the Supreme Court's membership has been dramatically transformed. With the appointment of Warren E. Burger as chief justice by president Richard M. Nixon in 1969 to replace the retiring Earl Warren, a conservative and Republican ascendancy began. Indeed, Republican presidents Nixon, Ford, Reagan, and Bush filled all of the vacancies between 1969 and 1991.[8] And even though President Clinton made two appointments in his first term (Ruth Bader Ginsburg and Stephen G. Breyer), a return to a philosophy of judicial restraint and deferral to the political branches dominated the Supreme Court's jurisprudence.

The Rehnquist Court had moved steadily away from the liberal Warren Court of the 1950s and 1960s, which was much maligned by the right for sweeping decisions checking the power of government in the name of civil liberties—decisions that covered a vast array of areas ranging from criminal law to national security. Rehnquist himself was the justice on the Burger Court "who was least supportive of civil liberties . . . [and] by his third term as chief justice a solid conservative majority had emerged with views that coincided with his."[9] The leading intellectual force for conservatism became Justice Scalia, who filled Rehnquist's seat when the latter was named chief justice.[10]

So imagine the widespread apprehension of civil libertarians as this Supreme Court, in the anxious times of the war on terror, prepared to render a historic judgment on the proper balance between national security and constitutional rights. With Congress maintaining a cowardly silence about the president's assertion of unfettered authority over national defense in the handling of enemy combatants, the Supreme

Court was placed in the role of "monitor[ing] the constitutional boundaries between the other two branches and protect[ing] civil liberties when they are threatened by efforts to secure the national defense."[11] The justices were the last, best hope, but history strongly augured that the executive—as in *Ex parte Quirin, Hirabayashi,* and *Korematsu*— would prevail, since "only rarely have the courts had any significant impact on the decisions of the political branches [in the exercise of war powers under the Constitution]."[12]

History will record that this Supreme Court had quite an impact.

Foreign Nationals

In *Rasul v. Bush,*[13] Justice John Paul Stevens, joined by Justices O'Connor, Souter, Ginsburg, and Breyer, sided with the two Australians and twelve Kuwaiti citizens—and in effect nearly six hundred similarly situated foreign nationals—who were captured abroad during hostilities between the United States and the Taliban and were still being held by the U.S. military at the naval base at Guantánamo Bay, Cuba.[14] The decision turned on narrow questions of the proper interpretation of the 1950 Supreme Court precedent in *Johnson v. Eisentrager* and whether the U.S. facility in Cuba was within the territorial jurisdiction of the United States.[15] In a larger policy sense, however, the Supreme Court was unprepared to declare that American courts were closed "to determine the legality of the Executive's potentially indefinite detention of individuals who claim to be wholly innocent of wrongdoing."[16]

Justice Stevens' opinion is grounded in the historical purpose of habeas corpus—dating back to the Magna Carta and the founding of the United States[17]—to serve as "a means of reviewing the legality of Executive detention" when there have been no charges or trial of the prisoner.[18] Federal courts have reviewed applications for habeas relief "in a wide variety of cases involving Executive detention, in wartime as well as in times of peace."[19] Two illustrations of the viability of habeas corpus in time of war were *Ex parte Milligan*[20] and *Ex parte Quirin.*[21]

The majority readily distinguished *Eisentrager*—a legacy of World War II involving twenty-one German citizens captured by U.S. forces in China, convicted of war crimes by an American military commission headquartered in Nanking, and incarcerated in a prison in occupied Germany. The Supreme Court found no right of habeas corpus for these petitioners. The Guantánamo Bay detainees, however, were different.

> They are not nationals of countries at war with the United States, and they deny that they have engaged in or plotted acts of aggression against the United States; they have never been afforded access to any tribunal, much less charged with and convicted of wrongdoing; and for more than two years they have been imprisoned in territory over which the United States exercises exclusive jurisdiction and control.[22]

Justice Stevens shredded the government's argument that the U.S. naval base at Guantánamo Bay was not within "the territorial jurisdiction" of the United States. By the express terms of the agreements with Cuba in 1903 and 1934, the United States exercises "complete jurisdiction and control" over the site, effectively in perpetuity. The government conceded that an American citizen held there could file a habeas corpus petition, and Congress had drawn no distinction in the statute between citizens and noncitizens held in federal custody. Accordingly, "[a]liens held at the base, no less than American citizens, are entitled to invoke the federal court's authority under [the federal habeas corpus statute]."[23]

Justice Kennedy concurred in the judgment. While he agreed with the majority that federal courts have jurisdiction to consider the lawfulness of the detention of the foreign nationals held in Cuba, he quarreled with its rejection of *Eisentrager* as the controlling precedent. Instead, applying the criteria of that precedent, Justice Kennedy considered the facts here distinguishable for two critical reasons.

> First, Guantanamo Bay is in every practical respect a United States territory, and it is one far removed from any hostilities. . . . [Second,] the detainees at Guantanamo Bay are being held indefinitely, and without benefit of any legal proceeding to determine their status. In *Eisentrager*, the prisoners were tried and convicted by a military commission of violating the laws of war and were sentenced to prison terms. Having already been subject to procedures establishing their status, they could not justify "a limited opening of our courts" to show that they were "of friendly personal disposition" and not enemy aliens. 339 U.S. at 778. Indefinite detention without trial or other proceeding presents altogether different considerations. It allows friends and foes alike to remain in detention. It suggests a weaker case of military necessity and

much greater alignment with the traditional function of habeas corpus. Perhaps, where detainees are taken from a zone of hostilities, detention without proceedings or trial would be justified by military necessity for a matter of weeks; but as the period of detention stretches from months to years, the case for continued detention to meet military exigencies becomes weaker.[24]

Justice Scalia, joined by Chief Justice Rehnquist and Justice Thomas, issued a strong dissent. He chastised the majority for "a novel holding . . . [contradicting] a half-century-old precedent [*Eisentrager*] on which the military undoubtedly relied" and "an irresponsible overturning of settled law in a matter of extreme importance to our forces currently in the field."[25] In Justice Scalia's view, Congress has not authorized in the federal habeas statute such extraterritorial jurisdiction over enemy aliens in Guantánamo Bay, Cuba. Since federal courts are courts of limited jurisdiction, that should be "the end of this case."[26]

Fearing a deluge of prisoner lawsuits, Justice Scalia rebukes the "carefree" majority for "boldly extend[ing] the scope of the habeas statute to the four corners of the earth."[27] If past is prologue, we should consider that the United States had in custody some two million enemy soldiers at the end of World War II, and nearly six hundred prisoners are currently detained at Guantánamo Bay. Indeed, the anomalous result of the majority's "clumsy, countertextual reinterpretation" of the federal habeas statute is to confer "upon wartime prisoners greater habeas rights than domestic detainees," who must petition in the district of their confinement, while the Guantánamo Bay detainees can file in any of the ninety-four federal judicial districts.[28]

Justice Scalia challenges the majority's conclusion that Guantánamo Bay lies within the territorial control of the United States at least for purposes of the federal habeas statute. "The Court does not explain how 'complete jurisdiction and control' without sovereignty causes an enclave to be part of the United States for purposes of its domestic laws. . . . [T]he Court's treatment of Guantánamo Bay, like its treatment of §2241, is a wrenching departure from precedent."[29]

Finally, Justice Scalia—taking a swipe at his colleagues for their "extraordinary" departure from stare decisis (adherence to precedent) and its "potentially harmful effect upon the Nation's conduct of a war"—reminds us that "Congress is in session" and could intelligently undertake to revise the federal habeas statute if it wanted to do so.[30] In characteristically caustic rhetoric, Justice Scalia scolds his fellow justices for conspicuous irresponsibility in siding with the accused enemy prisoners. "For this Court to create such a monstrous scheme in time of war, and in frustration of our commanders' reliance upon clearly stated law, is judicial adventurism of the worst sort."

Reckless or not, six justices rejected the Bush administration's carefully crafted strategy designed to prevent these prisoners of the war on terror from being able to challenge their indefinite confinement and alleged abusive treatment in violation of international humanitarian law.[31] As much as anything else, the *Rasul* decision breathed new life into the separation of powers doctrine in time of war. Not surprisingly, Congress, as it has in so many instances involving civil liberties in wartime and national emergencies, did nothing except appropriate the funding for the prison facilities at Guantánamo Bay that enabled the executive to attempt to create a "law-free" zone off the coast of Florida. Thus, how ironic that Justice Scalia should complain that the detainees there are being allowed to "forum-shop"!

The people's elected representatives are accomplices in President Bush's attempt to subvert international humanitarian law. An AWOL "Congress has largely abdicated its own duty to restrain the wartime president . . . [who claims the] power to seize anyone in the world, at any time, and hold him incommunicado, perhaps for decades, with no semblance of due process."[32] It thus fell to the third branch to restore some balance by checking what Anthony Lewis has aptly characterized as "[t]he extreme reach of the administration's view that a war president is not subject to check by the other branches of government."[33]

U.S. Citizens

In the two cases involving U.S. citizens, the Supreme Court's deliberations yielded mixed results—one on the merits and the other on procedure.

Padilla

In *Rumsfeld v. Padilla*, five justices voted to reject Jose Padilla's habeas challenge to his indefinite confinement by the military. Apprehended at Chicago's O'Hare International Airport on May 8, 2002, he had been detained as a material grand jury witness in connection with an investigation of the 9/11 attacks. After being initially held in the Southern District of New York, he was transferred to military custody and transported to a naval brig in Charleston, South Carolina, upon the president's designation of him as an enemy combatant. Padilla's removal occurred before his lawyer managed to file on his behalf a federal habeas petition in the Southern District of New York.

For over two years, Padilla had been relegated to a state of legal limbo, held incommunicado by the military without charges, counsel, or a hearing to contest his confinement. In short, he was afforded none of the procedural guarantees provided by the U.S. Constitution to persons accused by the government of committing a crime. Nor had he enjoyed any of the rights of prisoners of war secured by the Geneva Convention of 1949. His habeas corpus petition, filed in the Southern District of New York, sought to challenge his indefinite confinement.

Chief Justice Rehnquist, joined by Justices O'Connor, Scalia, Kennedy, and Thomas, wrote the majority opinion. Ducking the issue of whether the president had the authority to detain Padilla, the Supreme Court held that the Southern District lacked jurisdiction over his petition naming Secretary of Defense Donald Rumsfeld as respondent instead of his immediate custodian, who exercised day-to-day control over Padilla but was not physically present within the Southern District of New York. Thus, the District of South Carolina, where Padilla was confined, was the proper forum in which to file his habeas petition. The Supreme Court therefore reversed the Second Circuit's opinion in favor of Padilla on the habeas jurisdictional issue and ordered that his petition be dismissed without prejudice.

The chief justice viewed the issue narrowly—"at bottom a simple challenge to physical custody imposed by the Chief Executive—the traditional core of the Great Writ."[34] Historically, the "rule has always been that the Great Writ is 'issuable only in the district of confinement.' "[35] Fearing "rampant" "forum shopping by habeas petitioners," the majority saw no reason to recognize in Padilla's case any exception to the immediate custodian and district of confinement rules.[36] The chief justice rejected the dissenters' plea, as he phrased it, "to bend the jurisdictional rules because the merits of this case are indisputably of 'profound importance.' But it is surely just as necessary in important cases as in unimportant ones that courts take care not to exceed their 'respective jurisdictions' established by Congress."[37]

Justice Kennedy, joined by Justice O'Connor, filed a concurring opinion. He viewed the issue as one not of subject-matter jurisdiction but of personal jurisdiction or venue. Since the government had not waived its objections to a proper forum in South Carolina and no established exception to the immediate custodian and district of confinement rules was presented, Justice Kennedy voted to dismiss the petition as improperly filed in the Southern District of New York.[38]

Justice Stevens, joined by Justices Souter, Ginsburg, and Breyer, dissented, asserting that the majority's arguments "do not justify avoidance of our duty" to decide this "exceptional case that we clearly have jurisdiction to decide."[39] Stevens first took issue with the government's "secret transfer" of Padilla out of Manhattan, by means of an ex parte motion to the district court, without informing his counsel beforehand. Armed with such knowledge of the government's intent to remove him from the Southern District, his attorney, Donna R. Newman, surely "would have filed the habeas petition then and there, rather than waiting two days [and] . . . respondent's immediate custodian would then have been physically present in the Southern District of New York carrying out orders of the Secretary of Defense."[40] The government should not be allowed "to obtain a tactical advantage" by flouting the rules requiring advance notice to an adversary of an intent to present a significant motion.

Even with the stealthy removal of Padilla to another district, Stevens found "ample precedent for affording special treatment to this exceptional case, both by recognizing Secretary Rumsfeld as the proper respondent and by treating the Southern District as the most appropriate venue."[41] The rules governing a district court's habeas jurisdiction—riddled with exceptions to the immediate custodian rule—are far from iron-clad.

> It is . . . disingenuous at best to classify respondent's petition with run-of-the-mill collateral attacks on federal criminal convictions. On the contrary, this case is singular not only because it calls into question decisions made by the Secretary himself, but also because *those decisions have created a unique and unprecedented threat to the freedom of every American citizen.*[42]

The Supreme Court's cases have tended to favor a functional approach to habeas jurisdiction, focusing on the person with the power to produce the petitioner's body. In this instance, President Bush entrusted Secretary of Defense Rumsfeld with control over Padilla. Since he is a proper custodian and amenable to service of process in the Southern District, the court can issue a writ "within its jurisdiction" requiring production of the prisoner—even if he is confined outside the issuing court's territorial jurisdiction. And from a practical standpoint, the Southern District is a more convenient forum to litigate Padilla's petition in light of the government's initial selection of that venue and the familiarity of the judge and his counsel with the legal and factual issues surrounding his detention.[43]

Justice Stevens' dissent is a stirring reminder that what is at stake

> in this case is nothing less than the essence of a free society. Even more important than the method of selecting the people's rulers and their successors is the character of the constraints imposed on the Executive by the rule of law. Unconstrained Executive detention for the purpose of investigating and preventing subversive activity is the hallmark of the Star Chamber. Access to counsel for the purpose of protecting the citizen from official mistakes and mistreatment is the hallmark of due process.[44]

Executive detention of enemy soldiers—to remove them from the battlefield and prevent them from committing destructive acts—may be justified. But, Justice Stevens warns, indefinite confinement is not permissible for extraction of information by unlawful procedures.[45] "Incommunicado detention for months on end"—not to mention for over two years in Padilla's case—is impermissible regardless of "[w]hether the information so procured is more or less reliable than that acquired by more extreme forms of torture."[46]

For the four dissenters in *Padilla*, America has gone to war to preserve its democratic values. How we treat our enemies defines us as a society. America must never abandon her ideals by stooping to conquer. "For if this Nation is to remain true to the ideals symbolized by its flag," Justice Stevens eloquently reminds us, "it must not wield the tools of tyrants even to resist an assault by the forces of tyranny."[47]

The net result is that Padilla—after two years of confinement with no charges and no opportunity to contest his enemy combatant designation—must start his habeas challenge all over again. One consolation is that he will be able to cite in support of his new petition the Supreme Court's ruling in *Hamdi*. Nevertheless, his ability to secure his day in court will be delayed for months. This is especially troubling since the government may not be able to establish that Padilla is an authentic enemy combatant even under the relaxed burden of proof in *Hamdi*.[48]

Hamdi

In *Hamdi v. Rumsfeld*, six justices voted to require that a U.S. citizen captured on the battlefield in Afghanistan be afforded some measure of due process to challenge the president's designation of him as an enemy combatant. In two opinions, one by Justice O'Connor, joined by Chief Justice Rehnquist and Justices Kennedy and Breyer, and the other by Justice Souter, joined by Justice Ginsburg, the Court mustered a majority for this modest proposition. In a stinging dissent, Justice Scalia, joined by Justice Stevens, went much further in rebuking the president and chiding his colleagues for not recognizing Padilla's constitutional right to the full panoply of protections guaranteed to anyone accused of a crime, including the right to a speedy jury trial and the assistance of counsel. Justice Thomas filed a separate dissent, arguing that neither the Constitution nor federal law placed any restrictions on the executive's power to hold a U.S. citizen indefinitely under these circumstances.

Tallying the votes, Hamdi won 8–1—but on three different theories, none of which commanded a majority. "In summary, eight members of the Court think Hamdi (and by implication Padilla) is at least entitled to a hearing, with four saying he should be sprung right away, albeit two on statutory and two on constitutional grounds."[49]

The Supreme Court was badly divided in *Hamdi*, with no opinion commanding an unqualified majority of the justices. Justice O'Connor's plurality opinion came the closest and formed the basis of the judgment of the Court thanks to the concurrences of Justices Souter and Ginsburg. Nevertheless, eight justices repudiated the Bush administration's extreme position on separation of powers in wartime. Justice O'Connor's opinion articulates the consensus view of four justices: "We hold that although Congress authorized the detention of combatants in the narrow circumstances alleged here, due process demands that a citizen held in the United States as an enemy combatant be given a meaningful opportunity to contest the factual basis for that detention before a neutral decisionmaker."[50]

While the Non-Detention Act forbids detention of a U.S. citizen "except pursuant to an Act of Congress,"[51] the Authorization for the Use of Military Force—enacted by Congress a week after the 9/11 attacks—explicitly authorized Hamdi's detention. The measure authorized the president to use "all necessary and appropriate force" against "nations, organizations, or persons" associated with the terrorist attacks.[52] "We conclude that detention of individuals falling into the limited category we are considering, for the duration of the particular conflict in which they are captured, is so fundamental and accepted an incident to war as to be an exercise of the 'necessary and appropriate force' Congress has authorized the President to use."[53]

In reaching this conclusion, Justice O'Connor heavily relied on *Ex parte Quirin*—and German saboteur Hans Haupt's U.S. citizenship—for the proposition that "[t]here is no bar to this Nation's holding one of its own citizens as an enemy combatant."[54] The fact that Congress did not authorize indefinite detention is hardly to the point because "[i]t is a clearly established principle of the law of war that detention may last no longer than active hostilities."[55] Given the unconventional nature of the war on terror and the improbability of it ending with a formal cease-fire agreement, however, Hamdi's concern about being detained for the remainder of his life "is therefore not far-fetched."[56]

How long can Hamdi be held? So long as "the record establishes that United States troops are still involved in active combat in Afghanistan."[57] In other words, a very long time.

The venerable Civil War precedent *Ex parte Milligan*—holding that a U.S. citizen could not be prosecuted by a military tribunal when the civilian courts were open and functioning—did not protect Hamdi from indefinite confinement by the military. Justice O'Connor distinguished the seemingly on-point precedent on the ground that

> Milligan was not a prisoner of war, but a resident of Indiana arrested while at home there. . . . The Court's repeated explanations that Milligan was not a prisoner of war suggest that had these different circumstances been present he could have been detained under military authority for the duration of the *conflict*, whether or not he was a citizen.[58]

Justice O'Connor's dismissal of *Ex parte Milligan*—and the "sweeping proposition" asserted by Justice Scalia's dissent that "the military does not have authority to try an American citizen accused of spying against his country during wartime"—supposedly found support in the unanimous Supreme Court opinion in *Ex parte Quirin*.[59] Haupt had been accused of being a spy, she reasoned, and "[t]he Court in *Quirin* found him 'subject to trial and punishment by [a] military tribunal [ ]' for those acts, and held that his citizenship did not change this result."[60] Justice Scalia's emphasis on the fact that Haupt conceded that he was a member of an enemy force, while Hamdi contests his classification as an enemy combatant, has no legal relevance. The dissenters can point to no authority, Justice O'Connor asserted, "that those captured on a foreign battlefield (whether detained there or in U.S. territory) cannot be detained outside the criminal process."[61]

While Congress may have authorized Hamdi to be detained once it is sufficiently clear that he is in fact an enemy combatant,[62] the Court had to decide "what process is constitutionally due to a citizen who disputes his enemy-combatant status."[63] The government argued that it satisfied any constitutional requirement by offering a declaration from a Department of Defense official that his agency had (undisclosed) evidence that Hamdi met the criteria for enemy combatants and that Hamdi confirmed in an interview that he surrendered and gave his firearm to Northern Alliance forces.[64] Once the government has offered "some evidence," the president's counsel asserted, that is the end of the matter—the courts must uncritically accept the government's say-so that the detainee is an enemy combatant. Hamdi's counsel, on the other hand, countered that he is entitled to counsel and a meaningful and timely hearing to contest a sworn statement based on thirdhand hearsay.

Justice O'Connor adopted neither position. The government's weighty interest not to be unduly burdened with legal proceedings at a time of ongoing military conflict had to be balanced against the competing interest of "our Nation's commitment to due process" even during "our most challenging and uncertain moments."[65] The balance struck by the Court would not have "the dire impact on the central functions of warmaking that the Government forecasts."[66] For example, she perceived a vast difference between initial captures on the battlefield—which require essentially no due process—and the military's determination to continue to hold people (such as Hamdi) who have been captured.

The Court flatly dismissed the government's assertion that "separation of powers principles mandate a heavily circumscribed role for the courts in such circumstances."[67] The president's argument that the judiciary must forgo any review of individual cases so long as the "broader detention scheme" is legal offends our historic hostility to condensing power into a single branch of government.[68]

> We have long since made clear that a state of war is not a blank check for the President when it comes to the rights of the Nation's citizens. . . . [The Constitution] most assuredly envisions a role for all three branches when individual liberties are at stake. . . . Likewise, we have made clear that, unless Congress acts to suspend it, the Great Writ of habeas corpus allows the Judicial Branch to play a necessary role in maintaining this delicate balance of governance, serving as an important judicial check on the Executive's discretion in the realm of detentions. . . . [I]t would turn our system of checks and balances on its head to suggest that a citizen could not make his way to court with a challenge to the factual basis for his detention by his government, simply because the Executive opposes making available such a challenge. Absent suspension of the writ by Congress, a citizen detained as an enemy combatant is entitled to this process.[69]

While not a picture of clarity or an expansive view of due process under the circumstances, the Court's holding tilted toward Hamdi's position.

> [A] citizen-detainee seeking to challenge his classification as an enemy combatant must receive notice of the factual basis for his classification, and a fair opportunity to rebut the Government's factual assertions before a neutral decisionmaker. . . . He unquestionably has the right to access to counsel in connection with the proceedings . . . [challenging his classification].[70]

In reality, the Court did not afford Hamdi anything remotely close to the array of fundamental rights afforded citizens accused of serious crimes and facing long-term imprisonment. First, Hamdi was not allowed the basic protection of trial by a jury under the normal rules of evidence and criminal procedure. Second, the detainee has the burden of rebutting a presumption in favor of the government's evidence—as opposed to the government bearing a heavy burden of proof.[71] Third, the government can satisfy its burden of proof with only hearsay testimony—making it difficult or impossible for the detainee to confront and cross-examine his accusers. Finally, habeas corpus review by a federal district court judge may be obviated because the neutral decision maker can be a military tribunal.

Justice Souter, joined by Justice Ginsburg, filed an opinion in which he selectively supported and opposed portions of Justice O'Connor's opinion. He agreed with the plurality's rejection of any limit on the exercise of habeas jurisdiction, but he departed from its conclusion that Congress authorized detention of American citizens in the Authorization for Use of Military Force. Absent any other evidence not presently in the record, the Non-Detention Act entitled Hamdi to be released.

Justice Souter traced the history of the Non-Detention Act's repeal of the Emergency Detention Act of 1950—a Cold War statute authorizing the attorney general in time of emergency to detain anyone reasonably thought likely to engage in espionage or sabotage. "That statute was repealed in 1971 out of fear that it could authorize a repetition of the World War II internment of citizens of Japanese ancestry; Congress meant to preclude another episode like the one described in *Korematsu v. United States.*"[72] For Justice Souter, the law's origin "provides a powerful reason to think that §4001(a) was meant to require clear congressional authorization before any citizen can be placed in a cell."[73]

Even without the cautionary example of Japanese American internment, the very nature of American constitutional government—with "its constant tension between security and liberty"—demanded unambiguous legislative authority to detain a citizen.[74] Our system of separation of powers requires that the Congress, not the executive (though directly responsible for national security), be the branch of government that strikes "the balance between the will to win and the cost in liberty on the way to victory."[75]

Justice Souter found no congressional authorization for Hamdi's detention. The Force Resolution passed a week after the 9/11 attacks is hardly a clear statement of authority to detain. In fact, the measure does not even mention detention. And given the "well-stocked statutory arsenal of defined criminal offenses" for terrorist-related acts, "there is no reason to think Congress might have perceived any need to augment Executive power to deal with dangerous citizens within the United States."[76] The government, Justice Souter points out, has in fact proceeded criminally against those who aided the Taliban, including John Walker Lindh, the American captured in Afghanistan who was sentenced to twenty years in the federal court in Alexandria, Virginia.

Nor did Justice Souter see any authorization for the president's actions on the basis of the law of war. He rebuked the government for arguing out of both sides of its mouth. On one hand, the White House stated in early 2002 that "the Geneva Convention applies to the Taliban detainees," thereby apparently entitling Hamdi to qualify as a prisoner of war under the Third Geneva Convention.

> By holding him incommunicado, however, the Government obviously has not been treating him as a prisoner of war, and in fact the Government claims that no Taliban detainee is entitled to prisoner of war status. . . . This treatment appears to be a violation of the Geneva Convention provision [Article 5] that even in cases of doubt, captives are entitled to be treated as prisoners of war "until such time as their status has been determined by a competent tribunal."[77]

Since it is questionable that the United States is acting in accordance with the laws of war, the government has failed to demonstrate that the Force Resolution authorized the detention of Hamdi for purposes of Section 4001(a).

Justice Souter dismissed the government's "hints of a constitutional challenge to the . . . [Non-Detention Act on the basis of] inherent, extrastatutory authority under a combination of Article II of the Constitution and the usages of war."[78] Congress has expressed its will that no citizen may be detained without its authorization, and that judgment must be respected. After all, "the President is not Commander in Chief of the country, only of the military."[79]

In times of genuine national emergency, the government may have to act with no time for consultation with Congress. Under those extremely limited circumstances, Justice Souter conceded, "the Executive may be able to detain a citizen if there is a reason to fear he is an imminent threat to the safety of the Nation and its people."[80] In Hamdi's case, however, no such justification is presented since he "has been locked up for over two years."[81]

In the final analysis, none of the government's justifications for indefinitely confining this U.S. citizen is credible. As *Ex parte Milligan* held, civil law can be supplanted by military authority only by an actual and present necessity not present here. "[W]e are heirs to a tradition given voice 800 years ago by Magna Carta, which, on the barons' insistence, confined executive power by 'the law of the land.' "[82]

Given the sharp division in the Court on how much due process Hamdi should be afforded, Justices Souter and Ginsburg cast the decisive votes about the outcome of the case. They would not reach the issue of what process was due in light of their view that the government has failed to justify holding him "in the absence of a further Act of Congress, criminal charges, a showing that the detention conforms to the laws of war, or a demonstration that §4001(a) is unconstitutional."[83] Nevertheless, desiring to give practical effect to "the conclusions of eight members of the Court rejecting the government's position," Justice Souter joined with Justice O'Connor's plurality opinion because it orders "remand [to the lower courts] on terms closest to those I would impose."[84] In so doing, however, Justice Souter cautioned that he was not implying "agreement that the Government could claim an evidentiary presumption casting the burden of rebuttal on Hamdi . . . or that an opportunity to litigate before a military tribunal might obviate or truncate enquiry by a court on habeas."[85]

Justice Scalia, joined by Justice Stevens, wrote the best-reasoned and most eloquent opinion, scolding the plurality for preferring the "demands of national security" over "our citizens' constitutional right to personal liberty."[86] His brilliant dissent—"a classic piece of Scalia biting invective," particularly when he savages the "uniquely crabbed process" afforded Hamdi by O'Connor's opinion[87]—is representative of his opinions, which usually "display a vigor and an incisiveness that is far removed from the turgidity of most judicial prose."[88] That he teamed with one of the Court's most liberal justices makes his opinion all the more poignant.

Justice Scalia pithily summarized his position at the very outset of his dissent:

Where the Government accuses a citizen of waging war against it, our constitutional tradition has been to prosecute him in federal court for treason or some other crime. Where the exigencies of war prevent that, the Constitution's Suspension Clause, Art. I., § 9, cl. 2, allows Congress to relax the usual protections temporarily. Absent suspension, however, the Executive's assertion of military exigency has not been thought sufficient to permit detention without charge. No one contends that the congressional Authorization for Use of Military Force, on which the Government relies to justify its actions here, is an implementation of the Suspension Clause.[89]

Reminding his fellow justices of the intentions of the framers of the Constitution, Scalia stressed that the origins of the protection of personal liberty dated from Magna Carta and were written into the Constitution by the Founders. "The very core of liberty secured by our Anglo-Saxon system of separated powers has been freedom from indefinite imprisonment at the will of the Executive."[90] The historic writ of habeas corpus was "the instrument by which due process could be insisted upon by a citizen illegally imprisoned"—and both found expression in the Constitution's due process and suspension clauses.[91]

Citizens accused of aiding the enemy in wartime were not constitutional pariahs—they "have been treated as traitors subject to the criminal process."[92] As far back as the fourteenth century, English subjects accused of levying war against the crown were routinely prosecuted for treason. The Founders adopted this understanding, providing in Article III, Section 3, clause 1 of the Constitution for treason as a criminal offense and requiring two witnesses for conviction. "In more recent times, too, citizens have been charged and tried in Article III courts for acts of war against the United States, even when their noncitizen co-conspirators were not."[93] Justice Scalia cites the cases of two American citizens implicated in World War I spying for Germany and "the famous German saboteurs of *Ex parte Quirin* . . . [who] received military process, but the citizens who [were] associated with them . . . were punished under the criminal process."[94] The only citizen other than Hamdi imprisoned for his ties to the enemy in Afghanistan was John Walker Lindh, who "*was* subjected to criminal process and convicted upon a guilty plea."[95]

The only exception to ordinary criminal process for citizens accused of serious offenses in wartime are "times when military exigency renders resort to the traditional criminal process impracticable. English law accommodated such exigencies by allowing legislative suspension of the writ of habeas corpus for brief periods."[96] Thus, the British Parliament passed numerous temporary suspensions in times of threatened invasion or rebellion, including the American Revolution. Massachusetts suspended its writ under the Commonwealth's constitution, crafted by John Adams, in order to quell Shays's Rebellion in 1786. Little wonder, then, that Article I, Section 9, clause 2 of the U.S. Constitution permits suspension, but only by Congress "when in Cases of Rebellion or Invasion the public safety may require it."

The suspension clause has been sparingly invoked over two centuries. President Jefferson unsuccessfully sought to suspend habeas to deal with Aaron Burr's conspiracy to overthrow the government. After President Lincoln was rebuked by Chief Justice Taney in *Ex parte Merryman*, Congress in 1863 enacted the first measure authorizing the president to suspend the writ of habeas corpus, followed by a similar suspension with the Ku Klux Klan Act in 1871 to enable President Grant to suppress a rebellion in nine South Carolina counties.[97]

Justice Scalia rejected any notion that a citizen can be indefinitely imprisoned merely on proof of reasonable suspicion or some other standard short of a jury finding guilt beyond a reasonable doubt. The common law as far back as the English Habeas Corpus Act of 1679 ruled out some "bobtailed judicial inquiry into whether there were reasonable grounds to believe the prisoner had taken up arms against the King."[98] This was also the Founders' view—"the only constitutional alternatives were to charge the crime or suspend the writ."[99] Those who wrote the Constitution did not want to give "the Executive authority to use military force rather than the force of law against citizens on American soil" because they had a "general mistrust of military power permanently at the Executive's disposal."[100]

Three cases decided during and immediately after the War of 1812 confirmed that the military lacked authority "to imprison citizens indefinitely in wartime—whether or not a probability of treason had been established by means less than jury trial."[101] Two of those decisions were cited with approval in *Ex parte Milligan*—"one of the great landmarks in . . . [Supreme Court] history"—where the justices unanimously "rejected in no uncertain terms the Government's assertion that military jurisdiction was proper 'under the "laws and usages of war." ' "[102] Since the courts are open, the law of war cannot be applied to Hamdi, whose "imprisonment without criminal trial is no less unlawful than Milligan's trial by military tribunal."

Justice Scalia disparaged *Ex parte Quirin* as "not this Court's finest hour."[103] Justice Scalia's unwillingness to follow *Ex parte Quirin* can be explained in part by his judicial philosophy. Rejecting a slavish adherence to precedent merely for the sake of stare decisis, he has plainly declared that it would be a violation of his oath to adhere to a mistaken precedent so that the Supreme Court "might save face."[104] In terms of the World War II decision, Justice Scalia was troubled by "a brief *per curiam* [opinion] issued the day after oral argument concluded" and the issuance of a full written opinion months after six of the German saboteurs were executed.[105]

Justice Scalia was convinced that *Ex parte Quirin*'s fundamental flaw was its misinterpretation of *Ex parte Milligan*. The case did not turn on whether Milligan was a nonbelligerent who was not subject to the law of war. Instead, the critical point was the availability of habeas corpus for citizens held by the military on American soil. Properly understood, *Ex parte Milligan* stands for the proposition that "[t]hough treason often occurred in wartime, there was, absent provision for special treatment in a congressional suspension of the writ, no exception to the right to trial by jury for citizens who could be called 'belligerents' or 'prisoners of war.' "[106]

By its own terms, *Ex parte Quirin* would not justify denial of Hamdi's writ. There the German terrorists admitted that they were in fact enemy invaders, and the Court's specific holding was merely that " 'upon the *conceded* facts,' the petitioners were 'plainly within [the] boundaries' of military jurisdiction."[107] But where, as in Hamdi's case, those jurisdictional facts are contested and the petitioner insists that he is not a belligerent, "*Quirin* left the pre-existing law in place: Absent suspension of the writ, a citizen held where the courts are open is entitled either to criminal trial or to a judicial decree requiring his release."[108] Responding to the plurality's criticism of his distinction of *Ex parte Quirin*, Justice Scalia argued that the fact that a citizen disputes his enemy combatant designation makes all the constitutional difference in the world. "[T]he whole point of the procedural guarantees in the Bill of Rights is to limit the methods by which the Government can determine facts that the citizen disputes and on which the citizen's liberty depends."[109]

Congress did not in any way suspend the writ of habeas corpus with the Authorization for Use of Military Force. Yet the Court is allowing the executive to eviscerate the suspension clause at the expense of Congress' power and the citizens' personal liberty by finding "a congressional authorization for detention of citizens where none clearly exists" and then improvising, "under the guise of the Due Process Clause . . . what procedural protections *it* thinks appropriate."[110] Justice Scalia is appalled by the Court's handiwork in writing a new constitution based on due process concepts associated with withdrawal of disability benefits when the issue is the due process rights of citizens facing loss of freedom and possibly execution. The plurality has decreed "an unheard-of system in which the citizen rather than the Government bears the burden of proof, testimony is by hearsay rather than live witnesses, and the presiding officer may well be a 'neutral' military officer rather than judge and jury."[111]

Not only has the plurality distorted the suspension clause, it "finishes up by transmogrifying the Great Writ" by instructing the district court to engage in some hybrid form of fact-finding as "judicial remediation of executive default."[112] Justice Scalia will brook no compromise here: if Hamdi is being imprisoned in violation of his constitutional right of due process of law, his habeas petition should be granted, thereby requiring the president to prosecute or release him.

Reserving some of his harshest criticism for the plurality's "Mr. Fix-it Mentality," he condemns such judicial legislating as a misguided "mission to Make Everything Come Out Right, rather than merely to decree the consequences, as far as individual rights are concerned, of the other two branches' actions and omissions."[113] Beyond the deprivation of a citizen's fundamental rights and aggrandizement of the Court's circumscribed role in a democratic society, this approach of the Supreme Court "repeatedly doing what it thinks the political branches ought to do . . . encourages their lassitude and saps the vitality of government by the people."[114] Wartime in and of itself is not an excuse to curtail civil rights by stealth or sleight of hand. "[I]t must be done openly and democratically, as the Constitution requires, rather than by silent erosion through an opinion of this Court."[115]

Justice Scalia concludes with an homage to a 215-year-old covenant drafted by Founders who "well understood the difficult tradeoff between safety and freedom" and "equipped us with a Constitution designed to deal with" balancing the two.[116] It is not for this generation of justices, in the midst of the latest threat to our nation's security, to rewrite this unambiguous charter of liberty and separated powers.

> Many think it not only inevitable but entirely proper that liberty give way to security in times of national crisis—that, at the extremes of military exigency, *inter arma silent leges*. Whatever the general merits of the view that war silences law or modulates its voice, that view has no place in the interpretation and application of a Constitution designed precisely to confront war and, in a manner that accords with democratic principles, to accommodate it. Because the Court has proceeded to meet the current emergency in a manner the Constitution does not envision, I respectfully dissent.[117]

Under the Court's decision in *Hamdi*, a U.S. citizen can be robbed of his liberty and confined for years (or the remainder of his life) on unreliable testimony from faceless accusers without proof beyond a reasonable doubt and trial by jury. In fact, a military officer can apparently suffice as the judge, and the government never has to produce in court anyone who claims that the American detainee is an enemy combatant. The noncitizen detainees at Guantánamo Bay have been promised far greater legal protections in their military trials than Hamdi, including a presumption of innocence, proof beyond a reasonable doubt, limitations on the use of hearsay evidence, and a right of appeal.[118] Yet Hamdi, like the Guantánamo prisoners, faces imprisonment for the rest of his life.

Justice O'Connor is long on rhetoric. She speaks of "an unchecked system of detention [that] carries the potential to become a means for oppression and abuse of [innocent people]"[119] and "the fundamental nature of a citizen's right to be free from involuntary confinement by his own government without due process of law."[120] Her plurality opinion, however, is short on mandating time-tested due process procedures that would equip a citizen detainee with adequate tools to prevent a miscarriage of justice. The promise of *Hamdi*—vindication of "a citizen's core rights to challenge meaningfully the Government's case"—is hollow. As such, the Court, in "[s]triking the proper constitutional balance [between civil liberties and national defense]," has "give[n] short shrift to the values that this country holds dear" and "the privilege that is American citizenship"[121]—just what Justice O'Connor expressly declared should not be done. As Ronald Dworkin has noted: "By the Supreme Court establishing rules of procedure that omit important traditional protections for people accused of crimes," the government can conceivably satisfy the Court's lenient procedural standards without actually altering its morally dubious detention policies.[122]

Justice Scalia got it right. The Constitution requires a charge-or-release approach to the treatment of U.S. citizens detained for terrorist-related acts. That the crimes are the most heinous that can be perpetrated against our nation does not diminish a citizen's rights. Affording Hamdi some "bobtailed judicial inquiry" is virtually worthless in discovering the truth about whether a citizen is in fact an enemy combatant. In the end, *Hamdi* appears to be the triumph of symbolism—and a defeat for civil liberties.

Chapter 27

History Lessons

Any great national crisis invariably places a severe strain on constitutional rights—whether protection of property rights, First Amendment–guaranteed dissent, liberty, or human life itself. Popular appeals to patriotism, national defense, and domestic tranquillity are powerful, often irresistible incitements to conformity and repression of unpopular minorities. Whether it is the jailing of antiwar protesters and "draft dodgers," the lynching of civil rights activists, or the seizure of steel mills, the promise of lawfully protected and fundamental liberty has not always been kept. As a nation, we must try to understand the causes of these periodic lapses in our noble commitment to protecting the minority from the tyranny of the majority. The greatest dangers to liberty are always accompanied by ignorance of the bitter lessons of history. America's greatness lies not only in her triumphs in war and social progress in peace, but also in the capacity for self-criticism and reform.[1] A country that can honestly confront its history and learn from its mistakes materially enhances the chances that history will not repeat itself.

As America struggles to combat international terrorism and preserve the very democratic society that is under attack, what can be learned from the German saboteurs' experience six decades ago about protecting civil liberties and national security in wartime? This assessment necessarily entails a critical evaluation of the performance of the three branches of government, measured against the backdrop of the times and their assigned roles in our constitutional system. Ultimately, we must be mindful of Benjamin Franklin's warning: "They that give up essential liberty to obtain a little temporary safety deserve neither liberty nor safety."

The genius of American democracy is its constitutional commitment to the separation of powers in the legislative, executive, and judicial functions of government. Over time, we have accepted as essential for the preservation of ordered liberty—and the protection of unpopular minorities from the tyranny of majority rule—an intricate system of checks and balances. Among those restraints on abuse of power and authoritarian rule, none is more critical than the right to judicial review of executive and legislative decisions challenged as unconstitutional. Throughout our history, presidents and Congress have bristled at attempts by the Supreme Court (and other federal courts) to curb executive and legislative assaults on civil liberties.[2]

Given President Roosevelt's unprecedented challenge in fighting a total war in the wake of a global depression, his vigorous execution of his war powers to protect and defend the nation was unquestionably required. While the death penalty may appear excessive in hindsight, the desire to send Hitler a warning and to bolster public confidence in the government's ability to prevent sabotage was surely legitimate. That the executive branch may have violated some aspects of the Articles of War—while also affording the unlawful combatants a trial not required by international law—is regrettable but nowhere as egregious as the deplorable internment of 117,000 Japanese Americans without any due process or proof of disloyalty. Roosevelt's evacuation order in 1942 is all the more unpardonable because he must have known that his action violated the Constitution, and he prolonged the misery and shame long after any putative "military necessity" could have justified the draconian measure.[3]

The president's prosecution team presented an airtight case based on the German defendants' own damaging statements and incriminating physical evidence. Biddle—one of the twentieth century's most outstanding attorney generals—admirably consented to Supreme Court review of the president's authority. All in all, the government struck hard but mostly fair blows in securing the Germans' inevitable convictions.

Yet even the most principled attorney general cannot curb all presidential excesses. While Biddle deserves great credit for resisting Roosevelt's considerable pressure to imprison newspaper editors and for vigorously fighting against Japanese American citizens' internment, he needed (but did not get) the assistance of the federal courts. The threat to individual liberties is all the more clear and present when the attorney general is not solicitous of civil rights, Congress is silent, and the judiciary is timid, leaving no effective checks on a headstrong president's usurpation of power in wartime.

Federal law enforcement amid national anxiety during World War II merits mixed reviews. The failure to respond to Dasch's initial call and the delay in apprehending the other saboteurs was a bureaucratic fiasco. The gathering of evidence and the suspects' statements was excellent police work without major violations of their legal rights. The cover-up of the instrumental roles of Cullen and Dasch in the saboteurs' apprehension—aided and abetted by the secret trial—was vintage Hoover spin control. And while Dasch is hardly a sympathetic figure, Hoover broke his promise of a swift presidential pardon in exchange for Dasch's cooperation.

The military commission—hardly a "court," as its president emphatically reminded Royall—did what was expected of it. While some rulings on admissibility of evidence were plainly wrong by civil court standards, the German saboteurs received a trial of sorts, not a summary court-martial. That they had already confessed to the charges without any coercion by the FBI had more to do with the outcome than any bias or predisposition on the part of the seven generals. The imposition of the death penalty on six defendants—all of whom except Kerling were hapless cogs in the wheel of Nazi aggression—was severe but authorized by the law of war.

The German terrorists' case cannot be cited as an excuse for denying enemy captives prompt appointment of counsel, a speedy trial, or access to habeas corpus.[4] In fact, the Guantánamo Bay detainees and imprisoned U.S. citizens have been afforded far less due process protections than Hitler's terrorists. President Roosevelt charged the saboteurs and assigned highly competent counsel at the very same time, and the German defendants enjoyed substantial legal rights, including a speedy trial, the preservation of confidentiality in their communications with counsel, access to all relevant evidence, and Supreme Court review of the legality of the military proceedings.[5] As Philip A. Laco-vara, a former high-ranking Justice Department lawyer, has persuasively argued: "Surely, if such procedural guarantees could be extended to acknowledged enemies prosecuted under the Articles of War applicable during World War II, they can also be accorded to the suspects the [Bush] administration wants to put on trial before specially constituted military commissions today."[6]

That a secret trial was not vigorously protested by the news media is a reflection of a wartime accommodation to national security concerns and the widespread perception that the courts would not intervene to compel public access. In truth, no sensitive information about law enforcement investigative techniques, military operations, or intelligence-gathering methods was disclosed in the closed military proceedings. Given judicial recognition of the modern-day role of the press as the eyes and ears of the citizenry, a total blackout of any trial of accused terrorists—civilian or military—should require much more justification than a mere assertion of "military necessity" without any particularized demonstration of need.[7] At a time when America's motives are being questioned by friend and foe alike, "the antiseptic glare of sunlight [should] be allowed to shine on politically sensitive trials."[8]

Congress played a largely passive role during World War II. After implicitly ratifying FDR's Japanese American evacuation order by enacting legislation making any violation of any exclusion order a misdemeanor, the legislative arm of the federal government remained on the sidelines. No legislator criticized President Roosevelt for using the law of war as well as the congressionally enacted Articles of War as the basis of his charges against the German agents. In the end, Congress deferred to the commander in chief in the exercise of his wartime powers.

Of all the players in the drama, the Supreme Court failed most miserably in preserving the delicate balance between security and liberty. The damage to the high court's reputation was largely a self-inflicted wound. Taking the politically charged case was questionable in light of the perceived need to rush a decision. The justices' predisposition to support their president in time of war—along with the conspicuous conflicts of interest, ex parte contacts, and President Roosevelt's threats—tainted the proceedings.

More than anything else, allowing the petitioners to be executed without a fully reasoned opinion was a gross dereliction of duty later acknowledged by several justices. As Justice Scalia remarked in *Hamdi*, it was not the Supreme Court's finest hour. *Ex parte Quirin* is a cautionary example of the danger of judges abandoning their historic role as impartial, deliberate, and wise guardians of justice. For this reason alone, the decision—a relic of vastly different times and a flawed process—is an unreliable authority for justifying today's sweeping scheme of secret military trials of accused domestic and foreign terrorists.

"It was bad law, and they knew it," concludes emeritus Stanford University professor David J. Danelski. "That's what is so frightening about the decision—it is being used as authority today."[9]

Ex parte Quirin—like its sister cases *Hirabayashi* and *Korematsu*, upholding Japanese American citizens' detention and internment[10]— were products of the same World War II judicial mind-set of total deference to unexamined claims of national security. As we have seen with President Bush's arguments in *Rasul*, *Hamdi*, and *Padilla*, the Supreme Court's decisions in those World War II cases—and more ominously the federal judiciary's supine acceptance of the executive branch's "military necessity" justification for denial of fundamental constitutional rights—remain, in the prophetic words of Justice Jackson, "a loaded weapon ready for the hand of any authority that can bring forward a plausible claim of an urgent need." Chief Justice Rehnquist has perceptively identified the Achilles' heel of these wartime decisions: the justices failed to press the government to determine whether it was "a case of genuine military necessity, where the power sought to be exercised is at least debatable," or whether "the threat is not critical and the power either dubious or nonexistent."[11] A primary justification for reposing awesome power in an unelected Supreme Court is to protect "the few against the legalized tyrannies, major or minor, of the many."[12] Unfortunately, as one legal scholar has noted, these World War II decisions "revealed the Court in its darkest hour; a time when the Court appeared to lose either faith in, or fealty to, core constitutional guarantees."[13]

The question remains whether *Ex parte Quirin* should have any bearing on the outcome of legal challenges to modern-day exercises of presidential power in dealing with global terrorism and curtailing the civil liberties of U.S. citizens and the rights of foreign nationals captured on the battlefield in Afghanistan and elsewhere.

A decision of the Supreme Court becomes binding precedent for future disputes raising similar factual and legal issues. Under settled principles of stare decisis, literally "let it (the previous ruling) stand," judges and public officials are duty bound to respect such governing authority absent some compelling justification. Three prominent reasons for *not* adhering to a precedent include a constitutional amendment effectively overruling a decision (the Thirteenth Amendment, abolishing slavery, preempted the 1857 *Dred Scott* decision declaring that African Americans were not U.S. citizens), the passage of time, and a fundamental change in sociocultural attitudes (*Brown v. Board of Education* in 1954 overruled the 1896 decision in *Plessy v. Ferguson* and declared segregated public schools unconstitutional violations of the equal protection clause of the Fourteenth Amendment), and "when such adherence [to a more recent decision] involves collision with a prior doctrine more embracing in its scope, intrinsically sounder, and verified by experience."[14]

As discussed in Chapter 23, another ground is suggested by the doleful experience with *Hirabayashi* and *Korematsu* in light of the disclosure that the government fabricated evidence of "military necessity"—in effect perpetrating a fraud on the justices. *Ex parte Qurin* poses a related problem in terms of its legitimacy. That a Supreme Court decision may have been more the product of bias, conflicts of interest, and outright intimidation than a dispassionate decision on the merits—and therefore not entitled to the status of a respected precedent—is uncharted territory in the annals of Supreme Court jurisprudence. Yet that is precisely the issue presented by *Ex parte Quirin* and the problem of relying upon the decision to support an expansive view of presidential power to employ military tribunals to handle modern-day terrorists, especially U.S. citizens.

While still on the books, the decision does not deserve to be treated as a binding precedent. Beside the material factual differences between World War II and the present undeclared war on terror, and between the German saboteurs and suspected Taliban and al-Qaeda combatants, the process by which the Supreme Court reached judgment in *Ex parte Quirin* was illegitimate. As discussed in Chapter 22, we now know, based on internal files, the justices' private papers and correspondence, and other contemporary records, that the impartial administration of justice, as reflected in the decision-making process, was materially tainted by the justices' conflicts of interest, bias, and President Roosevelt's ex parte threats to execute the German saboteurs if the Supreme Court did not uphold his actions. That the decision was the product of undue influence on the justices should undermine any moral claim to legitimacy. For that reason alone, Justice O'Connor's heavy reliance on *Ex parte Quirin* in her concurring opinion in *Hamdi* significantly weakens the soundness of her substantial deference to the president in wartime in balancing citizens' fundamental rights against national security. Accordingly, the issue of presidential power—to detain citizens without charges or trial and to imprison indefinitely foreign nationals captured on the battlefield without complying with U.S. and international law—should be decided afresh by the Supreme Court without further polluting the stream of justice by relying on *Ex parte Quirin*.

In terms of the merits of the decision in *Ex parte Quirin*, the principled rule of law was sacrificed, in the name of national security, on the altar of expediency as the justices admittedly turned a blind eye to a popular president's violations of law. Portions of Chief Justice Stone's opinion embody a conspicuously erroneous interpretation of the Constitution, laws, and *Ex parte Milligan*. *Ex parte Quirin* is a discredited relic of a different time when the judicial branch had not yet wised up to the perils of uncritical acceptance of the executive's assertions of military necessity. For this additional reason, *Ex parte Quirin*, like *Dred Scott*, *Plessy v. Ferguson*, *Hirabayashi*, and *Korematsu*, should not tie the hands of federal courts—and especially the Supreme Court—in adjudicating the lawfulness of modern-day exercises of presidential power in time of war.

Indeed, it is little wonder that Justice Frankfurter himself, echoing the judgment of history, later disparaged *Ex parte Quirin* as "not a happy precedent."[15] No one knew better its illegitimacy. Tragically, the "Roosevelt Court"—from its rushed decision making without the benefit of careful study, research, and reflection to the unprincipled compromises reached to achieve a cosmetic consensus—disserved the American ideal of the reasoned rule of law and equal justice for even the most unpopular litigants. In the end, the justices, not the laws, were unconscionably silent in time of war.

The passage of sixty years has brought tectonic changes in constitutional law and a strengthened national commitment to civil liberties.

With the advent of the Warren Court in the mid-1950s, the Supreme Court signaled a willingness to shake off "its total war mentality and displayed an invigorated concern for civil liberties."[16] Today a secret trial would be severely challenged, separate counsel would be appointed for each defendant, a co-conspirator's confessions would not be admissible against other co-defendants, and ex parte contacts with Supreme Court justices might be impeachable offenses.[17] As Chief Justice William H. Rehnquist cogently predicted, modern courts will likely pay "more careful attention . . . to the basis for the government's claims of necessity as a basis for curtailing civil liberty. The laws will thus not be silent in time of war, but they will speak with a somewhat different voice."[18]

In a post-9/11 world beset by terrorists committed to destroying the American way of life and its commitment to the rule of law and personal freedom, the German saboteurs' case should serve as a reminder that military necessity is easily invoked—but not as easily proven by objective evidence—as a justification in wartime for trumping civil liberties. Now that the Supreme Court in *Rasul* has correctly upheld federal court jurisdiction to decide habeas corpus petitions by prisoners held in Guantánamo Bay, the federal courts should rule that those captives must be treated as prisoners of war under the Third Geneva Convention. The outcome of that issue will reveal how much we have really advanced in six decades as a democratic society in rationally balancing national security interests against individual rights preserved in the Constitution, statutes, and international law. One thing is certain, however: *Ex parte Quirin*'s "crumbling foundation" cannot support a "new and more expansive claim of executive authority."[19]

As Secretary of State Colin Powell urged in a losing battle within the Bush administration, applying the Geneva Convention to the Guantánamo Bay detainees is the correct legal conclusion. It is also morally correct. Ronald Dworkin has urged that we should

> not subject those we hold without trial to harsh treatment and objectionable methods of interrogation. But we should be willing, out of respect, for our traditions and values, to accept whatever unknown loss of efficiency this deference to morality may entail. . . . The world is shocked by our willingness to abandon what we claim to be our most fundamental values just because our victims are foreigners. We must hope that Camp X-ray and Abu Ghraib soon became symbols of a national aberration, like the Japanese-American internment camps of World War II.[20]

It is to be hoped that we have learned another valuable lesson from our history: national security is not physical safety alone. Preserving the rule of law and protecting individual liberties are equally fundamental components of security. Justice must always remain a treasured goal in a free society, and human rights must be at the heart of any credible search for justice, whether punishing crime at home or abroad. In preserving liberty, we strengthen our democracy's ability to withstand the fear and uncertainty of terror.

The liberty-security balance is delicate, but liberty and security are not a zero-sum game, where one profits from the loss of the other. Unquestionably, America faces a real and ongoing threat of terrorist attacks with no foreseeable end. Nor is there any doubt that abuses of constitutional rights have occurred in this war on terror and other wars in American history. Striking the right balance requires constant vigilance. The 9/11 Commission put the struggle succinctly:

> We must find ways of reconciling security with liberty, since the success of one helps protect the other. The choice between security and liberty is a false choice, as nothing is more likely to endanger America's liberties than the success of a terrorist attack at home. Our history has shown us that insecurity threatens liberty. Yet, if our liberties are curtailed, we lose the values that we are struggling to defend.[21]

Indeed, security is enhanced by freedoms and liberties and vice versa. Bruce Schneier, a respected security expert, has aptly warned that

> the reason the U.S. Constitution and the court system have put limits on police power is that these limits make all citizens more secure. We're more secure as a society because the police have limited powers. We're more secure as a society because we have the right to free speech—even the right to criticize the very government that gives us that right—and the right to freedom of the press. . . . Constitutionally protected liberties are more important to individual security than are democratic elections, and taking away liberties in the name of security is an enormous trade-off.[22]

Tipping the scales radically in favor of national security will not make us safer. Indeed, just the opposite will result. History has demonstrated the paradox of increasing military power and decreasing national security.[23]

We have also learned that citizens of open societies—where police and military powers are held in check—are more secure generally than those unfortunate people who live in totalitarian nations where surveillance is commonplace and personal freedoms and the rule of law are restricted. The genius of open societies—with firmly established laws governing everything from contracts to criminal justice—is to allow dissent and innovation, to keep secrecy to an absolute requisite minimum, and to share information widely. For the same reasons that open societies have led in scientific and technological revolutions, democratic societies are far more likely to devise "innovative defensive ideas and new defensive technologies" in the war on terror. Thus, "[e]ven if we give up our freedoms, we wouldn't be more secure as a result."[24]

The indefinite detention of hundreds of suspected terrorists will undoubtedly prevent any actual terrorists in the group from committing terrorist acts. But the cost—in terms of depriving many possibly innocent persons of their freedom and loss of respect for American justice—has been far too high.[25]

Abraham Lincoln got it right: we must defend our country against all enemies and sometimes—rarely, we hope—temporarily curtail civil liberties in wartime for the greater good. We must defeat terrorism just as we defeated totalitarianism and communism. In the process, however, we must reject knee-jerk reactions to limit our basic rights—such as the right to counsel and trial by jury—absent a compelling justification (necessity) and only after a searching debate over a proposed measure's efficacy (benefit) and the price paid in personal liberty (cost).

Appeals to national security, military necessity, and state secrets have historically been abused by presidents and the military to cover up official misconduct, corruption, and illegalities. Indeed, just like the outright falsehoods leading to the internment of Japanese Americans in World War II and the cover-ups in the German saboteurs' case, it has now been revealed by the *Los Angeles Times* that a half century ago, the government lied to the federal courts in claiming national security as the justification for not releasing information about a fatal B-29 aircraft crash. As it turns out, "the Air Force was protecting lies about the airplane's safety, not state secrets."[26] This revelation is just one of many examples of how any institution—when allowed at its sole discretion to cloak its operations in secrecy—will use this empowerment not only for justifiable reasons but also for self-protection from accountability. Such hedgehog tactics are highly relevant to our times because the Bush administration has relied heavily upon the Supreme Court's 1953 landmark decision in that case, *United States v. Reynolds*—upholding a claim of state secrets to trump three widows' negligence lawsuits[27]—as a cornerstone of its response to the 9/11 attacks, sweeping USA Patriot Act powers, and its legal position on the executive's unilateral authority to detain indefinitely suspected terrorists and to impose strict security restrictions.

Time and time again, history has shown that excessive secrecy in government is the handmaiden of abuse of power. The cone of silence around the detentions of suspected terrorists—from not informing detainees of the charges and evidence against them to preventing their unfettered access to counsel to abusing and torturing them—has spawned unconstitutional actions in the name of national security. *Ex parte Quirin*, *Korematsu*, and *Reynolds* are haunting testaments to the ominous threat to government accountability and civil liberties from entrusting government officials with "the sole power to decide what citizens should know." As two senior senators of widely differing views, Trent Lott and Ron Wyden, have observed: "The United States cannot preserve an open and democratic society when one branch of government has a free hand to shut down public access to information. . . . As we fight the war on terror, it's a legacy [of excessive secrecy] we can no longer afford."[28]

Only a few months after assuring the Supreme Court in oral argument that the indefinite military confinement of Hamdi was vital to national security and winning the war on terror, the Bush administration released him in late September 2004 without any criminal charges. Even with the Supreme Court's watered-down procedures heavily favoring the government, the United States could not establish Hamdi was in fact "an enemy combatant." In a deal negotiated by his lawyers, Hamdi, in exchange for moving to Saudi Arabia, agreed to renounce his U.S. citizenship and not sue the government for civil rights violations.[29] Hamdi's release after nearly three years of detention, as noted by Deborah Pearlstein, a lawyer with Human Rights First, represents "a huge victory for the rule of law."[30]

Not only was freeing Hamdi without charges or a trial "a huge embarrassment for the [Bush] administration,"[31] it cast into grave doubt the government's claims about Padilla and many of the Guantánamo Bay detainees. Hamdi's release also raised profoundly troubling questions about allowing the government to become immune from critical scrutiny by the media, Congress, and the public by cloaking its actions in a shroud of secrecy.

Padilla may also have to be released. Justice Department lawyers fear that, despite Attorney General John Ashcroft's much-publicized denunciation of Jose Padilla as a terrorist,[32] the government may not be able to develop a conventional criminal case with admissible evidence against Padilla for providing "material support" to al-Qaeda. The prosecution's theory from the outset—that Padilla was sent to the United States for the express purpose of detonating a radioactive "dirty bomb"—has turned out to be wrong.[33] Perhaps that is why Padilla's resolute lawyer, Donna Newman, has always insisted that "we want our day in court."[34]

Turning again to Lincoln's example, once Chief Justice Roger Taney rebuked the president for unilaterally suspending habeas corpus during the Civil War, Congress suspended the writ pursuant to the suspension clause in the Constitution because of the "rebellion."[35] Whether it is imprisoning suspected Taliban and al-Qaeda partisans in Guantánamo Bay and not complying with the Third Geneva Convention or interning indefinitely U.S. citizens for terrorist-related acts, Congress and the American people must be full partners in the resolution. President Bush is not the only stakeholder in the war on terror.

The war on terror is being waged on many fronts at home and abroad. Domestically, we are fighting to preserve the American way. The Preamble to the Constitution is a covenant among "the People of the United States . . . to insure domestic Tranquility, provide for the common defence, promote the general Welfare, and secure the Blessings of Liberty." The terrorists want to destroy us physically and spiritually. Just as we must protect our airports, harbors, and buildings in the "the common defence," so, too, we must "secure the Blessings of Liberty" by preserving the fundamental values that justify the nation's continued survival. How we, the American people, strike that delicate balance will define America in the twenty-first century. Ultimately, we are defending the rule of law.

As Lord Peter Goldsmith, attorney general of Great Britain, re-marked on June 25, 2004:

> It is a bitter pill to swallow for those who have seen and experienced the devastation that results from terrorist outrages to see systems estab-lished to protect the legal rights of those they believe responsible for them. And those who are responsible, let it be admitted, do not have a single shred of concern for the legal or human rights of those they would kill, maim and terrorise. So why should we care, some would say, about theirs? The answer to this is that the rule of law is the heart of our democratic systems.[36]

Is it too late to reverse this dangerous erosion of fundamental rights and fairness? While Congress has shown some renewed interest in the issue[37] and the media has intensified their news and editorial coverage, public discourse on this issue is almost nonexistent. The last and best hope lies in the federal courts. On a policy level, there are feasible alternatives.

First, the cases of any U.S. citizens detained by the military any-where as "enemy combatants" should be promptly brought before grand juries, and if any of them are indicted, they should receive speedy trials in federal court and should be accorded the full panoply of rights typically enjoyed by criminal defendants.

Second, with regard to the detainees in Guantánamo Bay and else-where, the United States should respect Article 5 of the Third Geneva Convention and immediately convene a hearing before a "competent tribunal" to determine each detainee's status and release those who should not have been imprisoned in the first place.

Third, the fatally flawed military-court scheme for prosecuting Guantánamo Bay detainees should be jettisoned.

Fourth, regular military courts, acting under the Uniform Code of Military Justice, should handle the trials of alleged "unprivileged combatants."[38]

In the final analysis, the war on terror—however necessary and urgent—can never justify a war on fundamental civil liberties. *The les-sons of history teach us to be most on our guard when our survival is most threatened.* In a democracy founded on the rule of law, the ends never justify the means, and all public officials must be held accountable for their actions. What good does it do America to wage a battle against the tyranny of terrorism while acquiescing in a president's unconstitutional usurpation of power? This is especially true when the drastic measures taken—particularly indefinite detention of suspected terrorists long after deriving any benefits from intensive interrogation—seem so attenuated. Now more than ever, the Supreme Court must reassert its historic role as the people's guardian. The justices have two pieces of urgent unfinished business after *Rasul* and *Hamdi*: uphold the primacy of the Constitution by correcting its mistakes in *Hamdi* and enforce our country's compliance with the letter of the Third Geneva Convention. There is no better or more exigent occasion to champion liberty, equality, and justice than in time of war.

America was sorely tested fighting totalitarianism sixty years ago. While one million of our countrymen were being killed and wounded abroad, the protection of constitutional rights at home was also a victim of war. Free speech and a free press were largely respected, but the rights of minorities suffered a major setback. Congress was a willing participant in the internment of loyal Japanese Americans and a major impediment to improving the lives of African Americans. As demonstrated by its decisions in *Hirabayashi*, *Korematsu*, and *Ex parte Quirin*, the Supreme Court marched in lockstep with the popular commander in chief.

Six decades later, America is again sorely tested. In the war on terror, the United States has mobilized in the wake of the deadly 9/11 terrorist attacks to confront a largely invisible, unconventional, and ruthless enemy. It is a challenge, a test of will, as daunting as that faced by our parents' generation in World War II. Then, as now, our soldiers, sailors, and pilots risked—and, tragically, so many lost—their lives in the defense of our democratic way of life.

It remains for us, the beneficiaries of this courage, to honor their sacrifices by keeping faith with the fundamental values that define the United States as a free society. Amid the gongs of war, we must redouble our commitment to civil liberties by respecting the rule of law at home and abroad. And we must learn from our past experiences during times of turmoil that when we allow the government to violate the rights of noncitizens, it is only a matter of time before citizens suffer the same deprivations.

A nation is defined by its actions, particularly in times of crisis. President Bush's open disdain for international humanitarian law and the Constitution has sullied America's image as a bastion of liberty in a world yearning for freedom from violence, terror, and oppression. While Congress slept, President Bush trammeled the rights of Guantánamo Bay detainees and interned U.S. citizens such as Hamdi and Padilla.[39] In affording prisoners of war a forum to challenge their indefinite detention, the Supreme Court properly filled the power vacuum caused by Congress' inaction. *Rasul* was a positive step toward mitigating the image of the United States in the world legal community as a rogue state. How the lower federal courts implement the decision—especially in light of the Bush administration's cynical attempt to avoid federal court habeas corpus jurisdiction by using military officers to review the detainees' status[40]—will be another important test of the separation of powers.

While the Supreme Court repulsed the president's absurdly extreme assertion of his war powers under the Constitution, *Hamdi* is nevertheless a setback for civil liberties. Just as their predecessors rejected President Nixon's attempt to enjoin the publication of the Pentagon Papers[41] and his claim of executive privilege in Watergate,[42] no self-respecting modern Supreme Court could countenance the executive's assertion of unlimited (and unreviewable) power to detain U.S. citizens indefinitely without due process. To have ruled otherwise would have left a gaping hole in the Bill of Rights.

But in fashioning a remedy, the Supreme Court shortchanged Hamdi in his ability to wage a fair fight for his freedom. Without Hamdi having the right to confront his accusers or compel production of exculpatory evidence at his hearing, much less force the government to prove his guilt before a jury, Justice O'Connor's high-minded statements about curbing presidential abuses of power dissolve into empty rhetoric.[43] War or no war, an American detained on American soil should be entitled to the constellation of constitutional rights afforded to anyone accused of criminal conduct. How can we reconcile guaranteeing a petty thief the right to trial by jury, proof beyond a reasonable doubt, right of confrontation, and right to appeal while denying a U.S. citizen accused of serious (and perhaps capital) crimes, if not treason, the very same rights?

The means for winning the war on terror should be the subject of a robust debate, including how the United States should treat suspected terrorists and prisoners of war, both citizens and noncitizens. It is counterproductive to demonize those who have conscientiously held opposing views about the most effective response. President Bush is not a "dictator" because, in his zeal, he has mistakenly struck the wrong balance between civil liberties and national security. Nor should civil libertarians be disparaged for allegedly failing to understand that we "are at war with stateless enemies abroad and Islamist infiltrators at home who will not stop plotting to kill us unless we kill them first overseas and nab them preemptively on our own soil."[44] This, too, is divisive rhetoric.

The place for this national dialogue is the people's forum—Congress. The time is now. Senator Robert C. Byrd has rightly placed a great deal of the blame on the erosion of civil liberties under President Bush on a "sleepwalking" Congress that enacted the Patriot Act without any debate and failed to exercise any effective oversight on the Bush administration's methodical erosion of essential liberties. "How can we be so comatose as a nation when so many damaging and radical changes are at once thrust upon us?"[45]

It is not too late for Congress to act. All it would require is another resolution declaring that the Supreme Court was wrong in *Hamdi* and that Congress has not authorized the detention of U.S. citizens as required by the Non-Detention Act. Congress should also make abundantly clear that U.S. citizens such as Hamdi and Padilla must be prosecuted or released. As Justice Scalia observed, *Hamdi* is as much an erosion of Congress' power as it is a cancer on the constitutional rights of Americans.

Congress should also pass legislation to correct the abuses at Guantánamo Bay, Abu Ghraib, and elsewhere. The people's elected representatives should insist on full compliance with the letter and spirit of the Third Geneva Convention (including immediate Article 5 status hearings), should outlaw all torture and abusive interrogation methods, and should replace the current flawed military commissions with military tribunals acting pursuant to the Uniform Code of Military Justice.

Congress should also repeal the Patriot Act and start afresh on new antiterrorism powers for the government based on a thoughtful process of thorough hearings and unrushed floor debate. As longtime civil liberties commentator Nat Hentoff has warned, however, this will be a formidable challenge. "A Congress that so overwhelmingly passed this antiterrorism bill is hardly likely to expunge parts of it unless there is rising citizen resistance."[46]

Preservation of our precious legal rights, like protecting America from those who would destroy her, is an unending struggle requiring eternal fidelity. In time of war, civil liberties are always on trial. Striking a sensible balance between safety and due process is never easy or risk-free.

Fortunately, in times of national emergency, American patriots have shown the way. John Adams unflinchingly defended the British soldiers in the Boston Massacre, and Chief Justice Roger Taney boldly told President Abraham Lincoln that he could not unilaterally suspend the writ of habeas corpus even during a civil war. Similarly, Colonel Kenneth C. Royall advanced the right to counsel by fearlessly defending the German terrorists in the darkest days of World War II. So, too, the military and civilian lawyers defending Hamdi, Padilla, and the more than six hundred Guantánamo Bay detainees are brave sentinels on the front line of freedom, keeping our nation true to her fundamental values in the war on terror.[47] America will eventually triumph against this latest threat, and when we do prevail, let us be able proudly to proclaim that the rule of law was not a casualty.

Less than a week after President Bush's reelection, a federal judge ruled that he had exceeded his constitutional authority and improperly disregarded the Geneva Conventions in establishing military commissions to try detainees as war criminals at the Guantánamo Bay naval base.[48] On November 8, 2004, U.S. District Court Judge James Robertson in Washington, D.C., issued a forty-five-page opinion granting a petition for writ of habeas corpus filed by Salim Ahmed Hamdan, a former driver for Osama bin Laden in Afghanistan who faced terrorism charges. The practical effect of the Bush administration's latest legal setback was to halt the thirty-four-year-old Yemeni citizen's pretrial proceedings. A few days later, the government announced that it was suspending all military commission proceedings at Guantánamo Bay while it pursued an appeal of Judge Robertson's decision.[49]

Judge Robertson's courageous decision hinged on the most fundamental point that critics had long been maintaining about the ad hoc military commission system's violation of the rule of law: a detainee's inalienable right under Article 5 of the Third Geneva Convention to a prompt determination by "a competent tribunal" of whether he is "an offender triable under the law of war."[50] The president himself could not make the determination, and no competent tribunal had ever been convened. The court also held that Hamdan must be tried under the Uniform Court of Military Justice and that the military commission procedures established by the president's order were "'contrary to or inconsistent' with those applicable to courts-martial."[51] In his scholarly opinion, Judge Robertson rejected all of the government's arguments about the inapplicability of the Geneva Convention, including the claims that al-Qaeda was not a state party to the Geneva Convention, al-Qaeda fighters did not carry arms openly and operate under the laws and customs of war, Hamdan was captured in an international conflict and not a local war, and the Geneva Convention is not "self-executing" and therefore does not give rise to a habeas corpus action.[52]

Judge Robertson dismissed *Ex parte Quirin* as precedent for sustaining President Bush's order. President Roosevelt's authority to appoint military commissions, the Supreme Court had clearly ruled six decades ago, "is found, not in the inherent authority of the presidency, but in the Articles of War (a predecessor of the Uniform Code of Military Justice) by which *Congress* provided rules for the government of the army."[53]

Indeed, *Ex parte Quirin* supported the detainee's argument that "'the law of war [includes] that part of the law of nations which prescribes, for the conduct of war, the status, rights and duties of enemy nations as well as of enemy individuals.'"[54] Since the law of war clearly includes the Third Geneva Convention and Article 102 requires the use of the same courts and same procedures used for U.S. armed forces personnel, Hamdan was entitled to trial by court-martial as long as his POW status is in doubt.[55]

Judge Robertson—a former navy officer—commented on the hypocrisy and danger of the government's position.

> The government has asserted a position starkly different from the positions and behavior of the United States in previous conflicts, one that can only weaken the United States' own ability to demand application of the Geneva Convention to Americans captured during armed conflicts abroad.[56]

The *Hamdan* decision, coupled with *Rasul* and *Hamdi,* are encouraging signs that the federal judiciary will eventually force the total dismantling of President Bush's "black hole" at Guantánamo Bay. In its place, the United States should resort to the highly regarded Uniform Code of Military Justice. Then and only then will America be able to begin to reclaim its leadership role as a champion of human rights and the rule of law.

Note on Sources

This book is literally "based on a true story." The facts are drawn from a wide variety of primary and secondary sources. The secret military trial transcript and exhibits were declassified, and the Supreme Court providently transcribed the oral argument in *Ex parte Quirin*. The never-before-seen papers of Kenneth Royall—and particularly the Columbia University Oral History Project interview in the form of the unpublished *Reminiscences of Kenneth Claiborne Royall*—were discovered uncataloged at the University of North Carolina at Chapel Hill Wilson Library. The records and personal diaries of major figures in Franklin Delano Roosevelt's administration—including President Roosevelt, Eleanor Roosevelt, Attorney General Francis Biddle, Secretary of War Henry Stimson, and FBI Director J. Edgar Hoover—provided a treasure trove of rich information about internal debates over the German saboteurs' case, Japanese American internment, and national security measures. The diaries, memoranda, private papers, and correspondence of the Supreme Court justices—especially Chief Justice Harlan Fiske Stone and Justice Felix Frankfurter—shed a great deal of light on the manner in which the justices decided the case.

A number of other sources helped bring to life the personalities in the drama. They include the archives of the German High Command and *Abwehr*, the U.S. Judge Advocate General's Office, the U.S. Coast Guard, the U.S. Army, and the International Military Tribunal at

Nuremberg. The contemporaneous newspaper reporting of the *New York Times*, the *Washington Post*, and the *Washington Daily News* was invaluable. The National Archives preserved a great number of photographs and political cartoons about the events. Over 150 books as well as more than 2,000 articles, Internet materials, legal treatises, and reported judicial opinions, many of which are cited in the endnotes, were consulted. Interviews with persons who knew the protagonists—especially Richard Winfield, William Glendon, and Lloyd Cutler—were particularly informative.

The protagonists' quotations were gleaned from the actual statements made by or attributed to them. Occasionally, a character's thoughts are set forth in italics; they are based on the historical record of what they were saying or doing at the time. Spelling and grammatical mistakes have been corrected.

In the endnotes, certain sources are frequently cited. For the sake of convenience, the following abbreviations are used:

TT	Trial Transcript
SCT	Supreme Court Transcript
RKCR	*Reminiscences of Kenneth Claiborne Royall*
TCTK	Eugene Rachlis, *They Came to Kill*
ESAA	George Dasch, *Eight Spies Against America*

Notes

Chapter 1: A World at War

1. German military intelligence was a complicated structure. Under OKW, military espionage was run by Abwehr I—Branch 1 of the Abwehr. The other two main branches were Abwehr II, dealing with sabotage and minority uprisings, and Abwehr III, dealing with counterespionage, which formed part of the Amt Auslandsnachrichten und Abwehr, or Foreign Information and Counterintelligence Department. Admiral Wilhelm Canaris was its head. Hitler fired Canaris in June 1944 and the foreign sections of the Abwehr were put under the control of Walter Schellenberg, head of Department VI of the RSHA (*Reichssicherheitshauptamt* or Reich Security Administration). The RSHA was the intelligence arm of the Nazi Party. Some elements within the RSHA were also known as the SD (*Sicherheitsdienst*, or Security Service), the intelligence and espionage arm of the Nazi elite SS, which was incorporated into the RSHA in 1939. Its departments included, among other sinister organizations, the Gestapo, the secret police. For further information see David Kahn, *Hitler's Spies* (New York: Collier Books, 1985), pp. 6, 47. Regarded as the author of one of the definitive works on German intelligence in World War II, Kahn makes a slight error (p. 6) in his statement that "Canaris had had a submarine land eight men near the eastern tip of Long Island."

2. Gary Cohen, "The Keystone Kommandos," *Atlantic Monthly*, February 2002.

3. David Alan Johnson, *Germany's Spies and Saboteurs* (Osceola, Wis.: MBI, 1998), p. 22.

4. Cohen, "Keystone Kommandos."

5. In their spare time, the saboteurs were supposed to bomb random Jewish-owned department stores "for general terror-inducing effect." Ibid.

6. Eugene Rachlis, *They Came to Kill* (New York: Random House, 1961), p. 11 (hereafter "TCTK").

7. Ibid.

8. Hitler was convinced that Roosevelt was under the influence of the Jews in devising his foreign policy toward Germany. See John Toland, *Adolf Hitler* (New York: Anchor Books, 1976), p. 693.

Chapter 2: Fear Itself

1. This was the high tide of German victories. America could no longer scoff at the concept of *Grossraum*, or Greater Germanic Estate, embracing Europe from the Atlantic to the Urals. Peter Calvocoressi, Guy Wint, and John Pritchard, *The Penguin History of the Second World War* (New York: Penguin, 1999), p. 233. As part of his grand scheme of establishing the German master race as overlords of an extensive slave empire from the Atlantic to the Ural Mountains, Hitler intended to exterminate all Slavs along with all Jews. In this "New Order," the races targeted for genocide were *Untermenschen* (subhumans) with no right to live except to work in the fields, mines, and factories for their Aryan masters. Hitler envisioned total obliteration of Slavic culture and the great cities of Moscow, Leningrad, and Warsaw. William L. Shirer, *The Rise and Fall of the Third Reich: A History of Nazi Germany* (New York: MJF, 1990), pp. 937, 951.

2. Correlli Barnett, *Engage the Enemy More Closely: The Royal Navy in the Second World War* (New York: W.W. Norton, 1991), p. 429.

3. Ibid., p. 184.

4. Ibid., p. 437.

5. In that dismal April, neither man had the comfort of knowing that Germany's submarine fleet commander, Admiral Karl Dönitz, could deploy only about thirty submarines in the Atlantic at any one time during this period (one that U-boat sailors called "the second happy time"), and that the glory days for the U-boats operating off America's shores would come to an end by the summer, when effective anti-submarine-warfare measures finally began to take effect. Nor could they know that by April Japan had reached almost the maximum extension of its perimeter in the Pacific or that in June the Battle of Midway would so devastate the Japanese navy that it would never again have any chance for naval supremacy, much less pose a direct threat to America's West Coast.

6. In reality, the only means Germany had for striking directly at the United States was the U-boat. Hitler's surface fleet was quite busy elsewhere.

7. Frank Freidel, *Franklin D. Roosevelt: A Rendezvous with Destiny* (New York: Little, Brown, 1990), p. 441.

8. Kenneth S. Davis, *FDR: The War President, 1940–43* (New York: Random House, 2000), p. 347.

9. Edward S. Corwin, *Total War and the Constitution* (New York: Alfred A. Knopf, 1947), p. 168.

10. Robert Stinnett, "December 7, 1941: A Setup from the Beginning," presentation to the Independent Institute, December 7, 2000, www.independent.org/newsroom/article.asp?id=103.

11. David Brinkley, *Washington Goes to War* (New York: Ballantine, 1998), p. 43.

12. Secretary of War Henry L. Stimson put it best when he said: "The question was how we should maneuver them [the Japanese] into the position of firing the first shot." James Perloff, *The Shadows of Power: The Council on Foreign Relations and the American Decline* (Appleton, Wis.: Western Islands, 1989), p. 67.

13. Brinkley, *Washington Goes to War*, p. 14.

14. Ibid., p. 36.

15. While he desperately needed FDR to come to Britain's aid, Churchill "had a true affection for Franklin." David Stafford, *Roosevelt and Churchill: Men of Secrets* (New York: Overlook Press, 2002), p. 298. "Meeting him was like opening your first bottle of champagne," Churchill once remarked. "He was the greatest friend Britain ever had." James C. Humes, ed., *The Wit and Wisdom of Winston Churchill: A Treasury of More than 1,000 Quotations and Anecdotes* (New York: HarperCollins, 1995), p. 159.

The warm feelings were mutual. Eleanor and Franklin found the cigar-chomping, eccentric prime minister "lovable." Doris Kearns Goodwin, *No Ordinary Time: Franklin and Eleanor Roosevelt: The Home Front During World War II* (New York: Simon & Schuster, 1994), p. 312. Churchill was a genuine Renaissance man of protean energy and diverse interests. "[W]ith all his idiosyncracies, his indulgences, his occasional childishness, but also his genius, his tenacity and his persistent ability, right or wrong, successful or unsuccessful, to be larger than life," he was the greatest prime minister ever to occupy 10 Downing Street. Roy Jenkins, *Churchill: A Biography* (New York: Farrar, Straus, and Giroux, 2001), p. 912.

16. Jenkins, *Churchill*, p. 667.

17. Arthur M. Schlesinger Jr., "The Supreme Partnership," *Atlantic Monthly*, October 1984.

18. Jenkins, *Churchill*, pp. 641–42.

19. On the heels of Germany's invasion of Poland on September 1, 1939, and England going to war, the Third Reich had enjoyed a series of military triumphs over the enusing two years that made the Nazis seem invincible. In rapid succession, German tanks and crack soldiers, aided by the indomitable Luftwaffe, waged their blitzkrieg warfare with seemingly little opposition from the overmatched armies and air forces of the European nations they overran.

20. Davis, *FDR*, p. 217.

21. Ibid., p. 216.

22. As an awestruck world looked on, Germany threw 3 million crack troops, 3,000 tanks, 2,000 planes, and 7,200 guns against an even larger Russian army with more troops, planes, tanks, and guns. In less than two weeks, the Germans had captured 150,000 Red Army troops as well as 600 large guns and 1,200 tanks.

23. Winston S. Churchill, *The Second World War: Triumph and Tragedy* (New York: Bantam, 1962), p. 405.

24. Indeed, such dread is claimed to have contributed to the breakdown of U.S. secretary of the navy James Forrestal's wife. David Fromkin, *In the Time of the Americans: FDR, Truman, Eisenhower, Marshall, MacArthur—The Generation That Changed America's Role in the World* (New York: Knopf, 1995), p. 423.

25. Davis, *FDR*, p. 277.

26. Ibid., p. 284.

27. Ibid., p. 286.

28. Ibid., p. 288.

29. Fromkin, *In the Time of the Americans*, p. 422. The transition to a wartime footing was proceeding at a snail's pace. In July 1941, for example, only one four-engine bomber had been delivered to the army. Ibid., p. 431. And then there was the pledge to supply the Soviet Union with a billion dollars' worth of goods by June 1942. Davis, *FDR*, p. 293. All in all, victory over Germany and Japan would cost hundreds of

billions of dollars, posing a challenge to the nation's productive capacity that Henry Stimson termed "staggering." Ibid., p. 296.

30. Davis, *FDR*, p. 289.

31. Ibid., p. 289; see also Fromkin, *In the Time of the Americans*, p. 422.

32. Freidel, *Franklin D. Roosevelt*, pp. 405–6.

33. The long wait—"the awful uncertainty"—was now over. Schlesinger, "The Supreme Partnership." That night, Churchill "slept the sleep of the saved and the thankful." Freidel, *Franklin D. Roosevelt*, p. 410. The Japanese had lifted off Roosevelt's shoulders the terrible burden of trying to persuade his fellow Americans to enter the war. No more debate. None of the bitter, shrill America First rant about coming to the aid of embattled Britain, occupied France, and other Allies. Roosevelt's "conscience was clear." Freidel, *Franklin D. Roosevelt*, p. 404.

34. At first blush, "[n]either was particularly the other's type"; they were somewhat of an "odd couple."

> They were very different men. They had different styles of humor. They had different tastes in people. . . . Churchill worked by night, Roosevelt by day. Churchill relaxed in the company of men, Roosevelt in the company of women. Churchill painted watercolors and laid bricks; Roosevelt collected stamps. Churchill drank all the time; Roosevelt had a martini or two before dinner. Churchill believed in confrontation, order, and hierarchy; Roosevelt in evasion, competition, and improvisation. Churchill was a traditionalist with a grand and governing fidelity to the past and a somber sense of the tragedy of history. Roosevelt had an antiquarian's interest in the past but was an experimenter and optimist, who confidently embraced the future. They were hardly made for each other. (Schlesinger, "The Supreme Partnership")

Nevertheless, these patrician-born politicians understood each other's aspirations. Freidel, *Franklin D. Roosevelt*, p. 410. United beyond sharing common enemies, they had abiding faiths in popularly elected governments and a fierce hatred of tyranny. It was not surprising that they developed a close friendship that made the pressures of war easier to tolerate. The two leaders shared many interests beyond the life-and-death struggle of the war. They had grown up loving the sea and the navy. "They knew a great deal of history and had somewhat similar tastes in literature [especially biography]," Eleanor Roosevelt observed. Eleanor Roosevelt, *The Autobiography of Eleanor Roosevelt* (New York: Da Capo Press, 1992), p. 235.

35. For more information, see F.L. Loewenheim, H.D. Langley, and Manfred Jonas (eds.), *Roosevelt and Churchill: Their Secret Wartime Correspondence* (New York: Saturday Review Press, 1975); Warren F. Kimball (ed.), *Churchill and Roosevelt: The Complete Correspondence* (Princeton, N.J.: Princeton University Press, 1984).

36. Schlesinger, "The Supreme Partnership."

37. Ibid.

38. Ibid.

39. Freidel, *Franklin D. Roosevelt*, p. 405. "Instantly, he became the commander in chief, the war leader." Ibid., p. 404. FDR was confident, poised, and prepared. He methodically issued a series of orders placing the nation on a war footing, including tightening White House security and authorizing the surveillance of Japanese citizens. Ibid., p. 405.

No one knew FDR better than his loyal wife and political partner. When Eleanor stopped by later in the day, she found Franklin "serene." Roosevelt, *The Autobiography of Eleanor Roosevelt*, p. 227. "His reaction to any event was always to be calm," she noted. "If it was something that was bad, he just became almost like an iceberg." Davis, *FDR*, p. 347.

In the hours immediately after the attack, a grim FDR sat quietly at his desk, absorbing with an eerie calm "the dreadful news that poured in upon him, his attention wholly focused on what must now be done." Ibid., p. 347. As much as anything, he was relieved. "[T]he boss must have a great load off his mind," Frank Knox remarked. "At least we know what to do now." Ibid., p. 348.

40. Freidel, *Franklin D. Roosevelt*, p. 407.

41. Former Republican president Herbert Hoover summed up the feelings of all Americans: "American soil has been treacherously attacked by Japan. Our decision is clear. It is forced upon us. We must fight with everything we have." Davis, *FDR*, p. 349.

42. Ibid., p. 350.

43. Freidel, *Franklin D. Roosevelt*, p. 407.

44. Louis Fisher, *Nazi Saboteurs on Trial: A Military Tribunal and American Law* (Lawrence: University of Kansas Press, 2003), p. 145.

45. See *Ex parte Zimmerman*, 132 F.2d 442 (9th Cir. 1942) (upholding imprisonment of defendant for suspicion of subversive and disloyal activities).

46. It took Congress only an hour to declare war on Germany. The Senate vote was unanimous, while the lone dissenter in the House of Representatives was Jeannette Rankin of Montana, who also voted against U.S. entry into World War I in 1917.

47. Freidel, *Franklin D. Roosevelt*, p. 408.

48. Davis, *FDR*, p. 350.

49. Ibid., p. 347.

50. David Stafford, *Churchill and the Secret Service* (New York: Overlook Press, 1998), p. 228.

51. Freidel, *Franklin D. Roosevelt*, p. 447.

52. Davis, *FDR*, p. 216.

53. Freidel, *Franklin D. Roosevelt*, p. 410. It was one thing to declare that America would be the "arsenal of democracy" producing "clouds of planes." Roosevelt was painfully learning, however, that it was quite another to make it happen. As a young Katharine Graham observed from her unique Washington insider vantage point: "The competition for the few supplies we were producing was fierce—from our own army, navy, and air force, as well as from the British, the Free French, and the Russians." Katharine Graham, *Personal History* (New York: Vintage 1998), p. 134. That the military had grossly underestimated the military equipment needed to win the war only compounded the crisis.

54. Fromkin, *In the Time of the Americans*, p. 442.

55. While their president may have been girded for some kind of Japanese aggression, the American people were psychologically unprepared for the war to come to American soil. This was a "shocking blow" to American power and pride, Stimson thought at the time. He "was as much dismayed as anyone by the incompetence of the American defense at Pearl Harbor." Henry Stimson and McGeorge Bundy, *On Active Service in Peace and War* (New York: Harper, 1948), p. 382.

56. Ibid., p. 370.

Chapter 3: Hitler's Terrorists

1. Earl R. Beck, *Under the Bombs: The German Home Front, 1942–1945* (Lexington: University Press of Kentucky, 1986), pp. 7, 9. The thirty-three Allied air raids of 1942 were a chief contributor to the decline in morale. The seemingly impenetrable German air defenses—consisting of highly advanced tracking systems along with over one million men deployed at antiaircraft stations—proved to be quite effective, but not impenetrable. Ibid., pp. 8–9.

2. When you were "asked" to join a military mission such as Operation Pastorius, the answer was preordained. The alternative was Nazi justice. From the mass killing of Jews to conscription into the armed forces, the government's vicious will was law, and dissent was not tolerated. Hitler and his Nazi regime ruled all aspects of German life with an iron fist. By mid-1942, Hitler still had a spellbinding effect on the vast majority of the German people. In particular, his massive use of radio—broadcasting his speeches within Germany and occupied Europe in thirty-six different languages—was highly effective in propagating Nazi propaganda. "Psychology of Radio," www.sit.wisc.edu/~pnpoltzer/psychology_of_radio.htm. Of all the Allied leaders, Winston Churchill had early perceived the threat posed by Hitler and the Nazi Party. By 1930, he was warning of Hitler's aggressive intentions, and when "Corporal Hitler"—"[a] bloodthirsty gutter-snipe" and "a maniac of ferocious genius of the most virulent hatred that has ever corroded the human breast"—was elected Germany's chancellor three years later, his dire predictions intensified. James C. Humes, *The Wit and Wisdom of Winston Churchill* (New York: Harper Collins, 1995), p. 154. Churchill also ripped Hitler as "[t]his wicked man, the repository and embodiment of many forms of soul-destroying hatred, the monstrous product of former wrongs and shames." Ibid. Driven by an "apocalyptic vision of aerial warfare," Churchill stressed time and again the imperative need to bring the British air force into parity with Germany. David Stafford, *Churchill and the Secret Service* (New York: Overlook Press, 1998), p. 149.

Opposition to the Nazi government grew steadily in 1942, albeit in a passive-aggressive manner. Dissenters were terrified to speak their minds in public or even write about their opinions in private journals since the SS killed anyone thought to be against the government.

At least one public protest was held at the University of Munich. A group of students and faculty members decided to publish a series of pamphlets and letters called the "White Rose Pamphlets." Anti-Nazi statements—such as "[i]t is certain that today every honest German is ashamed of his government" and "[e]very word that comes from Hitler's mouth is a lie"—peppered each of the publications, and soon the pamphlets made their way into the "mood" reports of the SD. Paul Giesler, the Gauleiter of Bavaria, came to the university to speak to the students. As Giesler spoke, students slowly walked out of the hall, refusing to listen to his anti-education remarks. But the entire hall erupted when Giesler, who had previously stated that women should do their part for the Reich by giving birth to children, preferably males, stated: "Of course, a certain amount of cooperation is required in these matters. If some of you girls lack a sufficient charm to find a mate, I will be glad to assign you one of my adjutants for whose ancestry I can vouch. I can promise you a thoroughly enjoyable experience."

This final insult sparked a massive walkout on his speech, followed by student marches through the streets of Munich. A state of emergency was called, and it took riot police to quell the uprising. The writers of the publications were eventually found and executed. Beck, *Under the Bombs*, pp. 27–29.

3. Beck, *Under the Bombs*, p. 30.

4. Ibid.

5. The biographical information about the eight saboteurs is drawn from a variety of sources, including their sworn statements taken by the FBI, their trial testimony, contemporary newspaper stories, Eugene Rachlis's *They Came to Kill* and Dasch's *Eight Spies Against America*. It is unclear whether Dasch's claims about his motives for undertaking the American sabotage mission—to escape Germany and to defeat the Nazis—are genuine or are after-the-fact rationalizations of his betrayal of the mission.

6. David J. Danelski, "The Saboteurs' Case," *Journal of Supreme Court History* 21, no. 1 (1996): 62.

7. Ibid.

8. Hitler had lost the 1932 election for the presidency of Germany. In the second round, he got 13.4 million votes, and during the campaigns that year (for the presidency, the Reichstag [parliament], and state governments), Hitler created a climate of violence throughout the country. In the November 1932 Reichstag elections, an improving economy cost the Nazi Party 2 million votes as public support dropped. But in January 1933 Hitler, in backroom negotiations, engineered the downfall of Chancellor Schleicher (the actual head of government); President Hindenburg (as head of state) bowed to pressure and appointed Hitler chancellor.

It took only a few months for Hitler and the Nazis to seize power. The Nazi Party secured 43 percent of the vote in the March 1933 elections for the Reichstag, giving the Nazis 288 deputies out of a total parliamentary membership of 647—not the majority Hitler wished to achieve in what turned out to be the last free election in Germany. He was able to overcome this lack of a majority by various nefarious tactics—notably through arrests of opposition deputies after the Reichstag was set on fire and pushing through an enabling act in March that gave him the power to rule by decree. Hindenburg, the Reichstag, and all the old instruments and institutions of government became irrelevant. Hitler moved quickly in the following year to make Germany a one-party state ruled by an absolute dictator (chancellor and president combined). Hitler would completely Nazify the country during the years before the outbreak of war.

9. Ron Grossman, "Hero, Traitor," *Chicago Tribune*, December 1, 1989.

10. Ibid.

11. TCTK, p. 63.

12. Ibid., p. 69.

13. Ibid., pp. 71–72.

Chapter 4: "Just a Scrap of Paper"

1. Eric Larrabee, *Commander in Chief: Franklin Delano Roosevelt, His Lieutenants, and Their War* (New York: Harper and Row, 1987), p. 13.

2. Ibid., p. 1.

3. Lord Moran, *Churchill at War 1940–45* (New York: Carroll and Graf, 2002), p. 160.

4. Henry L. Stimson and McGeorge Bundy, *On Active Service in Peace and War* (New York: Harper, 1948), pp. 664, 666.

5. Ibid., pp. 664–65.

6. Henry Landau, *The Enemy Within: The Inside Story of German Sabotage in America* (New York: G.P. Putnam's Sons, 1937).

7. David Stafford, *Churchill and the Secret Service* (New York: Overlook Press, 1998), p. 175.

8. Ibid., p. 180; David Stafford, *Roosevelt and Churchill: Men of Secrets* (New York: Overlook Press, 2002), p. 144. Some of the detainees included hapless German Jewish refugees.

9. Stafford, *Churchill and the Secret Service*, p. 177.

10. Stafford, *Roosevelt and Churchill*, p. 146.

11. Ironically, many if not most of Churchill's bitterest enemies were in his own party. He was regarded as a turncoat (because he had abandoned the Conservative Party, crossed over to the Liberals, and served in Liberal governments as a cabinet minister before later returning to the Tories), an adventurer, a drunk, a warmonger, an opportunist who was untrustworthy, and perhaps just a little bit crazy—among other things. Churchill's return to power after years in the political wilderness had been aided by a distinct minority in the Conservative Party. Understandably, there were plenty of Members of Parliament in the Labour and Liberal parties who also took a very dim view of Churchill and were not happy to see him return and join Chamberlain's cabinet.

12. In all fairness to Lord Halifax, he slowly moved away from appeasement—but a bit too slowly for Churchill's taste, which accounts for Churchill's consternation when Chamberlain replaced the staunchly pro-Churchill and anti-Hitler foreign secretary Anthony Eden with Halifax. He ultimately (but rather late in the day, as British forces lurched through successive disasters to the almost miraculous evacuation at Dunkirk) agreed with Churchill that attempts to broker any sort of deal with Hitler or express anything other than resolve to wage war to the bitter end would place Britain "on a slippery slope." On Churchill's instructions, Halifax firmly rejected the peace offer Hitler made to Britain in his July 19, 1940, speech. The Halifax "problem" was finally solved when Churchill brought Anthony Eden back as foreign secretary in December 1940 and sent Halifax off to be ambassador to the United States. Two of the most vivid accounts of what faced Churchill in the 1930s and the early years of the war can be found in the diaries of Sir Harold Nicolson and in John Lukacs's riveting account of the run-up to the crucial days in May 1940, *Five Days in London, May 1940* (New Haven: Yale University Press, 1999), which deals with the critical period from May 24 to May 28. Lord Halifax's side of the story is somewhat problematic. The "Holy Fox," as he was known, covered his tracks rather well, rendering a rosy account of his behavior and beliefs during that period. His diaries and other personal papers were carefully weeded shortly after the war, and some of this material is still withheld from historians.

13. Kenneth S. Davis, *FDR: The War President, 1940–1943* (New York: Random House, 2000), pp. 361–62.

14. Francis Biddle, *In Brief Authority* (Garden City, N.Y.: Doubleday, 1962), p. 207.

15. Timothy L. Hall, *Supreme Court Justices: A Biographical Dictionary* (New York: Facts on File, 2001), p. 350.

16. Roosevelt's frustration with the Supreme Court's interference with his New Deal legislation—and his ill-fated, heavy-handed attempt to pack the Supreme Court with his appointees by expanding the number of justices from nine to fifteen (discussed in Chapter 18)—illustrates more FDR's pragmatic bent than a wholesale disdain for the Constitution.

17. Davis, *FDR*, p. 247.

18. "Since everything depended, he believed, on winning the war, anything that threatened that prospect had to be dealt with boldly and harshly." Doris Kearns Goodwin, *No Ordinary Time: Franklin and Eleanor Roosevelt: The Home Front in World War II* (New York: Simon & Schuster, 1994), p. 322. Roosevelt would later admit that he regretted the burdens and hardships imposed by the evacuation, but he signed Executive Order 9066 without the slightest hesitation. Ibid.

19. Davis, *FDR*, p. 350.

20. In March 1942, Roosevelt had told Churchill, " 'That delightful god . . . The Freedom of the Press' . . . was one of the 'additional burdens' by which they were 'both menaced' in time of war." Robert Dallek, *Franklin D. Roosevelt and American Foreign Policy, 1932–1945* (New York: Oxford University Press, 1981), p. 335.

21. Ibid.

22. After campaigning against the law in 1800, Thomas Jefferson pardoned those convicted under it when he became president.

23. U.S. Constitution Article I, §2, cl. 3.

24. *In re Stacy*, 10 Johns. 328; 1813 N.Y. LEXIS 125 (August 1813).

25. *Brown v. United States*, 12 U.S. (8 Cranch) 110 (1814).

26. Henry David Thoreau, "Civil Disobedience," *The Portable Thoreau*, ed. Carl Bode (New York: Penguin Books, 1849, 1982), pp. 113–14. African Americans were not the only slaves in the mid-nineteenth century. Native Americans were bought and sold in New Mexico. The most devastated tribe was the Navajos, who lost 25 to 35 percent of their people—upwards of forty-five hundred, mostly women and children—to ruthless slavers.

27. Peter Grier, "Fragile Freedoms: Which Civil Libierties—and Whose—Can Be Abridged to Create a Safer America," *Christian Science Monitor*, December 13, 2001, www.csmonitor.com/2001/1213/pls2-usju.html.

28. 17 F.Cas. 144.

29. Charles Adams, "Lincoln's Presidential Warrant to Arrest Chief Justice Roger B. Taney: 'A Great Crime' or a Fabrication?" available on www.lewrockwell.com (citing Frederick S. Calhoun, *The Lawmen: United States Marshals and Their Deputies, 1789–1989* [Washington, D.C.: Smithsonian Institution Press, 1989]). The warrant was never served.

30. Because the base was allegedly procured by means of coercion, Fidel Castro annually refuses to cash the $4,000 check from the U.S. Treasury.

31. Some estimates put the number of people prosecuted at two thousand. See Peter Grier, "Fragile Freedoms." For an excellent discussion of the Palmer Era and the suspension of civil liberties during wartime, see Geoffrey R. Stone, *Perilous Times: Free Speech in Wartime from the Sedition Act of 1798 to the War on Terrorism* (New York: W.W. Norton, 2004).

32. 249 U.S. 47 (1919).

33. In his book *Case Against the Reds* (1920), Palmer reported that he had "discovered the hysterical methods of these revolutionary humans. . . . The whole purpose of communism appears to be the mass formation of the criminals of the world to overthrow the decencies of private life, to usurp property, to disrupt the present order of life regardless of health, sex or religious rights. . . . These include the IWWs, the most radical socialists, the misguided anarchists, the agitators who oppose the limitations of unionism, the moral perverts and the hysterical neurasthenic women who abound in communism." Quoted in "Red Scare," www.spartacus.schoolnet.co/uk/USAredscare.htm.

34. In *Facing the Chair: Sacco and Vanzetti* (1927), John Dos Passos blasted Palmer for his "invented" revolution. See "Red Scare."

35. Felix Frankfurter, *The Case of Sacco and Vanzetti: A Critical Analysis for Lawyers and Laymen* (Boston: Little, Brown, 1927).

36. Jane Addams noted at the time that "poor laboring men and women are being thrown into jails and police stations because of their political beliefs. . . . [All] these radicals seek . . . is the right of free speech and free thought, nothing more than guaranteed them under the Constitution of the United States, but repudiated because of the war." Quoted in "Red Scare."

37. Davis, *FDR*, p. 414.

38. Goodwin, *No Ordinary Time*, p. 320.

39. Kevin Starr, *Embattled Dreams: California in War and Peace, 1940–1950* (New York: Oxford University Press, 2002), pp. 89–90.

40. John Costello, *The Pacific War* (New York: Rawson Wade, 1981), pp. 150, 562.

41. Starr, *Embattled Dreams*, pp. 34, 35, 63.

42. Davis, *FDR*, p. 419.

43. While Roosevelt apparently did not know exactly where the Japanese fleet would strike, his administration was not surprised by, and may have provoked, the attacks. Roosevelt's secretary of war, Henry Stimson, wrote in his diary on October 16, 1941: "We face the delicate question of the diplomatic fencing to be done so as to be sure Japan is put into the wrong and makes the first bad move—overt move." The United States did this by freezing all Japanese assets in the United States, closing the Panama Canal to all Japanese shipping, joining Britain in an all-out embargo against Japanese trade that cut off nearly 90 percent of their oil supply, and other acts. The British minister of production, Oliver Lyttelton, reminisced in 1944 that "Japan was provoked into attacking America at Pearl Harbor. It is a travesty of history to say that America was forced into war." James Perloff, "Pearl Harbor: The Facts Behind the Fiction," *The New American*, June 4, 2001. No credible evidence supports the claim that Roosevelt turned a blind eye to the attack on Pearl Harbor. Goodwin, *No Ordinary Time*, p. 293.

44. Starr, *Embattled Dreams*, p. 34.

45. Ibid., p. 36.

46. Goodwin, *No Ordinary Time*, p. 321.

47. Starr, *Embattled Dreams*, p. 36.

48. Goodwin, *No Ordinary Time*, p. 321.

49. Starr, *Embattled Dreams*, p. 98.

50. Costello, *The Pacific War*, p. 27.

51. The appointed commission included as its chairman Supreme Court justice Owen J. Roberts, two retired navy admirals, a retired army general, and an active army general. Davis, *FDR*, p. 363.

52. Dallek, *Franklin D. Roosevelt and American Foreign Policy*, p. 334.

53. Goodwin, *No Ordinary Time*, p. 321. A submarine shelled a radio station at Estevan, Vancouver Island, B.C., in mid-June 1942. A few days later, shore guns at Astoria, Oregon, were shelled by a Japanese submarine. On September 9, 1942, a Japanese plane dropped incendiary bombs in the vicinity of Brookings (Mount Emily), Oregon. On June 3, 1942, Dutch Harbor, Alaska, was attacked by carrier-based planes. Four days later, the Japanese occupied the islands of Attu and Kiska in the Aleutians. See William H. Rehnquist, *All the Laws but One: Civil Liberties in Wartime* (New York: Vintage Books, 2000), pp. 197–98.

54. Stafford, *Roosevelt and Churchill*, p. 147.

55. Ibid.

56. Davis, *FDR*, p. 419.

57. Actually, the order did not mention Japanese or Japanese Americans by name. The exceptionally broad decree empowered the secretary of war and his subordinates "to 'prescribe military areas . . . from which any and all persons may be excluded' and to place such further restrictions as they deemed necessary upon 'the right of any person to enter, remain in, or leave' these areas." Their forcible evacuation to the "Zone of the Interior" was also authorized. While Japanese were not singled out as a class in the order, they were the only persons evacuated from the designated military areas and interned against their will. Davis, *FDR*, pp. 418–19. The camps were located in desolate, remote areas of California, Arizona, Utah, Idaho, Arkansas, Colorado, and Wyoming.

58. Executive Order 9066 drew no distinction between issei (immigrants from Japan who were not citizens) and nisei (children of those immigrants who were born in the United States and citizens as a result of that fact). Nor did the order require any proof of disloyalty as a condition of forcible evacuation.

59. Frank Freidel, *Roosevelt: A Rendezvous with Destiny* (New York: Little, Brown, 1990), p. 407.

60. Roosevelt's desire to ease public anxiety by relocating all Japanese in the western coastal areas was not accomplished. In fact, the mass relocation of so many Japanese Americans did little to reassure edgy Americans still fearful of Japanese sabotage.

61. FDR "was aware that his actions violated the Constitution and constituted racial bias against the Japanese." Dallek, *Franklin D. Roosevelt and American Foreign Policy*, p. 336.

62. Stafford, *Roosevelt and Churchill*, p. 147.

63. Dallek, *Franklin D. Roosevelt and American Foreign Policy*, p. 335.

64. In truth, the forcible evacuation of 117,000 Japanese Americans had "no sound military justification." Ibid. Over a half century later, Chief Justice William H. Rehnquist, in a thoughtful, balanced assessment, concluded that the "military representations as to the necessity for evacuation . . . were undoubtedly exaggerated, and they were based in part on the view that not only the Issei but the Nisei were different from other residents of the west coast." Rehnquist, *All the Laws but One*, p. 203.

65. *Korematsu v. United States*, 323 U.S. 214, 241 (1944) (Murphy, J., dissenting).

66. Dallek, *Franklin D. Roosevelt and American Foreign Policy*, p. 335. As James McGregor Burns has noted, " 'Roosevelt was not a strong civil libertarian,' and 'the wartime White House was not dependably a source of strong and sustained support for civil liberties in specific situations.' " Quoted in ibid. The president could also count on strong support from editorialists and pundits. Thus, Walter Lippmann, a liberal on most issues, supported internment. In a gush of hyperbole, Lippmann wrote: "[N]obody's constitutional rights include the right to reside and do business on a battlefield." Stafford, *Roosevelt and Churchill: Men of Secrets*, p. 147.

67. Biddle, *In Brief Authority*, p. 219.

68. On March 21, 1942, Congress passed legislation making it a crime for anyone to violate an order relating to restrictions governing the military areas covered by Executive Order 9066, including curfews and evacuation. Three days later, General de Witt issued a proclamation establishing a curfew for all alien Japanese, alien Germans, and alien Italians and all persons of Japanese ancestry, and he issued a series of evacuation orders pertaining only to all persons of Japanese descent, both alien and citizen alike.

69. Dallek, *Franklin D. Roosevelt and American Foreign Policy*, p. 336. While he remained silent, Ickes privately thought internment was "both stupid and cruel."

70. The Supreme Court's decisions on Japanese American internment are discussed in Chapter 22.

71. "[It] was a compromise with the ideas the nation was supposed to be fighting." James MacGregor Burns, *Roosevelt: The Lion and the Fox* (New York: Smithmark, 1996), p. 463.

72. Goodwin, *No Ordinary Time*, p. 322.

73. Dallek, *Franklin D. Roosevelt and American Foreign Policy*, p. 335.

74. In all, 33,000 Japanese Americans served in the U.S. Army, and more than 16,000 nisei served in military intelligence in the Pacific theater, providing great assistance in defeating the Japanese by translating captured documents. Goodwin, *No Ordinary Time*, p. 514.

75. Bettina Boxall, "Reassembling a Sad Chapter of History," *Los Angeles Times*, Dec. 11, 2002, p. A28.

76. Ibid.

77. Goodwin, *No Ordinary Time*, p. 321. Even the ACLU's response was weak and contradictory at the time. One of its senior advisors and a noted civil libertarian, Alexander Meiklejohn, wrote Roger Baldwin, the ACLU's founder and head, defending the evacuation order. In mid-March 1942, Meiklejohn stated: "The Japanese citizens, as a group, are dangerous both to themselves and to their fellow citizens. And that being true, discriminatory action is justified." Davis, *FDR*, p. 783 n. 16.

78. Ibid., p. 419.

79. Dallek, *Franklin D. Roosevelt and American Foreign Policy*, p. 334. "If Roosevelt shrewdly understood the strength of America's democracy, he failed miserably to guard against democracy's weakness—the tyranny of an aroused public opinion. As attitudes toward Japanese-Americans on the West Coast turned hostile, he made an ill-advised, brutal decision." Goodwin, *No Ordinary Time*, p. 321.

80. One notable exception was General Ralph Van Deman, the World War I head of American military intelligence with a keen nose for subversives, who wrote an impassioned letter to Roosevelt defending the loyalty of the Japanese American community. Stafford, *Roosevelt and Churchill: Men of Secrets*, p. 147.

81. Roosevelt's myopia about the gross unfairness of his treatment of Japanese Americans starkly contrasted with his attitude toward conscientious objectors (COs). Even though World War II was the most popular and justifiable war of the twentieth century, Congress and FDR recognized CO status as a legitimate moral or religious stand for the first time. Objectors had two choices: they could serve in the military medical corps or perform other noncombatant duties or they had to do "alternative service" at home performing "work of national importance under civilian direction." In the five years from the passage of the Selective Service and Training Act in September 1940 to the end of the war, 34.5 million men registered for the draft, and 72,354 applied for CO status. About 6,000 men—pacifists morally incapable of cooperating with violence, regardless of how just the cause—refused the draft and opted to go to prison instead of supporting "the good war" effort. Even those COs who served honorably were often "outcasts in a world convinced of the necessity, the inevitability and the glory of war. Taking a stand against the popular war could mean being ostracized by society, by family, friends, in the workplace." "The Good War and Those Who Refused to Fight It," www.pbs.org/itvs/thegoodwar/story.html.

Conscientious opposition to war has a long history dating back at least to the earliest Christian pacifists in Roman times. Among America's Founders were pacifists fleeing from persecution for their beliefs and seeking religious tolerance in the New World. For example, William Penn, a Quaker and pacifist, founded New Jersey, Delaware, and Pennsylvania.

During the Revolutionary War, General George Washington issued a call to all young men of suitable age to be drafted, except those with "conscientious scruples against war." In his original proposal for the Bill of Rights, James Madison included a military exemption for any person "religiously scrupulous of bearing arms." In the Civil War, religious objectors and others in the North educated freed slaves and served in hospitals and noncombatant assignments or could buy their way out of the draft; conscientious objectors were treated most severely in the South. "Conscientious Objectors in the Civil War," www.civil/wartime.com/conscientiousobjectors.htm. In World War I—a war notorious for its intolerance of civil liberties—the first draft since the Civil War was enacted, and some 450 of the 3,500 conscientious objectors were jailed. "The Good War and Those Who Refused to Fight It." Abraham Lincoln's policies toward conscientious objectors were far more lenient than those of Woodrow Wilson's administration.

82. Biddle, *In Brief Authority*, p. 219.

83. Burns, *Roosevelt*, pp. 463–64.

84. Dallek, *Franklin D. Roosevelt and American Foreign Policy*, p. 336.

85. Ibid.

86. Ronald Kessler, *The Bureau: The Secret History of the FBI* (New York: St. Martin's Press, 2002), p. 64.

87. Stimson and Bundy, *On Active Service in Peace and War*, p. 406.

88. Goodwin, *No Ordinary Time*, p. 322.

89. Kai Bird, *The Chairman: John J. McCloy, the Making of the American Establishment* (New York: Simon & Schuster, 1992), pp. 149–50. The Departments of War and Justice were two of the original four executive departments established in the first administration of President George Washington. Henry Knox was the first secretary of war, while Edmund Jennings Randolph, a forebear of Francis B. Biddle, was the first attorney general.

90. See Stimson and Bundy, *On Active Service in Peace and War*.

91. Ibid., pp. xxi–xxii.

92. "Henry L. Stimson," www.spartacus.schoolnet.co.uk/USAstimson.htm.

93. Davis, *FDR*, p. 414.

94. Ibid., pp. 460–61. The president wanted to "bring home to Japan some measure of the real meaning of war." The Army Air Force plotted an extremely risky raid on the mainland of Japan. On April 18, 1942, eighty servicemen flying in sixteen B-25 bombers took off from the USS *Hornet* some 650 miles off the Japanese coastline, flew into Japan, and dropped their payloads on several Japanese cities. When the U.S. newspapers received word of the attacks, headlines such as the *Columbus Evening Dispatch*'s "U.S. Warplanes Rain Bombs on Leading Jap Cities of Jap Empire" were everywhere. When asked at a press conference where the planes had taken off from, Roosevelt, fully aware the planes had taken off from the USS *Hornet* but wanting to keep this aspect of the raid a secret, remarked: "They came from our new secret base at Shangri-La," a reference to James Hilton's fantasy novel *Lost Horizon*. The report of the "Doolittle Raid"—followed by U.S. victories at the Coral Sea, Midway, and Guadalcanal—helped lift the spirits of the American people, demonstrating that the Japanese were just as vulnerable to attack as the United States was at Pearl Harbor. While defeat was certainly

still possible, faith in ultimate victory was rising. Edward Oxford, "Jimmy Doolittle: Against All Odds," *American History Magazine*, August 1997.

95. *Richmond Independent*, "Spy Activity Is Virtually Halted, Says Hoover," January 8, 1942.

Chapter 5: The Landing

1. Joseph E. Persico, *Roosevelt's Secret War: FDR and World War II Espionage* (New York: Random House. 2002), p. 200.

2. David J. Danelski, "The Saboteurs' Case," *Journal of Supreme Court History* 21, no. 1 (1996): 63.

3. Homer H. Hickam Jr., *Torpedo Junction: U-Boat War off America's East Coast, 1942* (New York: Dell, 1989), p. 296.

4. Persico, *Roosevelt's Secret War*, p. 200.

5. The exchange between Dasch and Cullen is taken from TCTK, pp. 100–103.

6. Persico, *Roosevelt's Secret War*, p. 200.

7. Hickam, *Torpedo Junction*, p. 269. The author describes the "agents" as "four civilians"—despite the undisputed fact that they were wearing German military uniforms when they landed. The author may be reflecting the disdainful attitude of a U-boat commander toward his passengers and not the legal status of the four saboteurs either in Germany or the United States at the time.

Chapter 6: "The Real McCoy"

1. Dennis L. Noble, "The Beach Patrol and Corsair Fleet," www.uscg.mil/hq/g-cp/history/h_beachpatrol.html.

2. George DeWan, "In the Middle of the Action," Newsday.com, www.newsday.com/community/guide/lihistory/ny-past1208,0,6688414.story?coll-y-lihistory-navigation.

3. Ibid.

4. Stephen McGuire, "In Our Midst: The Day Nazi Terrorists Came To Queens," *Queens Tribune*, www.queenstribune.com/archives/featurearchive/feature2002/0131/feature_story.html.

5. Ronald Kessler, *The Bureau: The Secret History of the FBI* (New York: St. Martin's Press, 2002), pp. 9–11.

6. Compiled from Christopher Lydon, "J. Edgar Hoover Made the F.B.I. Formidable with Politics, Publicity and Results," *New York Times*, May 3, 1972, www.nytimes.com/learning/general/onthisday/bday/0101.html.

7. Kessler, *The Bureau*, p. 12.

8. Ibid., p. 17.

9. Ibid., p. 23.

10. Ibid., p. 20.

11. Lydon, "J. Edgar Hoover Made the F.B.I. Formidable."

12. Gangster George "Machine Gun" Kelly first used the moniker "G-man." Kessler, *The Bureau*, p. 32.

13. Kessler, *The Bureau*, p. 30.

14. Lydon, "J. Edgar Hoover Made the F.B.I. Formidable."

15. Kessler, *The Bureau*, pp. 47–48.

16. Ironically, Hoover's domestic spying was exploited by savvy public figures. Thus, Negro civil rights leaders such as A. Philip Randolph made statements at rallies urging FDR to issue an executive order banning discrimination, knowing that Hoover would send a surveillance report to the White House. Kenneth S. Davis, *FDR: The War President, 1940–1943* (New York: Random House, 2000), pp. 202–3. In retaliation, at least one top government official, William "Wild Bill" Donovan, OSS chief during World War II, kept his own file on FBI blunders "and initiated a covert investigation into one of Washington's most persistent rumors, that Hoover and his chief aide, Clyde Tolson, were engaged in a homosexual liaison." Joseph E. Persico, *Roosevelt's Secret War: FDR and World War II Espionage* (New York: Random House, 2002), p. 198.

17. Hoover kept tabs on Roosevelt's private life. FDR had taken Lucy Mercer as a mistress while she was his wife's social secretary and he was serving as assistant secretary of the navy during World War I. Mercer was a "beautiful, stately young woman with the melting smile. . . ." Ibid., p. 206. When Eleanor discovered a packet of love letters between her husband and secretary, Franklin solemnly vowed to end the affair. Eleanor and Franklin stopped sleeping together. Over the years, the outgoing, gregarious Franklin became an increasingly "lonely man, hungry for the warmth and intimacy of a woman's companionship." Ibid. Lucy came back into the president's life in 1941—an event duly discovered and memorialized in his secret dossiers by the avid collector of private indiscretions of public officials, J. Edgar Hoover. Ibid., pp. 207–8.

18. Kessler, *The Bureau*, p. 24.

19. Hoover played his secret dossier wild card during the civil rights movement years later. When Rev. Dr. Martin Luther King Jr. attacked the FBI, saying that Southern blacks could not turn to their local FBI officials for any help in the civil rights movement, Hoover quickly produced taped conversations from Dr. King's hotel rooms as evidence that "moral degenerates" were leading the civil rights movement.

20. Frances Biddle, *In Brief Authority* (New York: Doubleday, 1962), p. 259.

21. Robert Dallek, *Franklin D. Roosevelt and American Foreign Policy, 1932–1945* (New York: Oxford University Press, 1981), p. 335.

22. Persico, *Roosevelt's Secret War*, p. 201.

23. The FBI chief relished this kind of challenge. "His eyes were bright, his jaw set, excitement flickering around the edge of his nostrils," Biddle recalled. Ibid., p. 201.

24. Ibid.

25. Ibid.

26. Biddle, *In Brief Authority*, p. 327; Persico, *Roosevelt's Secret War*, p. 201.

27. David Stafford, *Roosevelt and Churchill: Men of Secrets* (New York: Overlook Press, 2002), p. 146.

28. Biddle was the only significant senior advisor who opposed Japanese internment, but "because he was new to the Cabinet, his opinion held little weight." Doris Kearns Goodwin, *No Ordinary Time: Franklin and Eleanor Roosevelt: The Home Front During World War II* (New York: Simon & Schuster, 1994), p. 322.

29. Kai Bird, *The Chairman: John J. McCloy, the Making of the American Establishment* (New York: Simon & Schuster, 1992), pp. 147–63.

30. Ibid., pp. 149–50.

31. Kenneth S. Davis, *FDR: The War President, 1940–43* (New York: Random House, 2000), p. 423.

32. Biddle, *In Brief Authority*, p. 219.

33. Davis, *FDR*, p. 423.

34. Ibid., p. 424.

Chapter 7: Mr. Dasch Goes to Washington

1. Paraphrased from TCTK, pp. 139–41.

2. Ibid., p. 142.

3. Ibid., p. 141.

4. David J. Danelski, "The Saboteurs' Case," *Journal of Supreme Court History* 21, no. 1 (1996): 64.

5. TCTK, p. 145.

6. Ibid., p. 147.

7. Ibid., p. 148.

Chapter 8: True Believer

1. David J. Danelski, "The Saboteurs' Case," *Journal of Supreme Court History* 21, no. 1 (1996): 61.

2. TCTK, pp. 129–30.

3. Ibid., p. 130.

Chapter 9: Citizen Haupt

1. For a detailed account of Haupt's activities in Chicago, see Richard Cahan, "A Terrorist's Tale," *Chicago Magazine*, February 2002.

2. TCTK, p. 115.

3. Ibid., p. 116.

4. Ibid., pp. 119–20.

5. Ibid., p. 123.

6. Robert Dallek, *Franklin D. Roosevelt and American Foreign Policy, 1932–1945* (New York: Oxford Press, 1981), p. 416.

7. Brennen Jensen, "Churchill's Crisis," *Baltimore City Paper*, March 14, 2001.

Chapter 10: Double Cross

1. George Dasch, *Eight Spies Against America* (New York: McBride, 1959), pp. 119–20 (hereafter "ESAA").

2. Ibid., p. 120.

3. Ibid., pp. 120–21.

4. Ibid., p. 133.

5. *Los Angeles Times* headline, June 28, 1942.

6. *New York Times* headline, June 28, 1942.

7. *Chicago Sunday Tribune* headline, June 28, 1942.

8. Quotes taken from "Haupt Planned to Marry," *New York Times*, June 29, 1942.

9. David J. Danelski, "The Saboteurs' Case," *Journal of Supreme Court History* 21, no. 1 (1996): 65.

10. Kai Bird, *The Chairman: John J. McCloy, The Making of the American Establishment* (New York: Simon & Schuster, 1992), p. 164.

11. Ibid.

12. David Alan Johnson, *Germany's Spies and Saboteurs* (Osceola, Wis.: MBI, 1998), p. 124.

13. ESAA, p. 135.

Chapter 11: Prisoners of War

1. During wartime, people tried to cope with shortages of everything from meat to gasoline. One precious item was paper. Indeed, in the almost four years of war, the national government would accumulate more records than in the preceding 150 years of the republic. David Brinkley, *Washington Goes to War* (New York: Ballantine, 1998), p. 109.

2. In fact, the social season was canceled until the end of the war.

3. Kenneth S. Davis, *FDR: The War President, 1940–1943* (New York: Random House, 2000), p. 353.

4. David Fromkin, *In the Time of the Americans: FDR, Truman, Eisenhower, Marshall, MacArthur—The Generation That Changed America's Role in the World* (New York: Knopf, 1995), p. 423. Before the war, it was, as David Brinkley observed, "a city moving slowly and doing little . . . a town and a government entirely unprepared to take on the global responsibilities suddenly thrust upon it." With the outbreak of war, however, this "languid Southern town with a pace so slow that much of it simply closed down for the summer grew almost overnight into a crowded, harried, almost frantic metropolis struggling desperately to assume the mantle of global power . . . [and] change itself into the capital of the free world." Brinkley, *Washington Goes to War*, pp. xi–xii.

5. The District of Columbia was ill prepared for the invasion of bureaucrats, journalists, and military personnel such as Kenneth Royall. In June 1942, the sleepy city on the Potomac—founded in 1790 on marshland and an underground river—was, wrote Malcolm Cowley in the *New Republic*, the worst of all possible places. In wartime, it was "a combination of Moscow (for overcrowding), Paris (for its trees), Wichita (for its way of thinking), Nome (in the gold-rush days) and Hell (for its livability)." Quoted in Brinkley, *Washington Goes to War*, p. vii.

6. Fromkin, *In the Time of the Americans*, p. 423. Washington wallowed in the backwaters of American arts and letters, hopelessly short of the original plan to become a focus of national culture. With the exception of Georgetown University, founded in 1789, its colleges and universities were small, struggling, and poor. The venerable Smithsonian Institution was derisively characterized as "the nation's junk closet." The lone standout was the magnificent Library of Congress, boasting the largest collection of books, maps, newspapers, documents, and manuscripts in the world. "Washington, D.C.," *Encyclopedia Britannica*, 15th ed. (2002), vol. 29, p. 715.

7. The Thirteenth Amendment, adopted in 1865, abolished slavery; the Fourteenth Amendment, adopted in 1868, was intended to make slaves equal citizens; and

the Fifteenth Amendment, adopted in 1870, prohibited denial of the right to vote by the federal and state governments "on account of race, color, or previous condition of servitude."

8. Alden Stevens, "Washington: Blight on Democracy," *Harper's*, December 1941.

9. Brinkley, *Washington Goes to War*, p. 16.

10. Among the more chilling subjects of Farm Security Administration photographers was a recurring scene of "hideous slums and black children in tattered clothes, with the gleaming dome of the Capitol of the United States in the background." Ibid., p. 17.

11. The small number of middle-class blacks who attended Howard University became lawyers, doctors, teachers, preachers, and morticians. Mostly, however, black employment meant menial, low-pay labor.

12. In 1964, Royall participated in the Columbia University Oral History Project. The interviews were typed but never published. The unpublished 347-page manuscript, *Reminiscences of Kenneth Claiborne Royall* (hereafter "RKCR"), was discovered in the uncatalogued Royall Papers at the Wilson Library at the University of North Carolina at Chapel Hill.

13. RKCR, pp. 8–9.

14. Ibid., p. 26.

15. Royall's use of the word *nigger* unfortunately reflected the ingrained prejudices of his native region; he would soon learn to purge that infamous word from his vocabulary.

16. RKCR, p. 19.

17. Ibid., pp. 19–20.

18. James MacGregor Burns, *Roosevelt: The Lion and the Fox* (New York: Smithmark, 1996), pp. 198, 285, 338, 339, 453.

19. Henry L. Stimson and McGeorge Bundy, *On Active Service in Peace and War* (New York: Harper, 1948), p. 461.

20. Ibid., p. 462.

21. "Eleanor Roosevelt and Civil Rights," Eleanor Roosevelt National Historical Site (2003), www.nps.gov/elro/teach-er-vk/lesson-plans/notes-er-and-civil-rights.htm.

22. Mrs. Roosevelt believed that government had a dual role: to develop policies that create economic opportunities for all Americans and to eradicate discrimination. "This means achieving an economic level below which no one is permitted to fall," Eleanor insisted. Ibid.

23. Ibid. Southerners openly branded the president's wife "a nigger-lover."

24. "Civil Rights in an Uncivil Society," American History 102, Lecture 26, University of Wisconsin (2003), p. 2, us.history.wisc.edu/hist102/lectures/lecture26.html.

25. In practice, the Fair Employment Practices Committee (FEPC) accomplished little because it could not take the initiative and could investigate reports of discrimination only after a complaint was filed.

Chapter 12: Military Justice

1. See Edward W. Knappman (ed.), *Great American Trials: From Salem Witchcraft to Rodney King* (Washington, D.C.: Visible Ink, 1994), pp. 142–45. One of the defendants sentenced to life imprisonment was Dr. Samuel Mudd, a Maryland doctor who treated Lincoln assassin John Wilkes Booth's broken leg sustained when he jumped to the Ford Theatre's stage from the presidential box after shooting Lincoln in the back

of the head at point-blank range. Little or no evidence linked Mudd to Booth's crime, but Mudd "was convicted by a military commission interested more in vengeance than justice." Ibid., p. 142. Mudd was later pardoned by President Andrew Johnson in 1868 for his humanitarian work in treating prisoners on Dry Tortugas Island in Florida during an epidemic. Substantial doubts about his guilt led President Jimmy Carter to write to Dr. Mudd's descendants expressing his belief in their ancestor's innocence. Nevertheless, the verdict of history is harder to erase. Thus, the expression "his name is mud" owes its origin to the taint of Dr. Mudd's conviction by the military commission for conspiring to kill President Lincoln. William H. Rehnquist, *All the Laws but One: Civil Liberties in Wartime* (New York: Vintage, 2000), p. 166.

2. Lincoln died on April 15, 1865, and the defendants were hung on July 7, 1865.

3. Jonathan Turley, "The Dark History of a Military Tribunal," *The National Law Journal*, October 28, 2002.

4. M.O. Lacey, "Military Commissions: A Historical Survey," *The Army Lawyer*, March 2002, p. 42.

5. Ibid., p. 43. Councils of war were used to try lawful combatants for Articles of War violations. Some five hundred Americans of Irish descent—known as St. Patrick's Battalion—defected to the Mexican cause reportedly because of the brutal, racist discrimination received from the United States, and also because they identified with their fellow Catholics. When captured, they faced court-martial trials for desertion from the U.S. Army. Jody Prescott and Joanne Eldridge, "Military Commissions, Past and Future," *Military Review*, March-April 2003, www.findarticles. com/p/articles/mi_m0PBZ/is_2_83/ai_106732243.

6. Ibid.

7. Diary of Henry L. Stimson, June 28, 1942, quoted in Louis Fisher, "Military Tribunals: The *Quirin* Precedent," Congressional Research Service Report, March 26, 2002, p. 4.

8. Cox "concluded that the saboteurs should be tried by court-martial for violating Article of War 82—relieving the enemy—and also for a possible violation of the law of war—coming through military lines in civilian dress for purpose of committing hostile acts." David J. Danelski, "The Saboteurs' Case," *Journal of Supreme Court History* 21, no. 1 (1996): 66.

9. Ibid.

10. Louis Fisher, *Nazi Saboteurs on Trial: A Military Tribunal and American Law* (Lawrence: University Press of Kansas, 2003), p. 48.

11. William H. Rehnquist, *The Supreme Court: How It Was, How It Is* (New York: Morrow, 1987), pp. 35, 74, 248.

12. Diary of Henry L. Stimson, June 29, 1942, quoted in Fisher, "Military Tribunals"; Danelski, "The Saboteurs' Case," p. 66.

13. Fisher, *Nazi Saboteurs on Trial: A Military Tribunal and American Law*, pp. 48–49 (paraphrased).

14. Joseph E. Persico, *Roosevelt's Secret War: FDR and World War II Espionage* (New York: Random House, 2002), p. 202; Francis Biddle, *In Brief Authority* (Garden City, N.Y.: Doubleday, 1962), p. 330. Major John André, an adjutant general in the British army, was caught in American territory in civilian clothes with incriminating documents following his negotiations with Benedict Arnold for the surrender of West Point, while Nathan Hale was an American engaged in espionage work who was caught by the British behind the lines. Biddle, *In Brief Authority*, pp. 330–31.

15. TCTK, p. 173. Prominent legislators—such as Congressman Carl Vinson and Senator George Norris—openly called for the death penalty.

16. William R. Glendon and Richard N. Winfield, "Colonel Royall Vigorously Defended Saboteurs Captured on U.S. Shores," *New York State Bar Association Journal*, February 2002, pp. 46–47.

17. Persico, *Roosevelt's Secret War*, p. 202.

18. Biddle, *In Brief Authority*, p. 330. For a thoughtful discussion of wartime treatment of civil liberties in the United States, see Rehnquist, *All the Laws but One*.

19. See generally Mark E. Neely Jr., *The Fate of Liberty: Abraham Lincoln and Civil Liberties* (New York: Oxford University Press, 1991).

20. Biddle, *In Brief Authority*, p. 331.

21. Vyvyan Tenorio, "White Shoes, Dot-Com," *The Daily Deal*, July 7, 2000, www.clm.com/news/new-970953_1.html. Carter, Ledyard & Milburn is still in business, with close to a hundred and twenty lawyers in New York and Washington, D.C.

22. In fact, Hoover had initially assumed that the Germans would be tried in a federal court. He was also convinced that the U.S. citizens could not be tried before a military court and "could obtain a writ of habeas corpus." Memorandum of J. Edgar Hoover to Special Agents Tolson, Tamm, and Ladd, June 29, 1942, quoted in Alex Abella and Scott Gordon, *Shadow Enemies: Hitler's Secret Terrorist Plot Against the United States* (Guilford, Conn.: Lyons Press, 2002) p. 130 n. 268.

23. TCTK, p. 172.

24. Ibid., p. 173.

25. The treatment of prisoners of war had evolved over thousands of years. From ancient times to medieval Europe, the general practice was to kill enemy prisoners of war without any sort of judicial proceeding. The Greeks generally put the entire adult male population of a conquered state to death. Prisoners captured by the Roman army were often brought back to Rome to fight to the death against exotic animals and one another in gladiatorial contests on the bloodstained sands of the Colosseum. The Muslim Ottomans executed thirty thousand Christian prisoners during the War of Candia (1667–68). With the rise of chivalry in late medieval Europe, however, the practice of brutally killing prisoners ended, for the most part, and the custom of showing mercy to captives took root. "Prisoners of War," *Microsoft Encarta Online Encyclopedia*, 2004, www.encarta.msn.com/encyclopedia_761563989/prisoners_of_war .html.

The humane treatment of POWs is a venerable American tradition dating back to the American Revolution. General George Washington instructed the American officer in charge of 221 British prisoners taken at the Battle of Princeton: "Treat them with humanity, and let them have no reason to complain of our copying the brutal example of the British army in their treatment of our unfortunate brethren." The commander of the American army was alluding to the British massacre of Americans who had surrendered during the Battle of Fort Washington. Washington openly wept as he personally witnessed the savage slaughter through a spyglass. Washington " 'often reminded his men that they were an army of liberty and freedom, and that the rights of humanity for which they were fighting should extend even to their enemies.' " George Will, "It Was Our Greatest Christmas," *Santa Barbara News-Press*, December 25, 2004, p. A9 (quoting David Hackett Fischer, *Washington's Crossing* (New York: Oxford University Press, 2004)

The humanitarian treatment of POWs was strengthened by a series of international agreements regarding the treatment of the wounded, prisoners of war, and civilians that became part of the law of war. The first of these treaties was the Geneva Convention of 1864, providing for the treatment and care of the wounded on the battlefield. Thirty-five years later, the Hague Conference of 1899 adopted numerous conventions, including the Second Convention (Laws and Customs of War on Land)—the first international agreement dealing with the status of prisoners of war and the rights of POWs. But the conventions of the Hague Conference of 1899 (and later the Hague Conference of 1907) proved to be insufficient in practice during World War I, leading to the Geneva Convention of 1929, which further expanded the protections of captured enemy soldiers. Notably, Japan and the USSR did not sign this convention. "Historical Attitudes Toward Prisoners of War," *Columbia Electronic Encyclopedia*, 6th ed. (New York: Columbia University Press, 2003); "Laws of War: Laws and Customs of War on Land" (Hegnett), July 29, 1899, the Avalon Project at Yale Law School, 2003, www.yale.edu/lawweb/avalon/lawofwar/hague02.htm.

Despite these new safeguards, the Geneva Convention of 1929 was not able to prevent some of the worst atrocities in history during World War II. Consequently, the Geneva Conventions of 1949 were established. Specifically, the Third Geneva Convention, Relative to the Treatment of Prisoners of War, was aimed at expanding and solidifying the rights of prisoners of war—which had been flagrantly violated by the Japanese war crimes in the Pacific theater. The death rate for American POWs in Japanese camps was nearly 40 percent, while the death rate for American POWs in Germany was below 2 percent.

Finally, the Geneva Convention of 1949 regarding the protection of civilians was born out of the millions of civilian deaths in the Holocaust in Nazi Germany and in bombing raids around the world. "World War II: Japan's Prisoner of War (POW) Camps," *VikingPhoenix.com*, www.vikingphoenix.com/public/rongstad/military/POW/PWcamps-2.htm.

26. Russian prisoners fared far worse. Out of nearly six million captured by the Germans, close to four million perished. William Shirer, *The Rise and Fall of the Third Reich: A History of Nazi Germany* (New York: MJF, 1990), pp. 951–52.

27. As the war intensified, however, Hitler decreed massive violations of the rules of war for treating commandos and later captured bomber crews. Thus, as the tide started to turn against him in 1942, the Führer personally ordered the extermination of Allied saboteurs, especially in the West. "From now on all enemies on so-called commando missions in Europe or Africa challenged by German troops, even if they are in uniform, whether armed or unarmed, in battle or in flight, are to be slaughtered to the last man." Ibid., p. 955 (quoting Hitler's "Top-Secret Commando Order" of October 18, 1942).

Hitler's secret order was a crime, an admitted contravention of expected treatment according to the Geneva Convention. Hitler's avowed goal was to deter commando raids by making it "clear to the enemy that all sabotage troops will be exterminated, without exception, to the last man." Ibid. The murder-on-sight policy had no discernible impact on the number or success of Allied sabotage missions behind German lines.

Similarly, Allied airmen came in for the same brutal treatment after the bombing of Germany became so intensive in 1943. Civilians were encouraged to murder the fliers as soon as they had parachuted to the ground. Hitler himself ordered the summary execution without court-martial of Allied crews who had killed civilians with machine-gun fire. Ibid.

28. Persico, *Roosevelt's Secret War*, p. 203.

29. Ibid.

30. Boris I. Bittker, "The World War II German Saboteurs' Case and Writs of Certiorari Before Judgment by the Court of Appeals: A Tale of Nunc Pro Tunc Jurisdiction," *Constitutional Commentary* 14 (1997), p. 431.

31. Article III, Section 3 provides: "Treason against the United States, shall consist only in levying War against them, or in adhering to their Enemies, giving them Aid and Comfort. No person shall be convicted of Treason unless on the testimony of two Witnesses to the same overt act, or on Confession in open court."

32. The Justice Department's research disclosed that the Supreme Court, in the few treason cases ever reviewed, had warned that "the crime of treason should not be extended by construction to doubtful cases." *Ex parte Bollman and Ex parte Swartwout*, 4 Cr. (8 U.S.) 75, 127 (1807).

33. Burger may not have been chargeable with treason since there was a strong argument that he had lost his United States citizenship by joining the German army. TCTK, p. 57.

34. Memorandum from Biddle to Roosevelt, June 30, 1942.

35. Biddle, *In Brief Authority*, p. 328.

36. Fisher, "Military Tribunals," p. 4.

37. The government might also have been able to proceed against the defendants for disobeying immigration laws by entering the country secretly and/or for violating customs laws by bringing articles into the United States when they landed from the U-boats. Undoubtedly, this approach was swiftly rejected because it would have been perceived as the proverbial slap on the wrist.

38. "[A] seasoned New Deal politician like Francis Biddle recognized that it was pointless to run head on against the direction the President was taking, especially in wartime." Bradley F. Smith, *Reaching Judgment at Nuremberg* (New York: Basic Books, 1977), p. 34.

39. Biddle, *In Brief Authority*, p. 328.

40. Jack Goldsmith and Cass R. Sunstein, "Military Tribunals and Legal Culture: What a Difference Sixty Years Makes," University of Chicago Law School, Public Law Research Paper no. 27, Olin Working Paper no. 153, p. 3, www.law.uchicago .edu/academics/publiclaw/resources/27.jg-cs.tribunals.pdf.

41. Persico, *Roosevelt's Secret War*, p. 203.

42. Committee on Communications and Media Law of the Association of the Bar of the City of New York, "The Press and the Public's First Amendment Right of Access to Terrorism on Trial: A Position Paper," 2002, p. 15 (quoting Lloyd Cutler, a junior attorney on the prosecution team).

43. This would later be the judgment of the defense team. One of the junior members was Lauson H. Stone, son of Chief Justice Harlan Fiske Stone. "The whole thing was kind of a legal farce," he recognized at the time, "because you knew what was going to happen from the beginning." Seth Kantor, "Secret Trial of 'German 8,'" *Atlanta Journal and Constitution*, July 5, 1980, p. 1-A, quoted in Committee on Communications and Media Law, "The Press and the Public's First Amendment Right," p. 15.

44. Diary of Henry L. Stimson, July 1, 1942, in Fisher, "Military Tribunals," p. 5.

45. Ibid.

46. Persico, *Roosevelt's Secret War*, p. 204.

47. Biddle, *In Brief Authority*, p. 331.

48. 7 Fed. Reg. 5101 (1942) p. 5.

49. Under a court-martial, a unanimous vote was required for the death penalty. Fisher, "Military Tribunals," p. 7.

50. The military review of any sentence and judgment ordinarily included the Judge Advocate General's Office. By appointing Cramer as one of the prosecutors, Roosevelt ensured that he would have a conflict in performing his normal appellate function.

51. Fisher, "Military Tribunals," p. 5. Congress had blessed the use of the law of war instead of the regular court-martial procedures by conferring "concurrent jurisdiction with respect to offenders or offenses that by statute or by the law of war may be tried by military commissions, provost courts, or other military tribunals." 10 U.S.C. Section 821 (1994).

52. Lewis Wood, "Army Court to Try 8 Nazi Saboteurs," *New York Times*, July 3, 1942, p. 3.

Chapter 13: "Sentence First, Verdict Afterward"

1. The first occupants moved into the new Pentagon on April 29, 1942. The 6,636,630-square-foot headquarters of the Department of War was built in sixteen months at a cost of $83 million.

2. Lewis Carroll, *Alice's Adventures in Wonderland* (New York: St. Martin's Press, 1977), pp. 201–2.

3. Louis Fisher, *Nazi Saboteurs on Trial: A Military Tribunal and American Law* (Lawrence: University Press of Kansas, 2003), p. 59.

4. William R. Glendon and Richard N. Winfield, "Colonel Royall Vigorously Defended Saboteurs Captured on U.S. Shores," *New York State Bar Journal*, February 2002, p. 47.

5. Behind the scenes, Biddle sent a memo to Roosevelt advising that it would be a "mistake" to deny Royall and Dowell authority to resort to the civil courts because it "might tend to give the public impression that the prisoners are not being given a fair trial." Fisher, *Nazi Saboteurs on Trial*, p. 65, n. 72. Characteristically, Roosevelt, avoiding a direct confrontation, did not send a draft letter furnished by Biddle. Instead, he had his secretary Marvin McIntyre convey an ambiguous "do what you think is best" message to the two defense lawyers.

6. RKCR, pp. 28–32.

7. ESAA, pp. 136–37.

8. TCTK, p. 180.

9. *Johnson v. Zerbst*, 304 U.S. 458, 462 (1938).

10. *Powell v. Alabama*, 287 U.S. 45, 69 (1932).

11. Ristine was appointed to defend Dasch on July 7, 1942—the day before the trial began. Louis Fisher, "Military Tribunals: The *Quirin* Precedent," Congressional Research Service Report, March 26, 2002, p. 6.

12. ESAA, pp. 148–49.

13. David J. Danelski, "The Saboteurs' Case," *Journal of Supreme Court History* 21, no. 1 (1996): 65.

14. ESAA, pp. 143–45.

Chapter 14: Kangaroo Court

1. Louis Fisher, "Military Tribunals: The *Qurin* Precedent," Congressional Research Service Report, March 26, 2002, p. 7.

2. Diary of Henry L. Simson, July 8, 1942, quoted in Fisher, "Military Tribunals."

3. TCTK, p. 177; Lewis Wood, "Spy Trial Starts in Grim Secrecy; 8 Saboteurs Hidden From Public," *New York Times*, July 9, 1942, p. A1.

4. Arthur Krock, "In the Nation: When Martial Law Was Proposed for Every-body," *New York Times*, July 14, 1942, p. A18.

5. Committee on Communications and Media Law of the Association of the Bar of the City of New York, "The Press and the Public's First Amendment Right of Access to Terrorism on Trial: A Position Paper," 2002, pp. 5–9. During the Civil War, military courts tried the cases of Confederate spies and soldiers, the federal government suppressed allegedly "disloyal" newspapers, and President Lincoln suspended the writ of habeas corpus, allowing "some northern civilians . . . [to be] tried and convicted by secret military tribunals for having engaged in 'disloyal' speech." Ibid., p. 11. While the military trial of Abraham Lincoln's assassins began in secrecy, "as criticism swelled, the trial was opened to the public and press." Thomas Reed Turner, "The Military Trial," in Edward J. Steers Jr. (ed.), *The Trial: The Assassination of President Lincoln and the Trial of the Conspirators* (Lexington: University Press of Kentucky, 2003), p. xiii. Chief Justice William H. Rehnquist concluded that the federal government during the Civil War "used a heavy-handed, blunderbuss approach" replete with "gross violations of the First Amendment." William H. Rehnquist, *All the Laws but One: Civil Liberties in Wartime* (New York: Vintage, 2000), p. 221.

6. A sharp debate about secrecy within the Roosevelt administration—between the Office of War Information and Secretary of War Stimson—was won by the prosecution. Louis Fisher, *Nazi Saboteurs on Trial: A Military Tribunal and American Law* (Lawrence: University Press of Kansas, 2003), pp. 53–55. Oklahoma Democratic congressman Mike Monroney criticized the total secrecy surrounding the trial, remarking that the suppression of "all news under guise of withholding military information strain[s] our credulity." "General M'Coy Predicts a Long Spy Trial," *New York Times*, July 11, 1942, p. A15.

7. "Spy Court Session Viewed by Press," *New York Times*, July 12, 1942, p. A1.

8. Interview with Lloyd Cutler, May 29, 2003.

9. Francis Biddle, *In Brief Authority* (Garden City, N.Y.: Doubleday, 1962), p. 333.

10. Ibid., p. 332.

11. Trial transcript, p. 3 (hereafter "TT").

12. In addition to Biddle and Cramer, three army colonels and two Justice Department officials served on the joint military-civilian prosecution team. James H. Rowe Jr., assistant to the attorney general, had strenuously opposed the internment of Japanese Americans a few months earlier. The other Justice Department representative was Oscar Cox, the assistant solicitor general who had written Biddle the memorandum outlining the charges against the accused. The youngest lawyer on the prosecution team was Lloyd Cutler, on loan from the Lend-Lease Administration.

13. TT, p. 5.

14. Louis Fisher, *Nazi Saboteurs on Trial*, p. 57.

15. Ibid., p. 59.

16. RKCR, p. 34.

17. TT, p. 30.

18. Interview with Lloyd Cutler, May 29, 2003.

19. Ibid.

20. TT, pp. 67–68.

21. Interview with William R. Glendon and Richard N. Winfield, June 15, 2003.

22. Ibid.

23. This quote is attributed to Edward Bennett Williams, the legendary trial lawyer for whom the author worked in the 1970s.

24. TT, pp. 100ff.

25. Later in the trial, over strenuous defense objection, Biddle tried to use Burger's confession against his fellow co-conspirators. Biddle argued that the lower standard of admitting evidence was designed by the president to allow "this body to disregard the highly technical and complicated rules of evidence and to consider whether or not . . . Burger freely and without duress" made the confession. TT, p. 306. Royall eloquently replied: "One thing we are proud of in this country . . . is our system of administering government . . . particularly in times like this. . . . [W]e are fighting . . . to protect our system of government. . . . [W]hen we deal with a fundamental principle of trying seven other men upon an unsworn, unexamined, and uninvestigated declaration of an eighth, we are encroaching, in our humble opinion, upon a fundamental element of our administration of justice." TT, pp. 308–9.

26. Wood, "Spy Trial Starts in Grim Secrecy."

Chapter 15: An Improbable Life

1. TT, p. 232.

2. William Hassett, *Off the Record with FDR* (New Brunswick: Rutgers University Press, 1958), p. 90.

3. TT, p. 610.

4. Ibid., p. 620.

5. The convictions of six defendants tried together in Chicago federal court were reversed by the appellate court for several reasons, including the failure to afford the accused separate trials. See *United States v. Haupt*, 136 F.2d 661 (7th Cir. 1943); *United States v. Cramer*, 137 F.2d 888 (7th Cir. 1943); and *United States v. Haupt*, 152 F.2d 771 (7th Cir. 1945).

6. TT, pp. 991–94.

7. Ibid., pp. 994, 996–97.

8. Ibid., p. 1600 and previous.

9. Francis Biddle, *In Brief Authority* (Garden City, N.Y.: Doubleday, 1962), p. 335.

10. Ibid., p. 336.

11. Ibid., p. 340.

Chapter 16: A Lion in Summer

1. TT, p. 1824.

2. Ibid., p. 1830.

3. Ibid., pp. 1833–34.

4. Ibid., pp. 1835–57.

5. Ibid., p. 1888.

6. Ibid., pp. 1889–91.

7. Ibid., p. 1894.

8. Ibid., p. 1924.

9. Ibid., pp. 1930, 1932.

10. ESAA, p. 153.

11. Ibid.

12. TT, p. 1937.

13. Ibid., p. 1939.

14. Ibid., p. 1945.

15. Ibid., p. 1941.

16. Ibid., pp. 1944, 1946–47.

17. Ibid., p. 1953.

18. Ibid., p. 1954.

19. Ibid., pp. 1957–58, 1960.

20. Ibid., p. 2018.

21. Ibid., pp. 2072–73.

22. Ibid., pp. 2078–79.

23. Ibid., p. 2099.

24. Ibid., p. 2104.

25. Ibid., pp. 2108–10.

26. Ibid., p. 2110.

27. Ibid., pp. 2111, 2114.

Chapter 17: They Don't Shoot Saboteurs in America

1. TT, p. 2265.

2. Ibid., p. 2343.

3. Ibid., p. 2457.

4. Ibid., p. 2458.

5. Francis Biddle, *In Brief Authority* (Garden City, N.Y.: Doubleday, 1962), p. 326.

6. Ibid. A prison psychiatrist later diagnosed Dasch as suffering from "obsessive, compulsive, neurotic, hysterical personality disorder." Ibid.

7. Ibid., p. 336.

8. TT, p. 2585.

9. Ibid., p. 2683.

10. Ibid., p. 2623.

11. Ibid., p. 2626.

12. Ibid., p. 2665.

13. Ibid., p. 2735.

14. Ibid., p. 2761.

Chapter 18: The Great Writ

1. The attribution of the jury trial's origins to the Magna Carta has been questioned. See *Duncan v. Louisiana*, 391 U.S. 145, 151, n. 16 (1968).

2. William Forsyth, *History of Trial by Jury* (New York: James Cockcroft, 1875), pp. 230–35.

3. William Blackstone, *Commentaries on the Laws of England* (San Francisco: Bancroft-Whitney, 1916), vol. II, p. 350.

4. Joseph Story, *Commentaries on the Constitution of the United States* (Boston: Charles C. Little and James Brown, 1851), vol. II, p. 527, quoted in *Thompson v. Utah*, 170 U.S. 343, 350 (1898).

5. Technically, the writ orders the person who is responsible for the petitioner's confinement (a warden or military officer, for example) to produce the petitioner

(i.e., the body, or *corpus*) in court for a judge to determine the legality of the detention.

6. Article 1, Section 9, clause 2. See Kermit L. Hall (ed.), *The Oxford Companion to American Law* (New York: Oxford University Press, 2002), p. 349.

7. *Ex parte Yerger*, 75 U.S. 85, 95 (1869).

8. The writ of habeas corpus was considered so important that the very first statute enacted by Congress (the Judiciary Act of 1789) empowered all federal courts "to grant writs of habeas corpus for the purpose of an inquiry into the cause of confinement."

9. *Fay v. Noia*, 372 U.S. 391, 401–2 (1963).

10. See *Ex parte Bollman and Ex parte Swartout*, 8 U.S. 75 (1807).

11. *Ex parte Merryman*, 17 Fed. Cas. 144 (No. 9487) (C.C.D. Md. 1861).

12. Taney was, to put it mildly, a thorn in Lincoln's side. A staunchly pro-slavery Southerner, he had led the Court in rendering the infamous *Dred Scott* decision (upholding the right of a slave's owner to recover that slave even if the slave had established temporary residence in a territory in which slavery, under the Missouri Compromise, was banned). The chief justice got it right in the *Merryman* case, even if his animus toward Lincoln was a potent factor in his admirable stand on habeas corpus.

13. 4 Wall. (71 U.S.) 2 (1866). In *Ex parte Milligan*, the Supreme Court made clear that when suspension occurs, the writ itself is not suspended, only the privilege. Thus, the writ would issue and the issuing court would then decide, when the government responded, whether the applicant could proceed.

14. 4 Wall. (71 U.S.) 2 at 120–21.

15. William R. Glendon and Richard N. Winfield, "Colonel Royall Vigorously Defended Saboteurs Captured on U.S. Shores," *New York State Bar Journal*, February 2002, p. 47.

16. Anthony Lewis, *Gideon's Trumpet* (New York: Random House, 1964), p. 169.

17. Roosevelt proposed that Congress enact legislation allowing him to appoint one additional justice for each incumbent justice who was over the age of seventy and declined to retire. FDR defended his plan as essential to relieve the Court's heavy workload. Of course, if Holmes, Brandeis, and Cardozo were still serving and supporting his economic legislation, Roosevelt would not have launched such an audacious assault on the "nine old men."

While the proposal was widely condemned by Republicans and Democrats, it was not unconstitutional. Congress is empowered by the Constitution to fix the number of seats on the Supreme Court. Over the first eighty years of the republic, Congress manipulated the Court's size for political purposes with as few as five seats and as many as ten seats. Sandra Day O'Connor, *The Majesty of the Law* (New York: Random House, 2003), p. 18.

18. Timothy L. Hall, *Supreme Court Justices: A Biographical Dictionary* (New York: Facts on File, 2001), p. 293.

19. Fred Rodell, *Nine Men: A Political History of the Supreme Court from 1790–1955* (New York: Random House, 1955), p. 11.

20. Hall, *Supreme Court Justices*, p. 297.

21. Roberts' frank self-assessment of his judicial career tells it best: "Who am I to revile the good God that did not make me a Marshall, a Taney, a Bradley, a Holmes, a Brandeis, or a Cardozo?" Ibid., p. 298.

22. The Roberts Commission was only the first in a series of inquests into questions of responsibility for and causes of the disaster. It was, like the later Warren Com-

mission, an attempt to deal with troubling questions expeditiously—and it also left a great many unsatisfied with its findings. These were delivered, with remarkable promptness, on January 24, 1942, and were fundamentally flawed because, among other things, the commission was not made aware of the degree to which the United States could intercept and read Japan's encoded diplomatic and military communications.

23. Hall, *Supreme Court Justices*, p. 309. Hugo Black "had been one of the fiercest allies of the New Deal as a senator from Alabama."

24. Rodell, *Nine Men*, pp. 251–52.

25. See Howard Ball, *Hugo L. Black: Cold Steel Warrior* (New York: Oxford University Press, 1996), pp. 60–62, 89–100.

26. Hall, *Supreme Court Justices*, pp. 303–6. In *Chambers v. Florida*, 309 U.S. 227 (1940), Black, writing for the majority, invalidated the state court convictions of four black defendants because of coerced confessions. Using the Fourteenth Amendment's due process guarantee, the Court held that fundamental fairness prohibited securing convictions and executing the accused on the basis of involuntary confessions.

27. *Chambers v. Florida*, 309 U.S. 227, 241 (1940).

28. Rodell, *Nine Men*, p. 252.

29. Hall, *Supreme Court Justices*, p. 307; Kermit L. Hall (ed.), *The Oxford Companion to the Supreme Court of the United States* (New York: Oxford University Press 1992), pp. 712–13.

30. Hall, *Supreme Court Justices*, p. 313.

31. Bruce Allen Murphy, *The Brandeis/Frankfurter Connection: The Secret Political Activities of Two Supreme Court Justices* (New York: Oxford University Press, 1982), pp. 189–90.

32. *West Virginia State Board of Education v. Barnette*, 319 U.S. 624, 646–47 (Frankfurter, J. dissenting).

33. Rodell, *Nine Men*, p. 253.

34. Bruce Allen Murphy, *Wild Bill: The Legend and Life of William O. Douglas* (New York: Random House, 2003), pp. 106–8, 183–84, 189, 191–92, 197–98, 209–11, 217–18, 212–32. In 1944, Douglas was touted as a possible vice presidential nominee, but Harry Truman was nominated as FDR's running mate and succeeded him when he died in 1945.

35. Hall, *Supreme Court Justices*, p. 320; see J. Woodford Howard Jr., *Mr. Justice Murphy: A Political Biography* (Princeton, N.J.: Princeton University Press, 1968).

36. Hall, *Supreme Court Justices*, p. 325. Byrnes resigned on October 3, 1942, to devote all his time to being "assistant president," serving President Roosevelt as director of economic stabilization and later as director of war mobilization.

37. *Edwards v. California*, 314 U.S. 160 (1941).

38. Hall, *Supreme Court Justices*, p. 327.

39. Ibid., p. 328.

40. William E. Leuchtenburg, *The Supreme Court Reborn: The Constitutional Revolution in the Age of Roosevelt* (New York: Oxford University Press, 1995), p. 180.

41. Francis Biddle, *In Brief Authority* (Garden City, N.Y.: Doubleday, 1962), p. 337.

42. TCTK, p. 252.

43. Lewis Wood, "Supreme Court Is Called in Unprecedented Session to Hear Plea of Nazi Spies," *New York Times*, July 28, 1942, p. 1.

44. Dillard Stokes, "Supreme Court to Meet in Test of Presidential War Power in Spy Case," *Washington Post*, July, n.d., 1942, Royall Papers, #4651, University of North Carolina at Chapel Hill (Wilson Library).

45. Interview with William R. Glendon and Richard N. Winfield, June 15, 2003.

46. Jack Betts, "The Trials of War," *Carolina Alumni Review*, March–April 2002, p. 37.

47. The sources for the newspaper quotes are collected in Jack Goldsmith and Cass R. Sunstein, "Military Tribunals and Legal Culture: What a Difference Sixty Years Makes," University of Chicago Law School, Public Law Research Paper no. 27, Olin Working Paper no. 153, p. 5, www.law.uchicago.edu/academics/publiclaw/resources/27.jg-cs.tribunals.pdf.

48. Arthur Krock, *New York Times*, July 30, 1942; editorial, "Habeas Corpus," *Washington Post*, July 31, 1942, p. 12.

49. Betts, "The Trials of War," p. 37.

50. Ibid.

51. Brief for Petitioners, *Ex parte Quirin*, pp. 363, 368–69.

52. See Philip B. Kurland and Gerhard Casper (eds.), *Landmark Briefs and Arguments of the Supreme Court of the United States: Constitutional Law* (Arlington, Va.: University Publications of America, 1975), pp. 402–63 (hereafter "SCT"); David J. Danelski, "The Saboteurs' Case," *Journal of Supreme Court History* 21, no. 1 (1996): 68–69.

53. Brief for the Respondent, *Ex parte Quirin*, pp. 429, 437, 447, 463.

Chapter 19: May It Please the Court

1. Boris I. Bittker, "The World War II German Saboteurs' Case and Writs of Certiorari Before Judgment by the Court of Appeals: A Tale of Nunc Pro Tunc Jurisdiction," *Constitutional Commentary* 14 (1997), p. 431.

2. Dillard Stokes, "Justices Question Plea 8 Took Role of Spies to Escape From Nazis," *Washington Post*, n.d., Royall Papers #4651, University of North Carolina at Chapel Hill (Wilson Library).

3. TCTK, p. 242.

4. Fred W. Perkins, "Aliens Taste Civil Rights Germany Denies Them," Royall Papers #4651 (Royall scrapbook, July–August 1942), University of North Carolina at Chapel Hill (Wilson Library).

5. *Moyer v. Peabody*, 212 U.S. 78, 85 (1909).

6. TCTK, p. 242.

7. "4 Justices Here, Others on Way for Spy Appeal," Royall Papers #4651 (Royall scrapbook, July–August 1942).

8. "Habeas corpus," Royall Papers #4651.

9. "Royall, True to Oath, Defended Spies With All His Legal Skill," Royall Papers #4651, University of North Carolina at Chapel Hill (Wilson Library).

10. Perkins, "Aliens Taste Civil Rights."

11. Kermit L. Hall (ed.), *The Oxford Companion to the Supreme Court of the United States* (New York: Oxford University Press, 1992), p. 102.

12. "The Republic endures and this is the symbol of its faith," proclaimed Chief Justice Charles Evans Hughes in laying the cornerstone in 1932. Designed by noted architect Cass Gilbert, the neoclassical-style building had been criticized for its scale and pomposity. "The place is almost bombastically pretentious," Hughes' successor, Chief Justice Stone, complained, "and thus it seems to me wholly inappropriate for a quiet group of old boys such as the Supreme Court." Anthony Lewis, *Gideon's Trumpet* (New York: Random House, 1964) p. 166.

13. For the first 146 years of the republic, the Supreme Court sat in three different cities, sharing space with other government entities, including the New York State Legislature (New York City), Pennsylvania Supreme Court and Independence Hall (Philadelphia), and the basement of the Capitol (Washington, D.C.). In 1809, the justices heard cases in a tavern near the Capitol, and for a few years after the British sacked the city in 1814, they met in a rented house.

14. Fred Rodell, *Nine Men: A Political History of the Supreme Court from 1790–1955* (New York: Random House, 1955), pp. 3–4 (emphasis in original).

15. Hall (ed.), *The Oxford Companion to the Supreme Court*, p. 44.

16. Rodell, *Nine Men*, p. 9.

17. See ibid., pp. 28–29. Justice Roberts most certainly read the 1936 election returns and newspapers detailing Roosevelt's court-packing plan when he inexplicably flip-flopped on the constitutionality of New Deal programs.

18. The Court's awe-inspiring pomp and circumstance "has invested the Court, in the popular mind, with a symbolic sacredness, an aura of being above such petty and temporal things as the making of political decisions and the wielding of political power." This myth of the justices as "politically sterile" projects an image of "apolitical persons, unaffected by what goes on in the nation outside their marble temple, aloof and remote from the workaday world." Rodell, *Nine Men*, pp. 27–29.

19. Jack Betts, "The Trials of War," *Carolina Alumni Review*, March–April 2002, p. 37.

20. Stimson Diary, June 29, 1942, cited in David J. Danelski, "The Saboteurs' Case," *Journal of Supreme Court History* 21, no. 1 (1996): 66.

21. Jonathan Turley, "The Dark History of a Military Tribunal," *The National Law Journal*, November 1, 2002.

22. Louis Fisher, "Military Tribunals: The *Quirin* Precedent," Congressional Research Service Report, March 26, 2002, p. 20; Turley, "Dark History."

23. James F. Byrnes, *All in One Lifetime* (New York: Harper and Brothers, 1958), pp. 148–54; Fisher, "Military Tribunals," p. 20.

24. Turley, "Dark History."

25. Tony Mauro, "A Mixed Precedent for Military Tribunals," *Legal Times*, November 19, 2001.

26. Turley, "Dark History."

27. TCTK, p. 255.

28. "Transcript: *Ex parte Quirin*," SCT, p. 496.

29. Lewis, *Gideon's Trumpet*, p. 167.

30. SCT, 497.

31. Ibid., 498.

32. Fisher, "Military Tribunals," p. 22.

33. SCT, p. 516.

34. Ibid., pp. 520–22.

35. Ibid., pp. 530–34.

36. Ibid., pp. 534–35.

37. Ibid., p. 536.

38. Ibid., p. 540.

39. Ibid., pp. 549–50.

40. Ibid., p. 550.

41. Ibid., p. 553.

42. TCTK, pp. 261–62.

43. TCTK, p. 264.

44. The XYZ Affair was an incident in the stormy diplomatic relations between the John Adams administration and the French government, which perceived the Americans tilting toward Great Britain, with whom France was at war. The French refused to accept the American delegation to Paris in what appeared to be an effort to embarrass the Federalist administration to the advantage of the pro-French Jeffersonian Republicans. Congress abrogated the 1778 treaties with America's ally in the Revolutionary War, suspended commercial relations, and prepared for war. For a short while, the United States even engaged in an undeclared naval war with France. Thus was the genesis of the much maligned Alien and Sedition Acts of 1798. See Robert A. Rosenbaum, *The Penguin Encyclopedia of American History* (New York: Penguin Reference, 2003), pp. 11–12, 134, 436.

45. Ibid., p. 11.

46. President Adams prosecuted fourteen cases under the Sedition Act that authorized punishment for making "any false, scandalous and malicious writing or writings" against either house of Congress or the president. Shortly after becoming president in 1801, Thomas Jefferson halted all pending prosecutions and pardoned those already convicted under the Sedition Act.

47. Robert E. Cushman, *"Ex parte Quirin* et al.—The Nazi Saboteur Case," *Cornell Law Quarterly* 28 (1942): 54, 58.

48. TCTK, p. 265.

49. SCT, pp. 650, 654.

50. Interview with Lloyd Cutler, May 29, 2003.

51. SCT, p. 666.

Chapter 20: Total Wipeout

1. TT, p. 2766.

2. Ibid., p. 2769.

3. Ibid., p. 2775.

4. Ibid., pp. 2780–81.

5. Ibid., p. 2785.

6. Ibid., p. 2800.

7. *Ex parte Quirin*, 317 U.S. 1, 18–19 (in footnote) (1942).

8. Lewis Wood, "Army's Spy Trial Upheld by Court; Case Nears Close," *New York Times*, August 1, 1942.

9. Ibid.

10. "Spies Denied Civil Trial: High Court Upholds F.D.," *Washington Daily News*, July 31, 1942, p. 1.

11. David J. Danelski, "The Saboteurs' Case," *Journal of Supreme Court History* 21, no. 1 (1996): 71. Danelski chronicles the behind-the-scenes discussions among the justices leading to completing the terse *per curiam* opinion only minutes before the eight justices took the bench.

12. TT, p. 2808.

13. Ibid., pp. 2815–21.

14. Ibid., p. 2822.

15. Ibid., pp. 2876, 2879.

16. Ibid., pp. 2889–90.

17. Ibid., pp. 2895–97.

18. Ibid., pp. 2907–8.

19. Ibid., pp. 2920–27.

20. Francis Biddle, *In Brief Authority* (Garden City, N.Y.: Doubleday, 1962), pp. 331, 332. Biddle also admired how Royall deftly balanced his two duties—to client and country—by the fact that he "wisely notified his chief, the Secretary [of War], before taking any important step on their behalf." Ibid., p. 332.

21. Interview with Lloyd Cutler, May 29, 2003.

22. TT, p. 2949.

23. Ibid., pp. 2959–61.

Chapter 21: Old Sparky

1. William Hassett, *Off the Record with F.D.R.: 1942–1945* (New Brunswick: Rutgers University Press, 1958), p. 98.

2. RKCR, pp. 32–34.

3. TCTK, p. 281.

4. Ibid., p. 283.

5. Ibid., p. 282.

6. Louis Fisher, "Military Tribunals: The *Quirin* Precedent," Congressional Research Service Report, March 26, 2002, p. 15.

7. TCTK, p. 284.

8. Ibid., p. 284.

9. Ibid., pp. 284–85.

10. ESAA, p. 168.

11. Memorandum from Brigadier General Albert L. Cox to the president of the United States, August 19, 1942.

12. Memorandum from Special Agent McGhee to FBI director Hoover, August 10, 1942, cited in Abella and Gordon, *Shadow Enemies: Hitler's Secret Terrorist Plot Against the United States* (Guilford, Conn.: Lyons Press, 2002), p. 201.

13. "Hitler's Rail-Wreckers," *Classic Trains*, Winter 2001, p. 47.

14. TCTK, p. 287.

15. Abella and Gordon, *Shadow Enemies*, p. 202.

16. Memorandum to the president from Brigadier General S.U. Marietta, August 15, 1942.

17. Today the presidential retreat is known as Camp David.

18. Joseph E. Persico, *Roosevelt's Secret War: FDR and World War II Espionage* (New York: Random House, 2002), p. 205.

19. Ibid., p. 205.

20. *New York Times*, August 8, 1942; *New York Times*, August 10, 1942; President's Secretary's Safe Files, FDR Library, Hyde Park, New York, http://www.fdrlibrary.marist.edu/psf/box5/a63a01.html.

21. Persico, *Roosevelt's Secret War*, p. 205.

22. TCTK, pp. 297–98.

23. "My Dear Kenneth," Justice Frankfurter began, "[n]ow that the grim business is over, I should like you to know how greatly I esteem the admirable manner in which you discharged the difficult and incongenial task entrusted to you by the Commander-in-Chief. You were in the service of both War and Law—and you served both with

distinguished fidelity." Justice Jackson wrote that "it is not unjudicial to say to you that you have acquitted yourself like an officer and a gentleman in a most difficult situation . . . an impressive demonstration that the right to counsel in our democracy is neither a fiction nor a formality." Ibid., p. 297.

Chapter 22: Fait Accompli

1. For a detailed account of the internal debate among the justices, see Alpheus Thomas Mason, "Inter Arma Silent Leges: Chief Justice Stone's Views," *Harvard Law Review* 69 (1956): 806; see also David J. Danelski, "The Saboteurs' Case," *Journal of Supreme Court History* 21, no. 1 (1996): 72–79; Michal R. Belknap, "Frankfurter and the Nazi Saboteurs," *Supreme Court Historical Society Yearbook*, 1982, pp. 66–71.

2. Mason, "Inter Arma Silent Leges," p. 821.

3. Melvin I. Urofsky, "The Court at War, and the War at the Court," *Journal of Supreme Court History* 21, no. 1 (1996): 6.

4. Danelski, "The Saboteurs' Case," p. 72.

5. Mason, "Inter Arma Silent Leges," p. 822.

6. Belknap, "Frankfurter and the Nazi Saboteurs," p. 68.

7. Louis Fisher, "Military Tribunals: The *Quirin* Precedent," Congressional Research Service Report, March 26, 2002, p. 29.

8. *Ex parte Quirin*, 317 U.S. 1, 46–47 (1942).

9. Fisher, "Military Tribunals," p. 32.

10. Belknap, "Frankfurter and the Nazi Saboteurs," p. 69.

11. Ibid., p. 71.

12. *Ex parte Quirin*, 317 U.S. 1, 25 (1942).

13. Ibid.

14. Ibid., at 26.

15. Ibid., at 27.

16. Ibid.

17. Ibid., at 27–28. That Congress elected to adopt by reference the Law of War was not objectionable. "Congress had the choice of crystallizing in permanent form and in minute detail every offense against the law of war, or of adopting the system of common law applied by military tribunals so far as it should be recognized and deemed applicable by the courts. It chose the latter course." Ibid., at 30.

18. Ibid., at 30–31 (emphasis added).

19. Ibid., at 36.

20. Ibid., at 37–38.

21. Ibid., at 38.

22. Ibid.

23. Ibid., at 39 (citations omitted).

24. Ibid., at 42 (footnote omitted).

25. *Ex parte Milligan*, 71 U.S. (4 Wall.) 2, 121 (1866).

26. *Ex part Quirin*, 317 U.S. at 45.

27. Ibid., at 46.

28. Ibid., at 47–48.

29. Danelski, "The Saboteurs' Trial," p. 61.

30. Michael R. Belknap, "The Supreme Court Goes to War: The Meaning and Implication of the Nazi Saboteur Case," 89 *Military Law Review* 59, 87 (1980).

31. Edward S. Corwin, *Total War and the Constitution* (New York: Alfred A. Knopf, 1947), p. 118.

32. Belknap, "The Supreme Court Goes to War," p. 87.

33. Ibid., p. 85.

34. Louis Fisher, *Nazi Saboteurs on Trial: A Military Tribunal and American Law* (Lawrence: University Press of Kansas, 2003), p. 44. Four justices filed a concurring opinion on the issue of whether Congress could have authorized a military commission to try a U.S. citizen in Indiana. On the main issue of whether the executive branch had the power to act unilaterally, the Supreme Court unanimously rejected any such notion, and the concurring justices expressly adopted the views expressed by Justice Davis in the opinion of the Court about "the inestimable value of the trial by jury, and of the other constitutional safeguards of civil liberty." The nine justices were united in the view, as stated by Chief Justice Chase in his concurrence, that: "The laws which protect the liberties of the whole people must not be violated or set aside in order to inflict, even upon the guilty, unauthorized though merited justice." *Ex parte Milligan*, 71 U.S. (4 Wall.) 2, 132 (Chief Justice Chase, concurring); see also ibid., p. 119 (opinion of the Court) ("[I]t is the birthright of every American citizen when charged with crime, to be tried and punished according to law").

35. "Martial law cannot arise from a *threatened* invasion. The necessity must be actual and present; the invasion real, such as effectively closes the courts and deposes the civil administration. . . . Martial rule can never exist where the courts are open, and in the proper and unobstructed exercise of their jurisdiction. It is also confined to the locality of actual war." 71 U.S. (4 Wall.) at 127 (emphasis in original).

36. 71 U.S. (4 Wall.) at 109. "Civil liberty and this kind of martial law cannot endure together; the antagonism is irreconcilable; and, in the conflict, one or the other must perish." Ibid., at 124–25.

37. Ibid., at 120–21.

38. Ibid., at 119.

39. Ibid., at 123.

40. Jonathan Turley, "The Dark History of a Military Tribunal," *The National Law Journal*, November 1, 2002.

41. RKCR, p. 34.

42. Jack Betts, "The Trials of War," *Carolina Alumni Review*, March–April 2002, p. 36.

43. RKCR, pp. 33–34.

44. Betts, "The Trials of War," pp. 32–34.

45. In at least this respect, Chief Justice Stone accomplished his goal that the Supreme Court's opinion would be praised as "as a striking demonstration that the law of the land still governed and that the jurisdiction of the courts was not ousted no matter what the President proclaimed." Mason, "Inter Arma Silent Leges," p. 828. Two decades later, the Court acknowledged that *Ex parte Quirin* was an example of how "*habeas corpus* has time and again played a central role in national crises." *Fay v. Noia*, 372 U.S. 391, 401 (1963), overruled in part, *Wainwright v. Sykes*, 433 U.S. 72 (1977).

46. Danelski, "The Saboteurs' Trial," p. 80.

47. Ibid., p. 79.

48. See Joseph A. Califano, *A Presidential Nation* (New York: Norton, 1975), pp. 53–79; Arthur Schlesinger Jr., *The Imperial Presidency* (Boston: Houghton Mifflin, 1998).

49. Danelski, "The Saboteurs' Trial," p. 80.

50. Mason, "Inter Arma Silent Leges," p. 831.

51. Belknap, "The Supreme Court Goes to War," p. 83.

52. Mason, "Inter Arma Silent Leges," p. 830 (footnote omitted).

53. One scholar charitably characterized the per curiam opinion as the product of "a hasty hearing and decision." Peter Irons, *Justice at War: The Story of the Japanese American Internment Cases* (New York: Oxford University Press, 1983), p. 233.

54. "The secrecy which surrounded the trial and FDR's review sorely nettled the Chief Justice. He was not happy in giving such proceedings a clean bill of health." Mason, "Inter Arma Silent Leges," pp. 823–24.

55. Louis Fisher, "Military Trials," p. 41.

56. John P. Frank, *Marble Palace* (New York: Knopf, 1958), p. 250.

57. As Douglas told an interviewer, the Supreme Court's experience with *Ex parte Quirin* made clear that "it is extremely undesirable to announce a decision on the merits without an opinion accompanying it . . . [because] sometimes those grounds [thought to be valid] crumble." Danelski, "The Saboteurs' Trial," p. 80.

58. After the decision, Frankfurter asked Frederick Bernays Wiener, a military justice expert, to evaluate *Ex parte Quirin*. In three analyses between November 5, 1942, and August 1, 1943, Wiener concluded that the opinion was seriously flawed. The Supreme Court had put its imprimatur on the president's use of a military commission despite Roosevelt's disregard for "almost every precedent in the books." Fisher, "Military Trials," p. 36. Particularly troublesome was the Court upholding the flagrant violation of Article of War 46, requiring the trial record of a military commission to be referred to the staff judge advocate or the judge advocate general. Ibid. Despite these errors, Wiener was of the view that a writ of habeas corpus should not have been issued. "Errors in procedure, and the question of petitioner's guilt or innocence, are beyond the scope of inquiry on habeas corpus to a military tribunal." Ibid., p. 37. Nor did Wiener entertain any doubt that the Germans had no constitutional right to a jury trial because of their status as unlawful belligerents by virtue of entering the United States in civilian clothes. Ibid., p. 38.

59. *Northern Securities Co. v. United States*, 193 U.S. 197, 400–1 (1904) (Holmes, J., dissenting).

60. Belknap, "The Supreme Court Goes to War," p. 95.

61. Belknap, "Frankfurter and the Nazi Saboteurs," p. 67.

62. Mason, "Inter Arma Silent Leges," pp. 830–31.

63. Turley, "Dark History."

64. Byrnes remained on the Supreme Court long enough for the full opinion in *Ex parte Quirin* to be issued and then formally resigned to become President Roosevelt's director of economic stabilization—an executive branch post that he planned to accept while deciding *Ex parte Quirin*.

65. Unquestionably, Frankfurter should have disqualified himself or at least disclosed his intimate involvement with the issue before the Supreme Court. Whether Frankfurter's undisclosed legal advice to Roosevelt's advisors on how to insulate the military commission from constitutional attack constituted an impeachable offense is debatable. Federal judges are appointed for life tenure during "good Behaviour." U.S. Constitution, Article III, Section 1. They can be removed only for "Treason, Bribery, or other high Crimes and Misdemeanors." Ibid., Article II, Section 4. Only one Supreme Court justice—Samuel Chase in 1805—faced an impeachment trial stemming from his unpopular views as a Federalist judge. He was acquitted when a Jeffersonian Republican-

controlled Senate could not muster the required two-thirds vote on any of the charges. See Emily Field Van Tassel and Paul Finkelman, *Impeachable Offenses: A Documentary History from 1787 to the Present* (Washington, D.C.: Congressional Quarterly, 1999), pp. 101–7; William H. Rehnquist, *Grand Inquests: The Historic Impeachments of Justice Samuel Chase and President Andrew Johnson* (New York: William and Morrow, 1992).

66. In his memoirs, Biddle hailed the decision as "an extraordinary example of justice at its best—prompt, yet fair—in striking contrast to what was going on in Germany." Francis Biddle, *In Brief Authority* (Garden City: Doubleday, 1962), p. 339.

67. George G. Battle, "Military Tribunals," 29 *Virginia Law Review* 255, 267 (1942).

68. James R. Agar II, "Military Commissions and the War on Terror," *Texas Bar Journal* 66 (2003): 60, 61.

69. Robert E. Cushman, "*Ex Parte Quirin* et al.—The Nazi Saboteur Case," *Cornell Law Quarterly* 28 (1942): 54, 65.

70. David McCullough, *John Adams* (New York: Simon & Schuster, 2001), p. 68.

71. Belknap, "Frankfurter and the Nazi Saboteurs," p. 71 n. 25.

72. Richard Cahan, "A Terrorist's Tale," *Chicago Magazine*, February 2002.

73. Jack Goldsmith and Cass R. Sunstein, "Military Tribunals and Legal Culture: What a Difference Sixty Years Makes," *Constitutional Commentary* 19, no. 1 (Spring 2002): 261, 280.

74. *Korematsu v. U.S.*, 323 U.S. 214, 248 (1944).

75. Thomas Keneally, *Abraham Lincoln* (New York: Penguin, 2003), p. 103.

76. Abraham Lincoln, special session message to Congress, July 4, 1861.

77. The assumption that an accused terrorist will fare better before a civilian jury is not necessarily the case. A credible argument can be made that trained military officers—especially under the Uniform Code of Military Justice enacted by Congress in 1951—may be more fair-minded and less vulnerable to emotional pressures and prejudices than a lay jury of average Americans. See Spencer J. Crona and Neal A. Richardson, "Justice for War Criminals of Invisible Armies: A New Legal and Military Approach to Terrorism," *Oklahoma City University Law Review* 21 (Summer/Fall 1996): 349, 379. Nor is it at all certain that military tribunals are nothing but staging areas for the accused's execution. Two of the German saboteurs were spared, ten of the twenty-two major Nazi war crime defendants at Nuremberg were either acquitted or given prison terms, and only twelve out of a hundred and seventy-seven other Nazi officials and SS members tried by U.S. military tribunals for crimes against the law of nations were executed. Ibid., p. 381. Moreover, the Uniform Code of Military Justice provides significant procedural protections to criminal defendants, some of which are not available in the civilian criminal justice system.

Chapter 23: "A Loaded Weapon"

1. *Hirabayashi v. United States*, 320 U.S. 81 (1943).

2. The petitioner was supported by amicus curiae ("friend of the court") briefs filed by the American Civil Liberties Union and the Japanese American Citizens League. The attorney generals of California, Washington, and Oregon supported affirmance of the conviction and the constitutionality of Executive Order 9066.

3. *Hirabayashi v. United States*, 320 U.S. at 93.

4. Kermit L. Hall (ed.), *The Oxford Companion to American Law* (New York: Oxford University Press, 2002), p. 432.

5. *Hirabayashi v. United States*, 320 U.S. at 99. Chief Justice Stone also noted that "[w]hatever views we may entertain regarding the loyalty to this country of the citizens of Japanese ancestry, we cannot reject as unfounded the judgment of the military authorities and of Congress that there were disloyal members of that population, whose number and strength could not be precisely and quickly ascertained."

6. *Hirabayashi v. United States*, 320 U.S. 1 at 100–101.

7. Peter Irons, *Justice at War: The Story of the Japanese American Internment Cases* (New York: Oxford University Press, 1983), p. 228.

8. Ibid., pp. 237–50.

9. Ibid., p. 250.

10. *Hirabayashi v. United States*, 320 U.S. 81 at 106 (Douglas, J., concurring).

11. Joel B. Grossman, "The Japanese American Cases and the Vagaries of Constitutional Adjudication in Wartime: An Institutional Perspective," *University of Hawaii Law Review* 19 (1997): 649, 676–77.

12. *Hirabayashi v. United States*, 320 U.S. at 11–12, 133 (Murphy, J. concurring).

13. The same parties who filed amicus curiae briefs in *Hirabayashi* also filed in *Korematsu*.

14. *Korematsu v. United States*, 323 U.S. at 218–19 (1944).

15. Grossman, "The Japanese American Cases," p. 661.

16. *Korematsu v. United States*, 323 U.S. at 226 (Roberts, J. dissenting).

17. Ibid., at 233–35, 239, 242 (Murphy, J., dissenting).

18. Ibid., at 243, 246 (Jackson, J., dissenting) (emphasis added).

19. David M. Kennedy, *Freedom from Fear: The American People in Depression and War, 1929–1945* (New York: Oxford University Press, 1999), p. 757.

20. Ibid., pp. 757–58.

21. Ibid., p. 758.

22. Ironically, just one day before the Supreme Court issued its *Korematsu* decision, the military announced that the period of "military necessity" had ended, rescinded General DeWitt's original evacuation order, and allowed camp residents to return home. Irons, *Justice at War*, p. 345.

23. In vacating Gordon Hirabayashi's conviction on the basis of government misconduct in suppressing evidence of doctoring the documentary record to reflect that General DeWitt had made a judgment of military urgency, one federal court found that the suppressed material, if submitted to the Supreme Court, would have materially affected the justices' decision. *Hirabayashi v. United States*, 828 F.2d 591, 599, 603–4 (9th Cir. 1987).

24. Kai Bird, *The Chairman: John J. McCloy, The Making of the American Establishment* (New York: Simon & Schuster, 1992), p. 162.

25. Doris Kearns Goodwin, *No Ordinary Time: Franklin and Eleanor Roosevelt: The Home Front in World War II* (New York: Simon & Schuster, 1994), pp. 428, 514.

26. Ibid., p. 514.

27. Kennedy, *Freedom from Fear*, p. 759.

28. Yasuko Ito of San Francisco testified years later that "[i]t is difficult to describe the feeling of despair and humiliation experienced by all of us as we watched the Caucasians coming to look over our possessions and offering such nominal amounts knowing we had no recourse but to accept whatever they were offering because we did not know what the future held for us." Commission on Wartime Relocation and Internment of Civilians, *Personal Justice Denied* (Washington, D.C., and Seattle: Civil Liberties Public Education Fund and University of Washington Press, 2000), p. 132.

29. Barry Denenberg, *The Journal of Ben Uchida: Citizen 13559, Mirror Lake Internment Camp* (New York: Scholastic, 1999), p. 139.

30. On December 18, 1944, a unanimous Supreme Court ordered that a loyal American citizen of Japanese ancestry be released from a detention camp. Writing for a unanimous Court, Justice William O. Douglas dodged the constitutional issues, holding that as a matter of statutory construction, the War Relocation Authority had no power to retain "citizens who are concededly loyal . . . [and] present . . . no problem of espionage or sabotage. . . . When the power to detain is derived from the power to protect the war effort against espionage and sabotage, detention which has no relationship to that objective is unauthorized." *Ex parte Endo*, 323 U.S. 283, 297, 302 (1944).

Justice Murphy concurred in the majority opinion, but he condemned the petitioner's detention as "another example of the unconstitutional resort to racism inherent in the entire evacuation program." Ibid., at 307 (Murphy, J., concurring).

Justice Roberts merely concurred in the result, chiding the majority for avoiding the serious constitutional questions posed by the detention of an admittedly loyal citizen for years in violation of the guarantee of the process of law. "Under the Constitution she should be free to come and go as she pleases." Ibid., at 310 (Roberts, J., concurring in the result).

31. Robert H. Jackson, *The Supreme Court in the American System of Government* (Cambridge: Harvard University Press, 1955), p. 25.

32. Earl Warren, "The Bill of Rights and the Military," 37 *New York University Law Review* 181, 193 (1962).

33. Edward S. Corwin, *Total War and the Constitution* (New York: Alfred A. Knopf, 1947), p. 91; see also Louis Fisher, *Nazi Saboteurs on Trial: A Military Tribunal and American Law* (Lawrence: University Press of Kansas, 2003), p. 147.

34. Eugene V. Rostow, "The Japanese American Cases—A Disaster," *Yale Law Journal* 54 (1945): 489, 533.

35. Grossman, "The Japanese American Cases," p. 650.

36. On the forty-third anniversary of Executive Order 9066, California congressman Norman Y. Maneta spoke on the floor of the House of Representatives in favor of a bill later enacted as the Civil Liberties Act of 1988. He described racial discrimination against over a hundred thousand loyal Japanese Americans as "a shocking and still unresolved abuse of the constitutional rights of those who were interned." 131 *Congressional Record* E 468 (February 19, 1985) (Remarks of Representative Mineta).

37. Secretary of War Stimson later acknowledged that "to loyal citizens this forced evacuation was a personal injustice." Attorney General Biddle, who had vigorously opposed the orders but did not force his lawyers to tell the truth to the Supreme Court about the bogus "military necessity," wrote in his memoirs that "the program was ill-advised, unnecessary and unnecessarily cruel." Justice Douglas, who twice voted to uphold the government's position, later claimed that this "was ever on my conscience." True to form, one prominent public official instrumental in the internment policy never repented. Assistant Secretary of War John J. McCloy, the so-called chairman of the American establishment, never waivered in his defense of the mass relocation of loyal Americans. His conscience was clear, he told the Commission on Relocation and Internment of Civilians on November 3, 1981, as Japanese Americans in the audience hissed at his claims that the relocation program "was as benignly conducted as wartime conditions permitted." " 'Men of real statesmanship and integrity'

had acted reasonably in ordering [this repressive measure]. . . . 'There is, I submit, nothing whatever for which the country should atone.'" Irons, *Justice at War*, pp. 352, 353–54.

38. President Gerald R. Ford, Proclamation 4417, Confirming the Termination of the Executive Order Authorizing Japanese-American Internment During World War II, February 19, 1976.

39. Address of President Gerald R. Ford at the University of Hawaii, December 7, 1975.

40. President Gerald R. Ford, Proclamation 4417.

41. Commission on Wartime Relocation and Internment of Civilians, p. 457. The commission was composed of former members of Congress, the Supreme Court, and the cabinet as well as distinguished private citizens.

42. President Reagan's "Remarks on Signing the Bill Providing Restitution for the Wartime Internment of Japanese-Americans," August 10, 1988.

43. Kennedy, *Freedom from Fear*, p. 759.

44. Grossman, "The Japanese American Cases," p. 670. The closest the Supreme Court has come to overruling the two Japanese American internment cases may be the statements in Justice Sandra Day O'Connor's opinion for the Court in *Adarand Constructors, Inc. v. Pena*, 515 U.S. 200, 214–15 (1995); see also 515 U.S. at 244 (Stevens, J., dissenting) (footnote omitted) ("The discrimination at issue in those cases was invidious because the Government imposed special burdens—a curfew and exclusion from certain areas on the West Coast—on the members of a minority class defined by racial and ethnic characteristics"); 515 U.S. at 275 (Ginsburg, J., dissenting) (*Korematsu* upheld "an odious, gravely injurious racial classification").

45. Fred Korematsu's 1944 conviction for violating an exclusion order was voided by a federal court in 1984 because the original verdict had been tainted by official misconduct. See *Korematsu v. United States*, 584 F. Supp. 1406 (N.D. Cal. 1984). Gordon Hirabayashi's conviction for violating curfew and exclusion orders was likewise vacated for the same reasons. *Hirabayashi v. United States*, 828 F.2d 591 (9th Cir. 1987), *affirming in part and reversing in part*, *Hirabayashi v. United States*, 627 F. Supp. 1445 (W.D. Wash. 1986). In vacating Korematsu's conviction. Judge Marilyn Patel observed: "Fortunately, there are few instances in our judicial history when courts have been called upon to undo such profound and publicly acknowledged injustice." 584 F. Supp. at 1413.

46. *Hirabayashi v. United States, supra*, 828 F.2d at 593 (footnotes omitted).

47. Grossman, "The Japanese American Cases," p. 685.

48. 18 U.S.C. §4001(a).

49. 50 U.S.C. §§812(a), 813(a) (1970) (repealed).

50. *Padilla v. Rumsfeld*, 352 F.3d 695, 720 (2nd Cir. Dec. 18, 2003) (opinion holding that the president exceeded his powers by authorizing the military to detain indefinitely—without counsel, charges, or a trial—as an enemy combatant an American citizen seized on American soil outside a zone of combat).

51. Ibid., at 68. In *Howe v. Smith*, 352 U.S. 473, 479 n. 3 (1981), the Supreme Court concluded that the Non-Detention Act "proscrib[ed] detention of *any kind* by the United States" (emphasis in original).

52. Hall (ed.), *The Oxford Companion to American Law*, p. 432.

53. 584 F. Supp. at 1420.

54. Grossman, "The Japanese American Cases," p. 649. In his 1997 article, Professor Grossman noted that while racist deprivations of civil rights on the scale of the

Japanese American internment are not likely to be repeated, he perceptively wondered: "Could a new national crisis of similar proportions, where national survival is (or is thought to be) at stake, precipitate a comparable compromise of individual rights by the political branches which would then be rationalized and accepted by the Supreme Court?" Ibid., p. 650. As discussed in Chapters 25, 26, and 27, the threat of global terrorism poses a national crisis that the government claims is a justification for abrogating traditional civil liberties of citizens such as indictment by grand jury, right to counsel, and speedy trial by jury.

Chapter 24: Winners and Losers

1. Germany formally surrendered on May 8, 1945, while Japan held out until August 15, 1945. In its mind-numbing wake, World War II left more deaths, casualties, and devastation than all the wars in history. Over 61 million military and civilian fatalities, more than 23 million wounded, and economic losses running in the billions of dollars. The United States sustained 291,557 combat deaths and 670,846 wounded compared to 27 million military and civilian deaths for the Soviet Union. The price in human misery and suffering is incalculable.

The Allies triumphed for a combination of reasons, not the least of which was the "arsenal of democracy" supplied by the United States. While the millions of Allied soldiers, sailors, and pilots were brave and skillful, "the single greatest tangible asset the United States brought to the coalition in World War II was the productive capacity of its industry." In total, the United States manufactured 297,000 planes, 86,000 tanks, 6,500 naval vessels, 64,500 landing craft, 5,400 cargo ships, 305,000 artillery pieces, and 17 million rifles. William E. Leuchtenberg et al., "Learning to Live with Less in a Land of Plenty," *Life History of the USA, 1933–1945*, http://sandysq.gcinet.net/uss_salt_lake_city_ca25/homefrnt.htm.

Adolf Hitler, who committed suicide just before the war's end, was justifiably concerned about American airplane manufacturing. The airplane plants targeted by Operation Pastorius made major contributions to the war effort. America defeated its enemies with a smaller army because it was able to construct "a gigantic, heavy-fisted air arm: bombers in fantastic numbers that would ultimately carry bombs of unimaginable destructive power." When his sabotage campaign against strategic aircraft manufacturing targets in the United States failed, Hitler, and certainly the German High Command, had to realize the inevitability of defeat. David M. Kennedy, *Freedom from Fear: The American People in Depression and War, 1929–1945* (New York: Oxford University Press, 1999), p. 631.

2. Patricia Shillingburg, "Roosevelt's Military Commission to Try Spies Started on Local Beach," www.shelter-island.org/german_spies.html.

3. Colepaugh and Gimpel were convicted of three counts: violation of the law of war by passing through military lines, violation of Article of War 82 for spying, and conspiracy. In this trial, neither Biddle nor Cramer prosecuted, the president was not the appointing official of the military tribunal, and the record was reviewed by the judge advocate geneal's office and not the president. Louis Fisher, "Military Tribunals: The *Quirin* Precedent," Congressional Research Service Report, March 26, 2002, pp. 44–45.

4. Ibid., p. 44; Francis Biddle, *In Brief Authority* (Garden City, N.Y.: Doubleday, 1962), pp. 342–43. Colepaugh brought an unsuccessful petition for writ of habeas cor-

pus, arguing that, as a U.S. citizen, he should not have been tried by a military tribunal. See *Colepaugh v. Looney*, 235 F.2d 429 (10th Cir. 1956), *cert. denied*, 352 U.S. 1014 (1957).

5. Gregory D. Kesich, "1944: When Spies Came to Maine," *Portland Press Herald*, April 13, 2003.

6. Henry Stimson and McGeorge Bundy, *On Active Service in Peace and War* (New York: Harper, 1948), pp. 612–13, 628–29; Henry L. Stimson, "The Decision to Use the Atomic Bomb," *Harper's Magazine*, February 1947.

7. Upon Biddle's appointment, Royall wrote a personal letter to his former adversary expressing his "genuine pleasure" and belief that he was "by far the best selection that could have been made." Letter from Kenneth C. Royall to Francis Biddle, dated September 13, 1945, Francis Biddle papers, Georgetown University.

8. Bradley F. Smith, *Reaching Judgment at Nuremberg* (New York: Basic Books, 1977), pp. xiii.

9. Erich Gimpel, *Agent 146: The True Story of a Nazi Spy in America* (New York: Berkley Books, 2003), p. 230.

10. Gary Cohen, "The Keystone Kommandos," *Atlantic Monthly*, February 2002.

11. Affidavit of Erwin Lahousen, dated January 21, 1946, in Office of United States Chief of Counsel for Prosecution of Axis Criminality, *Nazi Conspiracy and Aggression* (Washington, D.C.: U.S. Government Printing Office, 1946), vol. VIII, pp. 588, 594.

12. *Haupt v. United States*, 330 U.S. 631, 644 (1947).

13. Ibid., at 649 (Douglas, J., dissenting).

14. *Cramer v. United States*, 325 U.S. 1 (1945).

15. TCTK, p. 293.

16. See, e.g., *In re Yamashita*, 327 U.S. 1 (1946).

17. RKCR, p. 341.

18. John A. Garraty and Mark C. Carnes (eds.), *American National Biography* (New York: Oxford University Press, 1999), vol. 19, p. 16.

19. William R. Glendon and Richard N. Winfield, "Colonel Royall Vigorously Defended Saboteurs Captured on U.S. Shores," *New York State Bar Journal*, February 2002, p. 49.

20. John F. Kennedy, *Profiles in Courage* (New York: HarperCollins, 2003), p. 216.

Chapter 25: Clear and Present Dangers

1. Thomas L. Friedman, "War of Ideas, Part I," *New York Times*, January 8, 2004, p. A33. The other two great totalitarian challenges were posed by the Nazis in World War II and the Marxists in the Cold War. Ibid.

2. Paul Berman, "Thirteen Observations on a Very Unlucky Predicament," in George Packer (ed.), *The Fight Is for Democracy: Winning the War of Ideas in America and the World* (New York: Perennial, 2003), p. 284.

3. The 9/11 Commission characterized America's latest enemy as

sophisticated, patient, disciplined, and lethal. The enemy rallies behind broad support in the Arab and Muslim world by demanding redress of political grievances, but its hostility toward us and our values is limitless. Its purpose is to rid the world of religious and political pluralism, the plebiscite, and equal rights for women. It makes no distinctions between military and civilian targets. *Collateral damage* is not in its lexicon.

The 9/11 Commission Report: Final Report of the National Commission on Terrorism Attacks upon the United States (New York: W.W. Norton, 2004), p. xvi (emphasis in original).

4. *Home Bldg. & Loan Assn. v. Blaisdell*, 290 U.S. 398, 426 (1934).

5. *United States v. Robel*, 389 U.S. 258, 264 (1967).

6. Final Report of the Independent Panel to Review Department of Defense Detention Operations ("Schlesinger Report"), August 24, 2004, p. 79.

7. Ibid. (quoting Chairman of the Joint Chiefs of Staff Instruction 5810.01B, Implementation of the Law of War Program). In a letter to Senator Patrick Leahy on June 25, 2003, Department of Defense general counsel William Haynes disclosed a Pentagon policy not to engage in any cruel, inhuman, or degrading treatment or punishment that would be prohibited by the U.S. Constitution—a policy applicable to all detainees regardless of whether they were considered lawful of "unlawful" combatants. Human Rights Watch, "U.S. Prison Abuse Panel Doesn't Go Far Enough," August 24, 2004, hrw.org/english/docs/2004/08/24/usint9261.htm.

8. "Military Order, Detention, Treatment, and Trial of Certain Non-Citizens in the War Against Terrorism," *Federal Register* 66 (November 16, 2001): 57831–36.

9. Brian Knowlton, "Powell and Bush Split on Detainees' Status," *International Herald Tribunal*, January 28, 2002, www.iht.com/articles/46171.html.

10. Memorandum of the president, February 7, 2002, p. 1. The president reasoned that the Taliban is not "a High Contracting Party" (i.e., a state that is a signatory) to the Geneva Convention. He also determined that "the provisions of Geneva will apply to our present conflict with the Taliban," but the Taliban were *all* "unlawful combatants" who did not "qualify as prisoners of war under Article 4 of Geneva" because Geneva does not apply to conflicts "of an international character." Ibid., p. 2.

11. Ibid. An essential feature of the Geneva Convention is that no person, even if an "unprivileged combatant," is an "outlaw," i.e., outside the protection of the laws of some legal entity.

12. It has been alleged that race is the basis for the gross disparity in the treatment of the Caucasian Lindh, who is from a comfortable San Francisco Bay area family, and Hamdi, who is of Saudi Arabian ancestry. Harold Hongju Koh, "Rights to Remember," *The Economist*, November 1, 2003.

13. While Hamdi's petition for review was pending in the Supreme Court, the government announced that Hamdi could see a lawyer but only as a matter of executive discretion and not as a matter of right.

14. Koh, "Rights to Remember." A renowned international law professor at Yale Law School who became dean in the summer of 2004, Koh makes a compelling case for championing human rights at the same time we wage the war on terror. "[W]e can both obtain our security and preserve essential liberty, but only so long as we have courage from our courts, commitment from our citizens, and pressure from our foreign allies. Even after September 11, America can still stand for human rights." Ibid.

15. These included William Webster, Lloyd Cutler, William Coleman, Newt Minow, Bernard Meltzer, Ruth Wedgwood, and Griffin Bell. Cutler was a member of the government team that prosecuted the German saboteurs in 1942.

16. Department of Defense, Military Commission Order 1, March 21, 2002.

17. The delay has been extraordinary, and the U.S. government seems to be in a stall mode. For example, some of the most senior military judges and their legal advisors necessary to operate the military commissions were not appointed until the very end of 2003. The first trials were set to begin in late 2004, but pretrial motions and court challenges could further delay the trials. See note 84, below.

18. Even if, as promised, the U.S. government, in its sole discretion, sends home wrongfully held prisoners, there will still be hundreds of captives left for trial.

19. "Human Rights Forgotten in USA's 'War on Terrorism,'" *Amnesty International*, March 2003, web.amnesty.org/wire/March2003/usa. According to Amnesty International, the United States may have transferred some terrorist suspects to countries such as Egypt and Jordan with less stringent safeguards against ill treatment and torture. The requests of this respected human rights watchdog to visit Guantánamo Bay and Basram were rebuffed. Ibid.

20. Barbara Starr, "Afghan Detainees' Deaths Ruled Homocides," CNN.com, March 5, 2003, www.cnn.com/2003/US/03/05/detainee.homicides.

21. Johan Steyn, "Guantánamo Bay: The Legal Black Hole," Twenty-seventh F.A. Mann Lecture, November 25, 2003, p. 9, www.nimj.org/documents/Guantánamo.pdf.

22. Katherine Q. Seelye, "An Uneasy Routine at Cuba Prison Camps," *New York Times*, March 16, 2002, p. A8.

23. Steyn, "Guantánamo Bay," p. 10.

24. Petition for Writ of Certiorari, *Rasul v. Bush* (No. 03–343), pp. 12–13 (quoting Albert Camus, *The Plague* [Modern Library ed., 1948], p. 66).

25. Patrick Jackson, "Life After Guantánamo," BBC News, July 27, 2004, http://news.bbc.co.uk/2/hi/world/americas/3929535.stm.

26. Ibid.

27. "They did everything to us, they tortured our bodies, they tortured our minds, they tortured our ideas and our [Muslim] religion" (claim by an Afghan ex-detainee, Mohammed Khan). Ibid.

28. Glenn Frankel, "Three Allege Guantánamo Abuse," *Washington Post*, August 5, 2004, www.washingtonpost.com/wp-dyn/articles/A41232-2004Aug4.html. The former detainees reported that they were also "forcibly injected with drugs, exposed to intense heat and cold and pressured to make false confessions." Ibid. For a detailed account of the treatment of prisoners and abuses of human rights at Camp Delta, see David Rose, *Guantánamo: The War on Human Rights* (New York: The New Press, 2004).

29. Ibid.

30. Vikram Dodd and Tania Branigan, "US Abuse Could Be War Crime," *Guardian Unlimited*, August 5, 2004, www.guardian.co.uk/Guantánamo/story/0,13743,1276441,00.html. In confidential reports to the U.S. government, the International Committee of the Red Cross, after an inspection in June 2004, concluded that the American military has intentionally used psychological and physical coercion "tantamount to torture" on prisoners at Guantánamo Bay. Neil A. Lewis, "Red Cross Finds Detainee Abuse in Guantánamo," *New York Times*, November 30, 2004, p. A1.

31. Frankel, "Three Allege Guantánamo Abuse."

32. Final Report of the Independent Panel to Review Department of Defense Detention Operations, p. 11.

33. Ibid., p. 13.

34. Richard A. Serrano and Mark Mazzetti, "Prison Abuse Panel Faults Leaders," *Los Angeles Times* (online edition), August 25, 2004; Human Rights Watch, "U.S. Prison Abuse Panel Doesn't Go Far Enough," August 24, 2004, http://hrw.org/english/docs/2004/08/24/usint9261.htm; "Latest Report on Abu Ghraib: Abuses 'Are, Without Question, Criminal,'" *New York Times*, August 26, 2004, p. A11. David Hicks, an Australian held at Guantánamo Bay, has told his father that he "had been abused by American forces, physically in the weeks he was held in Afghanistan and

psychologically during his many months at Guantánamo." Neil A. Lewis, "Australian Pleads Not Guilty to Terrorism Conspiracy," *New York Times*, August 26, 2004, p. A14. David Rose's compelling exposé of prisoner mistreatment at Guantánamo Bay fully supports Hicks's claims. Rose, *Guantánamo.*

35. Final Report of the Independent Panel to Review Department of Defense Detention Operations, p. 13.

36. U.S. Army, "Investigation of Intelligence Activities at Abu Ghraib," executive summary, August 25, 2004, www4.army.mil/ocpa/reports/ar15-6/AR15-6.pdf.

37. Final Report of the Independent Panel to Review Department of Defense Detention Operations; Serrano and Mazzetti, "Prison Abuse Panel Faults Leaders."

38. Human Rights Watch, "U.S. Prison Abuse Panel Doesn't Go Far Enough" (quoting Reed Brody, special counsel with Human Rights Watch).

39. See also Anthony Lewis, "Making Torture Legal," *New York Review of Books*, July 15, 2004 (online edition).

40. "Still, the dots are there, making it clear that the road to Abu Ghraib began well before the invasions of Iraq, when the administration created the category of 'unlawful combatants' for suspected members of Al Qaeda and the Taliban who were captured in Afghanistan and imprisoned at Guantánamo Bay, Cuba." "Holding the Pentagon Accountable: For Abu Ghraib," *New York Times*, August 26, 2004, p. A26.

41. Dahlia Lithwick, "No Smoking Gun," *New York Times*, August 26, 2004, p. A27.

42. National Public Radio, "Human Rights Tasks More Difficult After Abu Ghraib," August 12, 2004, www.npr.org/features/feature.php?wfld=384897.

43. Kevin Phillips, "History Haunts Bush and Kerry," *Los Angeles Times*, August 29, 2004, p. M6. Retiring Nebraska congressman Doug Bereuter, vice chair of the House Intelligence Committee and originally a supporter of the Iraqi war, told his constituents that "it was a mistake to launch military action [against Iraq]" and that America's "reputation around the world has never been lower." Ibid.

44. A succinct defense was offered by the president's counsel, Alberto R. Gonzales: "[Military commissions] spare American jurors, judges and courts the grave risks associated with terrorist trials. They allow the government to use classified information as evidence without compromising intelligence or military efforts. They can dispense justice swiftly, close to where [the] forces may be fighting, without years of pretrial proceedings or post-trial appeals." Alberto R. Gonzales, "Martial Justice, Full and Fair," *New York Times*, November 30, 2001.

45. Joanne Mariner, "O.J. and Osama: The Fear of a Highly Publicized Bin Laden Trial, and the Problem with Military Commissions," *Find Law's Writ*, November 26, 2001, writ.news.findlaw.com/mariner/20011126.html.

46. John Dean, "The Critics Are Wrong: Why President Bush's Decision to Bring Foreign Terrorists to Justice Before Military Tribunals Should Not Offend Civil Liberties," *Find Law's Writ*, November 23, 2001, writ.news.findlaw.com/dean/20011123.html.

47. Gonzales, "Martial Justice."

48. Ibid.

49. Alberto R. Gonzales, "Marital Justice, Full and Fair," op-ed, *New York Times*, November 30, 2001.

50. *Ex parte Quirin*, 317, U.S., 1, 44 (1942).

51. Ibid., at 31.

52. Senator Patrick J. Leahy (D-Vt.), chairman of the Senate Judiciary Committee, chided the president for not at least consulting with Congress before issuing the order. The Senate held hearings on the issue. See Department of Justice Oversight:

Preserving Our Freedom While Defending Against Terrorism: Hearings Before the Senate Committee on the Judiciary, 107th Congress, 2001.

53. *Application of Yamashita*, 327 U.S. 1, 4 (1946).

54. In fact, the president cited two congressional authorities in issuing his order on military tribunals—the 1951 Uniform Code of Military Justice revising the earlier Articles of War and the September 25, 2001, joint resolution authorizing the president to use military force to respond to the September 11 attacks.

55. Some defenders, such as former White House counsel and Watergate defendant John Dean, went so far as to argue that prosecution of enemy belligerents by civilian law enforcement authorities "would set a horrifically bad precedent. Wars, including this war, are fought under well-understood rules. They don't include providing *Miranda* warnings when capturing an enemy, nor employing the legal niceties of the Federal Rules of Criminal Procedure when punishing them." Dean, "The Critics Are Wrong." Dean's analysis was based in part on a scholarly article by Spencer J. Crona and Neal A. Richardson, "Justice for War Criminals of Invisible Armies: A New Legal and Military Approach to Terrorism," *Oklahoma City University Law Review* 21 (Summer/Fall 1996): 349.

56. "Should Osama bin Laden be extracted from the rat hole in which he is hiding, it would then be reasonable to bring him before a military commission for trial." "No Kangaroo Courts: Trying Terrorist Before Military Tribunals Plays Into Our Enemies' Hands," found in "Civil Liberties," About.com, March 21, 2002. While lawful, such exercise of power might be imprudent, civil libertarians have suggested, because "his trial according to the highest standards of due process, with every advantage of an adversarial legal system, will go a long way toward proving that America got the right man and dealt him justice." Ibid.

57. Ibid.

58. Ibid.

59. Ibid.

60. As discussed later in this chapter, the real answer may be that the president and his advisors are worried about federal judges, not federal juries. Federal courts have historically been willing to entertain defendants' arguments about abuse of executive authority, and the writ of habeas corpus has been expressly cited by presidents such as Abraham Lincoln and Franklin Roosevelt as an inconvenient impediment to their imposition of martial law within the nation.

61. "No Kangaroo Courts."

62. See, e.g., Human Rights First, "Military Commission Proceedings Violate International Law," August 17, 2004, www.humanrightsfirst.org/media/2004_alerts/0817.htm; Human Rights First, "Ending Secret Detentions," June 2004, pp. 19–28, www.humanrightsfirst.org/us_law/PDF/EndingSecretDetentions_web.pdf; Human Rights Watch, "Briefing Paper on U.S. Military Commissions," August 2004, www.hrw.org/backgrounder/usa/2004/commission.pdf.

63. ACLU, "ACLU Troubled by Reports that Potentially Secret Military Tribunals Could Place Life or Death of Defendant Solely in Hands of President," press release, March 20, 2002, www.aclu.org/news/NEWSPRINT.cfm?ID=10182&C=111.

64. "No Kangaroo Courts."

65. In *Youngstown Co. v. Sawyer*, 343 U.S. 579 (1952), the Supreme Court invalidated President Harry Truman's seizure of private steel mills to avert a national strike during the Korean War. In his majority opinion, Justice Hugo Black stressed the fact that despite a "grave emergency "and "potential national disaster," Congress had not

authorized this drastic act and the Constitution did not give Truman the power. "The order cannot properly be sustained as an exercise of the President's military power as Commander in Chief of the Armed Forces. . . . The Founders of the Nation entrusted the lawmaking power to the Congress in both good and bad times." Ibid., at 587, 589.

66. William Safire, "Seizing Dictatorial Power," *New York Times*, November 15, 2001.

67. Ibid.

68. William Safire, "Kangaroo Courts," *New York Times*, November 26, 2001.

69. Ibid. Even John Dean admits that the German saboteurs got a raw deal and were tried in secret and executed to spare "the deceitful blow-hard" J. Edgar Hoover and his agents from the press and public learning that the FBI had not been the heroes in the saboteurs' capture but rather had bungled the whole affair. "[T]he secret trials of the eight Nazi saboteurs . . . were used to mislead Americans. The arrest of these Nazis was given much publicity by the FBI. Director J. Edgar Hoover had the world believing that his intrepid and invincible G-men had caught the Nazi spies as they had arrived—law enforcement at its best. . . . In fact, . . . one of the eight men, George Dasch . . . had turned everyone in within days of their arrival in the United States. . . . Thus, the story . . . did not reflect the efficacy of law enforcement; rather, it reflected a single individual's actions and decisions." Dean, "The Critics Are Wrong."

70. William Safire, " 'Voices of Negativism,' " *New York Times*, December 6, 2001.

71. Safire, "Kangaroo Courts."

72. Ibid.

73. Safire, "Seizing Dictatorial Power."

74. Ibid.

75. Ibid.

76. Ibid. Safire was hardly going soft on terrorists. He sprinkled his article with tough-talking rhetoric about turning bin Laden's "cave into a crypt . . . with 15,000-pound daisy-cutters and 5,000-pound rock penetrators."

77. William Safire, "Military Tribunals Modified," *New York Times*, March 21, 2002.

78. Ibid.

79. Ibid.

80. Safire, " 'Voices of Negativism.' "

81. Safire, "Military Tribunals Modified."

82. Jonah Goldberg, "Civil Liberties Debate Reveals Chasm on Right," TownHall .com, November 22, 2001. The *Wall Street Journal* enthusiastically supported military tribunals.

83. Senator Leahy also expressed his continuing concern about "the mass arrests and secret detentions that followed the terrorist attacks [on 9/11]" and the Bush administration's bias against Muslims and Arabs in enforcing immigration policy. Statement of Senator Patrick Leahy, Hearing on America After 9/11: Freedom Preserved or Freedom Lost? November 18, 2003.

84. Pretrial proceedings for the first four defendants began in late August 2004. The consensus among observers was that the "mind boggling" proceedings are "fatally flawed." John Hendren, "Trials and Errors at Guantánamo," *Los Angeles Times*, August 29, 2004, p. A28. A press observer, commenting on the five-member military commission (only one member of which is an attorney), described the opening round of the tribunals as seemingly "mired in uncertainty, inexperience and confusion." Ibid., p. A1. All Guantánamo proceedings were halted in November 2004. See pp. 361–62.

85. Letter to President Bush from Secretary-General Louise Doswald-Beck, December 6, 2001.

86. Several of the ICJ's concerns—including appointed counsel, beyond a reasonable doubt standard, specification of charges, confrontation of adverse witnesses, presumption of innocence—were satisfactorily addressed by Secretary Rumsfeld's regulations. Others were not changed, including possible secret proceedings, a two-thirds vote for conviction and execution, no detailed definition of what constitutes "acts of international terrorism," and appeal only within the executive branch. One of the practical problems caused by President Bush's plan was the reported reluctance of European allies such as Spain, Germany, and Great Britain to turn over al-Qaeda suspects to the United States because the contemplated military trials violate the United Nations Human Rights Treaty. Safire, "'Voices of Negativism.'"

87. Letter to President Bush from Secretary-General Louise Doswald-Beck, December 6, 2001.

88. Ibid.

89. Ibid.

90. Koh, "Rights to Remember."

91. The Department of Defense regulations for the military trials do not create "any right, benefit, or privilege, substantive or procedural." Detention, Treatment, and Trial of Certain Non-Citizens in the War Against Terrorism, Military Order of November 13, 2001. Thus, the secretary of defense can change the rules at any time.

92. "A Necessary Evil?" *The Economist*, July 12, 2003.

93. "Just Don't Kill Them," *The Economist*, July 12, 2003.

94. See, e.g., Steyn, "Guantánamo Bay," pp. 6–7.

95. "A Necessary Evil?"

96. Steyn, "Guantánamo Bay," pp. 1, 15.

97. *The Guardian* commented that the United States "received the searing indictment that it deserves . . . from Lord Steyn, one of the most senior judges on Britain's highest court, and in the most scathing language. . . . Remember, this was a law lord speaking, steeped in the need to use words with care and precision. . . . The lecture won immediate applause from international lawyers." "Quality of Judgment," *The Guardian*, November 27, 2003.

The Independent called Lord Steyn's speech "an unprecedented attack" on U.S. treatment of prisoners, and human rights lawyers "praised Lord Steyn for his courage." Shami Chakrabarti, director of the civil rights group Liberty, remarked: "Lord Steyn is a man of principle and courage and one of our most respected law lords." Robert Verkaik, "Guantánamo Treatment Is 'Monstrous,' Says Law Lord," *The Independent*, November 26, 2003.

98. Steyn, "Guantánamo Bay," pp. 11, 13, 21.

99. Ibid., pp. 10–11. "As matters stand at present the United States courts would refuse to hear a prisoner at Guantánamo Bay who produces credible medical evidence that he has been and is being tortured. They would refuse to hear prisoners who assert that they were not combatants at all. They would refuse to hear prisoners who assert that they were simply soldiers in the Taliban army and knew nothing about Al-Qaeda. They would refuse to examine any complaints of any individuals. The blanket presidential order deprives them all of any rights whatever." Ibid., p. 15.

100. Ibid., p. 13. Lord Steyn further dismisses *Ex parte Quirin* as involving vastly different circumstances, including the lack of a declared war, no congressional authorization of military commissions for this purpose, "military prosecution for violations never

before considered war crimes," and deprivation of "the right of confidential communications with their lawyers; access to all relevant evidence; and judicial review—all of which were afforded to the German saboteurs." Ibid., p. 13.

101. Ibid., p. 15.

102. Ibid., p. 16. The importance of prompt hearings is underscored by the experience in the Gulf War a decade earlier where the military held about twelve hundred hearings on the status of captured prisoners and found two-thirds of them not to be combatants. "It is surely likely that in the chaos of the Afghanistan war and its aftermath the United States military forces picked up a great many who were not even combatants." Ibid. This has proven to be true. Rose, *Guantánamo*.

103. Ibid., p. 18.

104. Ibid.

105. Ibid., p. 17.

106. Ibid., p. 11.

107. Ibid., p. 20. Two other adverse consequences are allowing repressive foreign governments to cite the U.S. treatment of the Guantánamo Bay detainees as justification for their own denials of human rights, and making martyrs of the prisoners in the moderate Muslim world, with which Western nations must work to promote world peace and stability. Ibid.

108. John McCain, commentary, *Wall Street Journal*, June 1, 2004, quoted in Human Rights First, "Ending Secret Detentions," June 2004, p. 25.

109. For an insightful analysis of the Bush administration's squandered opportunities in foreign policy in the wake of 9/11, see John Newhouse, *Imperial America: The Bush Assault on the World Order* (New York: Alfred A. Knopf, 2003); Koh, "Rights to Remember" ("The Bush doctrine . . . is less a broad manifestation of American national character than short-sighted decisions made by a particularly extreme American administration").

110. See Lewis, "Making Torture Legal."

111. In recommending that the government be given even broader powers on top of the USA Patriot Act to prevent terrorism by increasing its presence in our lives, including biometric identifiers, increased information sharing among many government agencies, and consolidation of authority over the intelligence community, the 9/11 Commission recognized the potential for "threats to vital personal and civil liberties . . . This shift of power and authority to the government calls for an enhanced system of checks and balances to protect the precious liberties that are vital to our way of life." *The 9/11 Commission Report: Final Report of the National Commission on Terrorism Attacks Upon the United States* (New York: W.W. Norton, 2004), p. 394.

112. John W. Dean, *Worse than Watergate: The Secret Presidency of George W. Bush* (New York: Little, Brown, 2004), p. 126. "The vast majority are being held on routine immigration charges under unprecedented secrecy. The government will not disclose most of their names. Their trials are held in secret, and their cases are not listed on any public docket." David Cole and James X. Dempsey, *Terrorism and the Constitution: Sacrificing Civil Liberties in the Name of National Security* (New York: The New Press, 2002), p. 149. The Justice Department's inspector general reported numerous beatings and episodes of mistreatment of these detainees. Dean, *Worse than Watergate*, p. 126.

113. John W. Dean, *Worse than Watergate*. Senator Patrick Leahy has complained about President Bush's penchant for secrecy. "In the quarter-century that I have served in the Senate, no administration has been more secretive, more resistant to congressional oversight, and more disposed to acting unilaterally, without the ap-

proval of the American people or their democratically elected representatives." *Congressional Record*, October 1, 2003 (Senate), p. S12278 (Statement of Senator Leahy).

114. Statement of Patrick Leahy, Hearing on Protecting Our National Security from Terrorist Attacks: A Review of Criminal Terrorism Investigations and Procedures, October 21, 2003.

115. Robert C. Byrd, *Losing America: Confronting a Reckless and Arrogant Presidency* (New York: W.W. Norton, 2004), p. 21.

116. For a thoughtful discussion of the civil liberties problems posed by the USA Patriot Act, see Cole and Dempsey, *Terrorism and the Constitution*, pp. 151–71.

117. Richard A. Clarke, *Against All Enemies: Inside America's War on Terror* (New York: Free Press, 2004), pp. 256–57. The 9/11 Commission was sufficiently concerned about the toxic atmosphere of public distrust caused by the USA Patriot Act to recommend that "a full and informed debate on the Patriot Act would be healthy." The 9/11 Commission also recommended:

> The burden of proof for retaining a particular governmental power should be on the executive, to explain (a) that the power actually materially enhances security and (b) that there is adequate supervision of the executive's use of the powers to ensure protection of civil liberties. If the power is granted, there must be adequate guidelines and oversight to properly confine its use.

The 9/11 Commission Report, pp. 394–95.

118. Within a week, the Senate had unanimously passed the Authorization for the Use of Military Force, and the House of Representatives had passed the bill by a vote of 420–1; www.ucc.org/jwm/911c.htm. Indeed, a poll conducted on November 26–27, 2001, found that 91 percent of the 1,012 adults surveyed approved of the presence of U.S. troops in Afghanistan. "USA Today/CNN/Gallup Pull results," *USA Today*, November 28, 2001, www.usatoday.com/news/sept11/2001/11/28/poll-results.htm.

119. Congress passed the Authorization for the Use of Military Force Against Iraq with a margin of 77–23 in the Senate and 296–133 in the House of Representatives. "Congress Approves Iraq Resolution," *Fox News*, October 11, 2002, www.foxnews.com/story/0%2C2933%2C65395%2C00.html.

120. Since the beginning of the war in Iraq, public support has consistently declined. A poll conducted in March 2003 found that 75 percent of Americans believed that sending troops to Iraq was not a mistake. By contrast, 50 percent of those polled in July 2004 felt that sending troops was a mistake. "Iraq," The Polling Report, 2004, www.pollingreport.com/iraq.htm.

121. President George W. Bush, State of the Union Address, January 28, 2003, www.whitehouse.gov/news/releases/2003/01/20030128-19.html.

122. Presidential Press Conference, July 30, 2003, www.whitehouse.gov/news/releases/2003/07/20030730-1.html.

123. According to a CNN.com report as of January 10, 2005, 1,516 coalition troops (1,356 Americans) had been killed since the start of hostilities in 2003. "Forces: U.S. and Coalition/Casualties," CNN.com, www.cnn.com/SPECIALS/2003/iraq/forces/casualties. That figure does not take into account the many deaths of civilian contractors in Iraq. An estimated 10,000 Iraqis have been killed. www.iraqbodycount.net/press/.

124. The Senate Intelligence Committee's ranking Democrat, Jay Rockefeller, stated: "Our credibility is diminished. Our standing in the world has never been lower.

We have fostered a deep hatred of Americans in the Muslim world, and that will grow. As a direct consequence, our nation is more vulnerable today than ever before." Associated Press, "Report Says Key Assertions Leading to War Were Wrong," *New York Times*, July 9, 2004.

125. The Senate Intelligence Committee reported that "[t]he key U.S. assertions leading to the 2003 invasion of Iraq—that Saddam Hussein had chemical and biological weapons and was working to make nuclear weapons—were wrong and based on false or overstated CIA analyses." Associated Press, "Report Says Key Assertions Leading to War Were Wrong," July 9, 2004. The report also stated that analysts fell victim to "group think" with their assumptions about Iraq. Ibid. Others have faulted the Bush administration for overstating the value of the intelligence and even for lying about it. The bipartisan 9/11 Commission found that there was no "collaborative relationship" between Iraq and al-Qaeda. In spite of this finding, President Bush persisted in contending that there was a relationship between the two in order to justify his decision to go to war in Iraq. After a cabinet meeting in June 2004, Bush stated: "The reason I keep insisting that there was a relationship between Iraq and Saddam and al Qaeda: because there was a relationship between Iraq and al Qaeda. . . . There's numerous contacts between the two." Dana Milbank, "Bush Defends Assertions of Iraq-Al Qaeda Relationship," *Washington Post*, June 18, 2004. Vice President Cheney has also been a fervent supporter of the purported link between Iraq and al-Qaeda. Ibid.

126. "Daschle Stands by Criticism of Bush," CNN.com, March 19, 2003, www.cnn.com/2003/ALLPOLITICS/03/18/sprj.irq.daschle.gop/. Democratic presidential nominee Senator John Kerry treaded more lightly, saying that Bush "has clumsily and arrogantly squandered the post-9/11 support and goodwill of the entire civilized world." Ibid.

127. Ibid.

128. Eleanor Clift, "Don't Betray the Family," *Newsweek*, March 21, 2003, msnbc.msn.com/id/3068508.

129. American Civil Liberties Union, *Freedom Under Fire: Dissent in Post-9/11 America*, May 2003, p. 1.

130. Dahlia Lithwick, "Tyranny in the Name of Freedom," *New York Times*, August 12, 2004, p. A25. The Secret Service has imposed so-called free-speech zones to keep dissenters away from President Bush, and they have arrested peaceful war protesters at Bush appearances. Ibid. Bob Barr, a former Republican congressman and conservative who staunchly supported President Bush's military tribunals, has sharply criticized the Bush administration's policy of preemptively identifying and interrogating possible demonstrators as "a serious threat to free speech. . . . The price of free speech should not be a high-profile FBI visit that makes all who know you wonder if you may be a criminal. . . . This is, of course, pure intimidation. . . . [Such] tactics . . . do chill free speech [and] usher in an era of intolerance and fear that has no place in American politics." Bob Barr, "The FBI's Pre-emptive Interrogations of 'Possible' Demonstrators: Chilling Free Speech," FindLaw.com.

131. "Ashcroft: Critics of New Terror Measures Undermine Effort," CNN.com, December 7, 2001, www.cnn.com/2001/US/12/06/inv.ashcroft.hearing.

132. "Patriotism," *Merriam-Webster Dictionary*, 2004, www.m-w.com/cgi-bin/dictionary?book=Dictionary&va=patriotism.

133. "Quotations of Theodore Roosevelt," Theodore Roosevelt Association, www.theodoreroosevelt.org/life/quotes.htm.

134. Statement of Senator Patrick Leahy, Hearing on America After 9/11: Freedom Preserved or Freedom Lost?, November 18, 2003.

135. The lawyers' ability to effectively assist the detainees was hampered by the tight secrecy surrounding their confinement and the government's refusal to allow lawyers and human rights organizations access to the prisons. A federal court has ordered that lawyers' visits with their clients must be free of government monitoring.

136. *Coalition of Clergy v. Bush*, 310 F.3d 1153 (9th Cir. 2002).

137. *Al Odah v. United States*, 321 F.3d 1134 (D.C. Cir. 2003), *cert. granted*, 2003 WL 22070725 (Nov. 10, 2003).

138. A chronology of the litigation prepared by the United States District Court for the Eastern District of Virginia can be found at www.vaed.uscourts.gov.hamdi/chronology.html.

139. *Hamdi v. Rumsfeld*, 294 F.3d 598 (4th Cir. 2002).

140. *Hamdi v. Rumsfeld*, 296 F.3d 278 (4th Cir. 2002).

141. *Hamdi v. Rumsfeld*, 316 F.3d 450, 459 (4th Cir. 2003).

142. *Hamdi v. Rumsfeld*, 337 F.3d 335 (4th Cir. 2003). The judges voted 8–4 against rehearing Hamdi's appeal.

143. Ibid., at 357 (Luttig, J., dissenting). Judge Luttig rebuked his colleagues for falsely promising Hamdi meaningful judicial review when the review "actually entailed absolutely no judicial inquiry into the facts on the basis of which the government designated that citizen as an enemy combatant." Ibid., at 358.

144. Ibid., at 368–69 (Motz, J., dissenting).

145. "In his June 9, 2002 Order, the President directed Secretary Rumsfeld to detain Padilla based on findings that Padilla was an enemy combatant who (1) was 'closely associated with al Qaeda, an international terrorist organization with which the United States is at war'; (2) had engaged in 'war-like acts, including conduct in preparation for acts of international terrorism' against the United States; (3) had intelligence that could assist the United States to ward off future terrorist attacks; and (4) was a continuing threat to United States security." *Padilla v. Rumsfeld*, 352 F.3d 695, 700 (2nd Cir., Nov. 18, 2003).

146. P.L. 107–40, 115 Stat. 224 (2001) ("Joint Resolution").

147. Ordinarily, the petitioner himself must sign his petition for writ of habeas corpus. Given the catch-22 that the government barred his lawyer's access to Padilla, the only choice was for her to sign the petition.

148. The government claimed Newman lacked standing to act as Padilla's next friend, Secretary Rumsfeld was not a proper respondent, and the federal court lacked jurisdiction over Padilla.

149. The court tried to fashion a procedure to allow Padilla to challenge the government's showing that he was an "enemy combatant," but his counsel was restricted in her access to him and the court's scrutiny of the government's proof was severely limited to only whether "the President had some evidence to support his finding that Padilla was an enemy combatant, and whether that evidence has been mooted by events subsequent to his detention." *Padilla ex rel. Newman v. Bush*, 233 F. Supp.2d 564, 569–70 (S.D.N.Y. 2002) (*Padilla I*).

150. See *Padilla ex rel. Newman v. Rumsfeld*, 243 F. Supp.2d 42 (S.D.N.Y 2003); *Padilla ex rel. Newman v. Rumsfeld*, 256 F. Supp. 2d 218 (S.D.N.Y. 2003).

151. On June 10, 2003, the Second Circuit granted an interlocutory appeal. By then Padilla had been in custody for fourteen months without any charges.

152. *Padilla v. Rumsfeld*, 352 F.3d at 698.

153. Ibid., at 699. The Second Circuit stressed that it was not addressing the detention of an American citizen such as Yaser Esam Hamdi, who was seized within a zone of combat in Afghanistan, or expressing an opinion as to the hypothetical situation of a congressionally authorized detention of an American citizen. Ibid., at 699.

154. Judge Richard C. Wesley dissented, arguing that "the President as Commander in Chief has the inherent authority to thwart acts of belligerency at home or abroad that would do harm to United States citizens . . . [and] I cannot see how the Non-Detention Act precludes [the president's actions]." Ibid., at 726 (Wesley, J. dissenting).

155. In its analysis, the Second Circuit rejected the argument that the president's authority was settled by *Ex parte Quirin*, 317 U.S. 1 (1942) and stressed that only Congress could suspend the writ of habeas corpus under Article I, Section 9, clause 2 of the Constitution.

> We do not agree that *Quirin* controls. First, and most importantly, the *Quirin* Court's decision to uphold military jurisdiction rested on express authorization of the use of military tribunals to try combatants who violated the laws of war. Ibid. [*Quirin*] at 26–28. Specifically, the Court found it "unnecessary for present purposes to determine to what extent the President as Commander in Chief has constitutional power to create military Commissions without the support of Congressional legislation." Ibid. [*Quirin*] at 29. Accordingly, *Quirin* does not speak to whether, or to what degree, the President may impose military authority upon United States citizens domestically without clear congressional authorization. We are reluctant to read into *Quirin* a principle that the *Quirin* Court itself specifically declined to promulgate.
>
> Moreover, . . . [b]ecause the *Quirin* Court did not have to contend with section 4001(a), its usefulness is now sharply attenuated.
>
> Second, the petitioners in *Quirin* admitted that they were soldiers in the armed forces of a nation against whom the United States had formally declared war. . . . Padilla makes no such concession . . . [here and] intends to dispute his designation as an enemy combatant, and points to the fact that the civilian accomplices of the *Quirin* saboteurs—citizens who advanced the sabotage plots but who were not members of the German armed forces—were charged and tried as civilians in civilian courts, not as enemy combatants subject to military authority.

Padilla v. Rumsfeld, 352 F.3d at 716 (footnotes omitted; citations omitted).

While rejecting *Ex parte Quirin* as controlling, the Second Circuit embraced *Ex parte Milligan*, 71 U.S. (4 Wall.) 2 (1866), which required congressional authorization for imposing military jurisdiction upon American citizens. Indeed, "*Quirin* and *Milligan* both teach that—at a minimum—an Act of Congress is required to expand military jurisdiction." *Padilla v. Rumsfeld*, 352 F.3d at 717.

156. See *Johnson v. Eisentrager*, 339 U.S. 763 (1950).

157. *Al Odah v. United States*, 321 F.3d 1134 (D.C. Cir. 2003), *cert. granted*, 72 U.S.L.W.3323 (U.S. Nov. 10, 2003) (No. 03–334) ("*Rasul*"), and 72 U.S.L.W.3327 (U.S. Nov. 10, 2003) (No. 03–343) ("*Al Odah*") (consolidated).

158. *Gherebi v. Bush*, 352 F.3d 1278, 1283 (9th Cir. 2003) (footnote omitted). Judge Rheinhardt specifically noted that Article 5 of the Third Geneva Convention and the army's own regulations require that "a competent tribunal" determine the detainees' status. Ibid., at 1283, n. 7. The Third Geneva Convention is a treaty that "is placed on

the same footing, and made of like obligation, with an act of legislation. Both are . . . the supreme law of the land." *Whitney v. Robinson*, 124 U.S. 190, 194 (1888).

In *Gherebi v. Bush*, a dissenting opinion was filed "with regret" by Judge Susan P. Graber, who urged that her colleagues await the Supreme Court's imminent decision on the issue of federal court jurisdiction in the *Rasul* and *Al Odah* consolidated cases. *Gherebi v. Bush*, 352 F.3d 1283, 1305 (9th Cir. 2003) (Graber, J., dissenting).

159. *United States v. Moussaoui*, 365 F.3d 292 (4th Cir. 2004). The majority opinion was written by Chief Judge Wilkins, the author of the Fourth Circuit's opinion in *Hamdi* upholding the indefinite confinement of a U.S. citizen apprehended on the battlefield in Afghanistan.

160. National Public Radio, "Review of This Week's Major News Stories," *Weekend Edition Saturday*, April 24, 2004, transcript, p. 3.

Chapter 26: Securing the Blessings of Liberty

1. Whether the United States is legally "at war" is debatable. A week after the 9/11 attacks, Congress did pass a joint resolution authorizing the president "to use all necessary and appropriate force against those nations, organizations, or persons he determines planned, authorized, committed, or aided the terrorist attacks . . . or harbored such organizations or persons." Authorization for Use of Military Force, P.L. 107–40 SS 1–2, 115 Stat. 224. This was not a formal declaration of war, the draft has not been reinstated, and no domestic emergency economic measures have been instituted. Increasingly, however, America has gone to war without a formal war declaration by Congress. With the advent of the Cold War and Congress authorizing funds for the buildup of a massive military establishment, a bipartisan political consensus developed that the president needed to be able to respond to military crises without a formal congressional declaration of war. Thus, the Korean, Vietnam, Persian Gulf, Afghanistan, and Iraq wars were waged without a war declaration. Indeed, on more than two hundred occasions, presidents have "sent military forces into combat without a formal declaration of war." Kermit L. Hall (ed.), *The Oxford Companion to the Supreme Court of the United States* (New York: Oxford University Press, 1992), p. 576.

2. See Stuart Taylor Jr., "Our Imperial, Unjudicial, Disingenuous, Indispensable Court," *Atlantic Monthly Online*, July 20, 2004 ("a stunning 8–1 vote"). "The Court's long-awaited decisions . . . have been widely hailed by editorial writers as an important defeat for the administration and a significant victory for civil and human rights." Ronald Dworkin, "What the Court Really Said," *New York Review of Books*, August 12, 2004 (online edition), p. 1.

3. "Stepping Back from the Fray: Five Who Argued Before the High Court This Term Talk About the Cases They Won—and Lost," *Legal Times*, August 9, 2004 (statement of Tony Mauro) (Westlaw), p. 4.

4. Human Rights First's comments on "War on Terror" court cases, "Security Detainees and the Supreme Court," www.humanrightsfirst.org/us_law/inthecourts/supreme_court.htm.

5. Ibid.

6. President Richard M. Nixon first appointed William H. Rehnquist as an associate justice in 1972, and President Ronald Reagan elevated him to chief justice in 1986. President Reagan appointed three other justices: Justice Sandra Day O'Connor in 1981, Antonin Scalia in 1986, and Anthony M. Kennedy in 1988. President Gerald

Ford appointed John Paul Stevens in 1975. President George Herbert Walker Bush appointed David H. Souter in 1990 and Clarence Thomas a year later. The only two justices appointed by a Democratic president were appointed by President William Jefferson Clinton: Justice Ruth Bader Ginsburg in 1993 and Justice Stephen G. Breyer the next year.

7. See Daniel Troy, "The Court's Mr. Right—Emergence of Justice Clarence Thomas as Masterful Interpreter of Constitutional Law," *National Review*, August 9, 1999.

8. President Jimmy Carter did not get to make any Supreme Court appointments— the first president since Andrew Johnson not to do so.

9. Hall (ed.), *The Oxford Companion to the Supreme Court*, p. 717.

10. "On taking his seat, Scalia quickly established a solidly conservative voting record, one that has made him the Court's most conservative member on many issues." Ibid., p. 756.

11. Ibid., p. 574.

12. Ibid.

13. The case (No. 03–334) was decided along with *Al Odah v. United States* (No. 03–343).

14. Two British citizens, who were among the original petitioners, had since been released from custody. At one point, Camp Delta had as many as 680 detainees, but some had been released by the time of the *Rasul* decision.

15. 339 U.S. 763 (1950).

16. *Rasul v. Bush*, 542 U.S. (2004) (slip. op., p. 17).

17. The federal habeas corpus statute originated in the very first grant of federal court jurisdiction in Section 14 of the Judiciary Act of 1789. Act of Sept. 24, 1789, ch. 20, §14, 1 Stat. 82. See *Rasul v. United States*, 542 U.S. at ___ (slip. op., p. 5).

18. 542 U.S. (slip op., p. 5) (quoting *INS v. St. Cyr*, 533 U.S. 289, 301 [2001]).

19. Ibid. (slip op., p. 6).

20. 71 U.S. (4 Wall.) 2, (1866).

21. 317 U.S. 1 (1942).

22. 542 U.S. (slip op., pp. 7–8). Justice Stevens further reasoned that the Supreme Court's decision in *Braden v. 30th Judicial Circuit Court of Ky*, 410 U.S. 484 (1973) overruled the statutory basis for *Eisentrager*. *Braden* held that a prisoner's physical presence within territorial jurisdiction of the district court was not an indispensable prerequisite to the exercise of district court jurisdiction under the federal habeas statute, so long as the custodian can be reached by service of process. Ibid. (slip. op., p. 10).

23. This conclusion also comported with the English common law that the historical reach of the writ of habeas corpus extended to the claims of aliens detained within the sovereign territory of the realm. 542 U.S. (slip. op., pp. 13–14).

24. 542 U.S. (slip op., pp. 3–4) (Kennedy, J., concurring in the judgment).

25. 542 U.S. (slip op., p. 1) (Scalia, J., dissenting). Scalia further accused the majority of "spring[ing] a trap on the Executive, subjecting Guantánamo Bay to the oversight of the federal courts even though it has never before been thought to be within their jurisdiction—and thus making it a foolish place to have housed alien wartime detainees." Ibid. (slip. op., p. 11).

26. Ibid. (slip op., p. 3).

27. Ibid. (slip. op., pp. 11, 12).

28. Ibid. (slip op., p. 20).

29. Ibid. (slip op., pp. 14, 18–19).

30. Ibid. (slip op., p. 19).

31. The United States has been accused of abusing some Guantánamo Bay detainees. See Chapter 25.

32. Taylor, "Our Imperial, Unjudicial, Disingenuous, Indispensable Court," p. 2.

33. Anthony Lewis, "The Court v. Bush," *New York Times*, June 29, 2004.

34. *Rumsfeld v. Padilla*, 542 U.S. (2004) (slip op., p. 13).

35. Ibid. (slip. op., p. 14) (quoting *Carbo v. United States*, 364 U.S. 611, 618 [1961]).

36. Ibid. (slip op., p. 19).

37. Ibid. (slip op., pp. 22–23).

38. Nor did Justice Kennedy believe that the Bush administration was guilty of forum shopping itself by moving Padilla to another district without first telling his lawyer. After all, "the Government's removal of Padilla reflected the change in the theory [from material witness to enemy combatant] on which it was holding him." 542 U.S. (slip op., p. 5) (Kennedy, J., concurring).

39. 542 U.S. (slip op., p. 1) (Stevens, J., dissenting).

40. Ibid. (slip op. pp., 4–5).

41. Ibid. (slip op., p. 6).

42. Ibid. (slip. op., pp. 6–7) (emphasis added).

43. Ibid. (slip op., p. 10).

44. Ibid. (slip op., p. 11). Lest there be any question, Justice Stevens expresses his full agreement with the Second Circuit's opinion that "the Non-Detention Act, 18 U.S.C. §4001(a), prohibits—and the Authorization for Use of Military Force Joint Resolution, 115 Stat. 224, adopted on September 18, 2001, does not authorize—the protracted, incommunicado detention of American citizens arrested in the United States." Ibid. (slip op., pp. 10–11, note 8).

45. In a footnote, Justice Stevens quotes Justice Felix Frankfurter's observation in *Watts. v. Indiana*, 338 U.S. 49, 52 (1949): "There is torture of mind as well as body; the will is as much affected by fear as by force. And there comes a point where this Court should not be ignorant as judges of what we know as men." Ibid. (slip. op. p. 11, note 10).

46. Ibid. (slip op., p. 11).

47. Ibid. (slip op, p. 12).

48. The government faces serious problems in proving the case against Padilla in a conventional criminal trial. See Chapter 27.

49. "Today's Trifecta—What Does It All Mean? (Pt. I: Hamdi)," June 28, 2004, Discourse.net.

50. *Hamdi v. Rumsfeld*, 542 U.S. (slip. op., p. 1) (opinion of O'Connor, J.). As discussed below, Justices Stevens and Ginsburg do not agree that Congress authorized Hamdi's detention in the Authorization for Use of Military Force Resolution.

51. 18 U.S.C. §4001(a).

52. 115 Stat. 224.

53. 542 U.S. (slip op., p. 10) (opinion of O'Connor, J.).

54. Ibid. (slip op. p. 11). See 317 U.S. 1, 37–38 (1942). ("Citizens who associate themselves with the military arm of the enemy government, and with its aid, guidance and direction enter this country bent on hostile acts, are enemy belligerents within the meaning of . . . the law of war.")

55. 542 U.S. (slip op., p. 12). Justice O'Connor cites as support for this proposition the Geneva Conventions of 1929 and 1949 and the Hague Conventions of 1899 and 1907—four of the most important cornerstones of international humanitarian

law. The irony of her reliance on the Geneva Convention of 1949 could not have been lost on the Bush administration, which has adamantly denied that its provisions apply to the Guantánamo Bay detainees, particularly Article 5, requiring prompt hearings on prisoner of war status before a competent authority.

56. 542 U.S. (slip op., p. 12).

57. Ibid. (slip op., p. 14).

58. Ibid. (footnote omitted, emphasis added).

59. Ibid. (slip op., p. 15). "*Quirin* makes undeniably clear that this is not the law today. . . . It both postdates and clarifies *Milligan*, providing us with the most apposite precedent that we have on the question of whether citizens may be detained in such circumstances." Ibid. Apparently Attorney General Francis Biddle was correct in his assessment at the time when he told President Roosevelt that *Ex parte Milligan* had been effectively overruled by the Supreme Court in *Ex parte Quirin*. Louis Fisher, *Nazi Saboteurs on Trial: A Military Tribunal and American Law* (Lawrence: University of Kansas Press, 2003), p. 125.

60. 542 U.S. (slip op., p. 15) (opinion of O'Connor, J.), quoting 317 U.S., at 31, 37–38.

61. Ibid. (slip op., pp. 16–17).

62. Justice O'Connor admits that the government has never defined "the legal category of enemy combatant . . . in great detail," but she is content to leave resolution of "the permissible bounds of the category" to the lower courts in subsequent cases. As for Hamdi, regardless of the definition, he would qualify as an enemy combatant since it is asserted that he "was carrying a weapon against American troops on a foreign battlefield." Ibid. (slip op., pp. 14–15, note 1).

63. Ibid. (slip op., p. 17).

64. The government conceded that except in the case of suspension by Congress—a rare event occurring only a few times—the writ of habeas corpus remains available to every individual detained within the United States. Ibid. (slip op., p. 18).

65. Ibid. (slip op., p. 25).

66. Ibid. (slip op., p. 27).

67. Ibid. (slip op., p. 29).

68. Ibid.

69. Ibid. (slip op., pp. 29–30).

70. Ibid. (slip op., p. 26, 32).

71. "Thus, once the Government puts forth credible evidence that the habeas petitioner meets the enemy-combatant criteria, the onus should shift to the petitioner to rebut that evidence with more persuasive evidence that he falls outside the criteria." Ibid. (slip op., p. 27).

72. 542 U.S. (slip op., p. 4) (opinion of Souter, J.).

73. Ibid. (slip op., p. 5).

74. Ibid. (slip op., pp. 6–7).

75. Ibid. (slip op. p. 7).

76. Ibid. (slip op., pp. 9–10).

77. Ibid. (slip op., p. 12). Justice Souter also concludes that the government has violated the military regulation adopted to implement the Geneva Convention "and setting out a detailed procedure for a military tribunal to determine an individual's status." Ibid.

78. Ibid. (slip op., p. 14).

79. Ibid.

80. Ibid.

81. Ibid. (slip op., p. 15).

82. Ibid.

83. Ibid. (slip op., p. 15).

84. Ibid.

85. Ibid. (slip op., p. 16).

86. 542 U.S. (slip op., p. 1) (Scalia. J., dissenting).

87. "Today's Trifecta."

88. Hall (ed.), *The Oxford Companion to the Supreme Court*, p. 756. Scalia's dissent is "a brilliant formalist opinion. It's very persuasive, perhaps because it's so simple and tidy." "Today's Trifecta."

89. 542 U.S. (slip op., pp. 1–2).

90. Ibid. (slip op., p. 2).

91. Ibid. (slip op., p. 3).

92. Ibid. (slip op., p. 6).

93. Ibid. (slip op., p. 7).

94. Ibid. (slip op., p. 8).

95. Ibid. (emphasis in original).

96. Ibid. (slip op., p. 8–9).

97. Justice Scalia cites two later congressional acts providing for broad suspension authority to governors of U.S. possessions—the Philippines (1902) and Hawaii (1900). Ibid. (slip op., p. 11).

98. Ibid. (slip op., p. 12).

99. Ibid.

100. Ibid. (slip op., pp. 16, 17).

101. Ibid. (slip op., p. 13).

102. Ibid. (slip op., p. 15, note 1, and 15).

103. Ibid. (slip op., p. 17).

104. *South Carolina v. Gathers*, 490 U.S. 805, 825 (1989).

105. *Hamdi v. Rumsfeld*, 542 U.S. (slip op. 17) (Scalia, J., dissenting).

106. Ibid. at 19 (footnote omitted).

107. Ibid. (quoting *Ex Parte Quirin*, 317 U.S. 1, 46 [1942]) (emphasis added).

108. Ibid. (slip op., p. 20) (footnote omitted).

109. Ibid. (slip op., p. 20, note 4).

110. Ibid. (slip op., p. 23) (emphasis in original). In *Ex parte Merryman*, 17 F. Cas. 144 (1861), Chief Justice Roger Taney ruled that, despite the fact that a rebellion was occurring, President Abraham Lincoln could not order that a citizen be detained without trial because Congress had not authorized suspension of the writ of habeas corpus. Congress thereafter suspended the writ.

111. Ibid.

112. Ibid. (slip op., p. 24).

113. Ibid. (slip op., pp. 24–25).

114. Ibid. (slip op., p. 25).

115. Ibid. (slip. op. p. 26).

116. Ibid. (slip. op. pp. 26–27).

117. Ibid. at 27. In a dissent that largely parroted the government's arguments, Justice Thomas advocated an uncritical deference to executive power in the prosecution of a war. He envisions no meaningful role for the courts, whose role is little more than that of a cheerleader on the sidelines, having the "institutional inability to weigh

competing concerns correctly." 542 U.S. __ (slip op., p. 1) (Thomas J., dissenting). For Justice Thomas, civil liberties are reduced to an unaffordable luxury in time of war. "In this context, due process requires nothing more than a good-faith executive determination," and Hamdi (who has never had even a hearing) "received all the process to which he was due under the circumstances." Ibid., at 12, 17. Justice Thomas even balks at affording citizens an attorney and notice of the factual basis for the government's determination. After all, "counsel would often destroy the intelligence gathering function." Ibid. at 21.

118. "Department of Defense Fact Sheet: Military Commission Procedures," www.defenselink.mil/news/Aug2003/d20030812factsheet.pdf. "The procedures and regulations already announced for those criminal tribunals [in Guantánamo Bay], though defective, provide more protection than O'Connor said was required to hold citizen-detainees indefinitely without trial." Ronald Dworkin, "What the Court Really Said," p. 7.

119. 542 U.S. (slip op., p. 23) (opinion of O'Connor, J.). In support of this proposition, Justice O'Connor cites *Ex parte Milligan*, demonstrating a too common judicial propensity to pick and choose among the holdings, rationales, and language of this landmark decision on protecting civil liberties in wartime.

120. Ibid. (slip op., p. 24).

121. Ibid. (slip op., p. 25, 28–29).

122. Ronald Dworkin, "What the Court Really Said," p. 1.

Chapter 27: History Lessons

1. For eloquent defenses of the essential role of dissent in time of war and particularly in the new war on terror, see Lewis H. Lapham, *Gag Rule: On the Suppression of Dissent and the Stifling of Democracy* (New York: Penguin, 2004), and Cynthia Brown (ed.), *Lost Liberties: Ashcroft and the Asssault on Personal Freedoms* (New York: The New Press, 2003).

2. One pertinent example is Congress repealing the Supreme Court's jurisdiction to entertain cases involving military trials and martial law in the wake of its landmark decision repudiating the use of military tribunals to try civilians in *Ex parte Milligan*, 71 U.S. (4 Wall.) 2 (1866). 14 Stat. 432, 433 (1867). See Louis Fisher, *Nazi Saboteurs on Trial: A Military Tribunal and American Law* (Lawrence: University Press of Kansas, 2003), p. 45.

3. Robert Dallek, *Franklin D. Roosevelt and American Foreign Policy, 1932–1945* (New York: Oxford University Press, 1979), p. 336.

4. The Supreme Court reaffirmed access to federal courts for review of military prosecutions of enemy leaders in *Application of Yamashita*, 327 U.S. 1 (1946).

5. Phillip Allen Lacovara, "Trials and Error," *Washington Post*, November 12, 2003, p. A23. Lacovara served as deputy solicitor general of the United States and counsel to the Watergate special prosecutor. An initial advocate of President Bush's military commissions for al-Qaeda and Taliban suspects, he eventually lost his enthusiasm, concluding that "the administration's approach to military commissions confirms many of the critics' worst fears." Ibid. Lacovara's most significant criticisms of the prescribed rules include the substantial departure from standards of fair procedure, undermining "the basic right to effective counsel by imposing significant legal constraints on civilian defense attorneys," negating traditional attorney-client confi-

dentiality, and authorizing the withholding of relevant and even exculpatory evidence from defendants and their civilian counsel. Ibid.

6. Ibid.

7. Critics of President Bush's military tribunals for "unlawful combatants" have expressed concern about undue secrecy in the proceedings. Committee on Communications and Media Law of the Association of the Bar of the City of New York, "The Press and the Public's First Amendment Right of Access to Terrorism on Trial: A Position Paper," 2002. Closure of conventional military trials is permitted only if genuinely classified information is involved and the decision is supported by individualized findings, is narrowly tailored, is no longer than necessary, and protects compelling government interests. *United States v. Grunden*, 2 M.J. 116 (C.M.A. 1977). The general public and the media have a qualified First Amendment right to access to criminal trials. *ABC, Inc. v. Powell*, 47 M.J. 363, 365 (1997); *United States v. Scott*, 48 M.J. 663 (Army Ct. Crim. App. 1998). At least portions of the military trial of President Lincoln's assassins, including the testimony of General Ulysses S. Grant, were opened to the public and press.

8. Lacovara, "Trials and Error." Fears about improper closure of terrorist-related court proceedings increased with the discovery of a totally secret federal court case involving the post-9/11 detention of an Algerian-born resident of south Florida who is one of more than a thousand Arab men swept up and imprisoned following the terrorist attacks of 2001. The case proceeded through the entire federal judicial system up to the Supreme Court in a virtually unprecedented blanket of secrecy. Linda Newhouse, "News Groups Seek to Open Secret Case," *New York Times*, January 5, 2004, p. A12.

9. Richard Cahan, "A Terrorist's Tale," *Chicago Magazine*, February 2002.

10. These two decisions are discussed in detail in Chapter 23.

11. Rehnquist, *All the Laws but One: Civil Liberties in Wartime* (New York: Vintage Books, 2000), p. 224.

12. Fred Rodell, *Nine Men: A Political History of the Supreme Court from 1790 to 1955* (New York: Random House, 1955), p. 23.

13. Jonathan Turley, "The Dark History of a Military Tribunal," *National Law Journal*, November 1, 2002.

14. *Helvering v. Hallock*, 309 U.S. 106, 119 (1940), quoted in *Adarand Constructors, Inc. v. Pena*, 515 U.S. 200, 229 (O'Connor, J.).

15. David J. Danelski, "The Saboteur's Case," *Journal of Supreme Court History* 21, no. 1 (1996): 61, 80 (quoting memorandum from Justice Frankfurter).

16. Michal R. Belknap, "The Supreme Court Goes to War: The Meaning and Implications of the Nazi Saboteur Case," 89 *Military Law Review* 59, 95 (1980).

17. Interview with Lloyd Cutler, May 29, 2003.

18. William H. Rehnquist, *All the Laws but One*, p. 225.

19. Turley, "Dark History."

20. Ronald Dworkin, "What the Court Really Said," *New York Review of Books*, August 12, 2004 (online edition), p. 10.

21. *The 9/11 Commission Report: Final Report of the National Commission on Terrorism Attacks Upon the United States* (New York: W.W. Norton, 2004), p. 395.

22. Bruce Schneier, *Beyond Fear: Thinking Sensibly About Security in an Uncertain World* (New York: Copernicus Books, 2003), p. 244.

23. The Israeli writer Amos Elon has noted: "Israel has been unable to resolve the painful paradox of increasing military power and steadily decreasing national secu-

rity." John Newhouse, *Imperial America: The Bush Assault on the World Order* (New York: Alfred A. Knopf, 2003), p. 27.

24. Schneier, *Beyond Fear*, p. 246.

25. Ibid., p. 250.

26. "Government's Ugly Secret," *Los Angeles Times*, April 21, 2004, p. B14. The two-part series by Barry Siegel, entitled "The Secret of the B-29," appeared on the front page of Section A of the *Los Angeles Times* on April 18 and 19, 2004.

27. The Supreme Court's decision in *United States v. Reynolds*, 98 U.S. 145 (1953), was decided on a 6–3 vote. While neither the district court nor the court of appeals judges accepted the military's argument, the Supreme Court was apparently influenced by the looming Cold War and the Korean War hostilities. *Reynolds* became the judicial foundation for national security law. Siegel, "The Secret of the B-29," Part II. Over the next half century, the "state secrets" privilege has morphed from "a shield to protect national security" into "a sword to kill litigations," allowing federal agencies to conceal misconduct, withhold evidence, and defeat embarrassing civil litigation, including lawsuits by whistle-blowers and alleged victims of civil rights violations by the CIA and FBI. Ibid. *Reynolds'* "ramifications reach beyond and civil law: By encouraging judicial deference when the government claims national security secrets, it provides a fundamental basis for much of the Bush administration's response to the September 11 terrorist acts, including the USA Patriot Act and the handling of terrorist suspects. . . . [T]he 'enemy combatants' Yaser Esam Hamdi and Jose Padilla, for many months confined without access to lawyers, have felt the breath of *Reynolds*. So has the accused terrorist Zacarias Moussaoui when federal prosecutors defied a court order allowing him access to other accused terrorists. So have hundreds of detainees at the U.S. Navy base at Guantánamo Bay, Cuba, held for more than two years without charges or judicial review." "Government's Ugly Secret."

28. Trent Lott and Ron Wyden, "Hiding the Truth in a Cloud of Black Ink," *New York Times*, August 26, 2004, p. A27.

29. After intensive negotiations, the United States and attorneys for Yasser Hamdi agreed in late September 2004 to his release from indefinite incarceration and return to his family in Saudi Arabia on certain conditions, including renouncing his U.S. citizenship, travel restrictions, and an agreement not to sue the United States for any injuries sustained while confined for more than two years at military brigs in Virginia and South Carolina. Hamdi's freedom represented another embarrassment for the government in the wake of "the resounding Supreme Court defeat for the White House." Richard B. Schmitt, "U.S. Will Free Louisiana-Born 'Enemy Combatant,'" *Los Angeles Times*, September 23, 2004, p. A25. That Hamdi obviously did not pose a dangerous threat to national security cast a long shadow over the Bush administration's strident claims to the contrary. Jerry Markon, "U.S. to Free Hamdi, Send Him Home," *Washington Post*, September 23, 2004, p. A1. Anthony Romero, executive director of the American Civil Liberties Union, noted: "This clearly shows that the government was not able to meet the burden of proof that the Supreme Court had set for it, and rather than risk further embarrassment in a failed prosecution, they've decided to send him out of the country. The whole case makes you wonder why he was being held in the first place." Eric Lichtblau, "U.S., Bowing to Court, to Free 'Enemy Combatants,'" *New York Times*, September 23, 2004, p. A1. The abrupt about-face also highlighted the importance of preserving judicial review of detentions. Shayana Kadidal, an attorney with the Center for Constitutional Rights, which filed amicus curiae briefs on Hamdi's behalf, noted: "This shows that if you don't have judicial review of

detentions, then the executive branch can take people who are essentially totally innocent . . . and hold onto to them for three years." Markon, "U.S. to Free Hamdi, Send Him Home"; see also ibid. ("The agreement freeing Mr. Hamdi reflects a striking reversal in a hotly debated test case regarding the limits of the Bush administration's prisoners in its pursuit of terror suspects.") As David Cole observed: "It is quite something for the government to declare the person one of the worst of the worst, hold him for almost three years, and then, when they're told by the Supreme Court to give him a fair hearing, turn around and give up." Lichtblau, "U.S., Bowing to Court, to Free 'Enemy Combatants.'"

30. David G. Savage, "American Detainee to be Freed, Sent to Saudi Arabia," August 13, 2004, Los Angeles Times–Washington Post News Service, http://www.gulf-news.com/Articles/Region2.asp?ArticleID=128840.

31. "U.S. Nears Deal to Free Enemy Combatant Hamdi; American Citizen Who Was Captured in Afghanistan Has Been Held Since 2001 Without Being Charged," *Washington Post*, August 12, 2004.

32. "In apprehending [Padilla] as he sought entry into the United States, we have disrupted an unfolding terrorist plot to attack the United States by exploding a radioactive 'dirty bomb.'" Michael Isikoff and Mark Hosenball, "Facing Defeat?" *Newsweek*, June 9, 2004, www.msnbc.msn.com/id/5175105/site/newsweek/site/newsweek (quoting Attorney General Ashcroft).

33. Ibid.

34. Ibid.

35. U.S. Constitution, Article 1, Section 9.

36. Attorney General Lord Goldsmith's speech on the issue of terrorism and justice at the Cour de Cassation, June 25, 2004. Russell Feingold, the lone dissenter in the Senate vote on the Patriot Act, passionately opposed the hastily conceived legislation. Presciently warning about the abuses that would in fact follow the law's enactment, Feingold spoke on the Senate floor about the fact that the Founders

> wrote the Constitution and the Bill of Rights to protect individual liberties in times of war as well as in times of peace. There have been periods in our nation's history when civil liberties have taken a back seat to what appeared to be the legitimate exigencies of war. Our national consciousness still bears the stain and the scars of those events. We must not allow this piece of our past to become prologue. . . . Preserving our freedom is the reason we are now engaged in this new war on terrorism. We will lose that war without a shot being fired if we sacrifice the liberties of the American people in the belief that by doing so we will stop the terrorists. (Statement of U.S. Senator Russell Feingold on the Anti-Terrorism Bill from the Sentate florr on October 25, 2001, http://feingold .senate.gov/~feingold/speeches/01/10/102501athtml.)

37. Hearings: U.S. Senate Committee on the Judiciary, Protecting Our National Security from Terrorist Attacks: A Review of Criminal Terrorism Investigations and Prosecutions, 108th Cong., 1st sess., October 21, 2003; U.S. Senate Committee on the Judiciary, America After 9/11: Freedom Preserved or Freedom Lost? 108th Cong., 1st sess., November 18, 2003.

38. Lord Steyn of Great Britain recommended an ad hoc international court because the Muslim world would more likely accept the trials as impartial justice.

39. Senator Robert C. Byrd, who has served in Congress for fifty-one years, has

acknowledged Congress' complicity in the Bush administration's assault on the balance of powers in our democratic system of government and the resulting "slow unraveling of the people's liberties." *Losing America: Confronting a Reckless and Arrogant Presidency* (New York: W.W. Norton, 2004), p. 13. Senator Byrd sees 9/11 as a cataclysmic event that "would spur the United States Congress to hand over, for the foreseeable future, its constitutional power to declare war. It would eventually lead this nation to an unprovoked attack on a sovereign nation. In consequence, that September morning would endanger cherished, constitutionally enshrined freedoms as had almost no other event in the life our nation." Ibid., pp. 11–12.

40. Secretary of the Navy Gordon England, "Implementation of Combatant Status Review Tribunal Procedures for Enemy Combatants Detained at Guantánamo Bay Naval Base, Cuba," memorandum, July 29, 2004, www.defenselink.mil/news/Jul2004/d20040730comb.pdf.

41. *New York Times v. United States*, 403 U.S. 713 (1971).

42. *United States v. Nixon*, 418 U.S. 683 (1974).

43. Ronald Dworkin, "What the Court Really Said," pp. 3–4 (pointing out the difficulties faced by a prisoner like Hamdi in meeting his burden of proving the government's hearsay allegations false without the ability to compel witnesses to testify on his behalf).

44. Peter-Christian Aigner, interview of Michele Malkin, "Racial Profiling in WWII and War on Terrorism," Townhall.com, August 9, 2004, www.townhall.com/columnists/GuestColumns/Aigner20040809.shtml.

45. Byrd, *Losing America*, p. 14. Beside "the ambivalence of the Congress," Senator Byrd also blames "the pandering nature of media coverage" and "the passive attitude of too many of our citizens" in "aiding and abetting a heinous process." Ibid., p. 13.

46. Nat Hentoff, *The War on the Bill of Rights and the Gathering Resistance* (New York: Seven Stories Press, 2003), p. 23.

47. These courageous counsel include Donna Newman, Frank Dunham, and Navy Lieutenant Commander Charles Swift, who is zealously representing Guantánamo Bay detainee Salim Ahmed Hamdan. Jonathan Mahler, "Commander Swift Objects," *New York Times Magazine*, June 13, 2004, pp. 42–47.

48. Neil A. Lewis, "Judge Halts War-Crime Trial at Guantánamo," *New York Times*, November 9, 2004, p. A1.

49. John Hendren, "Trials of Terror Suspects Halted," *Los Angeles Times*, November 13, 2004, p. A1.

50. *Hamdan v. Rumsfeld*, Civil Action No. 04-1519 (JR), Memorandum Opinion, p. 1, www.dcd.uscourts.gov/04-1519.pdf.

51. Ibid., pp. 31–42. Judge Robertson determined that at least one critical aspect of the military commission procedures was hopelessly flawed. Contrary to the guarantees in Article 39 of the Uniform Code of Military Justice, Hamdan's confrontation rights were abridged since he could be excluded from the proceedings and evidence could be withheld from him.

52. Ibid., pp. 14–26.

53. Ibid., p. 9 (emphasis in original).

54. Ibid., p. 13, quoting *Ex parte Quirin*, 317 U.S. 1, 27-28 (1942).

55. Ibid., pp. 13–14.

56. Ibid., p. 21.

Index